On a Darkling Plain

Introduction by Oliver James

Edited by Ivan Ward

ICON BOOKS UK · TOTEM BOOKS USA

Published in the UK in 2002
by Icon Books Ltd., Grange Road,
Duxford, Cambridge CB2 4QF
e-mail: info@iconbooks.co.uk
www.iconbooks.co.uk

Sold in the UK, Europe, South Africa
and Asia by Faber and Faber Ltd.,
3 Queen Square, London WC1N 3AU
or their agents

Distributed in the UK, Europe,
South Africa and Asia by
Macmillan Distribution Ltd.,
Houndmills, Basingstoke RG21 6XS

Published in Australia in 2002
by Allen & Unwin Pty. Ltd.,
PO Box 8500, 83 Alexander Street,
Crows Nest, NSW 2065

Distributed in Canada by
Penguin Books Canada,
10 Alcorn Avenue, Suite 300,
Toronto, Ontario M4V 3B2

ISBN 1 84046 343 0

Published in the USA in 2002
by Totem Books
Inquiries to: Icon Books Ltd.,
Grange Road, Duxford
Cambridge CB2 4QF, UK

Distributed to the trade in the USA
by National Book Network Inc.,
4720 Boston Way, Lanham,
Maryland 20706

ISBN 1 84046 384 8

Typesetting by Hands Fotoset

Printed and bound in the UK by
Mackays of Chatham plc

And we are here as on a darkling plain
Swept with confused alarms of struggle and flight,
Where ignorant armies clash by night.

(Matthew Arnold, 'Dover Beach', 1848)

Contents

Introduction

Oliver James

The essays in this volume reconnect psychoanalytic thinking with its roots in everyday psychology and contemporary culture. Drawing on diverse referents, from Ovid and Sophocles to pop music and television, each essay brings alive a specific psycho-analytic concept for the general reader – and not before time. In doing so, they reaffirm psychoanalysis as *the* modern paradigm for understanding the human condition.

It is often forgotten that Freud focused much of his thinking, especially his early work, on everyday psychology and that there was virtually nothing about us which he did not consider worthy of analysis. Whether it was dreams, jokes, slips of the tongue or children's games, no aspect of normality was too insignificant and commonplace for his attention. What is more, living as he was in the shadow of Darwin, Marx and Durkheim, and in an era of huge creativity in the social sciences, Freud never restricted his canvas to the merely individual. Biology, literature and anthropology were just a few of the many disciplines in his intellectual palette; indeed, he once claimed to have read more archaeology than psychology. Had he been writing today it is safe to assume that he would have delighted in explicating the unprecedentedly complex and bizarre manifestations of humanity which developed nations present, relishing the chance to employ new disciplines and research methodologies. Regrettably, psychoanalytic thinking has been more introspective during the last twenty years. The breadth, confidence and modernity of Freud's vision, and that of his descendants from the 1930s to the 1970s, has largely disappeared.

In the 1930s, psychoanalytic anthropologists like Abraham Kardiner linked patterns of childcare in societies to their structure and culture, and Geza Roheim trawled diverse cultures in search of psychoanalytic absolutes. Others turned the psychoanalytic spotlight onto their own societies, prefiguring the discipline that was to become 'cultural studies'. During the Second World War, analysts set up the Mass Observation method for recording what was happening in ordinary lives, and after it, the likes of Anthony Storr and Charles Rycroft developed analytic explanations for the Nazi holocaust. History had taught us that we could no longer ignore the deeply irrational roots of human behaviour. With the 1950s came diverse engagement with major social issues, from Donald Winnicott's BBC radio broadcasts on mothering, to Kate Friedlander's creation of a child guidance service. This was also the decade which saw the beginnings of individual psychoanalytic psychotherapy, of counselling, of Michael Balint's work with doctors and the beginnings of family, group and marital therapies.

By now, psychoanalysts and their ideas were often at the forefront of progressive social change in health and education: John Bowlby and James Robertson persuaded government that toddlers should not be left unaccompanied in hospital wards, Anna Freud set out the psychological basis for the legal framework of what was in the best interests of the child. From the 1960s onwards, diverse analytic treatments became increasingly available to people with low incomes, and it was the decade in which the rogue analyst R.D. Laing sought to redefine sanity. The 1970s was the decade that gave us Juliet Mitchell's scholarly, yet popular, attempt to reconcile Freud's theory with feminism and Winnicott's seminal attempt to link playing with reality.

But after this extraordinary richness came ossification and impermeability to living culture. Apart from the polemics of Alice Miller and Jeffrey Masson in the 1980s, both of whom, regrettably, came to reject psychoanalytic treatment completely, it is hard to think of any analyst who has succeeded in communicating psychoanalytic ideas to a wide audience, using the currency of modern culture and everyday reality. That is why these essays are such an important initiative, not solely drawing on clinical cases, although these, naturally, are employed to elucidate the psychic mechanisms under discussion.

The new blinkers are partly a response to a perception within the analytic community of being under siege. Hardly a week passes without the broadsheet newspapers reviewing a book exposing Freud as a charlatan or drug addict or creator of a religious cult. Therapists bemoan the lack of new patients and fear that their profession is at risk of extinction by drug treatments, such as antidepressants.

These perceptions are completely incorrect, a loss of perspective. They largely result from the tendency of publishers to publish books hostile to Freud, of newspaper books-page editors to review them and of journalists to be generally resistant to analytic thinking, giving it a bad press. Freud-bashing is now a popular pastime, and the perception of psychoanalysis suffers as a result.

It is also because the analytic community is not at all good at publicising itself, compared, for example, to the British Psychological Society, with its active press office and frequent conferences covering 'sexy' subjects. Nor do the analysts do much to counter the steady drip of hostility from the psychiatric profession that infests the media. This misperception of analysis as on the wane ignores the fact that Freud's legacy is all-pervasive and almost unstoppable, and so are the clinical practices that have flowered from it. In surveys of academic psychologists, a group notorious for their hostility to psychoanalysis, Freud is usually nominated as the most influential psychologist of all time. Freudian ideas are now ubiquitous in common parlance. Many of the subjects of the essays in this book are Freudian concepts that have become part of popular argot, so that even little-educated people can be heard to say that something they did was 'unconscious', that something they long for is a 'fantasy', that their 'libido' is in overdrive or low. Therapy and therapists were always widespread in American films from the 1940s onwards, but now they are commonly found across most television genres from drama to documentary.

What is more, far from there being a dearth of patients, there are actually many times more. If you include all therapies that are ultimately traceable back to Freud, like counselling or Relate marriage guidance, the numbers of patients at any one time is in the millions whereas, only a generation ago, it was a matter of thousands. Whilst there may be only 470 or so practising psychoanalysts in Britain, some of whom are represented in this book, there are now many thousands of graduates of analytically orientated trainings. Clinicians from the Behaviourist tradition have tried to get on this bandwagon by speciously incorporating 'psychotherapist' as part of their professional self-description; that they should seek to appropriate it shows how potent the notion has become. Though more patients than ever are prescribed anti-depressants, that has done nothing to stem the flow of unhappy people seeking analytic understanding of their problems. Despite the best efforts of Stuart Sutherland, Lewis Wolpert and others, we still live in a culture where many people would prefer to avoid drug treatment.

But perhaps most exciting of all is the new evidence, nearly all of it American, emerging from scientific disciplines which would once have regarded Freud's ideas as anathema and untestable. While many analytically minded folk are aware of the attempts to reconcile evidence from neuroscience with Freudian theory, there is even more exciting work being done by a handful of academic psychologists, of which few seem to be aware. In December 2000,

The Psychologist, the house magazine of academic psychology, devoted a whole edition to 'Freud in a modern light', detailing research that seems to prove many of Freud's basic contentions, mostly studies done in the last decade. Such work provides a scientific foundation for many of the essays published in this book.

Freud was right that we have an unconscious and that it governs much of our thought, feeling and behaviour. He was right that we repress what we cannot bear into this unconscious and that much of our mental life is devoted to elaborate defensive activity designed to keep it there. He was right that our inner lives are immensely complex, with conflicting wishes and paradoxical impulses, coexisting and fighting for expression. But the single most important of his discoveries to have been confirmed is the sheer extent to which our childhood family scripts govern the way in which we interpret the adult present, that transference is everywhere.

Recent research has shown what psychoanalysts have been saying for a century, that the sort of people we get close to are the ones whom we can persuade to play the role that we demand of them from our past. And we play a role for them too. Friendship and love, it seems, go beyond two people finding compatibility based on their pasts; it also requires that both feel at home with being fashioned by the other to fit their precise childhood prototypes. Within psychoanalysis itself, scientific testing of attachment theory reveals strong links between the kind of care you receive in childhood and the sort of parent you become yourself, as well as your proneness to mental illnesses and relationship problems.

Although nearly all academic psychology courses still give Freud short shrift, the engagement of just a few empirical psychologists is bearing rich reward. Whilst the essays in this book are not based on such empirical studies, the ideas they explore are increasingly backed by the findings of science. But the ideas of psychoanalysis do not stand or fall with such efforts. If physicists have not yet been able to solve the problem of turbulence in fluid mechanics, how much more difficult will it be to solve the problem of turbulence in the human mind, the most complex single object in the universe?

Both my parents were psychoanalysts, so I was raised in a home where the application of Freud's ideas to everyday life happened every day. It gives me great pleasure to introduce ten essays which, while acutely aware of the insights that come from clinical practice, reclaim normality and mass culture as fit subjects for analytic thinking.

Sit back and enjoy the ride with a cry of 'Two pickets to Tittsburgh, please!', as Phil Mollon starts the journey in the first essay.

1

The Unconscious

Phil Mollon

The concept of the unconscious has long been knocking at the gates of psychology and asking to be let in. Philosophy and literature have often toyed with it, but science could find no use for it.

(Freud, 1940)[1]

The Lewd Interloper

A man approaches the ticket desk of an airline in the USA intending to buy tickets to Pittsburgh and is served by an extremely attractive young woman endowed with very ample breasts. Somewhat flustered, the man blurts out, 'Two pickets to Tittsburgh, please!' His mistake reveals, in a rather obvious fashion, desires other than his *conscious* wish to purchase a ticket for his journeys.[2] A competing lust has lewdly interlocuted, disrupting his speech.

An author, highly irritated by some of his editor's suggestions for changes to the submitted text, dutifully complied with the request and revised the manuscript. He then attempted to send the new version to the editor by e-mail. Some days later, not having heard from the editor, he phoned to enquire and discovered that the e-mail had not been received. He then checked his e-mail folder and found, to his acute embarrassment, that he had mailed it to another publisher's address! Although this had not been his conscious intention, his mistaken action was congruent with a wishful fantasy of turning to an alternative publisher. A competing intention had infiltrated and hijacked the writer's actions.

Towards the end of the nineteenth century, the President of the Austrian Parliament opened a sitting with the words: 'I take notice that a full quorum of members is present and herewith declare the sitting *closed*.'[3] Naturally, what he intended consciously to say was that the sitting was open, but instead he made a slip of the tongue which revealed what he really felt. A number of the sittings

1

of the House shortly before had been stormy and unproductive, so it would be understandable that the President would far rather he were making his closing rather than opening speech. Although intending to *open* the sitting, a competing wish expressed itself instead.

In such ways the unconscious speaks – often embarrassingly, as if in humiliating mockery of our illusions of conscious awareness and control over our desires and intentions. Consciousness can appear as merely a fragile bubble on the deep waters of emotion, desire and fear.

Is the Unconscious a Valid Concept?

The unconscious is by definition unknowable . . . The psycho-analyst is therefore in the unfortunate position of being a student of that which cannot be known.[4]

The idea of unconscious motivation is an inference that provides an explanation for the gaps and distortions in our consciousness. This hypothesis, which brings coherence to behavioural and mental data that would otherwise appear incoherent, was first explored systematically by Sigmund Freud. He saw that slips of the tongue or pen, failures of memory, bungled actions and other mistakes can be, at a deeper level, not random errors but unconsciously intended. His genius was to see that such seemingly trivial phenomena were worth studying, and moreover to recognise the link between these and other mental creations like dreams, jokes and neurotic symptoms.

People sometimes express scepticism about the existence of an unconscious mind – as if reasoning along the lines of 'If we cannot perceive something with our consciousness then it does not exist.' Certainly, 'the unconscious' can seem an elusive concept. By definition, if a part of the mind is unconscious then we are not conscious of it. Does that mean that a hypothesis, or 'interpretation', regarding an unconscious content of the mind is completely beyond scrutiny in the light of evidence – a pronouncement inspired by dogma and to be swallowed by the patient unquestioningly on the supposed 'authority' of the psychoanalyst? Fortunately, the epistemological position is not quite so bleak. It is possible to think in terms of *gradations* of consciousness. In the examples given above, the individual's competing intentions were not very far from consciousness.

A moment's introspection, combined with a minimal degree of psychological mindedness, would have brought the less conscious wish into the person's full awareness. Similarly, in the course of psychoanalytic therapy, where the patient is encouraged to speak and think freely as far as possible, his or her previously unconscious wishes and fears become gradually closer to consciousness.

A psychoanalytic interpretation that went quite beyond the patient's potential awareness, so that it could only be accepted on faith, would be quite useless. Interpretations given in analysis are tentative hypotheses about what might be going on in the patient's mind, or between patient and analyst. They are based on the evidence of the patient's behaviour and words, and are assessed in the light of the patient's response.

Psychoanalysis is a co-operative venture undertaken by analyst and patient with the aim of expanding the domain of consciousness, so that the latter can conduct his or her life with more awareness, freedom and choice. However, it is a journey of exploration into the unknown, in which any sense of certainty must be eschewed.

The question of the plausibility of the unconscious can be turned around. We might ask instead, 'How plausible is it that we are conscious of all our mental processes?' or 'What is the function of *consciousness*?' For most of its history, experimentally based psychology has been as uncomfortable with the notion of consciousness as it has of unconsciousness, since both have seemed beyond the scope of laboratory investigation.

Radical behaviourists of the early twentieth century regarded consciousness as merely an 'epiphenomenon', without scientific significance or interest.[5] As more sophisticated psychology has developed, both consciousness and unconsciousness have become open to scientific investigation of their processes and functions.[6]

The idea of consciousness is actually similar to that of attention. We are conscious of what we attend to, and not conscious of what we do not attend to. We could become conscious of some things quite easily if we turned our attention to them – corresponding to what Freud[7] called the 'preconscious'. We might actively avoid attending to other things because we find them painful or disturbing – the repressed unconscious.

Perhaps a contemporary analogy might help. Consciousness could be compared to what is visible on a computer screen. Other information could be accessed readily by scrolling down the document or by switching to a different 'window'. This would be analogous to the conscious and the preconscious parts of the mind. However, some files on the computer may be less easily explored. They may have been encrypted or 'zipped', or they may require a password or be in other ways rendered 'access denied'. Some may also have been corrupted, so that information is scrambled and thereby rendered incomprehensible. While the Internet potentially makes available (to people collectively) all kinds of information and images (analogous to Jung's 'collective unconscious'), a program may have been installed that restricts access to Internet sites, *censoring* some that contain material considered unacceptable. Moreover, most of the activity of the computer is not visible on the screen; this is analogous to Freud's idea of the bodily based instincts, or 'id',[8] in themselves inaccessible to the mind, only to be discerned through their derivatives (desires and phantasies).

Yet another aspect of the unconscious is suggested by the peculiar frustration that this writer personally experienced in the early stages of getting to grips with a computer and in my initial attempts to access the Internet. I felt at times utterly bewildered. What added to the agony of this perplexity was that I could not even begin to identify and formulate in words the questions for which I needed the answers; at times it seemed that nothing made sense. This is analogous to what might be termed the 'presymbolic unconscious'[9] – those areas of experience of which we cannot be properly conscious because we have not been able to generate words or any other form of mental representation of them. These phenomena may at times be associated with anxiety, perplexity or 'presymbolic dread'. The concept of the presymbolic unconscious would also apply to earliest infancy before the development of language.

Farts, Stains and Lies

Other examples of slips of the tongue bring us closer to the realm of psychological illness or psychopathology.

A patient was referred to a clinic with an exaggerated fear of losing control of his bowels and an associated persisting pain in his anus (although there appeared to be no physical abnormality). The psychotherapist asked the man to describe more about this problem and how it was experienced. In speaking of his fear of losing control and expelling faeces or flatus, the man inadvertently said he was afraid of letting his 'feelings' out. This was almost certainly not what he consciously intended to say, but it did accurately express his unconscious anxieties. It provided a clue, which then enabled the psychotherapist to enquire about certain areas of the patient's life that could be troubling him emotionally.

The patient acknowledged that he did at times experience worry about a particular problem, but he said he tried to expel such thoughts from his mind. Thus, his worries were evacuated into his body, but the problem was merely displaced. A common example of a similar process is that of a child complaining of physical discomfort, such as a tummy ache, when worried about school or some other situation.

Another patient experienced states of panic at work when in the presence of his boss. In describing these he stumbled over his words, saying: 'I had an ang . . . anxiety attack.' Further exploration revealed that he was indeed troubled by conflicts over his feelings of *anger* towards his boss (which were derived from earlier feelings of anger towards his father) – and that it was his unconscious fear of his anger bursting out that led to his anxiety.

A second window into the unconscious is revealed by an unravelling of the meaning of seemingly bizarre and inexplicable neurotic symptoms. Freud[10] gives the following example of a severe obsessional neurosis.

A lady of thirty years of age felt compelled to repeat a particular action many times each day: she would run from one room to another one, take up a particular position beside a table, ring the bell for her housemaid, send her on some errand, then run back into her own room. Initially, neither Freud nor the patient had the faintest idea what on earth this ritual was about. However, the lady eventually provided the crucial clue. Ten years previously she had married a man who was impotent on their wedding night. On several occasions throughout the night he had to run from his room to hers in order to try again to have intercourse, but without success.

In the morning he had declared angrily that he would feel ashamed in front of the housemaid when she made the bed if there were no evidence of sexual activity. He had then procured a bottle of red ink and poured some of it over the sheet, although not quite in the right place where a blood stain would have been appropriate. Having told Freud this account, the lady then took him into the room where she would sit at her table during her ritual. She showed him a big red stain on the tablecloth. Apparently she would sit at the table in such a position that the stain was immediately apparent to the maid whom she summoned.

Freud's explanation of the obsessional ritual, in the light of this information, was as follows. The patient was identifying with her husband in her act of running from room to room. The table and tablecloth represented the bed and sheet. Thus the patient's ritual appeared to be a representation and repetition of the wedding night scenes. Through summoning the maid before whose eyes the stain was displayed, she was symbolically both repeating the scene and putting it right – the stain was in the right place. According to Freud's interpretation, the obsessional action was saying: 'No, it's not true. He had no need to feel ashamed in front of

5

the housemaid; he was not impotent.'[11] The ritual expressed a wish – to deny her husband's impotence.

This interpretation of the ritual becomes more plausible in the light of information about the patient's general life circumstances. She had lived apart from her husband for many years but could not contemplate divorce. In order to avoid temptations to be unfaithful to her husband, she withdrew from the world and in her imagination she created an elevated image of him. The obsessional ritual had the meaning of repudiating her own potential criticisms of him. Freud comments:

> *Indeed, the deepest secret of her illness was that by means of it she protected her husband from malicious gossip, justified her separation from him and enabled him to lead a comfortable separate life. Thus the analysis of a harmless obsessional action led directly to the inmost core of an illness, but at the same time betrayed to us no small part of the secret of obsessional neurosis in general.*[12]

Freud also notes that the interpretation of her symptom was discovered essentially by the patient herself, through her making the connection with a troubling event – one that linked to her most intimate areas of unhappiness, personal circumstances too painful to be tolerated in consciousness. Unconsciously she still struggled with the issues regarding her sexual life and her relationship with her husband, trying again and again to deny the humiliating reality. By generating a neurotic illness, her unconscious mind created a kind of solution to her conflicts, allowing her to live separately while preserving her husband's reputation, and moreover enabling her, in unconscious fantasy, to undo the unacceptable facts of her sexual unhappiness. This is typical of the way in which the unconscious mind can be quite ingenious in finding creative adaptations to mental conflict.

While the meaning of this ritual was readily understood by the patient, it is easy to imagine how the interpretation of the unconscious solution to a conflict may be strongly resisted in some cases. Undoing the unconscious disguise completely undermines the unconscious solution, thus exposing the individual again to whatever was the unbearable aspect of reality. For this reason, psychoanalysis has always been hated and feared (but unconsciously).

Freud and later psychoanalysts have described many ways in which human beings attempt to hide emotional truth from themselves. These are the *mechanisms of defence*,[13] which include repression (banishing from consciousness), projection (attributing to another person an unwanted aspect of oneself), rationalisation (concocting spurious explanations of one's motivations), splitting (keeping contradictory attitudes or feelings in separate compartments of awareness), manic defences (ways of denying feelings of depression) and many other subtle variations on these themes.

Such forms of 'lying' to oneself are both important and commonplace. They reveal how flimsy our conscious knowledge of ourselves is. However, there is a deeper reason for our dread of psychoanalysis – beyond its revelation of motivations that are unconscious. It is the threatening encounter with the utter 'otherness' of the unconscious – the life that dwells inside us, unknown to us, directing us and yet not speaking our language – the terrifying oracle that utters or mutters incomprehensibly during our sleep.

Dreams

The interpretation of dreams is the royal road to a knowledge of the unconscious activities of the mind.[14]

Dream analysis is the central problem of the analytical treatment, because it is the most important technical means of opening up an avenue to the unconscious ... Dreams are objective facts. They do not answer our expectations and we have not invented them ...[15]

The third point of access to the unconscious is through exploring the meaning of dreams. Freud felt that his major book *The Interpretation of Dreams*[16] was his most important work – and indeed the insights he presents there are profound and of lasting importance. Although psychoanalysis has branched in many directions since Freud's original theories and technical methods, all analysts make use of aspects of the understanding of the unconscious that is outlined in his book on dreams. Here, Freud offered not just a theory of dreams and a method of interpreting them, but also he discerned and dissected the modes of thinking and representation employed by the unconscious mind – modes that are quite different from those employed by our conscious mind.

Freud arrived at the hypothesis that dreams represented a disguised fulfilment of a wish – just as the neurotic symptom may do. This can be clearest in the dreams of children. Freud gives the following rather simple example of a wish expressed in a dream, which may be compared with the case described above, of the obsessional patient's expression of a wish through her ritual.[17]

A woman often dreamt as a child that 'God wore a paper cocked-hat on his head'. Taken on its own, without further information from the dreamer, there is no obvious meaning to this dream idea.

However, the lady recalled that she used to have such a hat placed on her head at mealtimes because of her habit of looking furtively at her brothers' and sisters' plates to see if they were given more than her. The hat was meant to act as blinkers and as a means of shaming her in order to discourage this looking. It was not difficult for the dreamer herself to arrive at the meaning of the dream, through an idea that suddenly occurred to her: 'As I had heard that God was omniscient and saw everything, the dream can only mean that I knew everything, even though they tried to prevent me.'[18]

As in the case of the lady with the ritual of the table-cloth and the stain, the unconscious managed to repudiate an aversive aspect of reality.

In another example, a little boy, Hermann, aged just twenty-two months, was told to hand over a basket of cherries to someone as a birthday present. It was obvious that he was unwilling to do so. However, next morning he reported a dream as follows: *Hermann eaten all the chewwies!*[19]

Freud comments that these and other examples illustrate how children's dreams are frequently short, clear, coherent and easy to understand. Moreover, they often contain an obvious fulfilment of a wish (which usually includes the broader wish to be able to defy adult prohibitions). Freud draws a conclusion from this: that dream distortion is not part of the essential nature of dreams. However, there is a subtle form of distortion even in these simple childhood dreams, insofar as the latent thought or wish (for example, *I would like to eat the cherries*) is transformed during sleep into an experience (for example, *I eat the cherries*). Freud also noted that people who are suffering deprivation of physical needs, such as those who are starving (rather than merely desiring a cherry), may dream of those physical needs being met. He quotes the dreams of members of an Antarctic expedition, which would often be concerned with eating and drinking large quantities. His own daughter, who had been forced to forgo food for a day owing to an upset stomach, dreamt of a menu, to which her name was attached: *Anna Freud; Stwawbewwies, wild stwawbewwies, omblet, pudden!*[20]

From such evidence Freud postulated that dreams are a means of preserving sleep through providing hallucinatory gratification of otherwise disturbing wishes.

In these examples, there is a continuity between a conscious wish and the dream transformation of that wish into a hallucinatory satisfaction. Freud gives an example of a dream whose wish-fulfilling meaning is a little more hidden, although readily apparent on reflection: a man reported that his young wife had dreamt that her period had started. Freud reasoned that if she had missed her period then she must have known she might be pregnant. Thus, by presenting her dream, the woman was both announcing her pregnancy and at the same time expressing a wish that it might be postponed.[21]

Where dreams become more obscure is in their dealing with wishes that are frightening or associated with emotional conflict – wishes that are therefore subject to mental censorship and rendered unconscious.

Freud showed that in order to discover the disguised meaning of a dream, it is necessary to explore the dreamer's associations – his or her spontaneous thoughts – in relation to the various elements of the dream (since there are no fixed universal meanings of dream symbols). One relatively simple example of this process is the following.[22]

A woman dreamt that she wanted to give a dinner party, but had no food in the house except for a little smoked salmon. She thought of going out to the shops, but remembered it was Sunday afternoon and they would all be shut. She tried to ring up some caterers, but the phone was out of order. So she had to abandon her wish to give a dinner party. The woman reported that the previous day her husband had remarked that he was putting on too much weight and had decided to adopt a regime of exercise and a strict diet. This would include accepting no more invitations to supper.

With more resistance, she then provided further associations: that the day before she had visited a woman friend who was admired by the patient's husband, thus evoking some jealousy. However, she was somewhat reassured by the fact that her friend was very thin and her husband usually was attracted to a fuller figure.

Freud asked what the two of them had talked about. The woman replied that the topic had been her friend's wish to put on weight. Her friend had enquired: 'When are you going to ask us to another meal? You always feed one so well.'

Freud concluded that the meaning of the dream was now clear and he interpreted to the patient as follows.

> *It is just as though when she made this suggestion you thought to yourself: 'A likely thing! I'm going to ask you to come and eat in my house so that you may get stout and attract my husband still more! I'd rather never give another supper-party.' What the dream was saying to you was that you were unable to give any supper-parties, and it was thus fulfilling your wish not to help your friend to grow plumper. The fact that what people*

eat at parties makes them stout had been brought home to you by your husband's decision not to accept any more invitations to supper in the interests of his plan to reduce his weight.[23]

Freud then enquired further about the smoked salmon element in the dream. The patient replied that smoked salmon was her friend's favourite dish. It is interesting to note that in terms of its *manifest content*, the dream portrayed the non-fulfilment of a wish, while its *latent* (unconscious) content did, in fact, fulfil the dreamer's wish.

In this example, the patient's thoughts and worries about her husband's attraction to her friend, and her resulting hostility and wish to reject the suggestion of a dinner party, were almost certainly not entirely conscious. This constellation of thoughts and emotions would probably have been associated with some anxiety and shame – and were therefore subject to censorship. Because they could not be experienced directly, they found expression in the form of a dream.

Freud likened the dream censorship to the political censorship that was prevalent during certain periods. He gives an example of a 'highly esteemed and cultivated' lady's dream in which the dreamer appears to be about to offer sexual favours to the local soldiers, ostensibly as part of her patriotic duty.[24] The lady herself dismissed the dream as 'disgusting stupid stuff'. One feature of the dream was that at several points where the narrative would lead to an expectation of some explicit sexual reference there appears instead of clear speech a mumble. For example, a soldier said to her: 'Suppose madam, it actually came to . . . (mumble).' The dreamer then thinks: 'Good gracious, I'm an old woman . . . it must never happen that an elderly woman . . . (mumble) . . . a mere boy.'[25]

Freud points out that the dream thus shows gaps, not in the dreamer's memory but in the content of the dream itself. At crucial points – where this respectable elderly lady might give expression to her sexual desires and fantasies – the content is 'extinguished' and replaced by a mumble. Freud comments:

> *Where shall we find a parallel to such an event? You need not look far these days. Take up any political newspaper and you will find that here and there the text is absent and in its place nothing except the white paper is to be seen . . . In these empty places there was something that displeased the higher censorship authorities and for that reason it was removed – a pity, you feel, since no doubt it was the most interesting thing in the paper – the 'best bit'.*

On other occasions the censorship has not gone to work on a passage after it has already been completed. The author has seen in advance which passages might expect to give rise to objections from the censorship and has on that account toned them down in advance, modified them slightly, or has contented himself with approximations and allusions to what would genuinely have come from his pen. In that case there are no blank places in the paper, but circumlocutions and obscurities of expression appearing at certain points will enable you to guess where regard has been paid to the censorship in advance.[26]

Freud hypothesised that if the wishes that arise during sleep are ones that might cause anxicty, guilt or shame, then the wish-fulfilment is disguised. As a result the meaning of the dream is no longer immediately apparent, in the way that it can be in the case of some rather transparent dreams of children. However, the dream may not be entirely successful in its effort to avoid anxiety. The dream may then contain highly alarming images and narrative.

Freud gives the following example of an anxiety dream.[27]

A young man reported that between the ages eleven to thirteen he had repeatedly dreamt that he was pursued by a man with a hatchet, and that he felt paralysed and unable to run away. In exploring his associations, the man recalled a story told by his uncle of how he had been attacked in the street by a threatening-looking man. Regarding the hatchet, he recalled that he had once injured his hand while chopping wood. Then he thought of how he used to ill-treat his younger brother, knocking him down and on one occasion kicking him in the head with his boot and drawing blood. His mother had said: 'I'm afraid he'll be the death of him one day.'

Finally, he thought of a memory from age nine when his parents had come home late and had gone to bed, while he pretended to be asleep. He had then heard panting and other noises, which had appeared to him 'uncanny', coming from their bed. Freud's explanation of this was as follows:

Further thoughts showed that he had drawn an analogy between his parents and his own relation to his younger brother. He had subsumed what happened between his parents under the concept of violence and struggling; and he had found evidence in favour of this view in the fact that he had often noticed blood in his mother's bed.

It is, I may say, a matter of daily experience that sexual intercourse between adults strikes any children who may

11

observe it as something uncanny and that it arouses anxiety in them. I have explained this anxiety by arguing that what we are dealing with is a sexual excitation with which their understanding is unable to cope and which they also, no doubt, repudiate because their parents are involved in it . . .[28]

What Freud does not quite spell out here is that the young man's own sexual arousal from the bodily and mental changes of puberty would have stirred his earlier impressions and fantasies regarding sex and aggression. The overhearing of his parent's intercourse would have been frighteningly overstimulating for him, especially if it were imagined as a violent exchange that was both pleasurably exciting and terrifying.

Moreover, the young man's earlier childhood Oedipal wishes – to be his mother's partner and do away with his rival father (readily observable among young children within families) – would have been evoked, giving rise to fears of violent retaliation. The man with the hatchet (a common theme in horror films dealing with adolescent sexuality)[29] would thus have represented the fantasised vengeful father, as well as the bullied brother – the dreamer's own violent and aggressive impulses were coming back at him. The sense of paralysis would have expressed the experience of being unable to escape the mounting tension of excitement. In this respect the dream would have been a 'failure' in its function of avoiding anxiety.

Freud's formula that dreams are disguised fulfilments of repressed (repudiated) wishes that have been rendered unconscious is a brilliantly succinct explanatory hypothesis, and he gave a great many examples in support of this. However, the above example of the young man's hatchet dream points to the way in which this formula can become a little strained. Dreams seem to combine many different mental elements – fantasies, perceptions, fears, thoughts, creative ideas, as well as wishes. Perhaps another, rather looser, way of expressing Freud's insight would be to say that dreams attempt to deal with areas of emotional life that are troubling and involve conflict – and which are partly unconscious during our waking hours.

Bion[30] presents the rather intriguing idea that dreams themselves function as a 'contact barrier' between the conscious and unconscious mind – a boundary that both expresses and conceals the unconscious. Its function is to prevent the conscious mind being overwhelmed with 'stuff' from the unconscious. For this reason, the idea of interpreting dreams – of violating their cover – can evoke the dread of being driven mad. According to Bion's theory, something akin to dreaming (which he terms 'alpha function') – the transformation of sense data into *emotionally meaningful* visual, auditory, olfactory and tactile representations that can be 'digested' and contribute to the growth of mind – must go on all the time. The failure to dream is a serious matter. Bion puts it (enigmatically) as follows:

> It used to be said that a man had a nightmare because he had indigestion and that is why he woke up in a panic. My version is: The sleeping patient is panicked; because he cannot have a nightmare he cannot wake up or go to sleep; he has had mental indigestion ever since.[31]

Is the psychoanalytic assumption that dreams are meaningful creations of unconscious thought valid in the light of current knowledge? With the discovery in the 1950s of rapid eye movement (REM) sleep and its correlation with dreaming, it was assumed by many psychologists that dreams were thereby shown to be merely meaningless images generated 'by noisy signals sent up from the brain stem'.[32] Those who took this view concluded that Freud's theory was so much nonsense. However, more recent research has revealed that dreaming is not exclusively linked with REM sleep; dreaming is not *caused* by REM sleep.[33] Indeed, Solms[34] has argued that the picture which current neuroscience shows of the dreaming brain is broadly compatible with the theory of dreams put forward by Freud a hundred years ago. Schore presents the view that Freud's general neuropsychological theory of the mind was far ahead of its time and that it is only recently that neuroscience has caught up with his nineteenth-century insights.[35]

How Dreams Represent Ideas: Condensation and Displacement

In addition to the distortion in dreams that is due to censorship and the need for disguise, Freud also drew attention to another source of their seeming obscurity. The language of the unconscious operates in quite a different way from that of the conscious mind. Thoughts expressed through the conscious mind are organised in a sequential, more or less logical and grammatical form, roughly following certain linguistic rules.

This 'lawful' use of symbols is what enables one person to understand another when using the shared language. By contrast, the unconscious mind, especially as expressed in dreams, employs largely visual images that may combine many different meanings at once – these multiple meanings being *alluded* to, or indicated by fragments, rather than being stated explicitly and in full. It is as if a great many thoughts were broken into pieces or scrambled, then squashed together into a seemingly small bit of meaning.

However, this analogy does not do justice to the astonishing creativity and ingenuity that the unconscious mind shows in constructing appropriate dream images to represent a constellation of thoughts, desires and fears.

Freud used the term *condensation* to refer to this capacity to combine many different elements of meaning. He described the processes involved as follows:

> *Condensation is brought about (1) by the total omission of certain latent elements, (2) by only a fragment of some complexes in the latent dream passing over into the manifest one and (3) by latent elements which have something in common being combined and fused into a single unity in the manifest dream.*[36]

He comments that the simplest form of this condensation is where there is a figure in a dream who is a composite of various people:

> *A composite figure of this kind may look like A perhaps, but may be dressed like B, may do something we remember C doing, and at the same time we may know he is D. This composite structure is of course emphasising something that the four people have in common. It is possible, naturally, to make a composite structure out of things or places in the same way as out of people, provided that the various things and places have in common something which is emphasised by the latent dream. The process is like constructing a new and transitory concept which has this common element as its nucleus. The outcome of this superimposing of the separate elements that have been condensed together is as a rule a blurred and vague image, like what happens if you take several photographs on the same plate.*[37]

A second feature of unconscious representation is that of displacement. Freud describes how this takes place in two forms: by the replacement of one element by a more remote element that alludes to the first; and by the shift of emphasis from an important element to one that is unimportant.

Later, the French psychoanalyst Jacques Lacan was to describe this process in terms of the 'sliding of signifiers'.[38] Whereas in conscious (particularly scientific) thought a word will have a fairly precise meaning, in the unconscious, meanings can slither easily from one representation (signifier) to another.

Yet another work of unconscious representation, particularly in dreams, is the transformation of thoughts into visual images and the substitution of an abstract idea by something more concrete. Freud gives the example of an idea such as 'adultery' (a breach of marriage), which is hard to represent in a picture, being portrayed by an image of another kind of breach, such as 'a broken leg'.[39]

Jung, an early collaborator with Freud, gives the following example – the dream of a 31-year-old unmarried man.[40]

I found myself in a little room, seated at a table beside Pope Pius X, whose features were far more handsome than they are in reality, which surprised me. I saw on one side of our room a great apartment with a table sumptuously laid, and a crowd of ladies in evening-dress. Suddenly I felt a need to urinate, and I went out. On my return the need was repeated; I went out again, and this happened several times. Finally I woke up, wanting to urinate.

The dreamer explained the dream in terms of a need to empty the bladder during sleep. However, further meanings emerged as his associations were explored. Jung asked him to say what came to mind in connection with each element of the dream, as follows:

Seated beside the Pope: 'Just in the same way I was seated at the side of a Sheikh of a Moslem sect, whose guest I was in Arabia. The Sheikh is a sort of Pope.' Jung privately conjectures that part of the dream thought derives from the point that the Pope is celibate, while the Sheikh is a Moslem – the young man is celibate but would like to have many wives like the Sheikh.

The room and the apartment with the table laid: 'They are apartments in my cousin's house, where I was present at a large dinner party he gave a fortnight ago.'

The ladies in evening-dress: 'At this dinner there were also ladies, my cousin's daughters, girls of marriageable age.' The man paused, displaying a resistance to continuing. Jung enquired about the young women. 'Oh nothing; recently one of them was at F. She stayed with us for some time. When she went away I went to the station with her, along with my sister.' He paused again and Jung asked what he was thinking. 'Oh I was just thinking that I had said something to my sister that made us laugh, but I have completely forgotten what it was.' Then he remembered. 'On the way to the station we met a gentleman who greeted us and whom I seemed to recognise. Later I asked my sister, "Was that the gentleman who is interested in – (the cousin's daughter)?"'

Apparently the dreamer was also interested in the young lady but she was now engaged to the man alluded to here.

The dinner at the cousin's house: 'I shall shortly have to go to the wedding of two friends of mine.'

The Pope's features: 'The nose was exceedingly well-formed and slightly pointed.' Jung asked who has a nose like that. 'A young woman I am taking a great interest in just now.' Jung asked if there was anything else about the Pope's features in the dream. 'Yes, his mouth. It was very shapely. Another young woman, who also attracts me, has a mouth like that.'

Jung explains how the figure of the 'Pope' illustrates a common form of highly economic unconscious representation:

> The 'Pope' is a good example of what Freud would call a condensation. In the first place he symbolises the dreamer (celibate life), secondly he is a transformation of the poly-gamous Sheikh. Then he is the person seated beside the dreamer during a dinner, that is to say, one or rather two ladies – in fact the two ladies who interest the dreamer.[41]

Jung enquired what came to mind in association with the idea of needing to urinate while attending a formal ceremony. The man replied:

> That did happen to me once. It was very unpleasant. I had been invited to the marriage of a relative, when I was about eleven. In the church I was sitting next to a girl of my own age. The ceremony went on rather a long time, and I began to want to urinate. But I restrained myself until it was too late. I wetted my trousers.[42]

Thus, from the dreamer's associations, it can be seen that the dream deals with themes of his sexual desires, his conflicts about celibacy, his interest in two women, defeat by a rival in love, his wishes to be able to let go of his bodily desires and impulses (represented by urination), and his fears of humiliation and shameful loss of control (the memory of wetting himself in the presence of a girl). No doubt the dream would allude to many other meanings as well, and Jung notes that the analysis of the material did continue much further.

Jung's account is also of interest because he indicates the dreamer's hesitations (resistances due to censorship) which are apparent as his associations are explored. The wish to understand one's own dream is never without ambivalence – and a certain dread of encountering unknown aspects of oneself.

The Cognitive Unconscious: The Mad Logician and the Mushroom of Meaning

It will be apparent from the above discussion of dreams that the qualities of the unconscious mind are more than merely that of being not conscious. The conscious and unconscious minds operate according to utterly different principles – as different as the modes of reasoning and representation of a scientist/philosopher on the one hand and a visionary artist on the other.

From the perspective of the reasoned and sequential mode of thought of the conscious mind, the cognitive methods of the unconscious mind seem like an insane mockery of our fragile strivings after logic.

Freud[43] identified a number of characteristics of the unconscious mind that are not found in the conscious mind.

1. Mutually incompatible impulses or ideas can exist without these appearing contradictory. Love and hate could both be expressed at the same time unconsciously, whereas the conscious mind would experience dissonance about this.
2. Meaning may be *displaced* easily from one image to another.
3. Many different meanings may be combined in one image – condensation.
4. The processes of the unconscious mind are timeless. Ideas are not ordered temporally and are not altered by the passage of time.
5. The unconscious pays no regard to external reality but represents internal psychical reality. Thus, dreams or hallucinations are perceived as real.

The implications of these points, if taken to their logical extreme, are rather startling. Whereas in conscious rational (especially scientific) discourse our language is ordered sequentially, one word following another, and each word having a more or less specific meaning, the process of condensation in the unconscious mind implies that all kinds of meanings may be presented concurrently without contradiction. The possibility arises, in principle, of a kind of total or ultimate condensation of all meaning and all potential. An analogy might be drawn with the contemporary scientific myth of the origin of the universe.

Prior to the Big Bang, all matter would be condensed into a point containing all potential forms and manifestations of matter and energy. We could picture the deepest unconscious mind as like this 'point', continually pouring out explosions of emotional meaning which then increasingly expand and differentiate as they manifest in consciousness. (We can never be in a position to know with any certainty how the universe began since we were not present at the time. The Big Bang theory could be essentially anthropomorphic mythology based on the structure of the human mind and the origin of our conscious thoughts.)

Freud seems to hint at something like this point of ultimate potential meaning in the following remarkable passage from *The Interpretation of Dreams*.

> *There is often a passage in even the most thoroughly inter-preted dream which has to be left obscure; this is because we become aware during the work of interpretation that at that point there is a tangle of dream-thoughts which cannot be unravelled and which moreover adds nothing to our knowledge of the content of the dream. This is the dream's navel, the spot where it reaches down into the unknown. The dream-thoughts to which we are led by interpretation cannot, from the nature of things, have any definite endings; they are bound to reach out in every direction into the intricate network of our world of thought. It is at some point where this mesh-work is particularly close that the dream-wish grows up, like a mushroom out of its mycelium.*[44]

Freud uses startling analogies here: the dream's navel – 'the spot where it reaches down into the unknown' – and the comparison with a mushroom growing out of its mycelium. These do suggest an ultimately hidden and unknowable source, a point containing, or leading to, all meaning.

As Freud implies, a dream can never be fully interpreted because the dream's associations would ultimately lead to every other association in every conceivable direction of a network (the mycelium) of thoughts and meanings – as one signifier leads endlessly to another.

A modern association to the idea of 'mushroom' might be the mushroom cloud of an atomic bomb. Is a mushroom a kind of 'explosion' of growth? Could we conceive that a dream is a kind of 'explosion' from the unconscious – arising at points of particular density and tension in the meshwork of meaning?

It will be apparent that the distinction between the relatively fixed meanings employed by the conscious mind and the very fluid quality of the meanings apparent in unconscious thought is not an absolute one. Poetry obviously draws heavily on the same processes of imagery and condensation of meaning found in dreams. Similarly, visual art may present an image to convey a welter of meanings simultaneously. Even scientific thought may make use of metaphor – Freud's reference to the 'navel' of a dream being an excellent example.

Freud expressed his insights into unconscious processes largely in terms of his instinct theory – his portrayal of the shifting investments (cathexis) of ideas with instinctual energy. He postulated that in the conscious mind these cathexes are relatively fixed, but in the unconscious mind they are relatively mobile, easily moving from one idea to another.

This theory of instinctual cathexis will seem rather obscure to the contemporary reader and in fact is rarely (if ever) used by psychoanalysts today. However, what remains timelessly valuable in Freud's observations are the following two points.

1. The unconscious does operate with a different 'logic' to that of the conscious mind.
2. The cognitive processes of the unconscious mind are determined partly by the interplay of conflicting emotional forces (psychodynamics).

Others have since clarified further the nature of the cognitive processes employed by the unconscious mind, and how these are apparent not only in dreams but also in schizophrenic and other psychotic states.

One point that Freud did not articulate, but is implicit in both Jung's idea of the 'collective unconscious' and Lacan's[45] concept that the unconscious is structured as a language, is that the unconscious does draw upon the pre-existing and externally existing words, images and cultural references. Thus, the unconscious is both personal and transpersonal.

The Unconscious Mode of Thought in Psychotic States

Silvano Arieti, who wrote arguably the finest book ever on schizophrenia – *Interpretation of Schizophrenia* – examined psychotic and dream thought in considerable detail.[46] He found that many of the peculiarities of thought which Freud had found in dreams and which were also displayed by schizophrenic patients could be accounted for by the following principle:

> *That the unconscious mind and the mind of the schizophrenic person may perceive two or more things as identical if they have some kind of associated attributes which are identical.*

The reasoning might be along the lines of: Bill is a British citizen; the prime minister is British; therefore Bill is the prime minister – Bill and the prime minister are regarded as identical because they have identical attributes of both being British.

Arieti gives the example of a patient who thought she was the Virgin Mary.[47] Her reasoning was:

> The Virgin Mary was a virgin; I am a virgin; therefore I am the Virgin Mary.

It was also apparent that her arriving at this delusional idea was motivated by her wish to deny her feelings of inadequacy and assert her identity with her ideal of femininity. Thus, the delusion depended on both a degraded form of logic and psychodynamic motivations.

The early investigator of schizophrenia, Eugene Bleuler, gave the example of a patient who was preoccupied with his wish for freedom and believed he was Switzerland.[48] His reasoning was:

> Switzerland loves freedom; I love freedom; therefore I am Switzerland.

The principle described by Arieti, of the unconscious and schizophrenic logic of identification of predicates, can be used to describe the formation of common dream symbols. For example, a snake, a cigar or a pen in a dream may symbolise a penis on the basis of a similarity of shape: a snake and a penis may be long and thin; therefore a snake is a penis. A box or a jewel case may represent a vagina because all are cavities.

Similarly, if a dream is representing an experience of the previous day, one attribute of the experience may be taken as the basis of a representation by an image that also possesses that attribute. An instance of this might be if a patient has experienced the psychotherapist as somewhat intrusive during a particular session and that night has a dream of being raped. The unconscious cognition here would be:

> My therapist was violating me in his comments today. A rape is a violation. Therefore the therapist is a rapist [and indeed a 'therapist' is 'the rapist'!].

These symbolic functions are not, of course, limited to dreams and schizophrenic thought. The story of Bill Clinton and the cigar provided a joke that required no explanation. A TV advertisement in which a beautiful young woman sensuously licks a stick of chocolate makes use of allusions that are scarcely unconscious for most viewers. Picture language, cartoons, religious iconography and so on employ similar means.

The richness of language and culture depends on an interplay between primary and secondary process cognition. However, for the schizophrenic patient the primary process mode of cognition may intrude into the capacity for secondary process logic, with the result that apparent metaphors are used but their abstract and 'as if' quality is lost. For example, a patient who was being kept under close observation in a psychiatric hospital stated her belief that she was in prison. Superficially this might have appeared a metaphor, a way of expressing her sense of her freedom being restricted. But on enquiry it became apparent that she believed she was actually and literally in a prison. There is here a failure of the capacity for abstract thought: the more abstract idea of a situation being *like* a prison becomes the more concrete idea of being *literally* a prison.

Disturbances of normal reasoning can also be revealed through the Rorschach inkblot test – where the subject is shown a series of coloured inkblots on cards, then asked what he or she perceives and to give reasons for those perceptions.

One patient kept seeing penises, vaginas and breasts in the inkblots and indignantly asked the psychologist: 'Doctor, why are you showing me all these dirty pictures?' For this patient the quality of looking *like* a sexual part of the body became instead equivalent to an *actual* picture of a sex organ. The degradation of logic was combined with the mental defence of projection, so that the sexual preoccupations were attributed to the psychologist rather than recognised as the patient's own.

Rapaport[49] gives the example of a patient who pointed to a coloured area of one of the inkblot cards and said: 'This bloody little splotch here – it's that bloody island where they had so many revolutions.'

Here the patient sees a patch of ink which looks like an island on a map; he sees also the red colour which he associates with blood, then fuses the two ideas to form the idea of a 'bloody island', and finally identifies it as a particular island where there were revolutions, which presumably were bloody. Rapaport referred to such instances of the loss of appropriate boundaries between concepts as 'contaminations'.

These various examples illustrate how psychotic patients may be trapped in a degraded form of cognition that does not work for them in negotiations with a world operating essentially according to conventional logic. For such patients words are no longer treated as symbols – that is, signifiers of objects that are absent – but instead are regarded as objects themselves. When a patient is in this state of cognition, the sound of the psychotherapist's voice may become more important than the *meanings* of the words; or the therapist's name may be repeated over and over as a source of reassurance. Thinking has become *concrete*.

Segal,[50] in her discussion of what she calls 'symbolic equations', gives the example of a schizophrenic patient who was asked by his doctor why he had stopped playing the violin. He replied indignantly: 'Why? Do you expect me to masturbate in public?' While it would be quite normal for a *dream* of playing the violin to represent masturbation – the violin unconsciously symbolising a penis – it is quite a different matter if it has that meaning in waking life.

The loss of capacity for abstract metaphor in psychosis is like a situation in which the actors in a play or film suddenly run off the stage or out of the screen and begin killing or raping the audience; the 'frame' that states this is 'as if' is lost.[51]

Various psychoanalysts have drawn attention to the way in which the structure of thought itself (as opposed to its content) is altered in psychosis. What is a matter of some debate is the question of whether this reflects a fundamental deficit (with neuropsychological underpinnings) or an active defence against the awareness of unbearable mental conflict (or indeed a combination of these factors).[52]

A related problem is that schizophrenic patients may experience difficulties both in being properly asleep and being fully awake.[53] The dreaming mind is not properly confined to sleep. It can be as if the person is dreaming while awake. Unconscious modes of cognition have invaded the conscious mind, with dire consequences for the capacity to understand and communicate with others.

On the other hand, it must be emphasised that a too exclusive reliance on purely secondary process, logical and rational language, would appear both dull and abnormal. The emotional colour of our language, art and culture depends on the contained penetration of the unconscious mode of thought into our waking life. Some intuitively or artistically gifted individuals may possess an unusual access to the normally unconscious, or primary process, modes of cognition. If contained and harnessed, the primary process is the source of creativity, but if unleashed it can overpower and destroy the capacity for rational thought. Here lies the fine line between genius and madness.

Psychotic Expulsion

To the extent that psychosis involves mechanisms of defence, a manoeuvre more radical than repression and related forms of disguise and self-deception must be involved. Normally, a content of the mind that has been rendered unconscious may reappear in a disguised symbolic form – in a dream, for example. It remains within a symbolic register, albeit disguised or encoded.

In psychosis, however, it is sometimes as if there has been an attempt to eject the objectionable content entirely from the mind, leaving a kind of hole in the fabric of representation. The ejected content may then return in the form of an experience of malevolent hallucination, continually rattling the psychic window. While dreams during sleep are a normal mode of representation, hallucinations while awake are not.

Freud noted, however, that psychosis is not restricted to those labelled mentally ill:

> [E]ach one of us behaves in some one respect like a paranoic, corrects some aspect of the world which is unbearable to him by the construction of a wish and introduces this delusion into reality.[54]

Unconscious Representations in Everyday Life

Just as dreams may represent an unconscious comment on a current situation in the dreamer's life, so we can also discern other forms of unconscious communication and representation that take place continually. These employ the same mechanisms of representation that are employed in dreams. Unconscious meanings are disguised and displaced, and use metaphor and imagery – or, as Robert Langs puts it, they are 'encoded'.[55]

Very common instances of this are those situations where a person is feeling angry and critical with someone but suppresses these feelings because it might be painful or anxiety-evoking to acknowledge them.

Such conflicts over anger or criticism usually occur in relation to someone who has an emotional significance to the person – such as a parent, a spouse, a boss and so on. Under these circumstances, what usually happens is that the suppressed feelings are communicated unconsciously in a disguised and displaced form – for example, by expressing criticism of someone else. Sometimes this disguised communication is done consciously and intentionally; it is then called 'hinting'.

A student social worker's supervisor told her that she was unexpectedly going to be away for a couple of weeks. The student's overt response was one of acceptance and an assurance that she could manage without supervision for this period. However, she then went on to mention a case she had heard of from a colleague, in which a mother had left her young toddler child at home while she went out to the local shops. The toddler had woken up and had been severely injured falling down stairs.

The unconscious communication is clear: the supervisor is unconsciously experienced as a neglectful and abandoning mother, while the student is represented as a toddler who cannot take care of herself and who might suffer a catastrophe if left alone. The reference to falling down stairs expresses the student's sense of not being held securely and protected from danger.

Thus, *consciously* the student speaks as if she is an adult who can manage without supervision quite adequately for a couple of weeks; *unconsciously* she is accusing the supervisor of criminal neglect of her parental responsibilities.

Langs[56] gives an example of a man (Larry) who was called into the office of his boss (Ken) and told that unfortunately he was to be made redundant. After a factual discussion of the situation, Larry suddenly stared at his boss and remarked: 'You know, the way you look now makes me think of a picture of a man in today's newspaper. There is a really strong resemblance. He murdered his boyfriend; they were homosexuals. He will probably get the electric chair.'

On the surface, these comments do not seem to fit the context of the discussion about being fired and appear superficially confusing. Nevertheless, it is not difficult to see the unconsciously encoded message. Langs explains what is going on here.

> It appears that Larry is under a strong compulsion to express and defend against an unconscious perception of his boss as a killer, and of his own wish to murder his boss in turn. The allusion to homosexuality touches upon unconsciously perceived (and never at all conscious) indications of a latent homosexual and seductive set of feelings in Ken towards Larry, and in Larry towards Ken. It appears that Larry is unconsciously (via an encoded expression) suggesting that a critical source of the decision to fire him involves these unconscious homosexual conflicts. Clearly, these are all powerful raw messages, many of which Larry was entirely unaware of; they required automatic and unconscious encoding in order to be communicated in disguised (displaced) form.[57]

Unconscious representations may also take the form of enactments. For example, Langs[58] describes the case of a man whose wife had separated from him and had locked him out of the house. He inadvertently locked himself out of his car and had to make a forced entry. The actions – of locking himself out and forcing his way back in – were an unconscious enactment of the situation with his wife and his rageful wish to re-enter his home. Langs adds that at a deeper level this could also be seen as expressing his wish to assault and penetrate his wife.

A formula begins to emerge here as we consider encoded unconscious representation and communication. It is that emotional meanings are encoded unconsciously if they are experienced as too dangerous or frightening to be represented or communicated consciously. Encodings may take various forms – including imagery, dreams, daydreams, enactments, ambiguous and disordered verbal messages, slips of the tongue, and emotional or neurotic symptoms of various kinds.

Warnings and Advice From the Unconscious

Although Freud considered that dreams are merely attempts to preserve sleep by organising, containing and disguising potentially disturbing unconscious wishes, most psychoanalysts and therapists find that dreams can often appear also to be *communications* from the unconscious. This is actually a more Jungian than Freudian notion, but in this respect, psychoanalytic therapists in general, even when trained in the tradition deriving from Freud, have become more 'Jungian'.

Dreams may reveal astonishing intelligence and creative ingenuity, provoking thought about their meaning – and in this way can stir a person to reflect on aspects of his or her life that may be neglected in conscious preoccupations. Moreover, this communicative function of dreams seems to increase often when a person is having therapy or analysis.

S.S. Radha[59] gives the following example of a woman's dream:

> *I saw myself in a train station, preparing to take a trip on my own. But I had five suitcases and nobody to help me with them. When I woke up I had the strong feeling that I really wanted to leave, but I simply didn't know if I could manage the heavy baggage. So I began to think that perhaps I would not go.*

As this was explored in therapy, the woman realised that the dream was expressing her repressed desire to leave her marriage, combined with her fear that if she were to do so she would not be able to look after her five children, represented by the five suitcases. A dream of this kind expresses an unconscious thought (which includes a wish) and potentially draws it to the attention of the conscious mind.

Sometimes the warning function of a dream is startlingly

apparent. A man, who was feeling drawn ever deeper into an affair with a highly attractive and seductive woman, dreamt that he was climbing a mountain, but left the path and his companion in order to admire and smell an extraordinarily beautiful rose. As he drank in the glorious scent he noticed that the ground in which the rose was growing was actually stinking manure. Moreover, he found his feet slipping as he stumbled near to a cliff edge where he could fall to his death. At this point he awoke. The meaning – and the message – is obvious.

Unconscious Representations of Frightening Reality

It sometimes happens that a dream will represent a frightening situation that is known unconsciously but is being ignored or denied by the conscious mind. Jung gives an example of a seventeen-year-old girl who presented with symptoms that could either be of an organic illness or of hysteria. He asked if she remembered any dreams and the girl replied that she frequently had terrible nightmares. She then narrated the following two dreams.[60]

> 1. *I was coming home at night. Everything is as quiet as death. The door into the living room is half open, and I see my mother hanging from the chandelier, swinging to and fro in the cold wind that blows in through the open windows.*
> 2. *A terrible noise broke out in the house at night. I get up and discover that a frightened horse is tearing through the rooms. At last it finds the door into the hall, and jumps through the hall window from the fourth floor into the street below. I was terrified when I saw it lying there, all mangled.*

In Jung's commentary on this dream he elaborates on the unconscious metaphors of the images of 'mother' and 'horse'. Although framed in terms of his theory of archetypes and the 'collective unconscious' – innate forms of representation found universally in the human psyche – this appreciation of the way in which a dream may use metaphor would be congruent with the perspectives of most analysts (even if the meanings derived would vary). The usual clinical practice is to allow the images of the dream to resonate with the associations of both the patient and analyst, rather like listening to poetry. There is no one definitive meaning of a dream.

Jung's own thoughts were as follows. He notes that 'mother' and 'horse' in the dream both commit suicide. The image of a horse may represent the forceful animal aspect of the psyche, the unconscious, the instincts. Mother may represent origins, the body, the nourishing vessel.

Jung concludes that the two dreams are expressing the same idea: 'The unconscious life is destroying itself' and 'The animal life is destroying itself'.[61] He adds: 'Both dreams point to a grave organic disease with a fatal outcome. This prognosis was soon confirmed.'[62]

Various Realms of the Unconscious

Of course, Freud was not the first to discover the unconscious mind.[63] Novelists and playwrights have long alluded to our human tendency for self-deception and to be unaware of our true motivations. Those practising hypnosis in the nineteenth century knew that a person could be programmed to carry out a particular action and be unconscious of the source of the impulsion.

More recently, cognitive psychologists have been happy to study non-conscious processing of information[64] and have even attempted experimental studies of unconscious psychodynamics.[65]

However, Freud was the first to study systematically the *dynamic* unconscious, which has remained predominantly the province of psychoanalysis. This concerns the process whereby unacceptable or frightening contents of the mind (wishes, thoughts, perceptions) are banished from conscious awareness, but continue to exert an influence, either by pushing to re-emerge into consciousness or by finding displaced and disguised expression through psychological symptoms, dreams, slips of the tongue or somatic disorders (physical illness). In addition to identifying the dynamic unconscious, Freud made a start on describing the peculiar modes of thought and representation of the unconscious mind.

However, there are other important realms of the unconscious. Robert Stolorow and George Atwood[66] have described two other forms in addition to the dynamic unconscious. One of these is the *prereflective unconscious*, which consists of the recurrent patterns, or *organising principles*, whereby a person perceives his or her relationships with others. For example, a patient in psychotherapy continually indicated her assumption that the therapist wished to turn her into a particular kind of person, while she in turn wished to rebel against this perceived pressure to mould her. She also seemed to experience people in other areas of her life as trying to control her. Moreover, at times she appeared to want to control the therapist by, for example, proposing all kinds of rules about what kinds of comments he was allowed to make.

Her recurrent organising principle, which determined her experience of herself in relation to others, was an assumption that the other person will try to control her – and that the only alternative is for her to control the other person. This organising principle appeared to be derived from experiences with her mother, whom she felt had established a life scenario for her even before she was born.

The notion of the prereflective unconscious is actually quite similar to Freud's concept of the *transference*. This idea can be quite complex and is used in somewhat varying ways by different groups of analysts, but basically it refers to the way in which a person will spontaneously, but without conscious awareness, repeat patterns of relationship that are based on relationships with parents in childhood.

Much of the work of psychoanalysis is to do with exploring this transference in relation to the analyst. It is unconscious, in that a person cannot be aware of the pattern except through exploring and reflecting upon what emerges in a relationship, but it is not *necessarily* repressed (although it may indeed contain repressed feelings, perceptions or wishes).

Is the transference (or prereflective unconscious) a kind of memory? Well yes, in a sense, it is a form of *procedural* or *implicit* memory.[67] Rather than consisting of a memory of facts or events, it is an expectation of what will happen in relationships, based on recurrent patterns in the original relationships of childhood.

Although there has been much discussion in recent years regarding so-called 'recovered memory' (and 'false memory'), the remembering of previously forgotten events plays a relatively small part in psychoanalysis, which, in most cases,[68] is much more concerned with the recurrent patterns of unconscious relationships. The Sandlers refer to this template patterning of unconscious relationships as the *present unconscious*, derived from, but distinguishable from, the relatively inaccessible historical experiences of relationships in childhood, which they term the *past unconscious*.[69]

However, Stolorow and Atwood describe another way in which harmful events in childhood can be denied access to consciousness, not because they are repressed, but because they never receive validation from the important figures in the child's environment and therefore cannot be acknowledged and thought about. They call this the *unvalidated unconscious* (which may relate to the concept of the 'presymbolic unconscious' mentioned earlier). An example they give is of a nineteen-year-old girl who suffered a psychotic breakdown.[70]

When she was younger, the girl's father had sexually abused her for several years. This had been a secret between father and daughter. He told her she must never mention it to others because most people had not evolved to the point where they could appreciate this special activity, which he claimed was enjoyed by royal families throughout history. Moreover, the sexual abuse contrasted utterly with the outward appearance of normality, the family playing a respected role in the community and being regular church attenders. Thus, there was a marked dissociation within the family and within the girl's experience.

The sexual abuse remained concealed until her mid-teens, when another child reported the father's behaviour. Prior to a psychotic episode she had dreamt that she was standing in the countryside, looking at a structure like an outhouse. She looked inside and saw a toilet. The water began gurgling up through the toilet bowl, foaming and overflowing. The flow became more and more agitated until it exploded with unidentified glowing material, increasing without limit. She awoke in terror.

Stolorow and Atwood argue that the dream represents the breakdown of repression, such that overwhelming emotions which had been in the *dynamic unconscious* – represented by the underground material – are now bubbling up in a terrifying and uncontrolled manner. The dream represents an aspect of the *prereflective unconscious* in its depiction of a division between the world above (alluding to the daylight and public world of a respectable family) and the world below (the experience of incest and betrayal), connected by the toilet. A dream image of a toilet does, of course, commonly represent the disposal of unwanted areas of experience. The unidentifiable and undifferentiated quality of the glowing material erupting from the toilet represents the *unvalidated unconscious*, overwhelming experiences that could not be named, thought about and spoken about.[71]

It will be apparent from this example that the three forms of the unconscious described by Stolorow and Atwood are, in practice, somewhat overlapping. However, the conceptual distinction between the dynamic, prereflective and unvalidated unconscious is helpful in drawing attention to different aspects of these phenomena.

Another important feature highlighted by Stolorow and Atwood's example is that repression is often best understood as taking place in a relational context. Areas of experience are repressed because they threaten needed emotional ties (especially that of a child to a caregiver).

Jennifer Freyd has a similar concept in her 'Betrayal Trauma' theory of forgetting of interpersonal trauma.[72] Repression can also be seen as an interpersonal process insofar as one partner in a relationship fails to offer validation of the other's experience in that relationship.

The Neuropsychological Unconscious

An exciting recent development is the convergence of psycho-analysis and the neurosciences (as Freud had always hoped), forming the new discipline of neuro-psychoanalysis. This is providing many interesting perspectives on unconscious emotional processing. Oversimplification is inevitable in describing these, but basically what emerges is that the right side of the brain, with its specialisation in visual perception, imagery and emotion, is the basis of the unconscious mind.[73] The left hemisphere, specialising more in linguistic and sequential logical processing, is the basis of the conscious mind. It matures slightly later than the right hemisphere.

During the first couple of years, the right brain is dominant and is strongly attuned to reading the mother's face. Through the orbitofrontal cortex the right brain links the perception of the external interpersonal environment with the deeper parts of the brain responsible for the autonomic nervous system and for generating emotion.

Later, the linguistic left brain becomes dominant. This imposition of slower sequential linguistic processing eclipses the rapid and holistic emotional information processing of the right brain, and creates a consciousness dominated by thinking with language. One way in which repression could occur would be through blocking communication from the right to the left hemisphere, with the result that emotional information is not processed into verbal language.

The unconscious mind, mediating between the conscious psyche and the soma, retains the visual and holistic imagistic thought processes of the right brain. Psychoanalytic therapy probably involves a shift towards more right-brain functioning in both patient and analyst during the session. Attention is drawn towards imagery and metaphor and other aspects of the language of the unconscious (the 'primary process'). The analyst listens with his or her right brain. This is in line with Freud's recommendation that 'he must turn his own unconscious like a receptive organ towards the transmitting unconscious of the patient'.[74]

Some analysts find that they often become sleepy or enter a dream-like state of mind for parts of a session, this alternating with other moments when understandings from the right brain are processed through the linguistic mode of the left brain (the 'secondary process').

The tendency towards either a left-brain or a right-brain mode of functioning may influence the bias towards one form of psychological therapy as opposed to another. Cognitive therapy is clearly a left-brain activity (often preferred by men and by those of a 'rational' or scientific outlook), as opposed to psychoanalysis which rests fundamentally upon right-brain receptivity.

A Hierarchy of Consciousness or Multiple Consciousnesses?

Freud's theory of repression implies a hierarchy of consciousness[75] and a metaphor of depth – as in commonly used phrases such as 'the deep unconscious', or 'buried in the unconscious'. Freud and Breuer[76] distinguished this *splitting of the mind* (repression) into consciousness and unconsciousness from *splitting of consciousness* (now termed dissociation), where there are alternating consciousnesses (as in Breuer's case of Anna O and the hysterical patients described by their French rival, Pierre Janet). However, a non-hierarchical model is required for those patients (often extensively traumatised) who show marked dissociation or splitting rather than repression.

Dissociation is a marked disruption of the normally integrative processes of the mind, such that what is known and felt in one state of mind is not experienced when in another state of mind. Some degree of dissociation is common among those who have suffered overwhelming trauma, whether in childhood or as an adult. It is also a core feature of what is called Borderline Personality Disorder. However, in a small number of cases, the dissociation may be so extreme that a person will experience his or her mind as divided into a number of alternating consciousnesses or personality states. These conditions are called multiple personalities, or Dissociative Identity Disorder.[77] Here the boundary of awareness is not between consciousness and unconsciousness, but is between the varying consciousnesses.

The recognition of dissociation is part of a trend among some psychoanalysts to place more attention on the shifts between states of mind rather than on the interplay between a conscious and unconscious mind.[78]

Interestingly, the French psychiatrist Pierre Janet, who was working at the same time as Freud at the turn of the century, had developed a sophisticated theory of dissociation based on trauma, which is highly compatible with contemporary understandings of trauma.[79] Freud's rival theory of repression became the more dominant notion, thereby eclipsing the understanding of trauma and dissociation for the best part of a century.

To understand the dynamics of the mind we need both the concept of repression (and related defences) and also that of dissociation in order to take account of the interplay between inner psychodynamic conflict and trauma resulting from external impingement.

The Infinite Unconscious

[T]*he system Ucs. resembles a child who is learning to speak and who at times conforms to the laws of grammar and at other times ignores them.*[80]

One of the most innovative psychoanalysts since Freud is Ignacio Matte-Blanco, who has brought his background in mathematics and philosophy to bear on the problem of understanding the unconscious. In his first book – *The Unconscious as Infinite Sets* – he argued that psychoanalysis has, in various of its developments, walked away from Freud's original astonishing insights into the ways of the unconscious mind.

Many of the later preoccupations of psychoanalytic theorists, such as mechanisms of defence, internal objects, attachment, ego functions, life and death instincts and so on, may be of interest and importance, but they can take attention away from an appreciation of the language and mode of being of the unconscious. This is evidenced, for example, in the way that some theorists, who are not themselves psychoanalysts, can take aspects of psycho-analytic ideas and build an essentially left-brain orientated theory of therapy which does not address the unconscious mind – for example, cognitive analytic therapy.

Matte-Blanco examined the mode of functioning of the uncon-scious, and presented a proposition that clarifies and unifies the diverse peculiarities of unconscious reasoning. This is that the unconscious follows a particular logic, although it is a very odd kind when viewed from the perspective of the Aristotelian logic of the conscious mind.

The unconscious adopts a principle of 'symmetry'. Whereas in our conscious thinking, asymmetrical relations are common – such as 'Paul is the father of Peter' or 'this leaf is part of the plant' or '2 o'clock is before 6 o'clock' – in our unconscious thought these relations may be regarded as symmetrical. As a result, Peter is also the father of Paul, the plant is part of the leaf, and 6 o'clock is before 2 o'clock.

Matte-Blanco[81] gives the example of a schizophrenic patient who sometimes complained that blood had been taken away from her arm and at other times that her arm had been taken away from her. Clearly, for her, blood *from* her arm and her arm itself were identical. This may seem like nonsense – and indeed it is from the point of view of the conscious mind – but all the characteristics described by Freud in his discussions of the unconscious and of dreams are explained by this principle – including, for example, the absence of contradiction and negation, timelessness, profound disorganisation in the structure of thinking, the part standing for the whole, condensation and displacement (where one thing is treated as if identical with another).

A further aspect of symmetrical thinking is that where there is categorisation of objects of pheno-mena within a particular 'set' (for example, mothers, breasts, forms of aggression or any kind of category imaginable), then the unconscious treats all the elements of the class as equivalent. This is because grouping elements into a category or set is in itself a form of symmetrical thinking (A is like B; B is like A), and the unconscious simply extends the symmetry into complete equivalence. As a result, the unconscious will perceive one mother, or father (and the analyst in the transference) as the same as all mothers, or fathers, and will also regard one form of aggression, or violation or seduction, as identical with the most extreme forms of murder or rape.

The 'logic' of this extreme or polarised thinking is as follows. Voicing a rude word is part of the category of aggressive acts; therefore all forms of aggressive acts are the same as a rude word (because the part is equivalent to the whole). Another way of putting this is to say that the unconscious deals in 'infinite sets'.

The attempt to consider the full implications of symmetrical logic can evoke something of the experience of confusion and difficulty with thinking that may be found in certain states of psychosis. However, as Matte-Blanco put it, 'The principle of symmetry is an external logical way of describing something which in itself is completely alien to logic.'[82]

The whole matter becomes a little more comprehensible when it is appreciated that thinking normally involves a varying mixture of symmetrical and asymmetrical reasoning. Purely rational and logical thought is predominantly asymmetrical, whereas the language of dreams contains much more symmetry.

However, common unconscious mechanisms of defence may rely crucially on asymmetry as well as symmetry. For example, displacement requires that one thing is treated as if it were another thing, but in addition the defence requires that there is some differentiation between these two objects in order that the disguise can operate.

Similarly, projection and stereotyping depends on symmetry (all Jews/Blacks/Whites/homosexuals are the same and embody all possible negative attributes) while simultaneously preserving asymmetry which differentiates self from other. Good thinking, whether for scientific or poetic purposes, depends on an appropriate mixture of symmetry and asymmetry. Too much symmetry results in thought disorder; too much asymmetry leads to a dry discourse that fails to resonate with our human depths.

The mixture of symmetry and asymmetry in thinking is about the degree of differentiation in perception. Asymmetrical thinking sees difference and individuality everywhere. Symmetry sees no differentiation. There appear to be *stratifications* of symmetry–asymmetry. At the deepest level of the unconscious, pure symmetry prevails. All is one and the whole is reflected in the smallest part – an insight as old as human culture. In the depths of the unconscious, in pure symmetry, we find the Godhead,[83] the awesome Other within – the 'Subject of subjects',[84] which can never be the object – the source of our being and fount of sanity and madness, of creation and destruction, of Grace and Terror.

Phil Mollon is a psychoanalyst and a clinical psychologist. He works in the National Health Service and in private practice in Hertfordshire. His psychoanalytic interests include memory, trauma, and psychosis.

Notes

Where no specific page references are given, it is because the references are to the works in general.

1. Freud, S., *An Outline of Psychoanalysis* (1940), in *Standard Edition of the Complete Psychological Works of Sigmund Freud*, London: Hogarth Press, 1953–74 (hereafter *SE*), vol. 23, p. 286.
2. Langs, R., *Unconscious Communication in Everyday Life*, New York: Jason Aronson, 1983, p. 85.
3. For example, Freud, S., *Introductory Lectures on Psychoanalysis* (1916), in *SE*, vol. 15, p. 34.
4. Ogden, T., *The Primitive Edge of Experience*. Northvale, NJ: Jason Aronson, 1989, p. 2.
5. For example, Skinner, B.F., *About Behaviourism*, New York: Knopf, 1974; and Watson, J.B., *Behaviourism*, New York: Harper Bros, 1925.
6. Baars, B.J., *A Cognitive Theory of Consciousness*, Cambridge: Cambridge University Press, 1988; and Horowitz, M. (ed.), *Psychodynamics and Cognition*, Chicago: University of Chicago Press, 1988.
7. Freud, S., 'The Unconscious' (1915), in *SE*, vol. 14.
8. Freud, S., 'The Ego and the Id' (1923), in *SE*, vol. 19.
9. Mollon, P. *Releasing the Self: The Healing Legacy of Heinz Kohut*, London: Whurr, 2001.
10. Freud, S., *Introductory Lectures on Psychoanalysis* (1917), in *SE*, vol. 16, pp. 261–4.
11. Ibid., p. 263.
12. Ibid., p. 263.
13. Brewin, C.R., 'Psychological Defences and the Distortion of Meaning', in Power, M. and Brewin, C.R. (eds.), *The Transformation of Meaning in Psychological Therapies*, Chichester: Wiley, 1997.
14. Freud, S., *The Interpretation of Dreams* (1900), in *SE*, vol. 5, p. 608.
15. Jung, C.G., *The Seminars: Volume One: Dream Analysis: Notes of the Seminar Given in 1928–30*, London: Routledge and Kegan Paul, 1984.
16. Freud (1900), op. cit.
17. Freud (1916), op. cit., p. 118.
18. Ibid., p. 118.
19. Ibid., p. 127.
20. Ibid., p. 132.
21. Freud, S., 'On Dreams' (1901), in *SE*, vol. 5, p. 646.
22. Freud (1900), op. cit., vol. 4, p. 147.
23. Ibid., p. 148.
24. Freud (1916), op. cit., p. 137.
25. Ibid., p. 137.
26. Ibid., p. 139.
27. Freud (1900), op. cit., pp. 584–6.
28. Ibid., pp. 584–5.
29. Ward, I., 'Adolescent Phantasies and the Horror Film', *British Journal of Psychotherapy*, vol. 13, (2), 1996, pp. 267–76.
30. Bion, W.R., *Learning From Experience*, London: Heinemann, 1962; reprinted in *Seven Servants*, New York: Aronson, 1977.

31. Ibid., p. 8.
32. Hobson, J. and McCarley, R., 'The Brain as a Dream-state Generator', *American Journal of Psychiatry*, vol. 134, 1977, p. 1374.
33. Mancia, M., 'Psychoanalysis and the Neurosciences: A Topical Debate on Dreams', *International Journal of Psycho-Analysis*, vol. 80 (6), 1999, pp. 1205–13.
34. Solms, M., 'New Findings on the Neurological Organisation of Dreaming: Implications for Psychoanalysis', *Psychoanalytic Quarterly*, vol. 64, 1995, pp. 43–67; Solms, M., *The Neuropsychology of Dreams*, Mahwah, New Jersey: Erlbaum, 1997; and Solms, M., 'Dreaming and REM Sleep are Controlled by Different Brain Mechanisms', *Behavioral and Brain Sciences*, vol. 23 (6).
35. Schore, A.N., *Affect Regulation and the Origin of the Self. The Neurobiology of Emotional Development*, New York: Erlbaum, 1994.
36. Freud (1916), op. cit., p. 171.
37. Ibid., pp. 171–2.
38. Leader, D. and Groves, J., *Introducing Lacan*, Cambridge: Icon Books, 2000.
39. Freud (1916), op. cit., p. 176.
40. Jung, C.G., *Dreams*, London: Routledge and Kegan Paul, 1974, p. 9.
41. Ibid., p. 11.
42. Ibid., p. 11.
43. Freud (1915), op. cit.
44. Freud (1900), op. cit., vol. 5, p. 525.
45. Lacan, J., *Ecrits* (1966), London: Tavistock, 1977.
46. Arieti, S., *Interpretation of Schizophrenia*, London: Crosby, Lockwood, Staples, 1974.
47. Ibid., p. 230.
48. Quoted in Arieti (1974), op. cit., p. 231.
49. Rapaport, D., *Diagnostic Psychological Testing*, Chicago: Year Book Publishers, 1946, p. 338.
50. Segal, H., 'Notes on Symbol Formation', *International Journal of Psycho-Analysis*, vol. 38, 1957, pp. 391–7.
51. See the discussion of art, illusion, frames and boundaries in Milner, M., 'The Role of Illusion in Symbol Formation', in Klein, M., Heimann, P. and Money-Kyrle, R.E. (eds.), *New Directions in Psycho-Analysis*, London: Tavistock, 1955. Also see Milner, M., *On Not Being Able to Paint*, London: Heinemann, 1950.
52. Grotstein, J., 'The Psychoanalytic Concept of Schizophrenia: 1 The Dilemma', *International Journal of Psycho-Analysis*, 58, 1977, pp. 403–25; Grotstein, J., 'The Psychoanalytic Concept of Schizophrenia: 11 Reconciliation', *International Journal of Psycho-Analysis*, vol. 58, 1977, pp. 427–52.
53. Bion (1962), op. cit., p. 7.
54. Freud, S., *Civilization and its Discontents* (1930), in *SE*, vol. 21, p. 81.
55. Langs (1983), op. cit.
56. Ibid., p. 82.
57. Ibid., pp. 82–3.
58. Ibid., p. 86.

59. Radha, S.S., *Realities of the Dreaming Mind*, Canterbury: Timeless Books, 1994, p. 119.
60. Ibid., p. 106.
61. Ibid., pp. 107–8.
62. Ibid., p. 108. Dreams should not, of course, be taken as a source of reliable diagnostic information regarding a physical illness.
63. Ellenberger, H.F., *The Discovery of the Unconscious: The History and Evolution of Dynamic Psychiatry*, London: Allen Lane, 1970.
64. Dixon, N., *Preconscious Processing*, Chichester: Wiley, 1981.
65. Horowitz, M. (ed.), *Psychodynamics and Cognition*, Chicago: University of Chicago Press, 1988.
66. Stolorow, R.D. and Atwood, G.E., *Contexts of Being: The Intersubjective Foundations of Psychological Life*, Hillsdale, NJ: Analytic Press, 1992.
67. Mollon, P., *Remembering Trauma: A Psychotherapist's Guide to Memory and Illusion*, Chichester: Wiley, 1998.
68. An example of memory recovery and reconstruction of childhood trauma is given in Casement, P., *On Learning from the Patient*, London: Routledge, 1985, pp. 102–67.
69. Sandler, J. and Sandler, A.M., 'A Psychoanalytic Theory of Repression and the Unconscious', in Sandler, J. and Fonagy, P. (eds.), *Recovered Memories of Abuse: True or False?*, London: Karnac, 1997.
70. Stolorow and Atwood (1992), op. cit., pp. 36–40.
71. Of course, a dream should not in itself be taken as providing reliable information about childhood events.
72. Freyd, J.J., *Betrayal Trauma: The Logic of Forgetting Childhood Abuse*, Cambridge, MA: Harvard University Press, 1996.
73. Schore, A., *Affect Regulation and the Origin of the Self*, New York: Jason Aronson, 1993; 'Attachment, the Developing Brain, and Psychotherapy', paper presented to the annual Bowlby Conference, London, 3–4 March 2000.
74. Freud, S., 'Recommendations to Physicians Practising Psychoanalysis' (1912), in *SE*, vol. 12, p.115.
75. Influenced by the theories of the neurologist Hughlings Jackson, a contemporary of Freud.
76. Breuer, J. and Freud, S., *Studies on Hysteria* (1893–5), in *SE*, vol. 2.
77. Mollon, P., *Multiple Selves, Multiple Voices: Working with Trauma, Violation and Dissociation*, Chichester: Wiley, 1996.
78. Horowitz, M., 'Unconsciously Determined Defensive Strategies', in Horowitz, M. (ed.), *Psychodynamics and Cognition*, Chicago: University of Chicago Press, 1988.
79. Van der Hart, O. and Horst, R., 'The Dissociation Theory of Pierre Janet', *Journal of Traumatic Stress*, vol. 2 (4), 1989, pp. 399–414.
80. Matte-Blanco, I., *The Unconscious as Infinite Sets*, London: Duckworth, 1975, p. 41.
81. Ibid., p. 137.
82. Ibid., p. 148.
83. Bion, W.R., *Attention and Interpretation*, London: Tavistock, 1970; reprinted in *Seven Servants*, New York: Aronson, 1977 (see especially pp. 26 and 88).

84. Grotstein, J.S., 'Bion, the Pariah of "O"', *British Journal of Psychotherapy*, vol. 14 (1), 1997, pp. 77–87.

Further Reading

Casement, P., *On Learning from the Patient*, London: Routledge, 1985.

Freud, S., *The Interpretation of Dreams* (1900), in *SE*, vols. 4 and 5. (Also published as a Penguin paperback.)

Langs, R., *Unconscious Communication in Everyday Life*, New York: Jason Aronson, 1983.

——*Decoding Your Dreams*, New York: Henry Holt, 1988.

Malan, D., *Individual Psychotherapy and the Science of Psychodynamics*, London: Butterworths, 1979.

Matte-Blanco, I., *The Unconscious as Infinite Sets: An Essay in Bi-Logic*, London: Duckworth, 1975.

——*Thinking, Feeling, and Being*, London: Routledge, 1988.

Mollon, P., *Freud and False Memory Syndrome*, Cambridge: Icon Books, 1999.

Orbach, I., *The Hidden Mind. Psychology, Psychotherapy and Unconscious Processes*, Chichester: Wiley, 1995.

Segal, J., *Phantasy in Everyday Life*, Harmondsworth: Penguin, 1985.

2

Anxiety

Ricky Emanuel

Introduction

As I begin to write this essay I am faced with many anxieties. Will I manage to finish it on time and get it to the publisher? Will it be good enough? Do I know what I want to say and can I say it clearly enough? This seems normal. Facing a new and potentially daunting task gives rise to anxiety in all of us. But how will I cope with these anxieties? Will they overwhelm me and lead to a paralysis of thought and writing, or will they spur me on to 'create' this essay? What exactly are these anxieties? And what function, if any, do they have?

If I try to examine exactly what I am anxious about – in other words, think about and name my own emotional experience – then perhaps the anxieties will be mollified. My anxieties are not necessarily irrational ones, although some of them may be. If I examine them more closely, I find that I am anxious about my performance. In other words, will I be judged harshly? Will I be exposed as fraudulent? Do I know enough about the subject to warrant having been asked to write this essay? Will I find inspiration from what psychoanalysts call my 'good objects', those mysterious guiding forces within me that are the basis of my security? Will my 'uncertainty cloud' about the whole enterprise be received and held by them, or will I let 'them' down?

This latter anxiety relates to an intimidating or tormenting feeling associated with the fear of being harshly judged, but also a different quality of anxiety, a dejected feeling concerning whether I can be worthy of my good object's expectations of me. This may be recognised by some readers as having something to do with one's conscience, Sigmund Freud's superego and the ego ideal in their relationship to my ego. There are also allusions to the psychoanalyst Melanie Klein's differentiation of the qualities of anxiety divided into persecutory and depressive anxiety, and the problem of containment of this anxiety described by the psychoanalyst Wilfred Bion. We therefore see that the subject of this essay is potentially a vast one, covering the whole spectrum of psycho-analysis.

Psychoanalyst Robert Hinshelwood writes: 'The history of psychoanalysis has been one of trying to understand the core anxiety of the human condition.'[1] In this essay I will attempt to trace how anxiety has been thought about in psychoanalysis from Freud to the present time, when the world of neuroscience has started to bring fresh insights into psychoanalytic formulations. I hope the examples I use are illustrative of the points I am trying to make, as this is not a theoretical exposition of the development of the concept of anxiety in psychoanalytic thought, but rather an attempt to make everyday life situations faced by all of us more comprehensible from a psychoanalytic point of view.

What is Anxiety?

Anxiety is certainly not just concerned with irrational fear. In many cases it would be irrational *not* to be anxious. For example, a person newly diagnosed as having cancer has every right to be anxious. We would be immediately alarmed if they were not. Although some of that person's fear may be irrational, the fact that he or she is frightened is not.

Irrational anxieties are often found in phobias, like the fear of spiders, thunder, open spaces and so on. Yet sometimes these phobic anxieties have a real basis. A more useful definition, which does not need to invoke real or imagined fears, is 'the response to some as yet unrecognised factor, either in the environment or in the self'. The response may arise from conscious or unconscious sources.[2] This definition captures uncertainty as a central factor in anxiety, and is close to the definition of anxiety coined by Bion as 'a premonition of emotion',[3] which highlights that anxiety is con-nected to an emotional experience that is likely to be experienced imminently, and emphasises the unknown nature of it.

The notion of premonition also captures something essential about anxiety, as it implies something close to a feeling of dread. Additionally, it firmly places the experience in the body of the person feeling it, as emotions are first and foremost bodily states. We all know what anxiety feels like: butterflies in the stomach, pounding heart, unpleasant sensations or a vague but persistent sense of unease (or dis-ease, as Bion liked to emphasise).

Hinshelwood writes that psychoanalytic theories of anxiety have proliferated over the years and are largely connected with problems arising from different forms of conflict.[4] Freud's thinking about anxiety changed throughout his career, and can be separated into three phases. In the first phase, he believed that anxiety was not directly connected to ideas or thoughts, but was the result of an accumulation of sexual energy or libido produced by abstinence or by unconsummated sexual excitement – for example, *coitus interruptus*. The libido that is unexpressed becomes 'dammed up' and, like a toxic substance, is converted into anxiety. Regular sexual practice was felt to release these blockages and liberate anxiety.

An increase in instinctual tension without any possibility of discharge gives rise to experiences of unpleasure, while discharge reducing the build-up of instinctual tension to regain equilibrium or homeostasis can be pleasurable. It is easy to see this in a crowd watching a football match. In football it is often difficult to score a goal, and this uncertainty and build-up of tension creates anxiety. There is an ever increasing anticipation of winning or losing in a stylised conflict situation, where triumph and humiliation are close at hand.

Most spectators in the crowd feel this, resulting in tension, which is easily observed in the faces of the crowd and is felt in a bodily manner by everyone. The shouting of the crowd itself is a socially acceptable method of discharging accumulated energy. Anxiety levels are raised as the supported team fails to score, and especially if the opposing team does. However, when the supported team *does* score, there is a massive release of tension in shouting, jumping and whooping, which is shared by everyone. The sense of pleasurable release is palpable and can seem orgasmic.

The fact that both the unpleasure of the rising tension and the pleasurable release is shared with a large group is helpful in managing the anxiety, as it is dispersed among everyone and thus easier to cope with. There is often an attempt to project the bad feelings into the opposing supporters by, for example, the gloating jeering at the losing team's supporters, when the supported team is winning, as crowds of fingers point at them, signalling the direction of the projection; and the supporters' chant: 'You're not singing, you're not singing anymore!'

It has frequently been said by ardent football supporters that watching your team winning a football match is better than sex. It has been shown that the level of the male sex hormone, testosterone, is raised in supporters when their team has lost at the end of a game. This 'blocked' sexual energy can become toxic in a similar manner to that described by Freud.

If there is no release of the build-up of this toxic tension when, for example, the team loses or the pleasure from the goal scored is removed as the other team equalise, then anxiety can increase and lead to attempts to discharge the tension in inappropriate ways in violent or anti-social behaviour. It is most commonly internalised, giving rise to a feeling akin to a low mood. I am aware that many other complex group and individual factors are at work in this example, and that it is oversimplified for the purposes of clearer exposition.

Repression

At the time when Freud was writing, Victorian sexual repression was rife and many problems encountered in clinical practice arose from the anxiety caused by unacceptable sexual desires. Freud's next theory of anxiety concerned repression. In this phase of his thinking, unacceptable sexual desires, impulses and urges arising from the primitive id come into conflict with 'civilised' societal norms internalised in the person in the form of the ego or superego.

The ego (or self), caught between the demands of its two 'masters', the id and the higher superego (or conscience), represses the ideas connected to the sexual instinctual urges and relegates them to the unconscious. The energy attached to the idea is liberated and can be used for other purposes, which Freud called *sublimation*. The stimulus for the repression is the anxiety in the ego, created by the conflict between the sexual instinct and societal norms.

This is still true today when, for example, a child's desire to 'marry mummy' brings him into supposed conflict with his rival father in external reality or his conscience in internal reality, when he wishes to get rid of his father so that he may have his mother all to himself. This conflict creates anxiety, and the ideas connected with these unacceptable sexual desires towards his mother are repressed and become unconscious. This Oedipal situation will be discussed later (see page 49), as it is the source of many anxieties.

The repressed idea may at times try to force its way back into consciousness – the 'return of the repressed' – and this too can generate anxiety once again in the ego by signalling the emergence of something dangerous.

Automatic and Signal Anxiety

Freud's later thinking about anxiety included a differentiation of two main types of anxiety. The more primitive and primary anxiety relates to a traumatic experience of total disintegration leading to possible annihilation, consequent on being flooded by overwhelming quantities of instinctual tension. Laplanche and Pontalis describe automatic or primary anxiety as *the subject's reaction each time he finds himself in a traumatic situation – that is, each time he is confronted by an inflow of excitations, whether of external or internal origin, which he is unable to master.*[5]

This so-called automatic anxiety is defended against by later signal anxiety, which serves as a warning about the potential emergence of the automatic anxiety – that is, a fear of annihilation.

Freud's later work[6] described '*signal* anxiety, not directly a conflicted instinctual tension but a signal occurring in the ego of an *anticipated* instinctual tension'.[7] Thus the classical psychoanalytic view of anxiety is a signal or warning that something really overwhelmingly awful is just about to happen, so you had better do something about it quickly if you are to survive physically and mentally. It can be likened to a massive electrical storm in the mind.

Freud thought it had connections to the overwhelming experience of birth. The signalling function of anxiety is thus seen as a crucial one, and biologically adapted to warn the organism of danger or a threat to its equilibrium. The anxiety is felt as an increase in bodily or mental tension, and the signals that the organism receives in this way allows it the possibility of taking defensive action towards the perceived danger, which the psychoanalyst Charles Rycroft describes as 'an inwardly directed form of vigilance'.[8]

Both forms of anxiety, signal and automatic, are seen as deriving from the 'infant's mental helplessness which is a counterpart of its biological helplessness'.[9] The automatic or primary anxiety denotes a spontaneous type of reaction connected to a fear of total dissolution arising from being utterly overwhelmed; it implies no capacity to judge or perceive the origin of the overwhelming stimuli and is thus differentiated from the signal type of anxiety. The function of the signal anxiety is 'to ensure that the primary [*automatic*] anxiety is never experienced by enabling the ego to institute defensive precautions' (my italics).[10] We are thus talking about a situation where we learn to distinguish warning signs or signals learnt from previous bad, unpleasurable or traumatic experiences, to try to avoid them again.

The anxiety thus has a crucial function in preserving the organism from physical or psychic danger. The 'never again' quality is familiar to all of us where we have been hurt or harmed, or overwhelmed. The fear of dissolution of the ego, or disintegrating or ceasing to be, is a primitive anxiety situation for us all. It was thought to have connections to the trauma of birth, but later psychoanalytic thinkers like Melanie Klein and Freud himself in his later works link it to a fear of the death instinct or aggression operating within. Other psychoanalysts like Ester Bick and Bion connect it to a failure of containment, and all these ideas will be discussed later (see pages 57–9).

It is easy to see these fears of disintegration, fragmentation or dissolution in many children's nursery rhymes or stories. Perhaps the best known is 'Humpty Dumpty'. He had a great fall and was in so many pieces that he could not be put back together again by all the King's horses and all the King's men. The anxiety about an irreparable Humpty has many sources. However, for this discussion I am focusing on the fear of disintegration or automatic anxiety.

One three-year-old child was so distressed when he heard the first bars of 'Humpty Dumpty' being played on a nursery-rhyme cassette (signal anxiety), that he clasped his hands together by his face and pleaded urgently, 'Fast forward Humpty, fast forward Humpty'. If there was no one available to do this, the child would run outside the room and wait until the song was over, at which point he would re-enter. Here we see the operation of signal anxiety in instituting defensive manoeuvres in order to prevent primary anxiety of total disintegration.

It is important to note that Freud's notion of anxiety derives from the fact of life that human infants are helpless creatures and utterly dependent for survival for longer periods of time than any other species on parenting functions to reduce states of internal tension arising from hunger, thirst, danger, cold and so on. This experience of helplessness is seen as the prototype of any situation of trauma. The trauma ensues when the organism cannot regulate its own state and thus becomes overwhelmed. Freud recognised that in any situation of trauma:

> What the internal dangers have in common is a loss or separation occasioning a progressive increase in tension until the subject finds himself incapable of mastering the excitations and is overwhelmed by them: this is what defines the state which generates the feeling of helplessness ... The infant's total helplessness over a relatively long period of time means that the dangers of the external world have a greater importance for it, so that the value of the object which can alone protect it against them and take the place of its former intrauterine life is enormously enhanced. This biological factor, then, establishes the earliest situations of danger and creates the need to be loved which will accompany the child through the rest of its life.[11]

This fact is crucial in understanding separation anxiety (discussed in more detail on pages 59–62). It is also the foundation for attachment theory developed by John Bowlby, a psychoanalyst and child psychiatrist, which emphasises the primary and biological function of intimate emotional bonds between individuals. The attachment behavioural system is a neurobiological organisation existing within the person, which monitors and appraises situations and events to maintain an internal sense of 'felt security' and safety by seeking proximity or contact with a specific caregiver, termed an attachment figure. Bowlby's use of the term 'anxiety' restricts it to situations of missing someone who is loved and longed for.[12] Child psychotherapist Juliet Hopkins writes:

> *Anxiety is experienced throughout life when we are threatened either by a hostile environment, or by the withdrawal or loss of our attachment figures.*[13]

Freud placed the loss of a loved object as one of the most central anxieties. His emphasis on the central role of castration anxiety or the fear of loss of bodily integrity – particularly the penis for the little boy – can also be understood as a variant of separation anxiety or loss. The loss of the penis not only signifies a loss of a source of pleasure; it also has a narcissistic value for the child. It also provides a means, in phantasy and in later sexual life in a symbolised form, of re-establishing the lost primary union with a mother figure.[14]

Emotional regulation through a relationship with a parental or attachment figure is thus crucial for human development. In fact, it has been shown that in situations of continual exposure to trauma in infancy where emotional regulation fails to reduce instinctual tension, the infant remains hyperaroused and hypervigilant to danger, resulting in the failure to acquire essential neurological structures necessary for development.[15]

Binding Anxiety

Anxiety therefore has a crucial signalling function for real or imagined dangers in trying to prevent the organism from being overwhelmed by emotion. The idea of anxiety as a 'premonition of emotion' thus implies the possibility that the emotion that may be experienced will be overwhelming and traumatic.

If the emotion can be recognised, it can be bound or attached in some way to an anticipated defensive response or memory or name, and this itself can reduce the anxiety. If you know what something is, at least you can begin to think about it and plan a course of action to try to deal with it. Predictability is a phenomenon that reduces anxiety, since it implies a reduction in uncertainty and helplessness which, as we have seen, are central factors in generating anxiety.

This is easy to observe in the way children love to have previously very frightening stories read to them again and again. One child watching the *Three Little Pigs* cartoon on a Disney video for the first time was terrified by the Big Bad Wolf who could 'eat you up'. The child developed a fear of wolves. Indeed, he would avoid looking at them in books and did not want to listen to the many fairy stories like *Little Red Riding Hood* that featured wolves. He did, however, want to watch the video, which he previously found frightening, again and again. He would anxiously wait for the appearance of the wolf, then start to laugh manically and over-loudly as if he had no fear of it at all. He seemed to be forcing himself to confront and master his fear. He used to play a game where he had to be chased, caught and eaten by the wolf, then reverse the situation by chasing and eating the pursuer.

While one could say that the child had developed a phobia about wolves and wanted to avoid situations where he may encounter them, he watched the video over and over again to convince himself he was not helpless and could triumphantly predict the appearance of the wolf. The phobia itself is a way of binding a more generalised anxiety to a specific situation that can then be controlled to some extent. This again reduces the helplessness at the root of the anxiety.

Many phobias are used in this way and are symbols for a deeper anxiety. And, luckily, most are only mildly disabling. Binding anxiety can also be seen in cases of deliberate self-harm, where people cut or inflict pain on themselves. While this can have many causes and meanings, it is often an attempt to localise a non-specific, uncontrolled pain or anxiety; to locate it in a particular area on the body under the control of the person. An adolescent girl aged sixteen described how, when she saw blood oozing from a cut she made on her arm, not only was inner tension relieved in a blood-letting sort of way, but also the source of the pain could be seen and controlled. It lessened her anxiety, although it had a negative side effect of creating guilt, which is a different type of mental pain.

Melanie Klein's Views of Anxiety

Melanie Klein's work radically altered how anxiety was thought about, as she moved the focus of attention from a generalised anxiety situation favoured by Freud to one of the inner phantasy *content* of the anxiety, to give meaning to it. Klein defined two clearly distinguishable classes of anxiety and defences – namely, the paranoid-schizoid position and the depressive position. She placed the study of anxiety in a central position in psychoanalytic work: 'From the beginning of my psychoanalytic work, my interest was focused on anxiety and its causation.'[16]

Anxiety was also seen to be the main motivation that promotes development, although excessive anxiety can have the opposite effect as well, and lead to an inhibition in development when it is overwhelming and unmanageable.

Klein asserted that infants have an innate quest for knowledge of all kinds, and that the baby's first object of curiosity is the mother's body – what goes on inside it, what it contains, how it relates to her outside appearance and how it is differentiated from the infant's own body. In line with Freud, Klein also felt that there was a continuous interplay within everybody between what may be called life instincts (or love) and the death instinct (or hate), giving rise to ambivalence.

Gratifying experiences with the mother generate loving impulses, while frustrating experiences generate hatred and rage. It is easy to observe how quickly a baby can flip between these two states and back again. A baby who is waiting to be fed and screaming with rage seems to be in the grip of an intense negative experience. As soon as he (I am using the pronoun 'he' to refer to the baby, with nothing implied by its gender) is picked up and put to the breast, the whole world changes. The baby calms immediately, as if by magic, and is soothed and comforted.

The rising unpleasant instinctual tension within the baby is felt as the presence of a 'bad breast' attacking him, rather than the absence of a 'good breast'. The relieving feed pushes the bad breast away and replaces it with the good breast. In common parlance, people talk of, for example, 'keeping the cold out', implying that they see the cold as a negative intrusive thing, rather than the thermo-dynamically correct idea of heat escaping or the absence of heat.

The other central tenet in Klein's theory concerns what she termed *unconscious phantasy*. Stated simply, this means that all bodily impulses and emotional experiences have a mental representation in the form of phantasies, which the infant uses to build up his own unique picture of the world. All the time, the baby is trying to make sense of his experience, to construct a model of the world – an internal representation that is continually being modified and tested throughout life. For example, the state of unpleasant instinctual tension arising from hunger can feel like being attacked by a bad object inside. Thus, from the beginning the infant carries within him a dynamic, ever-changing, *alive*, internal world. This world is peopled with representations of the self in relationship to significant others, termed internal objects or parts of the self in relation to each other. The state of these internal objects changes according to what is attributed to them and what is taken in from people outside, our external objects. As psycho-analyst Betty Joseph says:

> We know that we build our characters by taking into ourselves – introjecting – our early relationships to our parents and close figures of our infancy and childhood as we experience them, and that we feel about ourselves according to the world we build up inside, our internal world.[17]

The baby's perception of outside reality is dependent on this internalised representation of the world and the relationships within it, and the baby can only make sense of his experience with reference to this. Klein called this the *primacy of psychic reality*. Many of her observations are being confirmed by modern infant research, which has shown that the baby's internal world is much more complicated than we previously imagined and that all perception is mediated by the meaning attached to it by the brain.

The 'world' for the foetus is the inside of the mother's body, and from the infant's point of view it contains everything there is. Klein surmised that the baby was intensely curious about it. She also believed that the baby had unconscious knowledge about intercourse in a rudimentary form, as well as unconscious know-ledge of the existence of the father's penis. The mother's body represents in unconscious phantasy 'the treasure house of every-thing desirable which can only be got from there'.[18]

When the baby is frustrated or angry or in a rage, *in his phantasies* he attacks the mother's body with anything and every-thing he has at his disposal. It may be through his biting using his powerful jaws and gums, and later teeth, in phantasy to rip, devour, tear, shred, chew up and so on the frustrating breast or nipple. His faeces may be felt to be potentially very dangerous, explosive like bombs that burst from his rectum, or poisonous or contaminating. His urine, experienced as hot or burning, can be used in phantasy to burn up, drown and so on. The mother's body and its contents – particularly the babies inside or the father's penis supposedly incorporated during intercourse – are then felt to be destroyed and damaged, and the infant becomes intensely persecuted by terrors and fears of retaliation for the damage he has caused.

This all sounds most bizarre and far-fetched, but anyone who closely observes children's play or drawings, or who listens to their dreams, will find confirmation of these types of phantasy.

Many films contain references to them – particularly horror films. In war atrocities, these phantasies often get acted out.

Klein felt that the most provoking and frightening figure for the infant is when the mother and father are felt to be combined together in a hostile way, which she called the 'bad combined object'. This may occur when the baby feels left out of the parents' bedroom or their private intimate relationship. If the mother is absent from the baby, the baby may assume that she is either with the father or with other children. This is part of the well-known Oedipal situation.

In his phantasy, in the inner world, the infant is felt to attack the parents together, or the mother with some representation of the father inside her, like his penis, resulting in a damaged combined figure which becomes the most frightening and anxiety-provoking object for the baby. These 'bad' internal objects may damage the infant from the inside by the same methods that he had used originally in his attacks, or be felt to be located in bad external objects. His own life is felt to be in danger.

It is quite common for babies to become very frightened of taking the breast, arching their backs, screaming or turning away after they have been angry and frustrated while having to wait during a separation. The absent breast may have been attacked in the baby's mind and thus the baby may fear that the returning breast is hostile to him. The infant is therefore anxious and fearful about retaliatory attacks on him arising from objects inside or outside of him, primarily motivated by the law of the talion – an eye for an eye and a tooth for a tooth – and he uses powerful defences to protect himself and his equilibrium.

This destruction of the mother's body and its parts and contents goes on in the infant's internal world; in external reality the baby can do very little damage except perhaps hurt the mother's nipple or scratch her. It is very reassuring for the baby when his mother returns to him in a friendly manner and the baby sees she has not been destroyed. This confirmation of her survival enables him to gain confidence that there is a distinction between internal and external reality, and that he is not omnipotent – that is, his thought and phantasy are not as magical and powerful as he believes them to be.

Play and Phantasy

I want to give an example of how close observation of the play of a three-year-old child, Jeff, and his four-year-old brother, Adam, in a nursery can illuminate the phantasies being expressed in the play. The children depict in their play a series of phantasied attacks on the mother, father and combination of them both. We see the children becoming persecuted following this.

The children were in foster care, having been abandoned by their single mother a few months before the observation took place. Jeff had ferocious tantrums, especially after waking up, when he curled up like a foetus and couldn't bear being looked at.

Jeff is walking around a room in the nursery dragging his jumper on the floor. His worker asks him to hang it on a peg.

'I can't do it,' Jeff says.

'I'm sure you can,' says his worker – with which, Jeff hangs the jumper on the peg. [*Here we see Jeff feeling he has nothing inside, feeling unable to do anything.*]

The worker is sitting at the pastry table with Jeff's brother Adam. Jeff sits down and says: 'I want to play with you. Can you make me a sausage?'

'You try,' his worker says. 'I'll help you if you can't.'

Jeff rolls a piece of pastry and says to his worker, 'Is this a sausage?'

'Yes,' the worker says. 'That's fine.'

Adam says, 'No, that's a snake.'

Jeff says, 'No, it's not a snake.'

Jeff then rolls the pastry flat with a rolling pin. He puts his rolling pin down and says to his worker, 'How do balls go?'

The worker shows him and says, 'You try and make one.'

Jeff picks up the pastry, rolls it like his worker showed him and says, 'This is not going to be a sausage.'

Then he says, 'Can you make a necklace for my arm?'

His worker does so and gives it to him. Jeff breaks it into small pieces, throws it on the table and bangs it angrily with the rolling pin. [*The necklace on his arm was something feminine he wanted, perhaps linked to the abandoning mother, and it provokes a smashing, flattening attack with the rolling pin. This flattening of things – potentially good things which turn bad, also like the masculine sausage changing to the snake and ending up flattened – seems connected to his flattened lifeless state in the beginning.*]

Jeff then gets up from the table, sits back down again, gets up again, goes to the corner and picks up a boy doll, saying, 'He has a willy.' [*Refer to the earlier references to sausages, snakes and balls.*]

Jeff puts the doll on the pastry table and Adam sticks pastry over its penis area. Jeff says, 'Willy, willy!', looks at the worker, then sticks pastry on the doll's tummy (the pastry is red) and says, 'Bleed *her* belly.' [*Notice the change of sex, and the association to the willy's damaging activity. It implies a bad combination of willy and belly, causing bleeding. Klein called this a phantasy of a bad intercourse. The figure now seems both female and male, a potentially damaged and thus dangerous bad combined object.*]

Adam says, 'We are going to put it on her face' – which he does.

Jeff then puts some pastry in his mouth (which is against the nursery's rules) and says in a challenging way, 'What am I eating?' [*I think he is trying to provoke punishment for his sadistic attacks, as well as identifying with the object of the attack – taking it into him as described above.*]

Adam takes the pastry off the doll's willy. Jeff says, 'Put it back on his willy.' [*That is to make it feminine by covering up the penis, or to represent the idea that the mother and father are fused and combined with each other. It could also represent castration anxiety as described by Freud, with the idea that a woman is like a man with his penis removed.*]

Jeff puts more pastry on the doll's face, saying, 'He doesn't even like me, he can see.' [*Jeff seems to be becoming persecuted by the attacked and damaged object, which may see him and retaliate – think back to his terror on waking up and not wanting to be looked at.*]

Jeff then sits back and watches Adam cover the whole doll with the pastry. Jeff says, 'We're firing her up.' [*That is, burning her up.*]

Adam uses all the pastry and says, 'I want some more.'

The worker says there isn't any more.

Jeff finds a tiny piece and says to Adam, 'Put the pastry on her toes, on *his* toes, sorry.' [*Here especially we see the switch between female and male, probably representing the combination of them both.*]

Jeff shows the worker the small piece of pastry he has in his hand, and says, 'Look, I have pastry; it's pink.'

He gets up and says in a dismissive voice, 'Look at that dolly.'

Then he walks away to the sand.

I think this observation shows vividly how an attack on the mother and her body, including references to the mother and father being combined with each other, leaves her bleeding and fired up, with the man not liking what he is able to see, ripe to retaliate – a very persecutory situation for these little boys. They then turn away and, in a spirit of denial, characteristic of one of the defences of the paranoid-schizoid position, dismiss the whole thing and walk off.

Hinshelwood cites Klein's use of Freud's term 'Early Anxiety Situation' which refers to

> *early situations of anxiety or danger for the infant and applied it to her own discovery of the fears arising from the sadistic phantasies of attacking the mother's body and the retaliation expected from it.*[19]

Although the early anxiety situation also involves fear of loss of the loved object in a similar manner to that described by Freud, mentioned earlier (see page 45), we are focusing at present on the persecutory anxieties, which involve primarily a threat to the self. The overriding principle is the safety and comfort of the self; poor me. There is little or no concern for the other, and an abdication of personal responsibility.

This persecutory early anxiety situation is responsible for many of the anxieties we all face. For example, if we return to the child frightened of the wolves and the phobia resulting from it (see pages 45–6), it is possible to see that child's fear of the biting wolf who can eat you all up as a fear of retaliation for his own wishes to devour his object, probably the breast in its earliest manifestation, then later his mother and the contents of her body – including his father.

You may remember the reversal game played to gain mastery of this anxiety, when first the child chased his mother and ate her up and then she 'retaliated'. Klein's formulations enable us to make some sense of these primitive yet ubiquitous anxieties and their manifestations in behaviour.

Terror

Terror is a paranoid (highly persecutory) anxiety, felt in nightmares and anxieties about monsters, ghosts and so on, which leads to a sense of paralysis which 'leaves no avenue of action'.[20]

Meltzer believes that the greatest source of terror arises from the intense fears about dead objects – particularly the mother's babies murdered in psychic reality. Meltzer comments that the 'object of terror cannot even be fled from with success'.[21]

Terror is such a common anxiety that people go to horror films to be terrified to try to gain some control over it, much in the same way as the little boy watched the *Three Little Pigs* video over and over again. Ghost stories also proliferate in literature. These highly persecutory anxieties surface commonly in bad dreams, and children's play is full of them. The play enables the child to try to express and so bind the anxiety.

A very common anxiety expressed by children (and adults alike!) is the fear of burglars and intruders. This is different from reality-based fears of intruders. Again, Klein's theories can help us make some sense of these fears if we remember that the child in phantasy invades the mother's body – his first house – in order to damage or steal. The resulting retaliatory fears, including robbers coming in the window at night to stab or 'get' the child, are very common. There are many examples of this type of intrusive behaviour that create this type of anxiety – for example, plundering the mother's handbag, or getting between the parents in their bed or when they are being affectionate to each other.

A more vivid example is shown by Peter. In psychotherapy, the child is given the opportunity to express his phantasies in a non-directive way through the medium of play and behaviour.

Peter, aged seven, turns his attention to the window of the psychotherapy room during one of his sessions. He notices that the catch is broken and becomes anxious. His therapist interprets that he is worried that he has broken it. Peter looks at his therapist squarely in the eye as he says this. [*Peter was anxious about damage he may have felt he caused to this portal of entry to the room.*]

Peter decides to become the fixer of the window. His efforts are increasingly complex, Sellotaping the window closed and trying to fix the broken latch. He sets up a complex trap for the intruders, reminding the therapist of the film *Home Alone*, where a child abandoned by his parents triumphs over intruders into the family home with a complex series of traps.

Peter goes over to his toy box, selects a toy tiger, ties it up and wraps it in Sellotape as if imprisoning it. He goes back to the windows and smears glue over the Sellotape, saying, 'If they touch it . . .'

The therapist asks who 'they' are.

'The baddie children who come in,' Peter replies.

'Are they coming to get you?' the therapist asks.

'At night time, when there is thunder, I go to Morris's bed.' [*Morris is his brother.*]

Peter continues, 'They will smash down the door, not the window.'

It is as if he cannot make the room safe enough, that even if the window is secure, they could still come in somewhere else. [*In dreams, often the persecutors cannot be killed; they get up again after being shot and so on, and continue their threat or chase.*]

A little later, Peter goes over to the window and pulls the Sellotape off to release it. [*This seems to signal an attack from the persecutors, although the timing is now under his control so he is not entirely at their mercy.*]

He dives onto the couch in the room and appears to be attacked by the couch cover. He struggles with the cover as if his life depends on it. He thrashes about on the couch, then runs over to his toy box and releases the tiger he had earlier tied up and Sellotaped. At this point he seems to metamorphosise into this tiger. He begins growling and padding around the room on all fours, jumping onto the furniture. He bounds about the room growling, having now become the persecutor rather than the persecuted. [*This identification with the aggressor is a common method for dealing with persecutory anxiety, as it allows the person to project the fear into someone else who becomes the victim of the attack.*]

As Peter pads ominously around the room growling, snapping and baring his teeth, he suddenly says 'Daddy'.

'Daddy?' his therapist enquires.

'He is drunk,' says Peter, then launches an attack on the pillows of the couch, throwing them about, screaming 'They are babies.'

He grabs the playdough and, throwing it hard against the wall, says it is a baby, too.

'The tiger daddy is having babies. He hates them. He kills them. There are too many babies. They may kill the Daddy.'

As he speaks he throws the playdough around, 'killing it', saying 'I hate babies' in a gruff man's voice clearly identified with the tiger/daddy. The therapist speaks about how frightening this tiger/daddy is, and how Peter tries to become him so as not to be as terrified and helpless as the babies who may be killed must feel.

In this vignette, although we see that Peter is very confused by the source of the anxiety, some clear elements emerge. He is obviously terrified about the intruders getting in, which at first are 'baddie children'. These persecutors quickly become joined with the extremely frightening drunk daddy. His hatred of the rival babies is projected into the daddy, who is now the one who hates babies and wants to kill them.

It is a common defence to project into the father, and especially his penis, the sadism and aggression arising from exclusion from the parental intercourse or 'primal scene' which produces rival babies. People find it strange that young children are interested in their parents' sexuality. They are interested not only because of their own sexual and bodily feelings but also because their parents' sexuality is potentially quite threatening to them.

Peter probably had such murderous wishes towards his parents' intercourse and the threat of other babies produced from it. These babies are attacked ferociously in his phantasy, like the playdough and pillows are in the play. These attacked babies are probably synonymous with the 'baddie children' who are coming to get him. The retaliation is clear, as is his attempt not to feel the primary anxiety of helplessness as discussed earlier. Instead, he identifies with the persecutor and stops being a frightened boy in his bed at night, becoming a fearsome tiger/daddy himself.

Depressive Anxiety

Anxieties about the dangerous condition of the mother's body and, by extension, external reality, interfere with the free exploration of the outside world. These kinds of anxiety based on fears of retaliation and annihilation of the self, termed *persecutory anxieties*, are contrasted with a different kind of anxiety where the prime concern is over the safety or condition of the object – for example, the mother and her body. These are termed *depressive anxieties* by Klein, and relate to the concern and fear of loss of a good object resulting from the child's sadistic attacks on it.

As mentioned earlier (see page 47), intimate relationships are imbued with ambivalence in that both love and hate are felt for the same person. When the baby apprehends the 'selected fact'[22] that the bad and good mother are one and the same person, then the hate and the destructive impulses he feels towards the 'bad' mother are also directed towards the 'good' mother the baby loves; a depressive crisis occurs. The baby becomes concerned about the damage he may have inflicted on the very person he loves most. It is captured in Oscar Wilde's 'Ballad of Reading Gaol': 'Yet each man kills the thing he loves.' It gives rise to a particularly painful kind of anxiety in the baby, and a wish to repair the damage for which he feels responsible. It is, in fact, more painful than persecutory anxiety, as the main focus is guilt, grief, 'What have I done?', remorse, regret and loneliness.

While depressive anxiety involves the fear of loss of love of the person, the quality defined in this anxiety is different from that discussed by Freud. Freud's conception seems more linked to the fear of loss of love leading to the loss of the parents' availability to reduce the instinctual states of the child. This seems to be a more self-centred conception than Klein's idea of depressive anxiety. Since concern for the welfare of the other predominates over concern for the self, characterised by 'poor you' (compared with, in persecutory anxiety, 'poor me'), it also forms the basis for tenderness, empathy and reparative wishes. It involves taking responsibility for one's own feelings and their consequences. Joseph writes:

> Of course, toleration of ambivalence with its resultant sense of guilt, if properly elaborated, can and should lessen anxiety, because the awareness of love and concern, and the attempt to do something about this will mitigate anger and resentment and this reduces anxiety.[23]

Thus, the capacity to bear depressive anxiety is a major

achievement in the developmental path towards maturity. Many achievements in the world and acts of creativity are thought to be related to the need to make a contribution, to make reparation, arising from tolerating depressive concern, thus demonstrating how anxiety stimulates development. Klein also writes how a baby's anxiety about an object, particularly the persecutory variety, can stimulate the search for new objects which may not be so imbued with persecution, thus enlarging the scope of people and things that the child may relate to in the world.

If either form of anxiety is too great, there can be an inhibition and constriction in the way of relating to the world. Similarly, there can be a marked increase in feelings of guilt, despair and hopelessness if the damage done is believed to be irreparable and thus unforgivable.

Anxieties About Learning

Many learning difficulties can arise from the situation where there is evidence of actual damage to the mother's body. Klein believed that:

> It is essential for a favourable development of the desire for knowledge that the mother's body should be felt to be well and unharmed . . . If it is not destroyed, not so much in danger and therefore dangerous itself, the wish to take food for the mind from it can more easily be carried out . . . If the woman's body is felt as a place full of destruction there may be a basic inhibition in the desire for knowledge. Since the inside of the mother's body is the first object of this impulse; in phantasy it is explored and investigated as well as attacked with all the sadistic armoury.[24]

This may sound odd, but think that 'mother nature' is a primary object of knowledge. Specific intellectual inhibitions may result from defences against sadism. These defences may be for perse-cutory or depressive reasons. So many words and expressions concerned with learning link learning to the feeding and digestive process – for example, 'an appetite for learning', 'take something in', 'food for thought', 'she devoured that book', 'she absorbed it', 'you don't spoon-feed children', 'something was not digested', 'it was just regurgitated', 'swallowed it whole', 'chewed things over' and so on. Psychoanalysts believe that early experiences and situations lay down templates for the personality that recur in different guises throughout development. Anxieties about the feeding process invariably intersect with primitive anxieties and thus can affect the capacity to learn. The phantasy accompanying the particular activity thus determines the outcome of that activity.

In order to be able to read or discover things, you have to be able to look beneath the surface of things, to 'get into' a subject. This implies a kind of penetrating mental activity.

> *A book is a house for a story.*
> *A rose is a house for a smell.*
> *My head is a house for a secret.*
> *A secret I never will tell.*[25]

A word is thus a house for a meaning, and the first house the baby occupies is its mother's body. If the mother's body is felt to be a place 'full of destruction', in Klein's terms, when for example the mother has suffered a stillbirth, miscarriage, abortion or serious illness, then many learning difficulties can stem from this, including reading inhibitions. There may be an anxiety that either she is too fragile to withstand phantasied attacks upon her unborn or born children, or that the child's sadistic phantasies really are as powerful in external reality as they are in internal reality.

It is very common to discover that in the families of children referred with learning difficulties to child and family consultation services, there has often been the death of a baby or child for one reason or another.[26]

As I mentioned earlier (see pages 52–3), the child may respond in a persecutory manner and be terrified and fear retaliation from the dead ghost babies about being alive or occupying their place, or he may react depressively and feel very guilty about what he imagines he has done. He may inhibit his achievements accordingly. Either way, the child's learning is affected.

There are, of course, many other kinds of anxiety that affect the ability to learn, including the operation of envy. A person may inhibit his or her achievements in order not to provoke spoiling and destructive attacks arising from the supposed envy of someone else. Also, there is a need to tolerate the frustration of not knowing something in order to learn something new. In order to discuss this further, since it is a critical point in thinking about growth and change of any sort, it is necessary to discuss the concept of containment of anxiety.

Containment of Anxiety

A central theme of this essay is that anxiety, which is a type of mental pain, lies at the heart of all psychoanalytical conceptions. I will use the words 'anxiety' and 'mental pain' interchangeably. A central tenet of the psychoanalytical view is that no development can take place without pain. As we have discussed, too much or too little pain impedes development. Thus the problem of containment and distribution of the mental pain connected with growth and development is our core subject of study. Anxiety is dealt with through the relations with objects, initially the primary attachment figure. The capacity to cope with mental pain in a developmentally enhancing manner depends on the availability from birth, or even pre-natally, of an emotionally receptive or attuned person who can *contain* the infant's primitive communications and help him make sense of his emotional experiences. What does this concept of containment actually mean?

In Bion's theory of container/contained,[27] the development of the capacity to think or be curious in any way, to pay attention or to learn, depends on the baby's experience of being thought about, or having had the experience of somebody being curious or emotionally attentive to him. The baby's psyche is not developed enough to contain powerful feelings of any kind, and is thus absolutely dependent on the availability of some object, usually the mother in the first instance, into whom the baby can rid himself of these feelings. Bion calls this object the *container*, and the raw, unprocessed, undigested emotional material projected into the container, the *contained*.

The baby's crying or other behaviour evokes distress or other feelings in the mother if she is emotionally attentive to her baby. She then has to try to make sense of what the baby is feeling or what his cries mean by reflecting and thinking about what the baby has made her feel, by relating it to her own experience and her experience of the baby, before responding accordingly.

This process, called *reverie* by Bion, is often unconscious. The baby, then, is not only made more comfortable by having his needs met, but is also able to take inside himself the experience of his mother having a space in her mind for him, and he feels understood. As the baby has more and more experiences like this, it enables him to take into his mind a thinking object, a representation of the container/contained experience. He can then use this thinking object, this container, to think for himself about his own experiences. Thus, he begins to develop his own capacity to think about his emotional experiences and have a space in his own mind. A baby thus needs a container to investigate his feelings, to find out what he is feeling and what it means.

What if the mother cannot accept these projections of raw emotion from the baby? What if there is no one to perform the function of containment – that is, bear the unbearable for the baby?

The infant's only recourse is to try even harder to evacuate the bad feeling, which is made worse by the experience of feeling misunderstood and not attended to. He does not internalise a container who can think about him or understand him, or help him 'name' his anxieties and differentiate his emotional states based on differential responses to them, but instead takes in a communication-rejecting container.

The infant then cannot make sense of his experience and cannot understand. He seems to experience the container's unwillingness to receive his communications as hostile, and a vicious circle is set up whereby the only choice available to the infant is to try to get rid of his bad experiences with increasing force or, more catastrophically, to give up trying to project his anxieties at all. He does not develop a growth-enhancing method for regulating his emotions, and instead identifies with the characteristics of the faulty container.

Bion describes how in any situation of anxiety there are three ways of dealing with the problem.

The first involves *modulating* the mental pain, 'primarily by thought, leading to understanding and actions that may success-fully modify or adapt to the external world, or internalise new qualities into the internal objects that can comfort or strengthen the personality'.[28] Bion talks of the need for us to respect the *facts* of a situation to try to real-ise whatever they are, then act accordingly.

This is to be distinguished from the second method of dealing with pain by trying to *modify* the situation, to try to fit it into how you want it to be. This involves a distortion of the facts by the use of any of the mechanisms of defence – for example, idealise-ing, or denigrate-ing them.

The third more extreme way of dealing with pain is to try to *evade* it altogether, by destroying the capacity to know about reality or ignoring the facts entirely. This leads to ignore-ance, according to Bion. Modulation through thinking, modification through defending, or evasion through obliteration are, then, three different ways of coping with anxiety. In order to illustrate these ideas, I want to give an example of one of the most familiar anxieties seen in everyone – separation anxiety.

Separation Anxiety

I mentioned earlier (see pages 57–9) that a baby is absolutely dependent on the existence of a parent to regulate his emotional states. The absence of such a figure, then, gives rise to a particular type of anxiety called separation anxiety.

The separation from a needed and loved figure mobilises attachment behaviour (mentioned on page 45). Separation anxiety can be felt by anyone, of any age, when a loved/needed person is absent, but its roots lie in infancy. How it is dealt with depends on the state of the person's mental apparatus and attachment history. We know that separation is best handled if the child can keep contact with a securely internalised object, or container or working model, that allows him to feel safe in the new environment. I am grateful for Paulo Carignani[29] for allowing me to use these following observations.

Tom, aged twenty-two months, is a child who is finding it excruciating to separate from his mother when she brings him into the nursery. In this observation, soon after he joined the nursery, he runs into the room with his mother and takes out a gun, laughing manically and shooting at everybody. [*From the beginning we see him trying to obliterate his anxiety about coming into this new situation, by being omnipotent and out of touch. All potential dangers are to be got rid of.*]

A teacher says 'Hello' to him, then invites him to come and sit near her and listen to the story she is telling other children. Tom doesn't answer, but instead shoots his gun, making a noise with his mouth. [*We could safely assume that persecutory anxiety prevails, as clearly he is trying to get rid of some baddie threat.*]

Tom subsequently turns towards his mother who is coming into the room, then towards another little boy, who has a little car in his hand. He suddenly grabs this car from the child. The child starts shrieking and tries to get his car back. Tom shouts, then bursts into tears, while the teacher and mother step forward to separate the two children. For a few minutes the teacher tries hopelessly to convince Tom to hand back the car. When she eventually scolds him in a high voice, Tom yells even more loudly.

The teacher takes the car from Tom and hands it to the other child. Tom throws himself to the floor, crying desperately. The mother looks terribly anxious. She stands near him and does not seem to know what to do. She tries to explain why the teacher did it. The teacher tries to invite Tom to go and listen to the story, but he does not go. He picks up some toys from a cupboard and starts throwing them on the floor. His desperate crying changes to furious shouting. Mother says this happens every day.

In this painful scenario, we see how Tom tries to cope. His attempts to obliterate his anxiety are unsuccessful. He tries to inflict his distress about the potential loss of someone he wants to cling to onto someone else by grabbing the other child's car just after he sees his mother about to leave. This is an attempt to modify his pain by projecting it onto someone else, and is a typical defence that is used in the presence of persecutory anxiety. The other child is to have something taken from him and suffer.

Through the interventions of the teacher, when the car is handed back to the child, Tom is forced to have the pain he cannot yet bear. His mother does not know how to contain him in this state, and all he can do is try to evacuate distress by throwing himself and all the toys on the floor, which is another attempt at evasion and a typical response to a communication-rejecting container. He cannot think; he just acts.

Through the intervention of the observer, Paulo, who spent time each day observing the child, Tom seemed to learn a different method of coping with pain over time, perhaps through identifying with the thoughtful approach of the observer.

In contrast, three weeks later Tom is sitting on the floor with many toys. He has a piece of cloth in his mouth and is sucking it. [*Was this how he tried to keep hold of his infant self's connection to his mother?*]

He holds a pistol in his right hand and a little plastic elephant in his left. With the fingers of his right hand, he touches the elephant's eyes and at the same time drops his pistol to the ground. [*Was Tom focusing on the eyes and seeing, perhaps realising, rather than needing to hold on to the methods of the obliterating gun?*]

He takes a little and big elephant and clears a space in front of him; he then makes the small elephant feed from the big one. He has to grasp the two animals all the time, or they would fall. He tries leaving them several times and when they do fall, Tom looks at his mother and brings them back to their original positions. He seems curious about how they fell. [*Was this curiosity an identification again with the observer's curiosity? I remind you how Tom himself was falling in the first observations.*]

After a time, Tom's mother comes to him and asks what game he is playing. 'It is a game about animals who fall,' he says.

Mother smiles at him and says she has to go. He looks at her with desperate, tearful eyes and asks if she could stay with him one moment more. Mother says she can't. She kisses him and walks out. Tom looks at his mother while she walks out, then bursts into tears. After a few seconds he stops crying. He dries his tears with his hands, stands up and comes near the observer, asking him to pick him up and 'take me to the window to see my mummy who is not there'.

The observer takes him in his arms and walks to the window. Tom stares out into the garden and after a few minutes of silent gazing asks to be put down and runs off to play with the other children.

Tom was trying to symbolise his experience, which served the function of naming and binding the anxiety. He seemed to be thinking in the sense of creating a space, trying to make sense of his emotional experience where a mother and baby can be together, but who separate (fall), and then come back together (are stood up). It has all the hallmarks of a container mother and a contained baby.

If Tom can internalise and hold on to this representation, which allows him to realise the facts of the situation he is in, his anxiety seems to be modulated. He copes with the pain in a different way. He does not inflict it on someone else but carries it himself, perhaps with the help of this internal object like the big elephant, who can help him, as the baby, contain it and bear it. This is more of a depressive reaction to his situation. His ability to 'see a mummy who is not there' suggests that he has an internalised representation of a mother and baby in his mind, who can be together and apart, and then come back together again. His silent gazing while being contained by the arms of the observer may have been how he looked into his internal space to find this internal mother and baby representation.

The ability to tolerate the frustration of the presence of a 'not there mummy' long enough to create a thought about it, which Tom verbalised, is a crucial developmental step. His thinking modulates his anxiety and also gives rise to hope.

The presence, then, of an internalised object (in the form of a functioning container/contained system) to receive distress and think about it (based on identification with these functions having been performed externally for the child) is crucial in developing his capacity to deal with all mental pain in a growth-enhancing manner – that is, to bear it in a manner that leads to thought. We are now in a position to return to the anxieties involved in learning and growing up, or in dealing with any new situation.

Knowing and Not Knowing: Anxieties Involving Learning, Growth and Development

For many children, growing up is not conceived of as learning to take responsibility for one's self. For many young children, it is felt as a way to shed one identity and assume a new one . 'I'm a big boy/ girl now.'

This usually means finding someone else to have the baby feelings or little feelings, as growth is not conceived as organic and developmental, starting from the roots in the infantile ground and growing up from there.

True learning and growing is a painful experience and involves a lot of anxiety. For learning to take place, a certain amount of frustration is inevitable – the frustration of not knowing something, or of being confused and anxious about being ignorant. The capacity to bear these feelings determines the capacity to learn. This pain is essentially the 'uncertainty cloud'[30] or the ability to tolerate uncertainty, 'without irritable reaching after fact and reason', defined as *negative capability* by Keats.[31] This refers to the ability to tolerate the uncertainty of a new idea/situation impacting on the old ideas and ways of functioning that necessitates change. All 'facts of the external world are knowable only by their secondary qualities as they impinge on our senses in the context of an emotional experience. The ability to think about these facts of an emotional experience requires that the emotionality, especially the [anxiety], is contained'.[32]

The difficulty of bearing the anxiety of feeling little is illustrated by the following example of four-year-old Alison. Alison was immaculately dressed by her mother as a little adult. She carried herself with an air of superiority and haughtiness. She seemed above it all. Her mother used to drop her off at the nursery and stalk off, not saying goodbye, but leaving Alison unmoved; she was a big girl, big girls don't cry, only babies cry.

On one occasion, Alison sees her friend Molly by the climbing frame with another girl, Victoria. She walks over to them, hovering nearby. No one greets her. Molly then turns to Alison and says, 'I've got navy sandals.'

Alison replies scathingly, 'No, don't be silly; they're navy blue.' [*We call this a put-down, because it is putting another down, in an attempt to raise yourself up.*]

Molly and Victoria go inside. Alison follows a few steps behind. The girls move over to the book corner and sit looking at some books. Molly enthusiastically comments on the pictures in her book. Alison, on the other hand, sits cursorily flicking through the pages of a book, not seeming to take things in, but appearing to be reading. Molly makes fun of an *Aladdin* book, saying that 'Aladdin is a girl'. Alison rather sharply retorts, without looking up from her book, 'It's not an *Aladdin* book; it's not that front, it's the other front.'

Molly is confused.

Here we see Alison as a know-it-all, putting up a front, who makes others confused. She wants to give an impression of a big girl who doesn't care by projecting herself into a big grown-up identity as someone who knows how to read and corrects the silly little children. The caricatured quality of the pseudo little adult is evident, as littleness and confusion is projected elsewhere.[33]

In Melanie Klein's original formulation, depressive anxiety was thought to be developmentally more advanced than persecutory anxiety. Bion, however, was able to show that all of us oscillate between the two sets of anxieties.

It is common for the pain, especially guilt, inherent in depressive anxiety to be too intense to be contained and managed, and usher the return of more persecutory feelings. Premature feelings of guilt experienced by a person not capable of bearing them can feel extremely persecuting. Similarly, persecutory feelings may give rise to depressive feelings.

A simple illustration of the latter situation was afforded when a ten-year-old boy crept downstairs on the morning of his birthday and opened all his presents before other members of the family woke up. He knew that this was not what usually happened on birthdays. When his parents woke up they were appalled; they felt angry and cheated.

At first the boy was uncaring, but then became terribly upset when he saw how spoilt things had become. He knew he had wrecked his birthday morning, having looked forward to it for so long. He cried bitterly and painfully, saying, 'Why did I do it? I didn't think. Please, please forgive me.'

He was able to use the experience and see that half the pleasure of getting presents is the sharing with others of the experience of giving and receiving. Having deprived others of this, he had deprived himself as well.

The child's couldn't-care-less, self-centred attitude had given way to depressive anxiety, which was very painful when he saw the damage he had done. With the help of his parents he was able to manage it and learn from experience.

Nameless Dread, Naming and Failures of Containment

Bion describes a situation in which the infant, fearing that he is dying – that is, suffering from the primary anxiety about dissolution as described earlier (see pages 42–3) – projects this anxiety into his mother, or container.

> *A well-balanced mother can accept* [this anxiety] *and respond therapeutically – that is, in a manner that makes the infant feel it is receiving its frightened personality back again, but in a form that it can tolerate – the fears are made manageable for the infant personality.*[34]

If, however, the mother cannot accept these projections into her and perform the function of containment for the infant, he may take back into him an experience of his feeling having been stripped of meaning, and thus receive back what Bion has called 'nameless dread'. This is worse than the fear of dying itself, since it is unbound by a name and thus manifests itself as a feeling of dread that cannot be located.

This scenario is common in people who have serious illnesses and cannot let themselves know that the feeling they have is a fear of dying. Instead, they carry within them a worse feeling of nameless dread. Very often, those people around the very ill person are also so overwhelmed by anxiety themselves at the potential loss of their loved one that they cannot think clearly and help the ill person name and contain his/her experience. People often try to 'protect' the ill person, by using euphemisms or false reassurance, rather than helping the ill person and themselves face the facts of their lives.

To name an experience of anxiety binds it. A name is used to prevent the scattering of phenomena, because it describes the elements of an experience as being interrelated. As Bion says:

> Having found the name and thereby bound the phenomena, the remainder of history, if so wished, can be devoted to determining what it means. The name is an invention to make it possible to think about something before it is known what that something is.[35]

It is extremely persecuting to live in an unnamed universe. It leads to what is termed 'free floating anxiety' which cannot be located. Anxiety can feel everywhere.

Susan, aged ten, told her therapist that she could not sleep at night. She thought something was under her bed. It might be a cat, she thought; but the cat was on the other side of the room. Then she said it might be zombies with their arms stretched out in front of them; these zombies wanted the blood of humans by biting their necks. But then Susan worried that her house had a ghost in it because the TV channels spontaneously changed. The ghost, called James, was a friend of her mother's who had died of a heart attack. They also had sharks in their fishtank at home, and rats were a problem, too. At this point, Susan pulled up the hood of her jumper. Then she put her finger into her mouth and bit it really hard.

Susan is a little girl whose anxiety is located all over the place and seems to shift about with alarming rapidity. It does not come to rest anywhere, but floods her. Her hard biting on her finger may be her way of giving the pain a definite location, as discussed in the case of the self-harming adolescent (see page 46).

Failures of containment give rise to all kinds of anxiety. Panic attacks occur when there is no containment of anxiety and the person feels flooded with unprocessed, unnamed emotion that is often discharged into somatic disturbances. The fear and anxiety engendered by the thought of a panic attack is enough to trigger such an attack.

The failure of an attachment figure to contain anxiety can also mean that instead of the anxiety being 'named' and bound, it is returned to the person in an intensified form, as in the nameless dread situation. The person then has to deal with a double dose of anxiety, since he has the original anxiety projected back into him in an intensified form, together with the anxiety that no container exists for him – and so he feels misunderstood.

I observed an example of this in an aeroplane which hit a patch of turbulence. A child looked up at its mother's face to read from her, 'What am I supposed to feel about this situation?'; this was clearly anxiety-provoking, as the plane shuddered and bumped. The mother's face was ashen, conveying the emotions of someone in a supposed life-threatening situation. The child instantly became hysterical, as he was not only having to cope with his own anxiety unaided, but also seemed to receive a full blast of his mother's anxiety which then completely overwhelmed him.

Premonition of Emotion

If we return to Bion's definition of anxiety, as 'premonition of emotion', and accept that emotions are at the heart of our human existence, then anxiety, too, and how we deal with it, also occupies a central place.

Damasio, a neuroscientist, convincingly argues that emotion assists reasoning and that neurological evidence suggests that 'well-targeted and well-deployed emotion seems to be a support system without which the edifice of reason cannot operate properly'.[36] This is congruent with Bion's ideas that thinking arises out of containment of emotional experiences.

The ability to regulate emotional states is thus crucial for social, emotional, cognitive and neurobiological development.[37] This can only happen if the infant has the experience of an intimate relationship to an attachment figure who is emotionally attuned to him. If there are chronic disturbances in this for any reason, the baby never learns how to contain his own emotional states and cannot cope with the intensity of intimate relationships. The child's capacity to cope with anxiety thus predicates how well he will cope with life itself.

Acknowledgements

I would like to thank Adie, Alex and Louise Emanuel, Anne Hurley and Ivan Ward for their help in producing this essay.

Ricky Emanuel is a Child and Adult Psychotherapist working as a Consultant Child Psychotherapist at the Royal Free Hospital in London, and Head of Child Psychotherapy Services for Camden and Islington Community NHS Trust. He teaches at the Tavistock Clinic in London.

Notes

1. Hinshelwood, R.D., *A Dictionary of Kleinian Thought*, London: Free Association Books, 1991, p. 218.
2. Rycroft, C., *A Critical Dictionary of Psychoanalysis*, Harmondsworth: Penguin, 1968, p. 8.
3. Bion, W.R., *Elements of Psychoanalysis*, London: Heinemann, 1963, Chapter 16, pp. 74–7.
4. Hinshelwood, op. cit., p. 221.
5. Laplanche, J. and Pontalis, J.B., *The Language of Psychoanalysis*, London: Hogarth Press–Institute of Psychoanalysis, 1985, p. 48.
6. Freud, S., *Inhibitions, Symptoms and Anxiety* (1926), in *Standard Edition of the Complete Psychological Works of Sigmund Freud*, London: Hogarth Press–Institute of Psychoanalysis, 1953–73, vol. 20, p. 77–175.
7. Hinshelwood, op. cit., p. 221.
8. Rycroft, op. cit., p. 8.
9. Freud, op. cit., pp. 77–175.
10. Rycroft, op. cit., p. 8.
11. Laplanche and Pontalis, op. cit., pp. 189–90.
12. Bowlby, J., *Attachment and Loss: Vol. 1: Attachment*, London: Hogarth Press, 1969, 1982.
13. Hopkins, J., 'The Observed Infant of Attachment Theory', *British Journal of Psychotherapy*, vol. 6, 1990, pp. 460–71.
14. Ward, I., *Introducing Psychoanalysis*, Cambridge: Icon Books, 2000.
15. Perry, B.D., Pollard, R.A., Blakley, T.L., Baker, W.L. and Vigilante, D., 'Childhood Trauma, the Neurobiology of Adaptation, and "Use Dependent" Development of the Brain: How States Become Traits', *Infant Mental Health Journal*, vol. 16, 1995, pp. 271–91.
16. Klein, M., 'On the Theory of Anxiety and Guilt', *Envy and Gratitude and Other Works: Writings of Melanie Klein*, vol. 3 (1948), London: Hogarth Press and Institute of Psychoanalysis, 1975, pp. 25–43.
17. Joseph, B., 'Envy in Everyday Life', in *Psychic Equilibrium and Psychic Change: New Library of Psychoanalysis: Selected Papers of Betty Joseph*, ed. E.B. Spillius and M. Feldman, London: Tavistock–Routledge, 1989, Chapter 13, p. 186.
18. Klein, M., 'A Contribution to the Theory of Intellectual Inhibition', in *Love, Guilt and Reparation and Other Works: Writings of Melanie Klein*, vol. 2 (1931), London: Hogarth Press and Institute of Psychoanalysis, 1975, pp. 236–47.
19. Hinshelwood, op. cit., p. 112.
20. Meltzer, D., 'Terror, Persecution and Dread', *Sexual States of Mind*, Perthshire: Roland Harris Trust Clunie Press, 1979, Chapter 14, p. 105.
21. Meltzer, op. cit., p. 105.
22. Bion, W.R., *Learning from Experience*, London: Heinemann, 1962, p. 73.
23. Joseph, B., 'Different Types of Anxiety and Their Handling in the Analytic Situation', in Joseph, op. cit., Chapter 7, p. 108.
24. Klein, M., 'A Contribution to the Theory of Intellectual Inhibition', in Klein (1931, 1975), op. cit., pp. 240–1.

25. Hoberman, M.A., *A House is a House for Me*, Harmondsworth: Penguin, 1986.
26. Beaumont, M., 'The Effect of Loss on Learning', *Journal of Educational Therapy*, vol. 2, 1991, pp. 33–47.
27. Bion, W.R., *Learning from Experience*, London: Heinemann, 1962.
28. Meltzer, D. and Harris, M., 'A Psychoanalytical Model of the Child-in-the-Family-in-the-Community' (1976), in Hahn, A. (ed.), *Sincerity and Other Works: Collected Papers of Donald Meltzer*, London: Karnac Books, 1994, p. 387.
29. Carignani, P., 'An Observation in School with a 22 Month Old Child', paper given at the opening of the Centro Studi Martha Harris, Palermo, Sicily, 1994.
30. Bion, W.R., *Elements of Psychoanalysis*, London: Heinemann, 1963, p. 42.
31. Quoted in Bion, W.R., 'Letter to George and Thomas Keats, 21 December 1817', *Attention and Interpretation*, London: Heinemann, 1970, Chapter 13, p.125.
32. Meltzer and Harris, op. cit., p. 412.
33. Emanuel, R., 'The Child-in-the-Family-in-the-Nursery', *The Psychology of Nursery Education*, London: Freud Museum–Karnac Books, 1998, pp. 43–65.
34. Bion, W.R., 'A Theory of Thinking', in *Second Thoughts: Selected Papers on Psycho-Analysis*, New York: Jason Aronson, 1962, Chapter 9, pp. 114–15.
35. Quoted in Bion, W.R., 'Letter to George and Thomas Keats, 21 December 1817', *Attention and Interpretation*, London: Heinemann, 1970, Chapter 13, p. 87.
36. Damasio, A., *The Feeling of What Happens: Body, Emotion and the Making of Consciousness*, London: Heinemann, 1999, p. 42.
37. Schore, A., 'Attachment and the Regulation of the Right Brain', in Steele, H. and Cassidy, J. (eds.), *Attachment and Human Development*, London: Routledge, 1999.

Further Reading

Beaumont, M., 'The Effect of Loss on Learning', *Journal of Educational Therapy*, vol. 2, 1991.
Bion, W.R., *Learning from Experience*, London: Heinemann, 1962.
——'A Theory of Thinking', in *Second Thoughts: Selected Papers on Psycho-Analysis*, New York: Jason Aronson, 1962, Chapter 9.
——*Elements of Psychoanalysis*, London: Heinemann, 1963.
——'Letter to George and Thomas Keats, 21 December 1817', in *Attention and Interpretation*, London: Heinemann, 1970.
Bowlby, J., *Attachment and Loss: Vol. 1: Attachment*, London: Hogarth, 1969, 1982.
Carignani, P., 'An Observation in School with a 22 Month Old Child', paper given at the opening of the Centro Studi Martha Harris, Palermo, Sicily, 1994.

Damasio, A., *The Feeling of What Happens. Body, Emotion and the Making of Consciousness*, London: Heinemann, 1999.

Emanuel, R., 'The Child-in-the-Family-in-the-Nursery', *The Psychology of Nursery Education*, London: Freud Museum–Karnac Books, 1998.

Freud, S., *Inhibitions, Symptoms and Anxiety* (1926), in *Standard Edition of the Complete Psychological Works of Sigmund Freud*, vol. 20, London: Hogarth Press–Institute of Psychoanalysis, 1953–73.

Hinshelwood, R.D., *A Dictionary of Kleinian Thought*, London: Free Association Books, 1991.

Hoberman, M.A., *A House is a House for Me*, Harmondsworth: Penguin, 1986.

Hopkins, J., 'The Observed Infant of Attachment Theory', *British Journal of Psychotherapy*, vol. 6, 1990.

Joseph, B., 'Envy in Everyday Life', in *Psychic Equilibrium and Psychic Change: New Library of Psychoanalysis*, London: Tavistock–Routledge, 1989.

——'Different Types of Anxiety and their Handling in the Analytic Situation', in *Psychic Equilibrium and Psychic Change: New Library of Psychoanalysis*, London: Tavistock–Routledge, 1989.

Klein, M., 'A Contribution to the Theory of Intellectual Inhibition', *Love, Guilt and Reparation and Other Works: Writings of Melanie Klein*, vol. 1 (1931), London: Hogarth Press–Institute of Psychoanalysis, 1975.

——'On the Theory of Anxiety and Guilt', *Envy and Gratitude and Other Works: Writings of Melanie Klein*, vol. 3 (1948), London: Hogarth Press–Institute of Psychoanalysis, 1975.

Laplanche, J. and Pontalis, J.B., *The Language of Psychoanalysis*, London: Hogarth Press–Institute of Psychoanalysis, 1985.

Meltzer, D., 'Terror, Persecution and Dread', in *Sexual States of Mind*, Perthshire: Roland Harris Trust Clunie Press, 1979.

——and M. Harris, 'A Psychoanalytical Model of the Child-in-the-Family-in-the-Community' (1976), in Hahn, A. (ed.), *Sincerity and Other Works: Collected Papers of Donald Meltzer*, London: Karnac Books, 1994.

Perry, B.D., Pollard, R.A., Blakley, T.L., Baker, W.L. and Vigilante, D., 'Childhood Trauma, the Neurobiology of Adaptation, and "Use Dependent" Development of the Brain: How States Become Traits', *Infant Mental Health Journal*, vol. 16, 1995.

Rycroft, C., *A Critical Dictionary of Psychoanalysis*, Harmondsworth: Penguin, 1968.

Schore, A., 'Attachment and the Regulation of the Right Brain', in Steele, H. and Cassidy, J. (eds.), *Attachment and Human Development*, London: Routledge, 1999.

Ward, I., *Introducing Psychoanalysis*, Cambridge: Icon Books, 2000.

3

Phantasy

Julia Segal

Introduction

Why do we do what we do? Some people insist that they know the answer to this question, that everything they do is rational and sensible. These people never find themselves thinking, 'Whatever got into me?' or 'I know I shouldn't do that; why did I do it again?' – whether 'that' is drinking too much, getting involved with the wrong sort of partner, or letting their mothers upset them. Such people may not be very interested in this essay. Neither will those who prefer to put things to the back of their minds for fear of opening cans of worms. However, many people find themselves doing things which take them by surprise, or which they thought they did not want to do. Some wonder what exactly the worms in those cans look like. These people may also find themselves wondering at the behaviour of others. The concept of phantasy is a tool which allows for quite subtle and complex understanding of behaviour and feelings, even though many of its ideas might initially seem ridiculous. It is only when these ideas have been observed in action that they begin to seem convincing.

The Basic Idea: Daydreams

Our perceptions of other people depend not only on their real characteristics, but also on what we bring to the relationship. For example, after we quarrel with someone, in our heads the quarrel goes on. Things are said on both sides, and our picture of the other person changes. When next we meet, we greet that person with the memory not only of what both of us actually said, but also with our interpretation of those things, as well as with the memory of the imaginary post-quarrel conversation. Our mood and that of the other will not be quite what they were when we parted; we have to find out where we stand now. Similarly, shortly after leaving home for the first time, we may start a telephone conversation with our mother, expecting her to be interested in us, our achievements, our worries – only to find that she is more interested in the neighbours, our siblings, or whatever she is doing; and in turn, she expects us to be interested in those things, too. We carry in our minds more than one picture of her. We know what she is actually like; at the same time we have a picture of the mother we would like her to be and which we somehow hope she will be.

In our heads we not only talk to people, but we also do things to and with them. In our heads we may send a bunch of flowers or a birthday card – only to be surprised when they do not actually arrive. Daydreams of friendly encounters with a pop star, perhaps, or the boy next door, merge into daydreams of sexual encounters. The other person may or may not know of these daydreams. We may be clear about what actually happened, but sometimes we become confused between reality and imagination. Do we remember going to the seaside that year, or is it just the photograph we remember? Did our friend's father actually throw her out of the house, or just threaten to? Brothers and sisters may have quite different memories of an event, and may be angry at the construction we put on the behaviour we remember. In their heads they have worked it over differently. They may even have heard different things, since not only memory but also perception can distort. When a man says, 'You didn't tell me we were going out next weekend', he may be right; he may only have been told such a thing in his partner's fantasy. Or he may not have actually heard his partner.

These fantasies which we continually weave around our memories and experiences affect our relationship not only with the person we dream about, but also with other aspects of the world. Actually meeting someone you have fantasised about is an embarrassing idea. Anger with a friend may fade over time, or it may remain as sharp as ever. Thirty years after a bruising encounter with a life insurance salesman, a woman wrote to the Managing Director of the company concerned, saying she still felt furious with them every time their advertising literature came through the door, and would they please stop sending it? A woman who had been in a crash while in the back seat of a car could not get into another back seat for fifteen years. Being given strawberries and ice cream after tonsillitis put a child off both for twenty years.

Daydreams with Long-term Effects

Which memories or fantasies leave long-term traces and continue to annoy or distress us depends on their significance. The woman who had problems with sitting in the back seat might also have had other reasons for not wanting to 'take a back seat' metaphorically.

The woman's encounter with the insurance salesman happened in the aftermath of dealing with her father's estate; powerful feelings displaced from members of her family may have played a part in elevating an ordinary instance of rudeness to a constant irritation. Strawberries and ice cream reminded the child of being miserable and alone upstairs while the family laughed below. The concept of unconscious phantasy allows us to understand how these things might happen; how we add powerfully emotive elements belonging elsewhere to a memory, and so translate it into something else: a reluctance to get into the back seat of a car; a fury at the appearance of a particular piece of advertising; a distaste for certain foods. These 'symptoms' encapsulate upsetting feelings without leading to their resolution.

Disguises

Daydreams are conscious and we can probably choose to have them or not. But less conscious fantasies go on without our awareness. We can pick these up in various ways.

A song may come into our heads for no apparent reason. With thought, we may discover the phantasies behind it. Looking out at the rain, a writer friend told me he found himself singing '*Uh oh, oh no, don't let the rain come down*'. He was puzzled, as he found it easier to write when it rains. It was only when I asked him how the song went on and he said '*My roof's got a hole in it and I might drown*', that he remembered a roofer had told him he should do something about the state of his roof and it was worrying him. Some time later he reminded me that his mother had recently had a stroke, which he visualised as holes in her brain. I wondered if he thought he would drown in tears if she died. The 'oh no' made sense here. Tracing back from a simple snatch of song we can find anxieties which are just below the surface, expressed in concrete images. Below those, there are others. The song functioned to keep at bay both his own anxieties and (magically) his mother's death while disguising them sufficiently to allow him to work.

The concrete images are phantasies, woven together to represent and express anxieties and needs (his anxieties about his mother; his need to work). They use his experience of the present (his recent encounter with the roofer) and the past (the song itself; the belief in magic); metaphors (the 'holes' in his mother's brain); unconscious magical thinking ('I can stop my mother dying by saying "oh no"'). Phantasies in this sense are actions (a piece of magic) as well as causing actions (the refrain going through his head).

Sometimes we are aware of no more than a vague irritability in ourselves or someone else. With a bit of thought, we may be able to diagnose its cause quite easily; but we have to take that thought and there may be good reason not to. Another person may be able to see more clearly than we can.

In counselling, a woman with multiple sclerosis talked about herself and her family. I began to get a sense that she did not expect to live much longer. I asked her about this and, rather surprised, she agreed this was the case. I asked her why this might be, since my expectation would be that she would live for many more years. She did not know. I asked if her parents were still alive – puzzled, she said her father had died when he was 52; she was now 48. Suddenly she became aware that she had always thought that she was like him, and she was sure she would die at the age he had. She realised she had been unconsciously preparing for her own death for several years, and that this had affected her whole attitude towards her children and her husband. In unconscious phantasy, we can say, she was identifying with her father, and her own imminent death was a certain fact.

Fantasies which go on in our heads without our being completely aware of them can come out in other ways too. The author Martin Amis in his autobiography describes how in 1977 an ex-lover showed him a photograph of a small girl, saying it was his daughter. He gave the photo to his mother. Later he met the girl amid some publicity. Amis describes the shock which made him 'jump out of his boots' when Maureen Freely, reviewing his work, 'noted the punctual arrival – just in time for my third novel, *Success* (1978), of a stream of lost or wandering daughters and putative or fugitive fathers, and that these figures recurred, with variations, in every subsequent book'.

Amis continues:

> There was nothing I could do about this diagnosis. It chimed with something Patrick had said during our first talk on the telephone: 'I expect it's been in the back of your mind'. Yes, exactly: in the back of my mind. Your writing comes from the back of your mind, where thoughts are unformulated and anxiety is silent. I felt there was something almost embarrassing about the neatness and obviousness of the Freely interpretation. But it also sharply consoled me, because it meant that I had been with Delilah in spirit far more than I knew.[1]

Once Amis knew about the existence of his daughter, she turned up again and again in his mind – but in a disguised form. She existed in his mind in unconscious phantasy only, determining his writing without his recognising it. I think he was wrong about anxiety being silent at the back of the mind, however. We cannot silence anxieties by pushing them to the back of our minds in phantasy; we have to work them through. Until we do, they seek expression in the song which catches us unawares; in a fight we did not really mean to have; in an inhibition; in a piece of writing which others can interpret and understand.

Interpretation

It is not only novelists and psychoanalysts who interpret behaviour. We interpret other people's behaviour all the time; and sometimes those being analysed agree with us and sometimes they don't. [*'You're just like your mother!' 'You are tired.' 'I'm sorry I was bad-tempered; I was just exhausted/I was feeling hormonal/I was hungry.' 'She's bossy and a bully.' 'No, she's not. She just can't see the problem others have with doing it her way.'*]

In these interpretations we are trying to make sense of our own and other people's behaviour and feelings; the construction we put on them involves some kind of phantasy. The phantasy involves motivations and often predictions for future expectations.

Sickness involves many phantasies. [*'She caught a cold; she got very wet/everyone has a cold at the moment.' 'She was bewitched by the woman next door.' 'This lady down the road put the evil eye on her.' 'It was stress.' 'With all those children, it's not surprising she got ill.' 'She prayed to the Lord and he healed her! Praise the Lord!' 'If I exercise all the time, I won't get ill.' 'We must go to the doctor/priest/shaman and ask him to find out what is wrong with her.' 'Every time his father went away, he got a chest infection.' 'It's all in the mind.' 'Whatever is wrong with me, I know it is NOT my mind; it is my BODY.'*]

These interpretations are explanations which can influence behaviour. They deal with the powerful anxiety of not knowing what caused misfortune and what we can expect to happen next. Phantasies serve to contain anxieties by giving us explanations, often based on little evidence. Some allow for questions and answers; others do not.

Illness and death are both interruptions to normal life. They shake a set of phantasies that rely on the assumption that tomorrow we will be much the same as we are today. We do not think, 'Tomorrow I will not have flu'; we just assume it will be the case. We assume we will go on living for the foreseeable future, or we may have a vague or a clear idea about when we expect to die – and this is very unlikely to be 'tomorrow'. These assumptions are embodied in the normal phantasies we have which prepare us to face the world when we wake up. In these phantasies we know, without thinking about it, what our bodies are doing, what our mind is like, what they will do for us tomorrow. We may get angry and upset when these normal phantasies are challenged. When flu or some other illness intervenes, it takes us unawares and we have to rearrange the phantasies on which we base our normal life. Phantasies encapsulate normal assumptions about the world. We become aware of them, if at all, when they no longer fit and we have to seek new ones.

The Freudian Background

Freud discovered phantasies when he began trying to understand various symptoms as a neurologist. Nowadays we would call these 'conversion symptoms': they convert an idea into a phobia or an apparently medical symptom which the doctors cannot explain. For example, in examining a woman who said she had no sensation in her arm, Freud found that the lack of feeling followed the sleeve area, rather than nerve pathways. He also found that he could replicate loss of sensation or movement with hypnosis. From this came the realisation that ideas and thoughts could control the body in a way which was completely unconscious. He found that by allowing patients to 'free associate', he could build a picture of the ideas at the back of their minds which explained the symptoms. Like Amis, his patients often did not like these ideas.

One case involved a young man who had to run back along the road and move a stone for fear that his fiancée's carriage would hit it and there would be an accident. By some tortuous reasoning, he then had to go and put the stone back in the road.[2] As Freud listened to the young man talk, it became clear that he was terrified of killing his fiancée, but at the same time he wanted her hurt or even dead. This idea was deeply disguised from the young man himself, and he had no idea it was affecting his behaviour.

Freud at first thought that it was unbearable memories which were converted into symptoms; eventually he came to realise that the root causes were fantasies, memories encapsulated in stories, of events which might or might not have taken place. As everyone knows, he found young girls with fantasies of having sex with their fathers and young men with fantasies of having sex with their mothers. Both sexes also had fantasies of killing their parents. None of them actually thought consciously, 'I have tried to kill my father' or 'I have had sex with my father'. Like any sensible person would, they rejected the idea.

I became convinced of the reality of these ideas only after several mothers I knew told me of their small sons getting upset at the realisation that they could not marry their mothers or 'have babies in their wombs'. Now adults, these boys deny all memory of this humiliating idea.

Freud's patients' symptoms functioned both to express and to fend off the thought (just as the 'Uh oh, oh no' song expressed and fended off the thought of the mother's death). Freud found that he needed a new concept to distinguish unconscious phantasy (rejected from conscious thought but having an effect 'from the back of the mind', where the patient was unaware of it) from conscious fantasies (such as daydreams). It was James Strachey, Freud's translator, who decided to use the 'ph' spelling to distinguish conscious from unconscious fantasy, in order to clarify a complex situation.[3]

Phantasy, then, was understood at first as a fantasy of an event such as killing one's father or having sex with him, which appeared to preoccupy a certain group of disturbed individuals and caused mental, or apparently physical, illness. These fantasies were never conscious, and when they became conscious they lost their power to create symptoms.

In 'Studies in Hysteria', Freud wrote up a series of cases which make fascinating reading. Fräulein Elizabeth von R. came to Freud with leg pains that had no neurological explanation. She agreed to allow Freud to try his 'talking cure', but after months of talking to Freud about whatever came into her mind, she was horrified to discover that the pains represented a form of self-flagellation for incestuous feelings towards her brother-in-law. Once the idea had become conscious, the physical pains went away (and so did she), though for a long time they were replaced with painful thoughts. Freud describes the case thus:

> The recovery of this repressed idea had a shattering effect on the poor girl. She cried aloud when I put the situation drily before her with the words: 'So for a long time you had been in love with your brother-in-law.' She complained at this moment of the most frightful pains, and made one last desperate effort to reject the explanation: it was not true, I had talked her into it, it could not be true, she was incapable of such wickedness, she could never forgive herself for it. It was easy to prove to her that what she herself had told me admitted of no other interpretation. But it was a long time before my two pieces of consolation – that we are not responsible for our feelings, and that her behaviour, the fact that she had fallen ill in these circumstances, was sufficient evidence of her moral character – it was a long time before these consolations of mine made any impression on her.[4]

Freud said that the girl's mother had known about her daughter's feelings towards her brother-in-law for a long time. Part of the humiliation of uncovering aspects of ourselves we thought were well hidden can be the discovery that others have not been fooled, only ourselves.

Dreams

In his attempts to elucidate the thoughts and memories which lay behind symptoms, Freud found himself being told dreams. In dreams, the 'censor' which kept ideas out of consciousness worked differently, and the disguises were easier to penetrate.

He described a young woman whose illness

> began with a state of confusional excitement during which she displayed a quite special aversion to her mother, hitting and abusing her whenever she came near her bed, while at the same period she was docile and affectionate towards a sister who was many years her senior. This was followed by a period in which she was lucid but somewhat apathetic and suffered from badly disturbed sleep. It was during this phase that I began treating her and analysing her dreams. An immense number of these dreams were concerned, with a greater or less degree of disguise, with the death of her mother: at one time she would be attending an old woman's funeral, at another she and her sister would be sitting at table dressed in mourning. There could be no question as to the meaning of these dreams. As her condition improved still further, hysterical phobias developed. The most tormenting of these was a fear that something might have happened to her mother. She was obliged to hurry home, wherever she might be, to convince herself that her mother was still alive.[5]

Freud saw this case as demonstrating the different ways in which hostility to the woman's mother was expressed, as physical aggression or symbolised in a dream, or defended against by the conscious substitution of the opposite idea as a negation.

It was in the analysis of mental disturbances, then, that Freud discovered symbolism, which he found often linked to disturbing sexual fantasies. When he examined Elizabeth von R.'s painful legs by pinching them, she did not react as someone in pain; instead

> her face assumed a peculiar expression, which was one of pleasure rather than pain. She cried out – and I could not help

thinking that it was as though she was having a voluptuous tickling sensation – her face flushed, she threw back her head and shut her eyes and her body bent backwards . . . Her expression . . . was probably more in harmony with the subject-matter of the thoughts which lay concealed behind the pain.[6]

A region of her legs had come to represent some aspect of her sexuality. Later Freud discovered that this was an area which had touched her father's swollen leg while she nursed him as he lay dying. Freud thought we symbolised only things which we did not want to know about, which were repressed, and that these repressed thoughts came out in symptoms. As in the case of Elizabeth von R., the symptoms were overdetermined; many unconscious thoughts or fantasies lay behind each one. But Freud saw the symptomatic leg and other symbols as existing in a world of more neutral objects which had no particular psychic significance.

Klein: Children's Play

Melanie Klein was a mother of young children when she read Freud's *Interpretation of Dreams* (1900). Watching her own son playing, making mountains out of her body and running his carriages and people over it; listening to him relating his fantasies about his 'wiwi' and 'making babies' with his 'poo'; telling the toilet paper he wiped himself with to 'eat it up', she realised that she could interpret his play and his stories as Freud interpreted dreams. In 'The Development of a Child', she gives a wealth of examples of her son's fantasies.[7] For example, 'the womb figured as a completely furnished house, the stomach particularly was very fully equipped and was even possessed of a bath-tub and a soap-dish. He remarked himself: "I know it isn't really like that, but I see it that way"'.[8]

Freud had begun to think that it was repression of sexual interest which kept phantasies out of conscious awareness and therefore made them liable to emerge as symptoms, so Klein decided she would try to bring her son up without this repression. She decided to tell him where babies came from. This was revolutionary at the time, and it is not surprising that she could not quite bring herself to explain about the role of the father: besides, the child did not ask. This led to an important discovery. Her son was interested in what she said, but after a while he began asking stereotyped questions about what different things were made of and how they were made. For instance, 'What is a door made of? – What is the bed made of? . . . How does all the earth get under the earth? . . . Where do stones, where does water come from?' Klein explained that

*there was no doubt that . . . he had completely grasped the
answer to these questions and that their recurrence had no
intellectual basis. He showed too by his inattentive and
absent-minded behaviour while putting the questions that he
was really indifferent about the answers in spite of the fact that
he asked them with vehemence . . .*[9]

When she saw him gradually losing interest in everything,
including being told stories by her, she remembered that a senior
analyst had pointed out that the boy was asking about the role of
the father in a disguised form. After she explained it to him, the
child completely regained his interest in the world, began to play
freely and to relate stories to her.[10]

She began to analyse her own children (though she warned her
pupils later against doing this, feeling it was too intrusive), then
other children and later, adults. Klein, like Freud, began to
see that unconscious phantasies could have powerful effects on
daily life. Her own son's temporary inhibition had been cured by
her answering an unconscious question, and she found other
children with symptoms, who also responded to analysis of their
play and speech. Her son had shown her evidence of considerable
aggression towards his brother, sister and father; for example, in a
game where he cut off their heads;[11] but he later became anxious
about these games. Klein realised that it was not just negative adult
attitudes towards sexual ideas which could cause children to
inhibit their interests or to change their games, but their own
internal conflicts, in particular about their fantasies of damaging
or destroying those they loved.

A child called 'Fritz', described in 'The Role of the School in the
Libidinal Development of the Child', had many difficulties at
school, including an inhibition about doing division sums. Klein
says that 'Fritz'

*told me that in doing division he had first of all to bring down
the figure that was required and he climbed up, seized it by the
arm and pulled it down. To my enquiry as to what it said to
that, he replied that quite certainly it was not pleasant for the
number – it was as if his mother stood on a stone 13 yards high
and someone came and caught her by the arm so that they tore
it out and divided her . . . He then related . . . that actually
every child wants to have a bit of his mother, who is to be cut in
four pieces; he depicted quite exactly how she screamed and
had paper stuffed in her mouth so that she could not scream,
and what kind of faces she made, etc. A child took a very sharp
knife, and he described how she was cut up; first across the*

*width of the breast, and then of the belly, then lengthwise so
that the 'pipi'* [in his imagination, mothers also had penises, it
seems], *the face and the head were cut exactly through the
middle, whereby the 'sense' was taken out of her head. The
head was then again cut through obliquely just as the 'pipi'
was cut across its breadth. Betweenwhiles he constantly bit at
his hand and said that he bit his sister too for fun, but certainly
for love. He continued that every child then took the piece of
the mother that it wanted, and agreed that the cut-up mother
was then also eaten. It now appeared also that he always
confused the remainder with the quotient in division, and
always wrote it in the wrong place, because in his mind it was
bleeding pieces of flesh with which he was unconsciously
dealing. These interpretations completely removed his inhibition with regard to division.*[12]

In a note, Klein adds: 'The next day in school to his and his
mistress's astonishment, it turned out that he could now do all his
sums correctly. (The child had not become aware of the connection between the interpretation and the removal of the inhibition.)'

Klein had discovered that children create frightening phantasies
based on misunderstandings of the world fuelled by their anxieties.
Uncovering these phantasies could reduce the fear and free children to use their minds fully and creatively. Klein says of her son:

*To begin with, before he starts relating things he enquires quite
cheerfully whether what he finds 'horrid' will, after I have
explained it to him, become pleasant again for him just as with
the other things so far. He also says that he is not afraid any
more of the things that have been explained to him even when
he thinks of them.*[13]

Klein's new insights turned Freud's upside down. She saw that we
endow the world and everything in it with meaning derived from
unconscious phantasies and the anxieties which lie behind these.
It is our anxieties, our conflicting impulses and the derived
phantasies which lead us to see the things we see and behave in
the way we do. In this sense, nothing is neutral. In phantasy all
kinds of things are going on, in our heads, in our bodies, in our
'inner world'. We do not always know it 'isn't really like that'; we
really do 'see it that way'. The pains in Elizabeth's legs were real
for her and really blotted out her 'immoral' thoughts for a while.
'Fritz's' phantasy about division sums was so convincing that it
stopped him doing them. People who believe in witchcraft are
really frightened by it. And it is possible that the real atrocities

of war which so frighteningly mirror some of the children's phantasies described by Klein are caused by people acting on infantile phantasies in which people are closer to terrifying monsters or things than to human beings.

Phantasies as Perception

We can now look at unconscious phantasies from a different point of view. Klein discovered that phantasies provide the basic tools we use to make sense of our perceptions. They create the basic assumptions we use to live by; affecting not just disturbed behaviour, but also ordinary, everyday behaviour. Sensations of all kinds, arising from inside or outside ourselves, are all interpreted through phantasies. Phantasies also motivate perception. Seeking confirmation of our goodness or badness, we find people and situations which will tell us we are good or bad.

Work is motivated as much by unconscious phantasies about making things in the world better as by the more conscious ones of needing the money. ('The world', like the mountains in Klein's son's play, often stands for some idea of an early phantasy of the mother, with or without the father, who once made up our world.) Even conscious motivations have unconscious roots. If we take seriously what people say when they lose their jobs, it seems that 'money' can represent their own value to themselves and others, as well as their life, potency, the capacity to take care of loved people, or even proof that they are not the failure their father always said, for example. In phantasy, 'money' may be endowed with all these meanings, and the reassurance and comfort that it brings as it comes in every week or month may be enormous. Likewise, the ordinary behaviour of seeking a lover is clearly governed by unconscious phantasies about what he or she will do for you, and what you will do for him or her. Not all of these are realistic. The details of names, ages, physical, emotional and mental characteristics of a partner are also all likely to resonate with those of family members. Phantasies derived from the earliest family situation create a basis on which people encountered subsequently are then met, welcomed, understood or rejected accordingly.

'Fritz's' dislike of long division is thus perhaps 'disturbed', but it is a common disturbance. His phantasies endowed his division sums with horror. When his mother was away, his need to deal with his anger against her (for abandoning him) created phantasies of a witch who might poison him. These phantasies were separate from the mother he loved and wanted back. Children do often behave badly after their parents have been away for any reason; it makes sense that there might be ordinary angry phantasies behind this behaviour.

Phantasies motivate and underlie ordinary play. Hormonal surges and external frustrations create anger, which is perceived through phantasies which then govern its expression. Ball and computer games allow violent phantasies safe expression, well away from any idea of wanting to kill a real person. (But ask for names of the combatants in a computer game and there may be a hint of an underlying phantasy.) Playing these games modifies the phantasies available to understand and control reactions the next time anger arises. Girls' play often expresses strong feelings and phantasies about 'insides and outsides', for example through making and breaking circles of friendship, rope or beads.

Children also make sense of their parents' behaviour by using their own experience, coloured by their anxieties and needs. A boy of twelve talked about how angry he was with his father for not helping in the house; he said he was lazy for not doing his fair share; why should he help if his father did not? The boy knew his father was ill, but he had no understanding of neurological fatigue. In his phantasy, his father was motivated as he would be himself. I do not think it was pure self-interest which motivated this boy, but a much deeper anxiety about his father's illness. I suspect that he did not want to think of his father as unable to do things, as ill, weak and vulnerable; it was far preferable to think of him as strong and resistant to his mother's demands – as the boy would have liked to be himself.

Basic expectations of the wider world develop from the earliest phantasies created out of the child's interpretations of his or her childhood world. For example, as a child, Sue took it for granted that women always told men what to do, because that was how it was in her extended family. It was quite a shock when she went to school and discovered that nurses (female) had to do what doctors (male) told them. In another instance, Frances's father left home when she was two and a half years old. Several sexual relationships throughout her twenties and early thirties lasted almost exactly two and a half years. Frances did not think that there was any connection and was annoyed when I suggested there might be.

The phantasies we use to understand our own children are also based on our phantasies about ourselves and our parents. We may see our children as stupid and ignorant as we always feared we were; or we might see them as able to fulfil our wildest dreams. We may love them as we feel that we loved our parents. We may fear that they want to punish us, as we wanted to punish our parents. Parents often seem to have fantasies of being worn out, or done to death by their own children, and not only when they are ill. A woman told her grandson that he would kill his mother by breastfeeding: 'You'll suck her dry, you know!' And of course, the Oedipus story is scary from the point of view of the adults in it.

Primitive Phantasies

The most primitive phantasies, we think, are there at birth. Babies are born with a capacity to recognise certain objects and to react in certain ways. They actively seek the breast and nipple, by smell, feel, recognition of the mother's voice and reacting to a dark spot in a lighter circle. When they find the nipple, they know what to do, though there may be a few false starts. A phantasy corresponding to nipple-in-the-mouth seeks something in the outside world to match it. The experience of being fed then modifies this phantasy, so that very soon it has to involve the mother's own familiar nipple, with the right voice, smell and feel attached to it.

The modification of phantasies continues throughout life, so that later experiences of eating may seem to bear little resemblance to the first feed; later experiences of loving and being loved may not appear to have much in common with the tiny baby's love affair with the mother's breast, or the older baby's wordless adoration of a bigger sibling. But a connecting thread leads from one to another, and sometimes it is possible to see. A baby who always grabbed the nipple with enthusiasm, almost biting it but not quite, may be recognisable in an adult who greets new experiences energetically, getting her teeth into them in a similar way. Another adult who always holds back suspiciously, who does not quite trust the world, may have greeted his or her first feeds in much the same way. Underlying assumptions about the world may create phantasies which remain active many years later, regardless of actual experience.

Another thread connects all good experiences with each other. Good sex has something in common with a good feed, even in adulthood; also with a good conversation, a jazz or rock concert, or even a good book. The underlying phantasies are derived from the same basic ones; later distortions have not completely done away with the connection. The baby at the breast having a good feed has a whole-body experience of pleasure; its skin is flushed, its mouth wonderfully full; it is held in bliss for a timeless moment; nothing must interrupt. The experience has a beginning (when the baby must work hard to start the milk flowing); it has a middle (when the sucking is long and slow and rhythmic); and it has an end (when the baby falls off the breast with a drunken look of pleasure). What is more, such pleasure is not easily won; it arises only (if at all) after mother and child have learned how to do it. Pain, difficulty, discomfort and awkwardness often accompany the first experiences at the breast, as well as the first experiences of penetrative sex. The parallels are clear (to me, anyway), and extend to other experiences. The rhythm and structure of a conversation, for example, can also reflect good or bad sex. It may be boring, never coming to the point, or exciting. It may reach a climax and leave a satisfied feeling, giving rise to creative thoughts; or it may be crude, brutal and short, leaving a bad taste in the mouth. The word 'intercourse' refers both to 'sexual union' and 'conversation', just as the word 'conversation' also used to have both meanings.

The structure of a phantasy used in creating a conversation, a piece of music, a meal, or a story may have its roots in the earliest pleasurable phantasies, long forgotten but still leaving discernible traces. Phantasies are more primitive than thought. They provide the mental representations of our experiences and needs; they define the assumptions we use to understand and make sense of our world *without having to think about it*. A small baby does not *think*, for example, 'that pain inside me is hunger'; it simply starts looking for food.

Hunger Phantasies

The example of hunger is a useful one. Adults do not in fact always start looking for food when they are hungry; they may decide to wait a while. The baby may only appear to be seeking food. In phantasy it may be seeking anything to fill a phantasy gap, to smother or to punish the phantasy biting monsters inside, or to hold onto until the biting stops. Adults may start looking for food when it is in fact the pain of loss, misery or anger which is hurting inside. Phantasies about eating are often unrealistic, or connected with experiences which are not just hunger for food.

A younger sister may choose what she eats by watching her bigger sister or brother, rather than responding to her own appetite. In phantasy she is perhaps being them, with their appetite, not her own. Another person may in phantasy use food to stuff down a dependent, miserable, weak, lonely child part of the self and prevent it howling. Hunger may evoke a phantasy of a fat, intrusive mother pushing food at her daughter, saying 'Come on, dear, you must eat', bringing instant revulsion. Or hunger pangs may be interpreted as guilt, so the search for food is complicated by needing to clean up first, or to choose 'self-denying' foods. Hunger may bring feelings about a lost father who smoked; so a cigarette allows a comforting phantasy of breathing him in with the tobacco smoke, while smothering the anger for his unexpected departure and keeping the body slim as he liked it. On the other hand, one woman insisted on eating butter in large quantities, because, she said, it meant the war was over: during the war she had always given her butter ration to her mother, and she never intended to give it up again. And so on. The phantasies governing food, drink and smoking are enormously complex. (Susie Orbach describes some phantasies to do with eating in her book *Fat is a Feminist Issue*.[14])

Many phantasies distort truth, telling us we are not hungry when we are, or that we are happy when we are not, for example. They distort our view of ourselves and our own feelings [*I'm not jealous.' 'Everything I do is bad.' 'I am the wrong sex.'*]. They also distort our view of our children [*'He hasn't noticed his father's absence.' 'She was such a good girl.'*].

The Importance of Truth

Whether our phantasies are close to reality or a long way short of it matters. The closer our phantasies come to reality, the less likely we are to be suddenly brought up short against facts that do not fit. However, just as there may be strong emotional reasons for holding onto unrealistic worldviews, so there are plenty of 'stories' we can tell ourselves to 'explain' discrepancies in our view of the world and others' (e.g., 'They are stupid'; or 'They are unbelievers and will go to hell'; or 'They don't really know me; if they did they would *know* I am really very bad/good'). Certain phantasies represent illusions about the world which are shared with others, and our acquiescence with these makes us more or less comfortable in our social world. For example, in a world with extremes of poverty and riches, we may seek justification for our own position relative to others in order to be able to function without a constant sense of guilt towards those less fortunate. However, if this involves in phantasy 'shutting our eyes' to what we know are injustices, it gives us blind spots which may have other consequences.

Klein believed that our relation to the truth was vitally important. She found that even uncomfortable reality was in the long term preferable to trying to live in an illusory phantasy-world; the phantasies we use to confuse ourselves, to pretend that the world is closer to our wishes than it really is, were all damaging in one way or another. Not only did they damage our capacity to see and feel and think truthfully, but they also threatened our relations with other people and ourselves. Attempts to hide a painful idea from ourselves do not remain static; they draw to themselves other ideas or thoughts which might remind us of the idea; we have to 'forget' those too; before long we can end up unable to take an interest in anything for fear it will lead to the painful idea.

Many people disagree with Klein about this, claiming that illusion can be better in many ways than reality. Those who watch soap operas or go to church are apparently happier in some measurable way than those who do not. I suspect that the conscious and unconscious fantasy worlds these supply have much to recommend them for many people. I also suspect that they often fail at certain points when they are really needed, such as at times of illness. The characters from *Neighbours* do not deliver hot meals when you need them, whereas real neighbours may bring more conflicts but real food. And as a counsellor for people with multiple sclerosis, I have found that many religious beliefs fail to provide comfort when people have an illness which does not get better.

My own experience has convinced me that Klein was right; but it is vital to remember how difficult she thought it was to recognise truth when we see it. I know how painful and humiliating truth can be; and it may not be my place to expose it, even if I am convinced I can see it. Giving painful information, for example, requires patience, time and understanding; one cannot just 'drop it and run'. I would need to be sure I could offer real substitutes for the many pleasures of soap operas or religion before trying to undermine them in an adult; with my own children I have more choices about what I offer in the way of explanations and pleasures in life.

To return to phantasies governing eating, it is clear that some unrealistic phantasies may result in good, normal eating, but many will not. In a similar way, unrealistic phantasies about the end of the world may result in social policies that help protect the environment; and Columbus's phantasies about the existence of a passage to India and the glory of God resulted in a journey to the West Indies. Other phantasies about God, however, bring holy wars, death and destruction of one kind or another.

Phantasies in Action

I want now briefly to look at some of the significant phantasies we use.

Phantasies of the Good Object

Some of the most important phantasies involve what Klein called the good object. She was talking about phantasies of a good, loving, holding, containing figure inside, available for comfort and for comforting communication. The mother-in-your-head who loves you and understands you and wants the best for you is a good object; so is a good father-figure. Analysts use the word 'object' here to mean 'not the subject'; i.e., 'not-me'; someone/thing who is generally bigger or stronger in some way; providing something that the self cannot provide for itself. As the child grows, phantasies of the good object change and grow too.

Not everyone has a sense of a solid, reliable good object. Premature independence which creates a 'false self', for example, can result from a phantasy of a good object which is unsafe and unreliable and which needs to be looked after by an immature self.

Phantasies of Being Merged

The earliest phantasies seem to include an awareness of someone/thing who is 'not me' and a desire to join up with this figure. The first rooting for the nipple is a search for something; but is that something outside the self, or something necessary to complete the self? Plato's story depicting men and women as originally one male/female, torn apart and forever seeking our 'other half' or 'better half' implies a phantasy of the good object which combines both self and other. It is not surprising if boundaries between the baby self and the mother are not clear, but adults too can have difficulty knowing where they begin and their partner or their mother or father ends. Close couples sometimes 'know' what the other is thinking or feeling, without words; 'talking for' a child or a partner implies some phantasy of being one, which the other may or may not appreciate. Loving sexual relationships often involve fantasies of merging, becoming one, uniting against the world, making an indissoluble bond. However, there is a difference between merging into one and bonding as two separate beings.

Being merged with the loved object brings difficulties. Parts of the self which are different from the other may begin to feel trapped, stifled. These phantasies have their effects on the external world, and the loved person too may feel excessively controlled. Phantasies of being merged with another can be found in babies, their mothers and in some adult relationships. Where these lead to phantasies of being stifled, they can even provoke asthma attacks. Recognising the loved good object as someone separate not only allows each to breathe; it also allows for feelings of love and concern freely given. In the case of some couples who think that they want a divorce, what they really need is to separate in their heads; the separation in reality may then not be necessary.

For example, a woman told me she could not live with her husband any more. He watched every step she took; he wouldn't even let her buy knickers without his permission. I asked her how this worked; did she not have her own money? No, she had her own money; it was just that she knew he would disapprove. And how did she know this? Did he tell her? No, in fact, he never said anything; she just knew how he felt. It gradually became clear that he was so constantly present in her mind in fantasy that she never felt the need to ask him what he actually thought about anything. She just '*knew*'. When I cautiously pointed this out, she was quite startled. I was curious to know if she would ask him or not about her buying knickers. The next time I saw her, she was astonished to report that now it had been sorted out; he had no objection to her buying knickers at all; he was less bothered about how she spent money than she was. She had had no idea about his true feelings. It seemed that the person who felt she should not buy knickers was herself, but with her husband's encouragement she was able to go and choose some that she really liked, for the first time in her life.

The woman did not want to leave her husband after all. The phantasy of having him inside her, watching over her and identified with a restrictive part of her, had changed to one in which she could bear to see him as different, outside her, needing to communicate in words. Disentangling herself from her husband in her mind enabled her to begin to live with a real husband who was different from her and who brought her things she could not give herself – including permission to enjoy herself. Both could now live and love each other without, in her phantasy, being completely confused with each other.

Fathers play an important role in helping babies and children to separate from their mothers. Mothers have to identify with the baby initially in order to understand what it needs, but this identification can become frightening for both mother and child. In phantasy as well as reality, fathers come between mother and baby, preventing them from stifling each other, allowing the mother to regain a sense of herself as an adult and the baby to relate to a different person in a different way. Just as the baby wants to merge with its mother, so in the baby's phantasy, its parents are sometimes allowed to merge with each other, and, when this feels painful, to be separated again. Adults are often confused about the differences between their parents, as if they have never quite separated them out correctly. And people with schizophrenia sometimes fear merging in a very concrete way. They may fear that they will get totally tangled up with another person, literally falling inside them, for example.

Giving Parts of the Self

When we love someone, we want to give him or her things: food, love, books to read, films to watch. In phantasy (as in love songs) we give our selves to those we love. We also give them parts of ourselves, not just our heart. We want to join our bodies, if only temporarily, in sexual acts. We may want to give them babies or have their babies or create something together such as songs or works of art. In phantasy we may give them our own capacities too. For example, they may be more optimistic or generous than we are; and we may be happy to let them be optimistic or generous for us too. After a time, however, it may seem that they never see the more pessimistic side of things; they never worry about money, leaving us alone with our fears for a joint future. Or they may be able to earn more money, and we may be happy to give up our job and let them take responsibility for earning; again, after a while this bargain may not seem so comfortable, especially if earning money seems to carry with it higher social esteem, or permission never to cook another meal or wash another dish. Equally, our loved ones may give us parts of themselves: the more-responsible-with-money part; or the thinking-about-the-children part; or the driving-the-car part, or the filling-in-forms or dealing-with-authorities part. In phantasy we can chop ourselves up into many parts and pass them around, as 'Fritz' did with his mother every time he was faced with a long division sum.

Sometimes in phantasy we give of ourselves out of love, or for safe keeping, or in hope of increasing everyone's happiness. Sometimes these phantasies are more cruel or desperate, however. We may give parts of ourselves to others to control them or hurt them or to save our own life at the expense of theirs. Ambitious women are sometimes accused of handing over their own ambition to a husband, chasing the husband to fulfil their ambitions and then complaining when he does not do it well enough. Marrying someone who likes to feel better than everyone else may enable a woman (or man) to get rid of her or his own sense of superiority safely for a while. But it may eventually lead to being treated with contempt by the husband (or wife). Equally, loading a lover with one's own sense of inferiority or badness or uselessness or impotence allows the self to feel superior. In phantasy there may be a fear that the other has been expected to hold too much; that he or she may have been filled up with too much of our anger, contempt or hatred. Fear of losing the good object sometimes arises from such phantasies.

If these transactions have been basically loving, we feel that a good object can survive, our fears of losing it are reduced, and we can feel that it is strong and resilient. The good object helps put us back together, not allowing us to lose touch entirely with our own capacities, encouraging us to develop aspects of ourselves we did not know before, and helping us to survive the knocks of life. In reasonably happy circumstances this is what our parents, united as a couple, did in our earliest phantasies, and what a partner, parent, close friend or child may do later in life. Our worst moments may be when we fear we have lost this good object, represented by any of these people. Because the good object contains much of ourselves, we can feel that we are falling apart and losing ourselves at the same time.

The Bad Object; Bad Parents; Bad Lovers; Bad Babies; the Bad Self

The development of the good object takes place in parallel with phantasies of a threatening bad one. Initially, when the good mother is not there the baby may simply feel the presence of a bad one. When parents are downstairs laughing, a child may sometimes lie in bed fearing the witch or the burglar under the bed, the spider or the scary daddy-long-legs on the wall, until a (real) parent is sought to banish it. Over time, the child may allow itself to be aware that it is angry with the parents for being downstairs together and may not need to create frightening monsters out of secret fury. This becomes easier as the child is able to make its own life which can exclude the parents. People outside the family can take on good and bad parent aspects.

Bad objects can also be created out of an attempt to idealise a good one. Those aspects which are not liked can be separated off in phantasy and attributed to someone else. A young adult may blame all his or her troubles on one parent and see the other as a helpless victim. The victim is supposedly loved and the oppressor hated; but actually the supposedly loved parent is diminished and reduced in phantasy, and in reality, patronised. (To be a victim means to be weak; collusion or manipulation of the other parent by the victim may be ignored.) Idealisation is often a defence against phantasies of persecution: the persecuting, bad, angry aspects of the supposed good parent are attributed to the supposed bad one who can then be hated with impunity. 'My mother would have taken more notice of me if my father had let her' has an implication that she is completely at his mercy. 'My father was a good, kind, sweet man; but my mother drove him to drink.' 'My mother was an angel and my father a devil.' Relationships are seldom this simple; the angel might turn out to be a devil in disguise. The 'can of worms' that people fear if they begin to unpick their childhood memories sometimes turns out to contain the shocking realisation that an angelic parent was not so angelic, and a devil parent perhaps guiltily and distressingly maligned.

As the child becomes a young adult, girlfriends and boyfriends can take the place of parents in terms of providing a reference group, and creating their own definitions of reality which may be different from those of the parents. Young adults may seek good objects, or they may seek bad ones, as lovers. Bad ones provide containment for unbearable bad aspects of the self and may be comforting in this way. Ultimately they may prove a great threat to the self; but if this self is at depth felt to be bad in phantasy, the threat may be welcomed as a deserved punishment. Dangerous or bullying lovers may also be felt to punish the parents inside. Real parents, of course, are also made to suffer when their son or daughter is in a bad relationship.

In good circumstances, phantasies of perfect parents, destroyed when they fail to live up to perfection, are replaced by more ordinary ones which can survive disappointment. Gradually the child stops wanting to kill the evil mother-who-is-not-there but can hold on to a phantasy of a loving mother who survives absences.

Functions of Phantasy: Dealing with Conflicts

There are many ways of dealing with conflicts in phantasy. An internal struggle can take place; do I do this, or do I do that? A conflict can also be externalised. Two people with the same internal conflict can argue with each other rather than inside their own heads. One may be arguing that he can do something; the other says he cannot. The internal conflict has been split between them and can be played out in the outside world. Sometimes the issue is close to the underlying unconscious conflict; sometimes it only represents it. For example, one partner may claim to want more sex and the other less, neither wanting to admit to any ambivalence over the subject. Some couples can have this fight; others may translate it into arguments about money or about time spent together, or about football or nights out with friends, any of which may be disguised ways of expressing anxieties connected to the question of whether they love each other or not.

Conflicts can also be dealt with in stories. A small girl has to cope with her conflicts over loving her mother and at the same time envying all her possessions and attributes, as well as her ability to tell the child what to do, to demand help from her, and to leave her behind while the mother goes out and has a good time. In addition, the girl may suffer terrible jealousy over the love her parents bear for each other and for their other children. There are many ways of dealing with this conflict in phantasy. Some girls deny that their parents love each other and in phantasy hold on to a belief that it is only they who are loved. Some deny that they want their parents to love them, and try to develop a 'don't care' attitude. They may seek the love they want in premature sexual relationships which are doomed to failure because they are based not on love of the parents, but revenge against them, which eventually re-emerges in revenge on the lover.

Most little girls end up with some form of coming to terms with their own mixed feelings towards their parents. The Cinderella story represents a phantasy in which the small girl can try out many mixed feelings towards her parents without having to see clearly what she is doing. Stories like this may be understood like computer games, as a means of children externalising and playing out conflicts and anxieties in a safe setting.

Cinderella's mother is split into a good (but dead) mother and a bad (but living) stepmother. Both are idealised and unrealistic. Reading the story, in phantasy identifying with Cinderella, a small girl can enjoy the pleasure of triumphing over a (step) mother who has beautiful clothes, daughters of her own and the love of the girl's father, while denying that this mother is the same one as the mother she loves. The ugly, envious feelings a real little girl cannot avoid when contemplating her mother's and older siblings' possessions are attributed to the ugly sisters when, at the end of the story, it is Cinderella who is the object of envy and admiration.

Phantasies of Splitting the Mother Mean Splitting the Self

The Cinderella story shows how phantasies of splitting the object – the real mother – can be experienced as deadly: the good mother is dead but Cinderella has no responsibility for this. The reader identified with Cinderella in phantasy has no guilt to bear. Phantasies of splitting the good mother from the bad one also involve splitting the self. The dead mother/stepmother split is reflected in the split between Cinderella and her stepsisters, but Cinderella herself is split again into the beautiful princess and the ragged girl who come together at the end of the story. The pairing of the shoes at the end also hints at Cinderella's need to bring two parts of herself/her object together. It suggests, perhaps, that the little girl will be able to bring these parts of herself together when she is old enough to have her own husband.

Phantasies of splitting the self can explain why we sometimes do things which take us by surprise; the 'me' which behaves like that is not one 'I' recognise as myself – or not one I want to recognise as me. Because splitting takes place unconsciously, it can be a real shock to recognise a split-off part of the self; as Amis did when he realised he had been writing about his daughter in a disguised form for years. It seems that the part of him which cared and was concerned and perhaps curious had been hidden from the self he knew.

Much of the work of counselling and psychoanalysis involves clarifying and mending splits in the self, bringing together aspects of the self in such a way that concern, love and reparative capacities are freer to express themselves without being swamped by phantasies of revenge or anger or destruction.

Denial

The phantasy that something can simply be ignored and then it will go away has many forms. 'Positive thinking' may mean consciously replacing unhappy thoughts with happy ones. The unhappy ones are then pushed under the carpet or 'stuffed down a well'. In phantasy the thoughts may be cut out, chopped to bits; we can shut the door on them, refuse to go down that road. Our language is full of hints about the kinds of phantasies we use [*No way! You must be joking! I won't countenance it! I don't know what got into me. It wasn't like her.*]. These last two imply phantasies in which some troublesome behaviour is acknowledged but ownership is somehow questioned. Some people *cocoon themselves; cut themselves off; hide under the bedclothes; roll up in a ball and shut their eyes tight; bury their heads in the sand.* They may use drink *to drown their sorrows.* In phantasy the drowned 'sorrows' are personified, perhaps as a small, dependent and miserable child self, or a vicious, uncaring, accusing adult bad object. The drink may represent debased milk or what 'Fritz' called 'wiwi'; alcohol in such phantasies is poison rather than good food.

The problem with all of these is that the unwanted thoughts remain in their original state and are not brought into contact with reality which can modify them. They remain active 'at the back of the mind'. A phantasy of the lover felt as uncaring, 'driving to drink', is not checked against reality but remains seen through an ancient phantasy of an uncaring parent or an uncaring self.

Denial can be helped along in other ways too. It is not so easy to *really* 'not see' what is there; something has to be done to the perception. One common way of dealing with it is to 'see' it elsewhere, to thrust it in phantasy into or onto a different person. For example, a car driver waiting at a roundabout pulls out into a bicycle coming off the roundabout in front of him. The car driver shouts at the cyclist that she should watch where she is going. Clearly his perception that *someone* should watch where he or she is going is accompanied by a powerful 'Not me!' Denial of reality can often be helped along by focusing on something different. The bad behaviour of other people, particularly on the road, is a useful source of aggrieved feelings which for some people can be relied on to keep their attention off what they have done themselves.

This driver probably went away swearing at cyclists. This is also an example of an attack used as a defence. Attacking, demanding punishment, and blame can all be used to help along denial; in particular, denial of guilt.

In phantasy we do not always distinguish one person from another. Just as in dreams a person may be one moment our father, the next a teacher or ex-lover, the next a husband or son, so we use phantasies derived from one person to understand the next. Children may accidentally call their teacher 'Mum' or their mother 'Miss'. This also provides possibilities for denial of unpleasant thoughts or feelings. It is simple in phantasy to substitute one person for another who shares some characteristic. A woman came for counselling because she felt that her husband no longer loved her. In her descriptions of daily life, it seemed that she 'knew' both that he did really love her, and at the same time was sure that he did not. Her own father had died when she was thirteen, the age her daughter was at the time. I suspected that her 'perception' of her husband's lack of love was a misattribution; she did not want to know that she feared that her father no longer loved her when he died. It was less painful to keep her idealised image of him and to see her husband as unloving. Unfortunately, this ultimately led to her own daughter being deprived of a parent as she had been herself. Not only did she misperceive the love of her husband, but she also actively created in her daughter feelings which came close to her own feelings when she was a child.

This is a form of denial helped along by a process we call 'projective identification'. Briefly, this involves feelings which cannot be tolerated being evoked in someone else, where their fate can be observed from a safer distance.

Counselling/Psychotherapy/Psychoanalysis

In my own work as a counsellor, I find that these ideas make sense of ordinary, everyday interactions. Most of the people I see are not mentally ill. They bring to counselling the normal difficulties of life: struggles with parents, with children, with relationships, brought into focus by the symptoms of multiple sclerosis. But uncovering the phantasies behind ordinary difficulties can change their lives – and give me a privileged view of the human mind at work.

A mother told me that her son had suddenly lost interest in school. He talked of leaving and getting a job near home, when previously he had wanted to go to university and to travel. I knew that she had been very anxious when she was seriously ill a few weeks previously, and I wondered aloud if her son knew that her fears were now much reduced. I wondered if he wanted to stay at home to keep an eye on her; ultimately, to keep her alive. I suggested that he might have been too scared to look at her to see if she were better. She went back and spoke to him directly about her health, and afterwards, she said that it was as if the weight of the world had been lifted off his shoulders. A few days later he almost confessed to actually liking school. She said she felt guilty; she had enjoyed his solicitousness and had been thoughtless not to notice his anxiety about her. I suspected that the child was probably working quite hard to hide his worries from his mother, for fear of killing her with his own anxiety. Instead, he preferred to kill his ambitious self.

The link between a child's anxieties about his mother's health and his anxieties about school is an important one. So too is the realisation that a child's worry about his mother's health can feel like 'the weight of the world'. Often it is not necessary to know what the child's exact phantasies are, and parents have good reason not to like intruding on their children's privacy. But children can have quite unrealistic anxieties, based on partial information which has been eked out by the child's own phantasies. Phantasies are usually answers rather than questions, so children may simply 'know' that they will have to look after their mother alone if their father dies; or 'know' that they and their mother killed him by not loving him enough; or 'know' that it was their own bad behaviour which caused him to leave. It may simply not have occurred to children that other adults will come to their aid, or that they cannot have made their mother's MS worse by hitting her in play, or that telling her about their homesickness would not cause her damaging 'stress'.

Using the Ideas Outside the Consulting Room

Klein's ideas also make sense of behaviour outside the consulting room, though sharing one's interpretations may be more problematic there. A girl of twelve called over the fence to a boy of five. 'Would you like this?' she asked, holding out something. When the boy tried to take it, she snatched it away, laughing. She did this three more times. Then she turned to her friend in triumph, saying, 'He's so stupid, he fell for it four times!' Clearly the girl felt that the boy was stupid to hope that the world might be a friendly place. We can wonder whether she was making him feel something which she was afraid applied to her. In fact, she had reason to be anxious about whether the good things of life would be forever snatched away from her, just as she had begun to trust in their permanency. She must have thought that she was stupid to be taken in by her own hopes. Taking her game as a representation of anxieties (rather than just as evidence of childish sadism or cruelty) puts me in a position where I can at least think whether any of the adults in her life might be able to help her. In her case, there is a good chance that they will, but telling them my observation clearly has social implications.

Psychoanalysis

Psychoanalysts who work with patients five times a week can help with much deeper and more long-standing anxieties than those of us who see people once or twice a week. Holding anxieties alone over six days is quite different from holding them over the weekend, knowing that there will be five daily hours to work them through the next week.

I would like to show how one woman experienced powerful changes in her phantasies of a containing good object through several years of psychoanalysis. I am grateful for her permission to use this material. Ann went into analysis in her thirties, because professional and personal success had not brought her freedom from a constant sense of apprehension and anxiety. Her first dream in analysis was of a ruined house held up by scaffolding: the walls were open to the sky. She was clinging to a lampshade she had made herself, standing on a rickety ladder held by her father. Gradually the buildings in her dreams changed. They began to have roofs, though these leaked, and water poured down the internal walls. The buildings had precarious balconies and helpful or quarrelsome friends living in them. They were often dilapidated and awaiting repair. Sometimes Ann was hopeful, sometimes despairing, about the amount of work needed to repair them. Gradually, over a period of years, the houses became firmer, more substantial. She still occasionally dreamed of ruins, but they were set in country parks, with grass growing over them. The final dream before she left analysis – feeling more secure than she had ever felt in her life – was of a large, substantial old house. Ann explained that 'it used to be a small convent, it had a history, but there were ordinary people having a meal on a big table in the garden, which was green and well-tended'.

Conclusion

The concept of unconscious phantasy was discovered by Freud and developed further by other analysts, in particular Melanie Klein and the analysts she inspired. Phantasies go on in our mind all the time without our knowing. Some are evident to other people; some are more concealed. These phantasies determine our interest in the world, our beliefs and assumptions, what attracts our attention and what we do with it. They are motivated by needs and desires. They deal with conflicts and anxieties in various ways by enabling us to work them through and test them against reality, both the reality of our own experience and the reality of the external world. We can also use phantasies to deny reality in various ways which are experienced as destructive; this destructiveness is itself often denied.

The idea that phantasies lie behind our every assumption, belief, thought, attitude, relationship and action may seem strange to begin with. We know that other people's beliefs are not always rational or sensible; that our own may not be based entirely on clear perception of reality may be harder to accept. What I like about the concept of phantasy is the way it allows both rationality and perception of reality their place. Phantasies may be perfectly rational and sensible; on the other hand, they may be based on simple misunderstandings arising from ignorance, and the whole structure of our thinking and behaviour will be affected – in a perfectly rational way. Many of the phantasies we use to understand ourselves and other people are fairly close to reality. These we can rely on; they will not let us down. Others are extremely primitive and unrealistic, yet they still allow us to get on with our lives in our own fashion.

Many of our normal phantasies, unrealistic but good enough to get us by in daily life, in fact create enormous amounts of anxiety. Others, created in an attempt to get rid of anxiety, deprive anxieties of the attention and thought necessary to allow them to resolve themselves peaceably, in their own good time. Understanding the way these phantasies work may allow us to find better ways of dealing with our own and others' anxieties.

Julia Segal works as a counsellor in the NHS. She has written extensively about the use of the ideas of Kleinian psychoanalysts in ordinary settings. She is particularly interested in the effect of parental illness on children.

Notes

1. *The Guardian*, 10 May 2000, p. 4. Amis, M., *Experience*, London: Jonathan Cape, 2000.
2. Freud, S., *The Standard Edition of the Complete Psychological Works of Sigmund Freud*, trans. James Strachey, London: Hogarth Press–Institute of Psychoanalysis, 1953–73 (hereafter *SE*), vol. 10, p. 190.
3. Freud, S., *SE*, vol. 1, p. xxiv.
4. Freud, S. and Breuer, J., 'Studies on Hysteria' (1895), *SE*, vol. 2, p. 157.
5. Freud, S., *The Interpretation of Dreams* (1900), *SE*, vol. 4, p. 259.
6. Freud (1895), op. cit., p. 137.
7. Klein, M., 'The Development of a Child' (1921), in *Love, Guilt and Reparation and Other Works 1921–45: Vol. 1: The Writings of Melanie Klein*, London: Hogarth Press–Institute of Psychoanalysis, 1975, p. 1.
8. Ibid., p. 35.
9. Ibid., p. 28.
10. Ibid., p. 42.
11. Ibid., p. 32.
12. Klein, M., 'The Role of the School in the Libidinal Development of the Child' (1923), Klein (1975), op. cit., p. 69.
13. Klein (1921), op. cit., p. 42.
14. Orbach, S., *Fat is a Feminist Issue*, London: Paddington Press, 1978.

Further Reading

Bell, D. (ed.), *Psychoanalysis and Culture: A Kleinian Perspective*, London: Duckworth, Tavistock Clinic Series, 1999.

Caper, R., *Immaterial Facts: Freud's Discovery of Psychic Reality and Klein's Development of his Work*, London and New York: Routledge, 2000.

——*A Mind of One's Own: A Kleinian View of Self and Object*, London and New York: Routledge, 1999.

Klein, M., *The Writings of Melanie Klein*, 4 vols., London: Hogarth Press–Institute of Psychoanalysis, 1975.

——and Heimann, P., Isaacs, S., Riviere, J. (eds.), *Developments in Psychoanalysis*, London: Hogarth Press–Institute of Psychoanalysis, 1952.

——and Heimann, P., Money-Kyrle, R. (eds.), *New Directions in Psychoanalysis*, London: Tavistock, 1955, 1971.

Menzies-Lyth, I., *Containing Anxieties in Institutions*, London: Free Association Books, 1988.

Segal, H., *Introduction to the Work of Melanie Klein*, London: Hogarth Press–Institute of Psychoanalysis, 1973.

——*The Work of Hanna Segal: A Kleinian Approach to Clinical Practice: Delusion and Artistic Creativity and other Psychoanalytic Essays*, London: Free Association Books, 1986.

Segal, J.C., *Phantasy in Everyday Life* (1985); reprinted in London: Karnac Books, 1995; USA: Aronson, 1996.

——*Melanie Klein: Key Figures in Counselling and Psychotherapy*, London: Sage Publications, 1992.

Spillius, E., *Melanie Klein Today*, 2 vols., London: Routledge, 1988.

4

Oedipus Complex

Robert M. Young

It has always seemed odd to me that the Oedipus myth and complex should lie at the heart of our humanity. It strikes me as so eccentric, so weird, in the same way that being sensually excited by dangling bits of fat with nipples on them, or an enlarged vein with a sac beneath it, seems undignified and comical. But there it is: evolution, culture and fashion have left us this way, with sexuality and the Oedipal triangle intermingled and as lifelong unconscious preoccupations which have ramifications throughout both personal and large-scale history.

Freudian Ideas of the Oedipus Complex

The idea of the Oedipus complex was developed by Sigmund Freud around the turn of the twentieth century. He drew on his clinical experience, his self-analysis and the Greek cycle of plays by Sophocles – in particular, *Oedipus Rex*, in which Oedipus kills his father and marries his mother with disastrous consequences. That is, Oedipus breaks the taboo against incest, and tragedy ensues. In practice, the Oedipus complex means that children from about three to six years have intense loving feelings towards one parent and seek to possess that parent exclusively, while having strong negative feelings towards the other parent. Boys love their mothers and hate their fathers. Girls do too, but they move on to hate their mothers and to seek to possess their fathers. At the unconscious level, these feelings are sexual towards the desired parent and murderous towards the same-sex parent. If all goes well in psychological development, the child comes to see how he or she benefits from the parental union and learns to contain possessive and hostile feelings. Out of the resolution of the Oedipus complex comes the conscience, or 'superego'. Children learn not to act on violent impulses and to obey the rules of civilisation and the conventions of culture and society, the incest taboo being the most basic of these. The intense Oedipal feelings get reprised in adolescence, when teenagers are typically rebellious, experiment with their sexual identities and make trouble, sometimes serious trouble, for their parents. Think of the anguished lack of communication between James Dean and his father in the film *Rebel Without a Cause* (1955), or the hopeless breakdown of communication between father and daughter, and the neighbour's son and his father, in the film *American Beauty* (1999).

People who do not successfully work through their Oedipus complex are left immature, unable to get on, feel hung up about one or both parents, get involved in acting out rather than containing their psychological difficulties and/or experience stasis in their careers and relationships, have impaired impulse control and difficulty with authority and are prey to all sorts of other troubles. Think of the stymied life of Brick Pollitt (played by Paul Newman) in his relationships with his wife (Elizabeth Taylor) and his patriarchal father, 'Big Daddy' (Burl Ives), in the film version of Tennessee Williams' play *Cat on a Hot Tin Roof* (1955), released in 1958. The vicissitudes of an unresolved Oedipus complex often get passed down the generations. Having a bad relationship with one or both parents makes one's own parenting more difficult. Some also say that the vicissitudes of the Oedipus complex affect sexual orientation. A too strong attachment to a domineering mother, coupled with a weak or absent father, was a fundamentally important factor in the aetiology of male homosexuality in *Suddenly Last Summer* (1958), another play by Tennessee Williams. Others hotly dispute this link.

These are weighty matters, ones which Freud claimed in *Civilization and Its Discontents* (1930) provide the historical and emotional foundations of culture, law, civility and decency. Once again, what are the bare elements? First, there is the Oedipal triangle, wherein a child somewhere between three-and-a-half and six wants exclusive access to the parent of the opposite sex – physically, emotionally and intellectually – and has to come to terms with the prior claims of the same-sex parent. The child fears retaliation and soon begins to feel guilty for his incestuous desire and murderous impulses. Guilt reveals the presence of the super-ego, which Freud described as the heir to the Oedipus complex. The whole thing comes up again in adolescence, with respect to sexuality and to authority, and may arise again when one or the other parent dies. Patients who have not negotiated these rites of passage have unresolved Oedipal problems. One of the big ones that inhibits achievement and satisfaction is fear of surpassing a parent, leading to fear of retaliation for so-called 'Oedipal triumph'. Another is the risk of believing that one can be an adult without growing up emotionally, expecting fairy-tale or magical solutions to life's problems.[1]

In addition to my reservations about the Oedipus complex in general, I have also been slow to accept the centrality of the Oedipal triangle in psychoanalysis and psychotherapy – to realise that the analytic space is an Oedipal space. Patients experience their therapists as parental figures and fall in love with them as they once did with their parents. Within the analytic frame, the familial Oedipal dynamic is reprised.[2] The analytic relationship involves continually offering incest and continually declining it in the name of analytic abstinence and the hope of a relationship that transcends incestuous desires. Breaking the analytic frame invariably involves the risk of child abuse, and sleeping with patients or ex-patients is precisely that.

Martin Bergmann puts some of these points very nicely in an essay on transference love, wherein the patient falls romantically in love with the therapist. He says:

> *In the analytic situation, the early images are made conscious and thereby deprived of their energizing potential. In analysis, the uncovering of the incestuous fixation behind transference love loosens the incestuous ties and prepares the way for a future love free from the need to repeat oedipal triangulation. Under conditions of health the infantile prototypes merely energize the new falling in love while in neurosis they also evoke the incest taboo and needs for new triangulation that repeat the triangle of the oedipal state.*[3]

With respect to patients who get involved with ex-therapists, he says that they claim that 'unlike the rest of humanity I am entitled to disobey the incest taboo, circumventing the work of mourning, and possess my parent sexually. I am entitled to do so because I suffered so much or simply because I am an exception'.[4] From the therapist's point of view, 'When the transference relationship becomes a sexual one, it represents symbolically and unconsciously the fulfilment of the wish that the infantile love object will not be given up and that incestuous love can be refound in reality'.[5] This is a variant on the Pygmalion theme. The analytic relationship works only to the extent that the therapist shows, in Freud's words, 'that he is proof against every temptation'.[6]

Looking further into the Oedipal dynamic as experiences in the clinical psychoanalytic relationship, one finds the phantasy of the copulating parental couple with which the patient has to come to terms – hopefully moving from an unconscious phantasy of something violent and feared to a more benign one, in the lee of which he or she can feel safe, benefiting from the parents' union. It was my clinical practice that slowly eroded my conceptual scepticism about the Oedipus complex. It simply came up before me in clinical material again and again. Some of my patients are stuck because they have *no* phantasy of their parents together and believe that they are in bed between the parents, preventing them from getting together, and cannot get on with relationships themselves because of the harm they unconsciously believe they have caused. Stasis, longing and lack of fulfilment are the likely results.

A Closer Look at Oedipal Dynamics

Let's turn to a more detailed exploration of psychoanalytic formulations of the Oedipal dynamic and start with a definite developmental scheme, the one which constitutes the classical chronological story of orthodox Freudianism, as modified and enriched by Karl Abraham and, some would say, Erik Erikson. We begin with primary narcissism and pass through several successive phases of focus on particular bodily zones: oral, anal, phallic and genital – oral for the first year and a half, anal for the next year and a half, and phallic beginning towards the close of the third year.[7] As I have said, the classical Oedipal period is from age three-and-a-half to six (some say five). This leads on to the formation of the superego and a period of relative latency, during which boys are quintessentially boyish and horrid, with their bikes, hobbies and play, and girls are sugar and spice and all things nice, playing nurse and mummy, or so it is said.[8] Things get fraught again in adolescence when biological changes coincide with agonising problems about gender identity,[9] sexual exploration and maturation, conflict with parents, competitiveness and achievement. Erik Erikson spells out a further set of stages, beginning with a psychosocial moratorium in late adolescence, followed by young adulthood, full adulthood and mature age, the last of which he characterises as a period in which the central conflict is between integrity, on the one hand, and disgust and despair, on the other.[10]

A detailed chronology of the phases of the Oedipus complex is spelled out in Humberto Nagera's orthodox Freudian exposition of *Basic Psychoanalytic Concepts on the Libido Theory* (1969).[11] I find it remarkable that there is not here or in Freud's writings or in Laplanche and Pontalis' *The Language of Psychoanalysis* (1973),[12] an agreed, straightforward account.[13] This is particularly true of the female Oedipus complex:

Throughout history people have knocked their heads against the riddle of the nature of femininity ... Nor will you have escaped worrying over this problem – those of you who are men; to those of you who are women this will not apply – you are yourselves the problem.[14]

Freud's impish humour does not obscure the fact that he is looking at femininity from a masculine point of view, and this has been the basis of much criticism of his idea within psychoanalysis and beyond. With regard to the female Oedipus complex, he was faced with a problem. Since all children – both boys and girls – are originally attached to the mother, how is it that the female child turns to her father to become a 'daddy's girl'? Something must break the bond with the mother. Freud's answer brought opprobrium on his head from feminists and traditionalists alike. The girl is said to discover that she has no penis, to suffer from 'penis envy' and to look to her mother to supply her with one. When this is not forthcoming, she is disappointed. She blames her mother for the sense of deficiency, turns to the father in search of one, and remains ungratified until she gets a symbolic penis in the form of a baby.[15] For the boy, it is the 'castration complex' that turns him away from his mother; fear of the consequences of his incestuous desires. For a girl child, the female version of the castration complex – penis envy – is what catapults her into the Oedipus complex. But since she is already 'castrated' and has suffered the fate that the little boy is trying to prevent, the rivalry with the mother takes on a different, and perhaps more lasting, quality. Freud argued that the fact that the girl's Oedipus complex is resolved much more slowly, more gently and less brutally and abruptly than the boy's, accounts for the fact that girls' consciences are less brittle than those of males. It has also been suggested that some men – black slaves and post-colonials – are perpetually under such real or symbolic threat of emasculation that they never resolve their castration complexes and that this (along with poor economic prospects) may help explain the tendency on the part of some to be inconstant and to avoid familial responsibilities.[16]

The orthodox story of the Oedipus complex in its various forms is much-disputed, most obviously and appropriately by feminists (some of whom, for example, counter the idea of female penis envy with the notion of males having 'womb envy') and also by gays and lesbians and Lacanians and I don't know who-all. It is called too naturalistic and biologistic, too literally linked to parts of the body, too deterministic. In the real world of human development, as Freud well knew, there is an infinite number of outcomes to this momentous story, for both men and women – an infinite number of partial resolutions, compromises and sublimations. It should also be said that Freud was forever revising his views on both the male and female Oedipus complex and that his account of the female one is the messier and less adequately theorised of the two. As I shall show below, there is a more abstract and Kleinian version of Oedipal dynamics which suffers less from being found implausible.

The debates about the details of the direct and indirect Oedipus complex and the role of bisexuality in the Oedipal process are many and labyrinthine and can be followed in the abundant literature. I shall not detail them here, since I believe that an overview should paint on a broader canvas and because there are two sorts of issues about the Oedipus complex which are at the centre of recent debates, and summaries of them are not readily accessible: Kleinian ideas about the Oedipus complex, and anti-naturalistic positions about sexuality which challenge the whole idea of a biologically given, psychosexual developmental scheme.[17]

Before turning to those topics, however, I want to linger over the classical Freudian story. Freud called the Oedipus complex 'the core complex' or 'the nuclear complex' of every neurosis. In a footnote added to the 1920 edition of *Three Essays on the Theory of Sexuality*, he made it clear that the Oedipus complex is the immovable foundation stone on which the whole edifice of psychoanalysis is based:

> It has justly been said that the Oedipus complex is the nuclear complex of the neuroses, and constitutes the essential part of their content. It represents the peak of infantile sexuality, which, through its after-effects, exercises a decisive influence on the sexuality of adults. Every new arrival on this planet is faced with the task of mastering the Oedipus complex; anyone who fails to do so falls a victim to neurosis. With the progress of psycho-analytic studies the importance of the Oedipus complex has become more and more clearly evident; its recognition has become the shibboleth that distinguishes the adherents of psycho-analysis from its opponents.[18]

In the first published reference to the incest taboo in 1905 (he had written about the 'horror of incest' and incest as 'anti-social' in an unpublished draft in 1897), Freud refers to it as 'a cultural demand made by society' that may get passed on by organic inheritance, and adds in a footnote of 1915, 'Psycho-analytic investigation shows, however, how intensely the individual struggles with the temptation to incest during his period of growth and how frequently the barrier is transgressed in phantasy and even in reality.'[19] In both the development of the individual and the history of mankind, Freud identified the incest taboo as the basis of all other prohibitions. Guilt was the essential weapon in the struggle against uncivilised, rapacious impulses, and sublimation of sexual energies provided the energy for *all* of culture and civilisation, concepts that he disdained to distinguish: 'Incest is anti-social and civilisation consists of the progressive renunciation of it.'[20] The rapacious, sexually polymorphous 'primal father', the patriarch of the 'primal horde', was opposed and killed by his sons, and thus was established the taboo against incest, the foundation stone of all moral and cultural prohibitions. 'We cannot get away from the assumption that man's sense of guilt springs from the Oedipus complex and was acquired at the killing of the father by the brothers banned together.'[21] The price we pay for the advance of civilisation 'is a loss of happiness through the heightening of the sense of guilt'. He calls this 'the final conclusion of our investigation', thus making vivid the juxtaposition of civilisation and discontent in the title of the book: civilisation *causes* discontents.[22] He saw all of the vast panorama of human history as being acted out in the emotional space between Eros and Thanatos – the constructive impulse to love and create, and the aggressive impulse to destroy and die.

Freud claimed that the Oedipus complex is universal, and there have been heated debates, some involving anthropological fieldwork, about this. These debates have become pretty arcane, and I have the impression that orthodox Freudians have stretched things a long way in the hope of retaining some version of universality of the Oedipus complex, while critics have been scathing about them and about Freud's historical speculations about the 'primal horde'.[23] We are privileged to have a useful summary of these debates in *Oedipus Ubiquitous: The Family Complex in World Folk Literature* (1996), by Allen W. Johnson and Douglass Price-Williams. They review the issues and conclude that the complex as specified by Freud is prevalent in advanced, authoritarian societies, while a much looser version involving inter-generational conflict is widespread among the 139 folk tales they review, though more of the ones similar to Freud's account are about boys than girls.[24] Freud's very concrete claims about this or that body part fare less well than the general inter-generational conflict. There is also interesting psychoanalytic work by Alan Roland (1988) which shows important cultural differences in this matter in India (where conflict in sons and fathers is deeply taboo) and Japan (where deference is deeply embedded in women's personalities).

I want to make two more points about Freud's views which I

offer as counterweights to the mistaken belief that Freud was too reductionist and biologistic and left little space for historical relativity. First, although he saw the Oedipus complex as universal and rooted in our biological inheritance, he also saw its resolution as freeing us to some extent from that very heritage. Freud wrote:

> Otto Rank, in a large volume on the incest complex (1912), has produced evidence of the surprising fact that the choice of subject matter, especially for dramatic works, is principally determined by the ambit of what psychoanalysis has termed the 'Oedipus Complex'. By working it over with the greatest variety of modifications, distortions and disguises, the dramatist seeks to deal with his own most personal relations to this emotional theme. It is in attempting to master the Oedipus Complex – that is to say a person's emotional attitude towards his family, or in the narrower sense towards his father and mother – that individual neurotics come to grief, and for this reason that complex habitually forms the nucleus of their neurosis.[25]

This developmental task which faces each individual is connected for Freud with universal features of human nature. He continues:

> It does not owe its importance to any unintelligible conjunction; the emphasis laid upon the relation of children to their parents is an expression of the biological facts that the young of the human race pass through a long period of dependence and are slow in reaching maturity, as well as that their capacity for love undergoes a complicated course of development. Consequently, the overcoming of the Oedipus complex coincides with the most efficient way of mastering the archaic, animal heritage of humanity. It is true that that heritage comprises all the forces that are required for the subsequent cultural development of the individual, but they must first be sorted out and worked over. This archaic heirloom is not fit to be used for the purposes of social life in the form in which it is inherited by the individual.[26]

Second, the universality of the Oedipus complex does not mean immunity from historical development and cultural relativity in how Oedipal forces are expressed. Freud compares social mores at the time of Sophocles with those at the time of Shakespeare. Immediately after the first mention of the Oedipus complex in *The Interpretation of Dreams* (1900), in which he advocates its universal nature, Freud emphasises the historical specificity of this momentous theme:

> *There is an unmistakable indication in the text of Sophocles'* *tragedy itself that the legend of Oedipus sprang from some* *primaeval dream-material which had as its content the* *distressing disturbance of a child's relation to his parents* *owing to the first stirrings of sexuality . . .*
>
> *Another of the great creations of tragic poetry, Shakespeare's* Hamlet, *has its roots in the same soil as* Oedipus Rex. *But the* *changed treatment of the same material reveals the whole* *difference in the mental life of these two widely separated* *epochs of civilisation: the secular advance of repression in the* *emotional life of mankind. In the* Oedipus *the child's wishful* *phantasy that underlies it is brought into the open and realised* *as it would be in a dream. In* Hamlet *it remains repressed; and* *– just as in the case of neurosis – we only learn of its existence* *from its inhibiting consequences . . . Hamlet is able to do* *anything – except take vengeance on the man who did away* *with his father and took that father's place with his mother, the* *man who shows him the repressed wishes of his own child-* *hood realised. Thus the loathing which should drive him on to* *revenge is replaced in him by self-reproaches, by scruples of* *conscience, which remind him that he himself is literally no* *better than the sinner whom he is to punish.*[27]

Kleinian Ideas

How do specifically Kleinian ideas relate to all this? First, Melanie Klein famously claimed to find what she called 'the Oedipal situation' much earlier in life, along with persecuting ideas from the superego, long before a Freudian would grant that there could *be* a superego. She found the internalised idea of the copulating parental couple – for ill or good – in very early phantasies.

Klein is Freud's most assiduous follower with respect to the dual instinct theory (Eros–Thanatos) and the sombre lessons of Freud's theory of civilisation and its discontents. But there is a quite fundamental divergence between them with respect to development, structures and, indeed, all of the signposts in the inner world that help Freudians to find their way about. Kleinian ideas in this area help us to see why it is so hard to get hold of Klein at all. I am going to spell out the history and present situation with respect to the Kleinian tradition on the Oedipus complex, but I shall offer my overall conclusion now.

I think it's a matter of background and foreground. This may appear at first glance a small matter, but I think it is of fundamental significance. At first I thought that developmental chronology and stages didn't matter at all for Klein. I thought the structural hypothesis of id, ego and superego[28] didn't matter to her either, but I was mistaken. These concepts are there – all of them. So are those of the oral, anal, phallic and genital stages, as well as the Oedipus complex, but they are not in the foreground. They are background. What is in the foreground is the interplay of emotions and positions. A 'position' for Klein is a constellation of anxieties and defences, object relations and impulses.[29] The fundamental dichotomy is between Eros and Thanatos, which, in turn, give us paired emotions such as love and hate, gratitude and envy – all directed to whole-object and part-object relations.

There is another general point to be put alongside this one about positions and emotions. It is that the primitive is never transcended in the way it is in the Freudian developmental scheme. In particular, psychotic anxieties continue to break through integrated perceptions, leading to a perpetual oscillation between two fundamental ways of being in the unconscious – the paranoid-schizoid and depressive positions, the latter of which is characterised by integrated, more mature thinking in relation to whole objects, whereas part-object relations dominate the paranoid-schizoid position. The two positions were eventually linked with a double-headed arrow to show the oscillation between them: **Ps ↔ D**. It is because the primitive continues to dominate that the developmental scheme is background, while the interplay of emotions is foreground. This notion about foreground and background is supported in the argument of a paper by Ruth Stein (1990) to which I will return below. I am suggesting that the problem of finding one's way in the Kleinian inner world is to a considerable extent explained by the fact that they have taken the signposts down, rather as the British did when they expected Hitler to invade. The result is that feelings are rushing around without the benefit of the sorts of roadmaps, boundaries and tramlines that make Freudians feel safe.

Oedipus Rex

I now want to ponder Oedipus a bit. In the light of all the recent revelations and controversies about child abuse, I had a sudden insight about old *King Oedipus*, the play Aristotle called the perfect tragedy, the inspiration for the other candidate, *Hamlet*.[30] If we ask when Oedipus committed incest, the answers can be seen in a very different light than the usual story gives. What really happened is that having heard from the oracle that his child would murder its father and marry its mother, Laius assaulted his son at birth. In Sophocles' writings, Jocasta tells it like this:

> *As for the child,*
> *It was not yet three days old, when it was cast out*
> *(By other hands, not his) with riveted ankles*
> *To perish on the empty mountain-side.*[31]

'Oedipus', the name he was given by his adoptive parents, Polybus and Meropé, means 'swollen-footed'. When he was older and heard from a drunkard that he was not the son of Polybus, who he believed to be his father, he asked his supposed parents who were distressed that anyone had said this. He went to an oracle:

> *. . . I went to Pytho;*
> *But came back disappointed of any answer*
> *To the question I asked, having heard instead a tale*
> *Of horror and misery: how I must marry my mother,*
> *And become the parent of a misbegotten brood,*
> *An offence to all mankind – and kill my father.*[32]

Oedipus fled from Corinth, 'never to see home again / That no such horror should ever come to pass',[33] in order to avoid harming Polybus, his supposed father, and to avoid sleeping with Meropé, the woman he believed to be his mother. As he did so, he had a chance encounter with Laius at a crossroad. Did his father greet him with open arms? No, he did not. He tried to bully him over the trivial matter of who should pass first at a crossroad.

> *When I came to the place where three roads join, I met*
> *A herald followed by a horse-drawn carriage, and a man*
> *Seated therein, just as you have described.*
> *The leader roughly ordered me out of the way;*
> *And his venerable master joined in with a surly command.*
> *It was the driver that thrust me aside, and him I struck,*
> *For I was angry. The old man saw it, leaning from the*
> *   carriage,*
> *Waited until I passed, then, seizing for weapon*
> *The driver's two-pronged goad, struck me on the head.*
> *He paid with interest for his temerity;*
> *Quick as lightning, the staff in this right hand*
> *Did its work; he tumbled headlong out of the carriage,*
> *And every man of them there I killed.*[34]

What has Oedipus done except get assaulted at birth and again when he was trying to run away from the Oedipal triangle?[35] Of course, he certainly over-reacted to the bullying, but he was assaulted twice. Then he answers the riddle – about the life cycle ('What walks on four feet then two then three?'), ends the tyranny of the Sphinx, gets the prize (which turns out to be incestuous union with his mother), learns the truth in veiled form from wise, blind old Teiresias, doubts him, pursues the truth relentlessly, and gets it confirmed by servants who were directly involved in the crucial events. Oedipus feels dreadful; Jocasta hangs herself. Oedipus puts out his own eyes and eventually attains wisdom from looking into the inner world. As I read the play, I realise he has had bad, uncontained and uncontaining parents, a far from good enough mother, a grossly and repeatedly abusing father and a bad press, one which could rival our own renditions of couples and triangles. This man was well and truly maltreated and has the scars to prove it.

But as close inspection reveals with respect to many of the abused, this is not the whole story. A very different one can be told about his unconscious. Indeed, there is some evidence that Sophocles was a proto-Kleinian, since, if we look at the inner world, Oedipus will have been having the impulses – which explained, though they did not justify, Laius's behaviour – at a *very* early age. He wasn't committing incest in his mind at three and a half, as he would have if he were a Freudian baby, but straightaway, like a good Kleinian baby. No primary narcissism, as a Freudian would have it, but object relations at birth.

As John Steiner has argued, there is evidence that all the people involved in the tragedy really did know the other story or could easily have worked it out, but they 'turned a blind eye'.[36] I've had another look at the *Theban Plays*, and I am here to tell you that Sophocles must certainly have intuited Klein's 1928 paper, though we cannot be sure about the 1945 one or the 1946 one, where the role of projective identification in the paranoid-schizoid position was fully formulated, thus providing all the elements of the modern Kleinian analogue of the Oedipal story.[37]

Freud and *Oedipus Rex*

It would be a truism to say that this play made a deep impression on Freud, but I think it might benefit us to dwell a moment on that fact. We know that he said to his close interlocutor, Wilhelm Fliess, in 1897, 'I have found in my own case too, falling in love with the mother and jealousy of the father, and I now regard it as a universal event of childhood . . . If that is so, we can understand the riveting power of *Oedipus Rex*'.[30] He tells about seeking out his own family story in that letter and suggests that the same tragic triangle is at the heart of the inter-generational dynamics in *Hamlet*.[39]

Freud wrote of *Oedipus* in *The Interpretation of Dreams*.

If Oedipus Rex *moves a modern audience no less than it did the contemporary Greek one, the explanation can only be that its effect does not lie in the contrast between destiny and human will, but is to be looked for in the particular nature of the material on which that contrast is exemplified. There must be something which makes a voice within us ready to recognize the compelling force of destiny in the* Oedipus*, while we can dismiss as merely arbitrary such dispositions as are laid down in . . . other modern tragedies of destiny. And a factor of this kind is in fact involved in the story of King Oedipus. His destiny moves us only because it might have been ours – because the oracle laid the same curse upon us before our birth as upon him. It is the fate of all of us, perhaps, to direct our first sexual impulse toward our mother and our first hatred and our first murderous wish against our father. Our dreams convince us that this is so. King Oedipus, who slew his father Laius and married his mother Jocasta, merely shows us the fulfilment of our own childhood wishes. But, more fortunate than he, we have meanwhile succeeded, in so far as we have not become psychoneurotics, in detaching our sexual impulses from our mothers and forgetting our jealousy of our fathers. Here is one in whom these primaeval wishes of our childhood have been fulfilled. And we shrink back from him with the whole force of the repression by which those wishes have since that time been held down within us. While the poet, as he unravels the past, brings to light the guilt of Oedipus, he is at the same time compelling us to recognise our own inner minds, in which those same impulses, though suppressed, are still to be found. The contrast with which the closing Chorus leaves us confronted –*

> *. . . fix on Oedipus your eyes,*
> *Who resolved the dark enigma, noblest*
> *   champion and most wise.*
> *Like a star his envied fortune mounted beaming*
> *   far and wide:*
> *Now he sinks in seas of anguish, whelmed*
> *   beneath a raging tide . . .*

– strikes a warning at ourselves and our pride, at us who since our childhood have grown so wise and so mighty in our own

eyes. Like Oedipus, we live in ignorance of these wishes, repugnant to morality, which have been forced upon us by Nature, and after their revelation we may all of us well seek to close our eyes to the scenes of our childhood.[40]

He added this note in 1919: 'Later studies have shown that the "Oedipus complex" which was touched upon in the above paragraphs in the *Interpretation of Dreams*, throws a light of undreamt-of importance on the history of the human race and the evolution of religion and morality'.[41] Freud had added the term 'complex' under the influence of Carl Jung in 1910, and, as we have seen, in *Totem and Taboo* claimed that an actual killing of a father by a primal horde lay at the foundation of human history.[42]

Freud's own family constellation was multi-generationally confused. His father was twenty years older than his mother and already a grandfather via a grown son from his first marriage when Freud was born. That son and another were at least as old as the new bride. Freud was the eldest son of his family but the youngest child in the broader family group. The other two young children were, respectively, a year older and the same age, but his nephew and niece. A brother once said to him that he was of the third generation, not the second, with respect to his father.[43] (I am reminded of a novelty song on the Hit Parade when I was a boy, which told of family relations and re-marriages so complicated that the singer could logically claim, 'I'm my own grandpa!') It is no wonder that when Freud was reflecting on finishing secondary school, the one bit of study he singled out for mention was *Oedipus Rex*, in which he came first in his class on the basis of a translation from the Greek of the opening speech of the priest, beseeching Oedipus to deliver the Thebans from a complex and bewildering pestilence which was caused by the breaking of the inter-generational incest taboo.[44]

The significance of all this was driven home dramatically when Freud's disciples presented him with a medallion on his fiftieth birthday. On one side was Freud's portrait in profile, and on the other side a design of Oedipus answering the Sphinx, with this line from the closing passage of the play: 'Who knew the famous riddles and was a man most mighty.' When Freud read it he became pale and agitated about an uncanny coincidence between this tribute and his own fantasies. As a student he had strolled around the arcade of the University of Vienna, inspecting the busts of the famous professors. He had imagined his own bust there in the future with that exact inscription. His identification with Oedipus could not have been more complete.[45] Even Freud was shaken by feelings of Oedipal triumph. In the light of this life-long preoccupation, it is all the more striking that he never wrote a systematic exposition of his mature views on the Oedipus complex – a concept which was, by his own account, the centrepiece of his theory.

Exposition of Klein's Views

I want to turn now to an exposition of Kleinian views on the Oedipus complex. Klein's answer to the question, 'When did Oedipus commit incest?', is that he did it from the beginning, at least in unconscious phantasy. I will offer you both a clear and a diffuse version of this point. The sharp one can be found in all the various attempts to delineate Kleinian accounts from Freudian ones. They all depend on the developmental scheme I outlined above and to holding fast to the chronology that that implies. If it were not for this distinct schema, there would be little or no conflict between the conceptions. If you read through the 'Controversial Discussions' between the Kleinians and the rest of the members of the British Psychoanalytic Society in the early 1940s, the point comes up again and again that Klein is thought to be, as they repeatedly put it, 'depreciating' the classical Oedipus complex which occurs at three or beyond.[46] Klein denies this but acknowledges that there is a conflict. It is a conflict about what can be in the child's mind very early in life. As I have already said more than once, it is also a conflict about structure and chronology, foreground and background, how the mind works and how to think about it, but I'll return to that later.

Let's start with a simple rendition of Klein on the Oedipus complex.[47] Klein makes a distinction between what she calls 'the Oedipal situation', which recurs throughout life, and the classical Oedipus complex of Freud: 'According to Freud, genital desires emerge and a definite object choice takes place during the phallic phase, which extends from about three to five years of age, and is contemporaneous with the Oedipus complex.'[48] The superego and the sense of guilt are sequelae of the Oedipus complex.[49] Klein's view is that emotional and sexual development *from early infancy onwards* includes genital sensations and trends, which constitute the first stages of the inverted [desire towards same-sex parent; aggression towards opposite sex one] and positive Oedipus complex; they are experienced under the primacy of oral libido and mingle with urethral and anal desires and phantasies. The libidinal stages overlap from the first months of life onwards.'[50] She dates the superego from the oral phase. 'Under the sway of phantasy life and of conflicting emotions, the child at every stage of libidinal organization introjects his objects – primarily his parents – and builds up the super-ego from these elements . . . All the factors which have a bearing on his object relations play a part from the beginning in the build-up of the super-ego.'[51]

At first, it is not the parent as a whole that is introjected but only particular aspects, i.e., significant part-objects:

> The first introjected object, the mother's breast, forms the basis of the super-ego . . . The earliest feelings of guilt in both sexes derive from the oral-sadistic desires to devour the mother, and primarily her breasts (Abraham). It is therefore in infancy that feelings of guilt arise. Guilt does not emerge when the Oedipus complex comes to an end, but is rather one of the factors which from the beginning mould its course and affect its outcome.[52]

Klein's final remarks begin with a passage which supports my impression that she intermingles concepts which would be carefully distinguished in a Freudian developmental scheme:

> The sexual development of the child is inextricably bound up with his object relations and with all the emotions which from the beginning mould his attitude to mother and father. Anxiety, guilt and depressive feelings are intrinsic elements of the child's emotional life and therefore permeate the child's early object relations, which consist of the relation to actual people as well as to their representatives in the inner world. From these introjected figures – the child's identifications – the super-ego develops and in turn influences the relation to both parents and the whole sexual development. Thus emotional and sexual development, object relations and super-ego development interact from the beginning.[53]

She concludes: 'The infant's emotional life, the early defences built up under the stress between love, hatred and guilt, and the vicissitudes of the child's identifications – all these are topics which may well occupy analytic research for a long time to come.'[54] As with Freud, it is striking that although she lived for a further fifteen years and remained intellectually productive, Klein did not provide an integration of her views on this topic with her mature versions of other characteristically Kleinian preoccupations.

Recent Kleinian Ideas

'The Oedipus Complex in the Light of Early Anxieties' (1945) was published a year before Klein coined a term to characterise what was almost certainly her most profound idea, the mechanism which she called 'a particular form of identification which establishes the prototype of an aggressive object relation. I suggest for these processes the term "projective identification".'[55] This lies at the heart of the paranoid-schizoid position, in which splitting, projective mechanisms and part-object relations predominate. One can see these mechanisms at work in racism and other forms of virulent hatred in which a despised out-group becomes the repository of disowned and projected 'bad' characteristics. Once again, this configuration is in a dynamic relation with the depressive position, in which whole-object relations, concern for the object and integration predominate. What has happened in the subsequent research to which Klein alluded is that these ways of thinking have been brought into relationship with one another. As David Bell puts it:

> The primitive Oedipal conflict described by Klein takes place in the paranoid-schizoid position when the infant's world is widely split and relations are mainly to part objects. This means that any object which threatens the exclusive possession of the idealised breast/mother is felt as a persecutor and has projected into it all the hostile feelings deriving from pregenital impulses.[56]

If development proceeds satisfactorily, secure relations with good internal objects lead to integration, healing of splits and taking back projections:

> The mother is then, so to speak, free to be involved with a third object in a loving intercourse which, instead of being a threat, becomes the foundation of a secure relation to internal and external reality. The capacity to represent internally the loving intercourse between the parents as whole objects results, through the ensuing identifications, in the capacity for full genital maturity. For Klein, the resolution of the Oedipus complex and the achievement of the depressive position refer to the same phenomena viewed from different perspectives.[57]

Ronald Britton puts it very elegantly:

> [T]he two situations are inextricably intertwined in such a way that one cannot be resolved without the other: we resolve the Oedipus complex by working through the depressive position and the depressive position by working through the Oedipus complex.[58]

We are provided here with a key to translating between the Freudian and Kleinian conceptual schemes. In both frames of reference, the child comes to terms with his or her place within the family triangle (whether this involves two real parents or one, with the idea of a third person held in the mind of the caring parent). In the recent work of Kleinians, this way of thinking has been considerably broadened. For example, it has been applied to development of the ability to symbolise and learn from experience. Integration of the depressive position – which we can now see as resolution of the Oedipus complex – is the *sine qua non* of the development of 'a capacity for symbol formation and rational thought'.[59] Greater knowledge of the object 'includes awareness of its continuity of existence in time and space and also therefore of the other relationships of the object implied by that realization. The Oedipal situation exemplifies that knowledge. Hence the depressive position cannot be worked through without working through the Oedipus complex and vice versa.'[60] Britton also sees 'the depressive position and the Oedipal situation as never finished but as having to be re-worked in each new life situation, at each stage of development, and with each major addition to experience or knowledge.'[61]

This way of looking at the Oedipal situation also offers a way of thinking of self-knowledge or insight:

> *The primal family triangle provides the child with two links connecting him separately with each parent and confronts him with the link between them which excludes him. Initially this parental link is conceived in primitive part-object terms and in the modes of his own oral, anal and genital desires, and in terms of his hatred expressed in oral, anal and genital terms. If the link between the parents perceived in love and hate can be tolerated in the child's mind, it provides him with a prototype for an object relationship of a third kind in which he is a witness and not a participant. A third position then comes into existence from which object relationships can be observed. Given this, we can also envisage being observed. This provides us with a capacity for seeing ourselves in interaction with others and for entertaining another point of view whilst retaining our own, for reflecting on ourselves whilst being ourselves.*[62]

I find this very helpful – indeed, profound.

I had an odd experience while I was working out what I had to say about this matter. I knew that an important source would be the 'Controversial Discussions' in the 1940s when Kleinians and Freudians debated, as I confidently supposed, this very matter.[63] I had done research in the compendious volume on these debates with respect to other topics: in particular, phantasy and psychotic anxieties, which have huge index entries – a whole page in one case and a half-page in the other. 'Oedipus complex' has only a few lines. After reading all the relevant passages, it took me the longest time to figure out this apparent inconsistency. The answer is that they are not separate topics. That is, the Kleinians were challenging the neat developmental scheme of classical and neo-Freudians. They were drawing attention to the *content* of early emotional processes, whereas Freudians tended to focus on scientistic models and metapsychological presentations of their *forms*. What I think was really novel and breathtaking about what Klein and her colleagues were reflecting upon was the primitive ferocity of the content of unconscious phantasies and psychotic anxieties which, as Hinshelwood puts it, lie 'beneath the classical Oedipus complex'.[64]

This role for unconscious threats is particularly true of the combined parent figure and the terrified phantasies – normal but psychotic anxieties – associated with it,[65] as well as the child's feelings about his or her role and situation – at risk, excluded, responsible. I experience a number of my patients as in stasis because of inactivity in this space due to depression, preoccupation or estrangement between the parents. (André Green has written a moving paper on this.[66]) They cannot get on with life, because there is no living relationship, no benign combined parent figure in the lee of which they can feel contained and can prosper. Sometimes they stay very still, lest the stasis give way to something far worse.

I often feel that the controversialists in the Freud–Klein debates were talking past one another – the Freudians about actual parents and conscious feelings and the Kleinians about internal objects, part-objects and utterly primitive unconscious phantasies of a particularly distressing and preverbal kind. The analogy occurs to me between the truths Oedipus thought he was seeking and the deeper ones which eventually emerged and which Steiner suggests were unconsciously known all along. One of the main features of recent Kleinian developments in this area is that the Oedipal situation is increasingly being seen as concerned with the prerequisites of knowledge, containment and that which is being contained. The focus changes to the riddle of the Sphinx and the search for the truth of origins which represent the Oedipal quest in its widest sense – that of the need to know at a deeper level: *epistemophilia*.

I now want to turn to those matters to which I promised to revert. There are a number of points to be made. First, Klein's views on the

Oedipal situation and the Oedipus complex were developing in ways which interacted with the development of other major concepts, in particular, the depressive position, the paranoid-schizoid position and projective identification. Something parallel happened with Freud's conscious, preconscious and unconscious (deep categories of topography) and id, ego and superego (important but not so deep categories of structure). Freud never explicitly replaced his topographic metapsychology with the structural one, nor did he make a clear distinction between the superego and the ego ideal.[67] Evolving theories are not tidy.

Second, my signposts about background and foreground can now be applied to the relationship between primitive processes, positions and emotions, on the one hand, and developmental schemes, chronology, topography and the structural hypothesis, on the other. Klein had no quarrel with the background, but it was not her central concern. It was the depths of the id and the unconscious that preoccupied her. People would take her to be writing and speaking in unorthodox ways about structures, when she was burrowing away at the core of a child's being. What was foreground for Klein – the interplay of unconscious feelings – was background for the Freudians, or they were silent about it, preferring to present things in scientistic analogies of forces, energies, structures, adaptations, etc.[68] Klein often chucks in the whole caboodle: the phrase 'oral, anal and phallic' recurs throughout her writings, as does 'mingle', as if she were making a salad or immersing us in a bubbling cauldron or maelstrom rather than referring to a chronological scheme.

In a very interesting paper in the *International Journal of Psycho-Analysis* in 1990, Ruth Stein took 'A New Look at the Theory of Melanie Klein'.[69] She argues that Klein's is fundamentally a theory of affect in which the focus is 'shifted from Freud's cathectic explanations to the concepts of objects and the feelings attached to them'.[70] 'Positions' become more important than structures, and these are 'built around different core feelings'.[71] There are basically two psychological configurations, corresponding to the two basic instincts. They 'differ fundamentally according to *the capacity of* the individual to tolerate unpleasant or conflictual feelings'.[72] Psychic life is the regulation of feelings.[73] She concludes that 'Klein has no theory of the mental apparatus, and feelings are not placed in any such frame'.[74] Anxiety and guilt are the inevitable outcome of the coexistence of love and hate, and the Oedipal situation generates them.[75]

What I find helpful about this point of view on Klein is that it – along with my own distinction between background and foreground – helps me to understand why I cannot find my way around using a map of the Freudian structures with which I was educated in my original reading of psychoanalysis in an American neo-Freudian context. Kleinian explanations ring true for me. They did when I was an analysand and continue to do so for me as a therapist and supervisor in individual therapy, group therapy and group relations work. In fact, group relations work was founded on the very point I am making here. Klein's distinguished analysand and perhaps the most original thinker in her lineage, Wilfred R. Bion, said in *Experiences in Groups* that there is nothing wrong with Freud's explanations in terms of id, ego and superego (which Freud insisted explained all individual and social phenomena) except that they didn't go deep enough and thereby missed out the 'ultimate sources' of group behaviour, just as they did the behaviour of individuals.[76] What he pointed to as more basic were psychotic anxieties, along with the paranoid-schizoid and depressive positions – and the emotions and basic assumptions that are derived from them and sunder sensible work in groups from time to time.[77]

I have so far tried to do two things concerning Kleinian ideas about the Oedipal dynamic. First, I have sketched Kleinian views on the Oedipus complex and how they differ from Freudian ones. Second, I have offered a couple of ideas which may help us to understand why these two ways of thinking about human nature seem so hard to bring into one framework of ideas – why they are so hard to mesh. I think it is because the fundamental determinants of human nature which are emphasised in the respective frameworks are on different levels. For Klein what matters is always the primitive processes, and the task is never-ending. What matters for Freudians, as Freud put it, is that, 'Where id is, there ego shall be. It's reclamation work, like draining the Zuider Zee.'[78] Some Freudians believe that you can resolve the Oedipus complex. Kleinians believe that you will be faced again and again with the Oedipal situation, more like Sisyphus than Prometheus.

Challenges to Developmental Determinism

The Kleinian position in the matter of developmental determinism is difficult, perhaps impossible, to square with recent arguments on behalf of 'plastic sexuality', whereby gays, lesbians and bisexuals claim that one can refuse the Oedipal path and choose another developmental trajectory.[79] The Kleinian view, according to some, makes the Oedipal configuration something one cannot evade and be a thoughtful, creative person. Of course, it is appropriate to show how failure to work through the Oedipal situation can, indeed, lead to perverse sexuality, as David Morgan has illustrated with moving case material.[80] However, there is in some Kleinian writing the tacit assumption that gay and lesbian sexuality is inherently ill, a position Freud never held. He regarded 'any established aberration from normal sexuality as an instance of developmental inhibition and infantilism'.[81] On the other hand, he did not regard homosexuality or perversion as illnesses.[82]

I am glad to say that some other Kleinians take a different view from the Kleinian orthodoxy and direct our attention to the qualities of unconscious phantasies rather than to sexual behaviours. In some 'Reflections on Perverse States of Mind', Margot Waddell and Gianna Williams argue that perversion of character involves 'the distortion and misuse of psychic and external reality: the slaughter of truth'.[83] Perverse states of mind involve 'a negativistic caricature of object relations'. There is an unconscious 'core phantasy of the secret killing of babies instead of parenting babies – an oblique form of attack on the inside of the mother's body . . . In this frame of reference, perversity has no connection with descriptive aspects of sexual choices – it can be equally present or absent in heterosexual or homosexual relationships alike'.[84] They conclude that this approach is

> *scintillating with possibilities for better understanding the nature of perversity as an aspect of character, as distinct from sexual behaviour or choice. It wholly subverts the current propensity to attach labels of 'perverse' or 'non-perverse' to categories of relationships – e.g., homosexual or heterosexual – and places the distinctions, rather, in the area of psychic reality and meanings as represented by different states of mind.*[85]

So, even when faced with behaviour which appears on the surface to some observers to be *inherently* perverse, one is still left with the clinical task of coming to understand the inner meaning, the object relations and unconscious phantasies, before diagnosing it as pathological. Perverse states of mind are one thing, while 'perversion' is a term that should be used with great care.

Anti-Naturalistic Critiques of the Oedipus Complex

Object Relations Theory

Where Kleinians have made the Oedipus complex much broader and have put the classical chronology of the libido theory in the background, advocates of various other persuasions have gone on to attack the concept and the assumptions underlying it. Certain broad – and other particular – developments in psychoanalysis can be seen as compatible with a very different approach to sexuality than that held by the heirs to Freudian orthodoxy. The broad movement is the decline in adherence to biologism and classical libido theory, and the rise of object relations. Object relations theory developed in the work of Melanie Klein, Ronald Fairbairn and Donald Winnicott.[86] There are important differences between their formulations (for example, Fairbairn was explicitly turning his back on biology in a way which Klein did not), but the effect on psychoanalytic thinking was to point to relations with the good and bad aspects of the mother and other important figures and part-objects, and to treat relations with objects, rather than the expression of instincts, as the basic preoccupation of psycho-analytic thinking and clinical work. The focus is on relations rather than drives, on '*the object* of my affection [who] can change my complexion from white to rosy red' (as the song says), *rather than the aim* of the instinct as specified in a biologistic meta-psychology.[87] Once you do this, sex, sexuality, sexual body parts and sexual energy no longer provide either the rhetoric or the conceptual framework for how we think about the inner world. Love, hatred, unconscious phantasy, anxiety and defences have come to the foreground.[88] For Freud, 'sexual' was all-embracing and meant any attribute of living tissue expressing negative entropy. This is what he meant by 'libido'.[89] Object relations theorists approach the matter the other way round: libido is not seen as pleasure-seeking but object-seeking.[90] Libido does not determine object relations; object relations determine libido.[91] It has been my recent experience that sex in its narrow sense plays a surprisingly small role in psychotherapy training and supervision and the literature. Indeed, some years ago I went to a public lecture by a psychoanalyst, Dr Dennis Duncan, with the title, 'What Ever Happened to Sex in Psychoanalysis?' Along with the turn away from the libido theory has come less attention to the psychosexual developmental scheme and the fairly strict chronology which it specified. As I said, if you read Klein and her followers, you find phrases like 'oral, anal and phallic elements' jumbled up and part of a *potpourri*. What emerged later in their scheme at specified developmental and chronological points in the libido theory somehow gets mixed in at an earlier stage in Klein's approach.

Alternative Developmental Schemes

The turn away from the libido theory and towards object relations theory is relevant to the topic of alternative developmental paths. Some of the most interesting writers in this debate make this their most important point: 'What's so wonderful about the developmental path specified by the libido theory?' In asking this question, they are attacking the centrality of the Oedipus complex in orthodox Freudianism. They write in explicit opposition to the Freudian 'Law of the Father' on which the importance of the Oedipus complex is based.[92] As the gay theorist John Fletcher puts it:

> What is refused here is not masculinity or the phallus in itself, but the polarity at the heart of the Oedipal injunction: 'You cannot be what you desire, you cannot desire what you wish to be.'[93]

What the Freudians claim as natural is what the sexual dissidents attack as a cultural norm to be struggled against. They argue for a re-symbolisation and re-investment in a new kind of sexuality. However, Freud himself said that

> a disposition to perversions is an original and universal disposition of the human sexual instinct and that normal sexual behaviour is developed out of it as a result of organic changes and psychical inhibitions during the course of development ... Among the forces restricting the direction taken by the sexual instinct we laid emphasis upon shame, disgust, pity and the structures of morality and authority erected by society.[94]

Support for this approach is found in the writings of the eminent French psychoanalyst, Jean Laplanche. The list of erogenous zones specified by the libido theory – mouth, anus, urethra, genitals – is accepted, but they are described less biologistically as places of exchange between inside and outside.[95] However, *any* bodily zone can take on a sexual level of excitement, as can ideas. The traditional understanding of perversion is an alteration or deviation from the fixed, biologically determined order of privileged zones, culminating in genital intercourse to orgasm. But if we refuse to accept this spontaneous unfolding of a unitary instinctual programme, sexuality itself can be seen as polymorphous and therefore, to put it ironically, perverse. Laplanche expresses this starkly by saying that:

> [T]*he exception – i.e., the perversion – ends up by taking the rule along with it. The exception, which should presuppose the existence of a definite instinct, a pre-existent sexual function, with its well-defined norms of accomplishment: that*

exception ends up by undermining and destroying the very notion of a biological norm. The whole of sexuality, or at least the whole of infantile sexuality, ends up becoming perversion.[96]

Fletcher puts this in symbolic terms, terms which increase the range, scope and flexibility of sexuality: 'The whole of sexuality as a mobile field of displaceable and substitutable signs and mental representations is a *perversion* of the order of biological needs and fixed objects.'[97] If perversion is ubiquitous, it cannot be called exceptional; it is commonplace, the rule, normal – hence 'perversion' as 'normal'. The pejorative connotations of the term become obsolete and, marching to the strict developmental requirements of the libido theory – with the Oedipus complex at its heart, it loses its authoritarian legitimacy and theoretical underpinnings.

Writing about bisexuality and lesbianism, Beverly Burch takes a similar line in opposition to biologism and in favour of social constructivism. She says that: 'Lesbianism *and* heterosexual identities are social constructs that incorporate psychological elements.'[98] These differ from one woman to another and have manifestations and sources as varied as individual biographies: 'The unity of heterosexual theory does not live up to the diversity of sexual orientations.'[99] She places sexual orientations on a continuum and argues that any point on it might be defensive, 'no position is necessarily or inevitably pathological'.[100] She surveys the literature and finds a relativism of theory to match her relativism of developmental pathways:

> *The point is that no one view is complete, and there are divergent routes on the way to final object choice. The road is not a straight one towards heterosexuality, and we cannot regard other destinations as a wrong turn.*[101]

Writers on these issues draw different lines between what they consider pathological and what they treat as merely human diversity. Robert Stoller defines perversion as 'the erotic form of hatred' and offers critical analyses of fetishism, rape, sexually motivated murder, sadism, masochism, voyeurism and paedophilia. He sees in each of these 'hostility, revenge, triumph and a dehumanised object'.[102] On the subject of homosexuality, however, he is a champion of pluralism:

> *What evidence is there that heterosexuality is less complicated than homosexuality, less a product of infantile-childhood struggles to master trauma, conflict, frustration, and the like? As a result of innumerable analyses, the burden of proof . . .*

has shifted to those who use the heterosexual as the standard of health, normality, mature genital characterhood, or whatever other ambiguous criterion serves one's philosophy these days ... Thus far, the counting, if it is done from published reports, puts the heterosexual and the homosexual in a tie: 100 percent abnormals.[103]

Another gem from Stoller is:

Beware the concept 'normal,' it is beyond the reach of objectivity. It tries to connote statistical validity but hides brute judgements on social and private goodness that, if admitted, would promote honesty and modesty we do not yet have in patriots, lawmakers, psychoanalysts and philosophers.[104]

Once again, with the rise in pluralism about alternative developmental schemes goes, for some, a demise in belief in the developmental pathway of the orthodox libido theory within which the Oedipus complex is the most important maturational rite of passage. Most psychoanalytically oriented practitioners would not be willing to go all the way down this path towards social constructivism in their approaches to development. An American neo-Freudian compendium, published in 1990, which purports to provide an integration of recent views, reports without comment: 'Indeed, [Leo] Rangell described the Oedipus complex as the climax of infantile instinctual life, the nucleus of the neuroses and the "organizing umbrella of future life".'[105]

Conclusion

I have tried to provide an exposition of the original idea of the Oedipus complex. Even though Freud claimed it as the basic concept in psychoanalysis, he never drew his thinking on the concept to a final formulation. There are many loose ends. Second, I have presented some ideas of Klein and later Kleinians in which the developmental scheme of the libido theory is placed in the background while Oedipal dynamics are broadened out into an 'Oedipal situation' which recurs throughout life. This less biologistic and more object-related idea is also linked to maturation of insight and to the paranoid-schizoid and depressive positions. Finally, I have sketched ideas about gender development whose proponents reject any notion of privileged developmental paths. Indeed, increasingly sophisticated theorisations of gay and lesbian views on gender identity have reached the point where they can claim that the exceptions overwhelm the rule, and can put forward the long-term goal of 'eschewing all forms of naturalism in psychoanalytic thinking'.[106] Exit the Oedipus complex.

My own view of the matter does not go that far. I find the original notion of the Oedipus complex inside the strict chronology of the libido theory too concrete and restrictive, too linked to specific body parts; although I should add that I often think of where a patient is developmentally and what stages he or she may have passed or be stuck at. More importantly, I have increasingly found that thinking in terms of the Oedipal situation – and difficulties in working through it – is appropriate in all my clinical work. In my opinion, the Oedipus complex belongs with the idea of the Unconscious and the concept of projective identification as one of the three most fruitful ideas in psychoanalysis. I have reached the conclusion that coming to understand the specific Oedipal dynamic between each of my patients and his or her parents (step-parents, children, etc.) lies at the centre of unravelling the tangles which have caused them anguish and have restricted their access to a fuller use of their capacities.

A Closing Note on Sophocles

When I read of Jocasta's last agony, an old joke I'd recalled about Oedipus was suddenly not so funny: 'There she bewailed the twice confounded issue of her wifehood – husband begotten of husband, child of child.'[107] And 'worse was yet to see'[108] when Oedipus found her, cut her body down and blinded himself with her golden brooches. I remembered that we are here in the realm of actual and phantasied violence, child abuse and incest, some-times nominally consenting, usually coerced, leaving deep scars. The failures to negotiate this complex are myriad in the present and throughout history. I think Kleinian psychoanalysis has shown that it is a never-ending battle, as we move back and forth – sometimes moment by moment and surely at every challenge-point in life – between fragmentation and integration, blaming and reparation, hate and love.

We can make a choice of levels. The first is the Yiddisha momma who brings her son to the psychologist, who examines the boy and calls the mother in to announce gravely that he has an Oedipus complex, to which she replies: 'Oedipus, Schmeedipus, as long as he loves his mother.' The historic Mrs Oedipus, the queen Jocasta, was equally keen to avoid deeper truths:

Fear? What has a man to do with fear?
Chance rules our lives, and the future is all unknown.

Best live as best we may, from day to day.
Nor need this mother-marrying frighten you;
Many a man has dreamt as much. Such things
Must be forgotten, if life is to be endured.[109]

Sophocles offers another punchline, one which evokes the tragedy in every life, where, as Teiresias put it,[110] each is the enemy of himself, as well as detective and criminal:

Sons and daughters of Thebes, behold: this was Oedipus,
Greatest of men; he held the key to the deepest mysteries;
Was envied by all his fellow-men for his great prosperity;
Behold, what a full tide of misfortune swept over his head.
Then learn that mortal man must always look to his ending,
And none can be called happy until that day when he carries
His happiness down to the grave in peace.[111]

Acknowledgements

I should like to acknowledge the particularly assiduous and insightful editorial comments and contributions of Ivan Ward.

Robert M. Young is Emeritus Professor of Psychotherapy and Psychoanalytic Studies at the University of Sheffield and a psychotherapist in private practice in London. He has written widely on psychoanalysis and on the history of ideas in human nature.

Notes

1. See Chasseguet-Smirgel, J., *Creativity and Perversion*, London: Free Association Books, 1985; *The Ego Ideal: A Psychoanalytic Essay on the Malady of the Ideal*, London: Free Association Books, 1985a.
2. Bergmann, M.S., *The Anatomy of Loving: The Story of Man's Quest to Know What Love Is*, New York: Columbia University Press, 1987, Chapter 18.
3. Ibid., p. 220.
4. Ibid., p. 222.
5. Ibid., p. 223.
6. Freud, S., 'Observations on Transference Love: Further Recommendations on the Technique of Psycho-Analysis III' (1915), in *The Standard Edition of the Complete Psychological Works of Sigmund Freud*, London: Hogarth Press, 1953–73 (hereafter *SE*), vol. 12, pp. 159–71 (p. 166).
7. See Brenner, C., *An Elementary Textbook of Psychoanalysis*, revised edition, New York: International Universities, 1973, p. 26; and Meltzer, D., *Sexual States of Mind*, Strath Tay: Clunie, 1973, pp. 21–7.
8. Cf. Dinnerstein, D., *The Mermaid and the Minotaur: Sexual Arrangements and Human Malaise*, New York: Harper and Row, 1976; and Chodorow, N., *The Reproduction of Mothering: Psychoanalysis and the Sociology of Gender*, Berkeley: University of California Press, 1978.
9. Cornwell, J., 'The Establishment of Female Genital Sexuality', *Free Associations*, vol. 1, 1985, pp. 57–75; Waddell, M., 'From Resemblance to Identity: A Psychoanalytic Perspective on Gender Identity', typescript, 1992, esp. pp. 9–10.
10. Erikson, E.H., *Identity and the Life Cycle: Selected Papers*, in *Psychological Issues*, vol. 1 (1), monograph 1, International Universities, 1959, p. 120. Reissued as *Identity and the Life Cycle*, New York: W.W. Norton, 1994.
11. Nagera, H. (ed.), *Basic Psychoanalytic Concepts on the Libido Theory*, London: Unwin Hyman, 1969, pp. 64–82.
12. Laplanche, J. and Pontalis, J.-B., *The Language of Psychoanalysis*, London: Hogarth Press, 1973, pp. 282–7.
13. See also Mullahy, P., *Oedipus – Myth and Complex: A Review of Psychoanalytic Theory*, New York: Grove Press, 1955, pp. 20–7.
14. Freud, S., *New Introductory Lectures on Psycho-Analysis* (1933), *SE*, vol. 22, pp. 3–182 (p. 113).
15. See Klein, M., 'The Oedipus Complex in the Light of Early Anxieties' (1945), in Britton, R. et al., *The Oedipus Complex Today: Clinical Implications*, London: Karnac, 1989, pp. 11–82 (pp. 72–5); Mitchell, J., *Psychoanalysis and Feminism*, London: Allen Lane, 1974; Dinnerstein, op. cit.; Temperley, J., 'Is the Oedipus Complex Bad News for Women?', *Free Associations*, vol. 30 (4), 1993, pp. 265–75.
16. Fletchman Smith, B., *Mental Slavery: Psychoanalytic Studies of Caribbean People*, London: Rebus, 2000.
17. Those interested in pursuing the fine texture of the debates about formulations of the Oedipus complex should consult, *inter alia,* Sigmund Freud ('The Infantile Genital Organization: An Interpolation into the Theory of Sexuality' (1923), *SE*, vol. 19, pp. 141–8; 'The Dissolution of

the Oedipus Complex' (1924), *SE*, vol. 19, pp. 171–9; 'Some Psychical Consequences of the Anatomical Distinction Between the Sexes' (1925), *SE*, vol. 19, pp. 243–60); Karl Abraham ('Psycho-Analytical Studies on Character-Formation' (1921–5), in *Selected Papers on Psycho-Analysis*, London: Maresfield, 1979, pp. 370–418; 'A Short Study of the Development of the Libido, Viewed in the Light of Mental Disorders' (1924), in Abraham (1979), op. cit., pp. 418–501); Victoria Hamilton (*Narcissus and Oedipus: The Children of Psychoanalysis*, London: Routledge, 1982); Adam Limentani ('The Oedipus Myth as Reflected in Problems of Ambivalence and Reparation in the Oedipal Situation', in *Between Freud and Klein: The Psychoanalytic Quest for Knowledge and Truth*, London: Free Association Books, 1989, pp. 18–34); George H. Pollock and John M. Ross (*The Oedipus Papers*, Madison: International Universities Press, 1988); Bennett Simon ('Is the Oedipus Complex Still the Cornerstone of Psychoanalysis?: Three Obstacles to Answering the Question', *Journal of the American Psychoanalytic Association*, vol. 39, 1991, pp. 641–68); Jay R. Greenberg (*Oedipus and Beyond: A Clinical Theory*, Cambridge, MA: Harvard University Press, 1991); and Juliet Mitchell (*Mad Men and Medusas: Reclaiming Hysteria and the Effects of Sibling Relationships on the Human Condition*, London: Allen Lane–Penguin, 2000).

18. Freud, S., *Three Essays on the Theory of Sexuality* (1905), *SE*, vol. 7, pp. 125–245 (p. 226n).
19. Ibid., pp. 225, 225n.
20. Freud, S., *Civilization and Its Discontents* (1930), *SE*, vol. 22, pp. 59–145 (p. 60).
21. Ibid., p. 131.
22. Ibid., p. 134.
23. See, e.g., Mullahy, op. cit., pp. 323–4; Johnson, A.W. and Price-Williams, D., *Oedipus Ubiquitous: The Family Complex in World Folk Literature*, Stanford: Stanford University Press, 1996, pp. 14ff.
24. Johnson and Price-Williams, op. cit., p. 6.
25. Freud, S., 'Preface to Reik's *Ritual: Psycho-Analytic Studies*' (1919), *SE*, vol. 17, pp. 256–63 (pp. 261–2).
26. Ibid.
27. Freud, S., *The Interpretation of Dreams* (1900), *SE*, vols. 4 and 5, pp. 263–4.
28. Freud, S., *The Ego and the Id* (1923), *SE*, vol. 19, pp. 3–66.
29. For further information on Klein's concept of the position, see p. 252 of 'Eros' in this volume. 'Eros' is also available as a separate book: Abel-Hirsch, N., *Eros*, Ideas in Psychoanalysis series, Cambridge: Icon Books, 2001 (see pp. 38–9).
30. See Freud (1900), op. cit., pp. 264–6; Jones, E., *Hamlet and Oedipus*, New York: Doubleday Anchor, 1949.
31. Sophocles, *King Oedipus*, in *The Theban Plays*, trans. E.F. Watling, London: Penguin, 1947, p. 45.
32. Ibid., p. 47.
33. Ibid., p. 47.
34. Ibid., p. 48.

35. Young, R.M., 'Consider Laius', *Free Associations*, vol. 13, 1988, p. 150.
36. Steiner, J., 'Turning a Blind Eye: The Cover Up for Oedipus', *International Review of Psycho-Analysis*, vol. 12, 1985, pp. 161–72.
37. See Klein, M.: 'Early Stages of the Oedipus Conflict' (1928), in *The Writings of Melanie Klein*, London: Hogarth Press, vol. 1, 1975, pp. 186–98; 'The Oedipus Complex in the Light of Early Anxieties' (1945), in Klein (1975), op. cit., vol. 1, pp. 370–419; 'Notes on Some Schizoid Mechanisms' (1946), in Klein (1975), op. cit., vol. 3, pp. 1–24.
38. Freud, S., *Extracts from the Fliess Papers* (1950), *SE*, vol. 1, pp. 175–280 (p. 265).
39. Cf. Freud (1900), op. cit., pp. 263–6.
40. Freud (1900), op. cit., pp. 262–3.
41. Ibid., p. 263n.
42. Freud (1910), op. cit.; Freud (1913), op. cit.
43. Rudnytsky, P.L., *Freud and Oedipus*, New York: Columbia University Press, 1987, p. 15.
44. Ibid., pp. 11–12. See also Rudnytsky, P.L. and Spitz, E.H. (eds.), *Freud and Forbidden Knowledge*, New York: New York University Press, 1994.
45. Rudnytsky, op. cit., pp. 4–5; Anzieu, D., *Freud's Self-Analysis*, London: Hogarth Press, 1986, Chapter 3.
46. E.g., King, P. and Steiner, R. (eds.), *The Freud–Klein Controversies: 1941–45*, London: Tavistock–Routledge, 1991, pp. 432–3.
47. Such a rendition can be found in two places – at the end of Klein's 1945 paper, 'The Oedipus Complex in the Light of Early Anxieties' (reprinted in Britton et al.'s collection, *The Oedipus Complex Today* (1989), summary, pp. 63–82). An up-to-date exposition is available in the entry on 'Oedipus Complex' in R.D. Hinshelwood's *A Dictionary of Kleinian Thought*, (revised edition, London: Free Association Books, 1991, pp. 57–67), and the issues are broadened and deepened in two papers by Ronald Britton ('The Missing Link: Parental Sexuality in the Oedipus Complex', in Britton et al., op. cit., pp. 83–102; 'The Oedipus Situation and the Depressive Position', in Anderson, R. (ed.), *Clinical Lectures on Klein and Bion*, London: Routledge, 1992, pp. 34–45) and one by Bell, D. ('Hysteria – A Contemporary Kleinian Perspective', *British Journal of Psychotherapy*, vol. 9, 1992, pp. 169–80).
48. Klein (1945), op. cit., p. 76.
49. Ibid., pp. 76–7.
50. Ibid., p. 78.
51. Ibid., p. 78.
52. Ibid., p. 79.
53. Ibid., p. 82.
54. Ibid., pp. 81–2.
55. Klein (1946), op. cit., p. 8.
56. Bell, D., 'Hysteria – A Contemporary Kleinian Perspective', *British Journal of Psychotherapy*, vol. 9, 1992, pp. 169–80 (p. 172).
57. Ibid., p. 172.
58. Britton, R., 'The Oedipus Situation and the Depressive Position', in Anderson, R. (ed.), *Clinical Lectures on Klein and Bion*, London: Routledge, 1992, pp. 34–45 (p. 35).

59. Ibid., p. 37.
60. Ibid., p. 39.
61. Ibid., p. 38.
62. Britton, R., 'The Missing Link: Parental Sexuality in the Oedipus Complex', in Britton et al., op. cit., pp. 83–102 (p. 87).
63. King and Steiner, op. cit.
64. Hinshelwood, R.D., 'Oedipus Complex', in Hinshelwood, op. cit., p. 57.
65. Ibid., p. 60.
66. Green, A., 'The Dead Mother', in *On Private Madness*, London: Hogarth Press, 1986, pp. 142–73.
67. Chasseguet-Smirgel (1985a), op. cit.
68. See Rapaport, D. and Gill, M.M., 'The Points of View and Assumptions of Metapsychology', *International Journal of Psycho-Analysis*, vol. 40, 1959, pp. 1–10; Rapaport, D., *The Collected Papers of David Rapaport*, New York: Basic, 1967.
69. Stein, R., 'A New Look at the Theory of Melanie Klein', *International Journal of Psycho-Analysis*, vol. 71, 1990, pp. 499–511.
70. Ibid., p. 500.
71. Ibid., p. 504.
72. Ibid., pp. 504–5 (emphasis in original).
73. Ibid., p. 508.
74. Ibid., p. 509.
75. Ibid., p. 505.
76. Bion, W.R.: 'Group Dynamics – A Re-view', in Klein, M. et al. (eds.), *New Directions in Psycho-Analysis: The Significance of Infant Conflict in the Patterns of Adult Behaviour*, London: Tavistock, 1955, pp. 440–77 (pp. 475–6); *Experiences in Groups and Other Papers*, London: Tavistock, 1961, pp. 187–90.
77. Young, R.M., *Mental Space*, London: Process Press, 1994, Chapters 5–7.
78. Freud (1933), op. cit., p. 80.
79. Giddens, A., *The Transformation of Intimacy: Sexuality, Love and Eroticism in Modern Societies*, London: Polity Press, 1992; and Young, R.M., 'Is "Perversion" Obsolete?', *Psychology in Society*, vol. 21, 1996, pp. 5–26.
80. Morgan, D., 'The Internal Couple and the Oedipus Complex in the Development of Sexual Identity and Sexual Perversion', in Harding, C. (ed.), *Sexuality: Psychoanalytic Perspectives*, London: Brunner–Routledge, 2001, pp. 137–52.
81. Freud (1905), op. cit., p. 231.
82. Abelove, H., 'Freud, Homosexuality and the Americans', *Dissent*, Winter 1986, pp. 59–69 (pp. 59, 60).
83. Waddell, M. and Williams, G., 'Reflections on Perverse States of Mind', *Free Associations*, vol. 2, 1991, pp. 203–13 (p. 203).
84. Ibid., p. 206.
85. Ibid., p. 211.
86. Greenberg, J.R. and Mitchell, S.A., *Object Relations in Psychoanalytic Theory*, Cambridge, MA: Harvard University Press, 1983.
87. Ibid., p. 126.
88. Ibid., p. 137.

89. Stoller, R.J., *Perversion: The Erotic Form of Hatred*, London: Maresfield, paperback edition, 1986, p. 12.
90. Greenberg and Mitchell, op. cit., p. 154.
91. Ibid., p. 157.
92. Fletcher, J., 'Freud and His Uses: Psychoanalysis and Gay Theory', in Shepherd, S. and Wallis, M. (eds.), *Coming on Strong: Gay Politics and Culture*, London: Unwin Hyman, 1989, pp. 90–118 (p. 113).
93. Ibid., p. 114.
94. Freud (1905), op. cit., p. 231.
95. Fletcher, op. cit., p. 96.
96. Laplanche, J., *Life and Death in Psychoanalysis* (1970), London: Johns Hopkins University Press, 1976, p. 23.
97. Fletcher, op. cit., pp. 98–9.
98. Burch, B., 'Heterosexuality, Bisexuality, and Lesbianism: Psychoanalytic Views of Women's Sexual Object Choice', *Psychoanalytic Review*, vol. 80, 1993a, pp. 83–100 (pp. 84–5).
99. Ibid., p. 85.
100. Ibid., p. 91.
101. Ibid., p. 97. See also Burch, B., *On Intimate Terms: The Psychology of Difference in Lesbian Relationships*, Urbana: University of Illinois Press, 1993b.
102. Stoller (1986), op. cit., p. 9.
103. Stoller, R.J., *Observing the Erotic Imagination*, New Haven: Yale University Press, 1985. Quoted in Burch (1993a), op. cit., p. 97.
104. Stoller (1985), op. cit., p. 41. Quoted in Burch (1993a), op. cit., p. 98.
105. Rangell, L., 'Aggression, Oedipus and Historical Perspective', *International Journal of Psycho-Analysis*, vol. 53, 1972, pp. 3–11 (p. 7). Quoted in Tyson, P. and Tyson, R.L., *Psychoanalytic Theories of Development: An Integration*, New Haven: Yale University Press, 1990, p. 59.
106. O'Connor, N. and Ryan, J., *Wild Desires and Mistaken Identities: Lesbianism and Psychoanalysis*, London: Virago, 1993, p. 246.
107. Sophocles, op. cit., p. 60.
108. Ibid., p. 61.
109. Ibid., p. 52.
110. Ibid., p. 36.
111. Ibid., p. 68.

Further Reading

Abel-Hirsch, N., *Eros*, Cambridge: Icon Books, 2001. Reprinted in *On a Darkling Plain*, pp. 239–66.

Abelove, H., 'Freud, Homosexuality and the Americans', *Dissent*, Winter 1986, pp. 59–69.

Abraham, K., 'Psycho-Analytical Studies on Character-Formation' (1921–5), in *Selected Papers on Psycho-Analysis*, London: Maresfield, 1979, pp. 370–418.

——'A Short Study of the Development of the Libido, Viewed in the Light of Mental Disorders' (1924), in *Selected Papers on Psycho-Analysis*, London: Maresfield, 1979, pp. 418–501.

——*Selected Papers on Psycho-Analysis*, London: Maresfield, 1979.

Anzieu, D., *Freud's Self-Analysis*, London: Hogarth Press, 1986 (esp. Chapter 3).

Bell, D., 'Hysteria – A Contemporary Kleinian Perspective', *British Journal of Psychotherapy*, vol. 9, 1992, pp. 169–80.

Bergmann, M.S., *The Anatomy of Loving: The Story of Man's Quest to Know What Love Is*, New York: Columbia University Press, 1987.

Bion, W.R., 'Group Dynamics – A Re-view', in Klein, M. et al. (eds.), *New Directions in Psycho-Analysis: The Significance of Infant Conflict in the Patterns of Adult Behaviour*, London: Tavistock, 1955, pp. 440–77; reprinted by Maresfield, 1977.

——*Experiences in Groups and Other Papers*, London: Tavistock, 1961.

Brenner, C., *An Elementary Textbook of Psychoanalysis*, revised edition, New York: International Universities, 1973.

Britton, R., 'The Missing Link: Parental Sexuality in the Oedipus Complex', in Britton et al., *The Oedipus Complex Today: Clinical Implications*, London: Karnac, 1989, pp. 83–102.

——'The Oedipus Situation and the Depressive Position', in Anderson, R. (ed.), *Clinical Lectures on Klein and Bion*, intro. by H. Segal, London: Routledge, 1992, pp. 34–45.

——et al., *The Oedipus Complex Today: Clinical Implications*, London: Karnac, 1989.

Burch, B., 'Heterosexuality, Bisexuality, and Lesbianism: Psychoanalytic Views of Women's Sexual Object Choice', *Psychoanalytic Review*, vol. 80, 1993, pp. 83–100.

——*On Intimate Terms: The Psychology of Difference in Lesbian Relationships*, Urbana: University of Illinois Press, 1993.

Chasseguet-Smirgel, J., *Creativity and Perversion*, London: Free Association Books, 1985.

——*The Ego Ideal: A Psychoanalytic Essay on the Malady of the Ideal*, London: Free Association Books, 1985a.

Chodorow, N., *The Reproduction of Mothering: Psychoanalysis and the Sociology of Gender*, Berkeley: University of California Press, 1978.

Cornwell, J., 'The Establishment of Female Genital Sexuality', *Free Associations*, vol. 1, 1985, pp. 57–75.

Dinnerstein, D., *The Mermaid and the Minotaur: Sexual Arrangements and Human Malaise*, New York: Harper and Row, 1976.

Erikson, E.H., *Identity and the Life Cycle: Selected Papers*, in *Psychological Issues*, vol. 1 (1), monograph 1, International Universities, 1959. Reissued as *Identity and the Life Cycle*, New York: W.W. Norton, 1994.

Fletcher, J., 'Freud and His Uses: Psychoanalysis and Gay Theory', in Shepherd, S. and Wallis, M. (eds.), *Coming on Strong: Gay Politics and Culture*, London: Unwin Hyman, 1989, pp. 90–118.

Fletchman Smith, B., *Mental Slavery: Psychoanalytic Studies of Caribbean People*, London: Rebus, 2000.

Freud, S., *The Standard Edition of the Complete Psychological Works of Sigmund Freud*, 24 vols., London: Hogarth Press, 1953–73 (hereafter *SE*). In particular:

——*The Interpretation of Dreams* (1900), *SE*, vols. 4 and 5.

——*Three Essays on the Theory of Sexuality* (1905), *SE*, vol. 7, pp. 125–245.

——'A Special Type of Choice of Object Made by Men' (1910), *SE*, vol. 11, pp. 163–76.

——*Totem and Taboo* (1913), *SE*, vol. 13, pp. 1–162.

——'Observations on Transference Love: Further Recommendations on the Technique of Psycho-Analysis III' (1915), *SE*, vol. 12, pp. 159–71.

——'Preface to Reik's *Ritual: Psycho-Analytic Studies*' (1919), *SE*, vol. 17, pp. 256–63.

——*The Ego and the Id* (1923), *SE*, vol. 19, pp. 3–66.

——'The Infantile Genital Organization: An Interpolation into the Theory of Sexuality' (1923a), *SE*, vol. 19, pp. 141–8.

——'The Dissolution of the Oedipus Complex' (1924), *SE*, vol. 19, pp. 171–9.

——'Some Psychical Consequences of the Anatomical Distinction Between the Sexes' (1925), *SE*, vol. 19, pp. 243–60.

——*Civilization and Its Discontents* (1930), *SE*, vol. 21, pp. 59–145.

——'Female Sexuality' (1931), *SE*, vol. 21, pp. 223–43.

——*New Introductory Lectures on Psycho-Analysis* (1933), *SE*, vol. 22, pp. 3–182.

——*Extracts from the Fliess Papers* (1950), *SE*, vol. 1, pp. 175–280.

Giddens, A., *The Transformation of Intimacy: Sexuality, Love and Eroticism in Modern Societies*, London: Polity Press, 1992; paperback edition, 1993.

Green, A., 'The Dead Mother', in *On Private Madness*, London: Hogarth Press, 1986, pp. 142–73.

Greenberg, J.R., *Oedipus and Beyond: A Clinical Theory*, Cambridge, MA: Harvard University Press, 1991.

——and Mitchell, S.A., *Object Relations in Psychoanalytic Theory*, Cambridge, MA: Harvard University Press, 1983.

Hamilton, V., *Narcissus and Oedipus: The Children of Psychoanalysis*, London: Routledge, 1982; reprinted by Karnac, 1993.

Hinshelwood, R.D., 'Oedipus Complex', in *A Dictionary of Kleinian Thought*, revised edition, London: Free Association Books, 1991, pp. 57–67.

Johnson, A.W. and Price-Williams, D., *Oedipus Ubiquitous: The Family Complex in World Folk Literature*, Stanford: Stanford University Press, 1996.

Jones, E., *Hamlet and Oedipus*, New York: Doubleday Anchor, 1949.

King, P. and Steiner, R. (eds.), *The Freud–Klein Controversies: 1941–45*, London: Tavistock–Routledge, 1991.

Klein, M., 'Early Stages of the Oedipus Conflict', *International Journal of Psycho-Analysis*, vol. 9, 1928, 167–80; reprinted in *The Writings of Melanie Klein*, London: Hogarth Press, vol. 1, 1975, pp. 186–98.

——'The Oedipus Complex in the Light of Early Anxieties', *International Journal of Psycho-Analysis*, vol. 26, 1945, pp. 11–33; reprinted in Klein (1975), Vol. 1, pp. 370–419, and in Britton et al. (1989), pp. 11–82 (see esp. summary, pp. 63–82).

——'Notes on Some Schizoid Mechanisms', *International Journal of Psycho-Analysis*, vol. 27, 1946, pp. 99–110; reprinted in Klein (1975), vol. 3, pp. 1–24.

——*The Writings of Melanie Klein*, 5 vols., London: Hogarth Press, 1975.

———et al. (eds.), *New Directions in Psycho-Analysis: The Significance of Infant Conflict in the Patterns of Adult Behaviour*, London: Tavistock, 1977; reprinted by Maresfield, 1977.

Laplanche, J., *Life and Death in Psychoanalysis* (1970), London: Johns Hopkins University Press, 1976; paperback edition, 1985.

———and Pontalis, J.-B., *The Language of Psychoanalysis*, London: Hogarth Press, 1973.

Limentani, A., 'The Oedipus Myth as Reflected in Problems of Ambivalence and Reparation in the Oedipal Situation', in *Between Freud and Klein: The Psychoanalytic Quest for Knowledge and Truth*, London: Free Association Books, 1989, pp. 18–34.

Meltzer, D., *Sexual States of Mind*, Strath Tay: Clunie, 1973.

Mitchell, J., *Psychoanalysis and Feminism*, London: Allen Lane, 1974.

———*Mad Men and Medusas: Reclaiming Hysteria and the Effects of Sibling Relationships on the Human Condition*, London: Allen Lane–Penguin, 2000.

Morgan, D., 'The Internal Couple and the Oedipus Complex in the Development of Sexual Identity and Sexual Perversion', in Harding, C. (ed.), *Sexuality: Psychoanalytic Perspectives*, London: Brunner–Routledge, 2001, pp. 137–52.

Mullahy, P., *Oedipus – Myth and Complex: A Review of Psychoanalytic Theory*, New York: Grove Press, 1948; reprinted, 1955.

Nagera, H. (ed.), *Basic Psychoanalytic Concepts on the Libido Theory*, London: Unwin Hyman, 1969; reprinted by Karnac as paperback edition, 1981, 1990.

O'Connor, N. and Ryan, J., *Wild Desires and Mistaken Identities: Lesbianism and Psychoanalysis*, London: Virago, 1993.

Pollock, G.H. and Ross, J.M., *The Oedipus Papers*, Madison: International Universities Press, 1988.

Rangell, L., 'Aggression, Oedipus and Historical Perspective', *International Journal of Psycho-Analysis*, vol. 53, 1972, pp. 3–11.

Rapaport, D., *The Collected Papers of David Rapaport*, New York: Basic, 1967.

———and Gill, M.M., 'The Points of View and Assumptions of Metapsychology', *International Journal of Psycho-Analysis*, vol. 40, 1959, pp. 1–10.

Roland, A., *In Search of Self in India and Japan*, Princeton: Princeton University Press, 1988.

Rudnytsky, P.L., *Freud and Oedipus*, New York: Columbia, 1987.

———and Spitz, E.H. (eds.), *Freud and Forbidden Knowledge*, New York: New York University Press, 1994.

Simon, B., 'Is the Oedipus Complex Still the Cornerstone of Psychoanalysis?: Three Obstacles to Answering the Question', *Journal of the American Psychoanalytic Association*, vol. 39, 1991, pp. 641–68.

Sophocles, *The Theban Plays*, trans. E.F. Watling, London: Penguin, 1947.

Stein, R., 'A New Look at the Theory of Melanie Klein', *International Journal of Psycho-Analysis*, vol. 71, 1990, pp. 499–511.

Steiner, J., 'Turning a Blind Eye: The Cover Up for Oedipus', *International Review of Psycho-Analysis*, vol. 12, 1985, pp. 161–72.

Stoller, R.J., *Observing the Erotic Imagination*, New Haven: Yale University Press, 1985.

——*Perversion: The Erotic Form of Hatred*, London: Maresfield, 1975; paperback edition, 1986.

Temperley, J., 'Is the Oedipus Complex Bad News for Women?', *Free Associations*, vol. 30, 1993, pp. 265–75.

Tyson, P. and Tyson, R.L., *Psychoanalytic Theories of Development: An Integration*, New Haven: Yale University Press, 1990.

Waddell, M., 'Gender Identity: Fifty Years On From Freud', *British Journal of Psychotherapy*, vol. 5, 1989, pp. 381–9; reprinted in *Women: A Cultural Review*, 1, 1990, pp. 149–59.

——'From Resemblance to Identity: A Psychoanalytic Perspective on Gender Identity', typescript, 1992.

——and Williams, G., 'Reflections on Perverse States of Mind', *Free Associations*, vol. 2, 1991, pp. 203–13.

Young, R.M., 'Consider Laius', *Free Associations*, vol. 13, 1988, p. 150.

——*Mental Space*, London: Process Press, 1994.

——'Is "Perversion" Obsolete?', *Psychology in Society*, vol. 21, 1996, pp. 5–26.

5

Guilt

Kalu Singh

Introduction

Imagine a world without guilt. Imagine a life, your life, without guilt. What do you feel right now? Puzzlement, fear, relief, hope, desire, joy, release – or perhaps even shame; but I hope not guilt. That would be the world's end, wouldn't it?

Try again. Try these words:

> I refuse to feel guilty. Guilt is a destructive emotion and doesn't fit in with my Life Plan.[1]

> Guilt is petit bourgeois crap. An artist creates his own moral universe.[2]

The first quotation is from the feckless Adrian Mole, responding to a crisis with typically pointless bravado. It is one of Woody Allen's fictional creations who makes the second remark, but after quoting it, biographer Marion Meade comments:

> Woody was about to find out that playing by his own rules would cost him millions in legal fees, the loss of his children, and abandonment by his audience.[3]

But what is guilt? Is it a sensation or a thought, or a medium for sensation and thought? Or a something, a force, sometimes internal, sometimes external, that is beyond thought and sensation? Most commonly, people say that guilt 'gnaws', capturing the sense of something inside and inaccessible, attacking one relentlessly. Or it is a burden that one can never shake off. There may be other metaphors: that it is like a pebble in one's shoe, a chafing thong, a polyp, leaking silicone, a throbbing phantom limb, a torn disabling gene, an irregularly beating transplanted pig's heart, a skin graft that tears and becomes septic, Dorian Gray's picture, the pall of volcanic ash.

Psychoanalysis takes up the challenge to heal guilt. Theology and its bastard aspect – organised religion – are outraged at the temerity of psychoanalysis to encroach upon its fiefdom. Surely all one needs to know about guilt – how to define it, explain it, contain it and heal it – is given within the paradigm of theology? How can there be non-religious guilt? Perhaps since the Renaissance, and certainly since the Enlightenment, this has been the paradox: that religion has failed in its promise to alleviate guilt – the guilt it had created in order to demonstrate the faith's power by healing it. The only remaining excuse is the perennial plea of the tension between the perfection of the theology and the culpability of the believers. But from the psychoanalytic point of view, clients arrive at the therapeutic realm variously crippled by guilts which religion has failed to heal, even if it didn't create them. Religion has had two to seven millennia, depending on your religion, to perfect its theology and its technique: psychoanalysis has had one century.

Ruling Passions: The Inheritance

'Guilt' is a concept that forms part of a matrix to do with moral division and reunion: 'transgression', 'fault', 'accusation', 'blame', 'plea', 'shame', 'contrition', 'remorse', 'repentance', 'apology', 'punishment', 'revenge', 'forgiveness', 'reparation', 'reconciliation'.

The typical narrative instantiating the above matrix begins with a morally capable and responsible person intending and performing an act which transgresses a rule or law – moral, civil or criminal – of the community which has defined itself partly by the instituting of those rules and laws, and among whom he lives. Ideally, the laws and rules were the product of the free dialogue of free citizens, and their purpose was to facilitate the free development of all. The purpose of the panoply of concepts listed above is to reintegrate the individual who through the transgression has separated himself from his community. The matrix can stand unvarnished by the religious and theological gloss with which it is usually associated. In the Christian revelation, the morally capable person carries from birth the stain of Original Sin. Though this is sometimes referred to as a *felix culpa* (happy fault), because it induced in God the compassion of the Incarnation, the doctrine demands a limitless fountain of individual guilt as part of the necessary mortal repentance. Perhaps the Judaic curse of 'visiting the iniquities of the fathers upon the children unto the third and fourth generation'[4] was attenuated somewhat by this new gospel, but it was also used by Christian states to justify anti-Semitism.

'There should be a statute of limitations ... why do you keep breaking our balls for that crime?', began a sketch by the American satirist Lenny Bruce, on the Law, which hounded him to death. 'Why, Jew, because you skirt the issue. You blame it on the Roman soldiers.' 'Alright. I'll clear the air once and for all. Yes, we did it. I did it, my family. I found a note in my basement. It said: "We killed him. Signed Morty."'[5]

This sketch seems facetious, even puerile. But a glance at the history of the Diaspora, let alone the horrors of the last century, reminds us how much ache and rage is in such humour. By a curious symmetry, many Jews remain outraged that the Catholic church, despite lavish Papal gestures of apology, still won't come clean about its culpability in the Holocaust.

Guilt seems so absolutely a personal, individual emotion that it seems difficult to talk about 'institutional guilt' or 'State guilt'. There is of course institutional failure and institutional culpability, whether by local-civic or international standards. But whereas in personal guilt there may be a crippling emotional cost to the individual, in institutional guilt there may be an economic cost of compensation, which is differently crippling. Hence the tobacco industry's decades-long guilty evasion of the apposite word 'addiction', or the London Metropolitan Police's guilty hesitation about imputing racist motives to criminals or themselves.

Out of the Holocaust came a re-examination of the familiar concepts of 'collective guilt' or 'guilt-by-association' – the shadow of the criminals; and the sharpest delineation of the rarer concept of 'survivor guilt' – the shadow of the victims. No secular citizen – and, I conjecture, almost no believer – would want Germans or Jews or Roma (the world's gypsies) yet to be born, to come into the world in 2100 under either of these shadows. But ascribing guilt even to those of that fatal generation is fraught with controversy, as the author of *Hitler's Willing Executioners* found.[6] Within the concept of 'survivor-guilt' there is, in addition to the ordinary layers of mourning and grief (here heightened by historical exigencies), the terrifying guilt that one's survival 'proves' that one failed as a human being to rescue those who died.

We are living through a period of re-examination, in philosophy and politics, of the concept of 'the bystander', both at the State level – as we saw in Kosovo in 1999 – and at the civic level. The moral ambiguities of the latter were wonderfully opened in the final episode of that masterpiece of situation comedy, *Seinfeld*. Stranded in 'Sticksville', the amoral, urban quartet witness a robbery. They can see only the comedic value in the victim's suffering. A local policeman observes their response and arrests them for breaking the new Good Samaritan Law, '[which] requires you to help or assist anyone in danger, as long as it is reasonable to do so'. Their Defence Counsel argues: 'You cannot be a bystander and be guilty. They want to create a whole new animal – the guilty bystander!'[7] But as the very title of the new law testifies, even these modern ambiguities seem unable to step from under the shadow of Biblical models.

The last tired punches between the combatants of the Reformation and the Counter-Reformation can be seen in the aphorism: 'Catholics have a sense of guilt, but no sense of sin. Protestants have a sense of sin but no sense of guilt. So it is that Catholics enjoy their sinning more than Protestants, who aren't allowed to enjoy anything.'[8] Jews and Buddhists would probably laugh at both for their casuistry and vain religiosity. Of course, both Christian denominations have an astigmatic concept of sin, focusing more on sexuality than avarice and wrath; most children would be surprised to learn that there are as many cardinal sins as there are Disney dwarves. The bathetic dimension to the casting of their mighty shadows on psychological development can be seen from the fact of the recent Catholic revaluation of the ordinary, albeit subversively named, activity of 'bashing the bishop' or, in the gender-blind phrase, 'making glue without boiling a horse'.[9] Just think how much emotion and thought, how many billions and billions of hours, have been wasted by men and women, priests and the laity, over two millennia, trying to manage the doctrinal guilt over masturbation. It's not that the Church has recently acquired a new scientific fact: more a belated gesture of compassion.

Can Fuck, Won't Cook: Freud's Account of Guilt

Sigmund Freud was aware of this inheritance, and especially of the wealth of narratives of fault-guilt-reconciliation in parable and literature. What did he imagine he could add to these 'explanations' of the human experience of guilt? Because he saw himself as a kind of hybrid between an ancient, questing hero and a modern detective, we might begin with some ordinary stories and the question: 'What kind and level of guilt do the following protagonists display?'

1. A woman runs into a room, straightens the tablecloth and rings for the maid. When the maid comes she sends her away instantly, though while they are briefly together she draws the maid's attention, silently and without accusation, to a stain on the tablecloth. She does this several times a day.

2. A man walking in the country accidentally kicks a pebble into the middle of the road. He pauses, and then moves the stone from the road. But then he pauses again, and this time he returns the stone to where his first kick had taken it.
3. A respectable person, during the course of an analysis in which he has appeared anxious, commits a pointless crime; and despite the possibility of punishment – in fact, partly because of its likelihood – he feels a tremendous sense of relief.
4. A woman goes on and on, and quite shamelessly on and on, saying how depressed she is. Why?

Freud was deeply sceptical of the ability of received rationality to describe what was happening in such stories – what they revealed about human desire, thought and action. The facts of ambiguity and complexity in human relations are signalled by language itself, by the ambiguity present in modal verbs. 'Can' is used for ability and for request; 'may' for probability as well as permission; 'will/shall' for intention, prediction and obligation. Thus the title of this section, my seemingly trivial gloss on an evocative example that even Freud characterised as 'absurd':

A maidservant refuses to go on cooking because her master has started a love-affair with her.[10]

The attempts of neurotics and obsessives and psychotics to manage the negotiations with the real or imagined forces and entities setting these ambiguous meanings, *viz.* parents, teachers, angels and devils, is marked by such hesitations and confusions of language.

Freud too began with ordinary notions of 'instinct', 'impulse', 'emotion', 'anxiety', 'pressure', as he attempted to explain the everyday experiences of pleasure and of sickness, and hence of guilt. One of his greatest achievements was to redefine the temporal scope and characteristics of human sexuality. With respect to time, he posits a sequence beginning with infantile sexuality, transmuting to an asexual/latency period and then a pubescent efflorescence enduring well past capability to death. To this characteristic of antiquity he added not only the imperious-ness and proneness to maldevelopment – recognised, in their own terms, by all religions – but also plasticity: its capacity to become something else.

Freud sought to show how psychic energy becomes the entities necessary for its management. The Id with its reservoir of instinc-tual energy (libido/Eros/someforce) first bodying forth, somehow, the Ego; and that in turn bodying forth the Superego. However the instinctual forces are conceived – whether *endosomatic* like hunger or *endopsychic* like love – their conflict generates four levels of developmental organisation: oral, anal, phallic and genital. Each phase articulates a kind of thinking: libidinous scopophilia (must see) becomes the more monastic epistemophilia (must know). The more familiar equation of knowledge, sexualised vision and guilt is demonstrated in the Edenic tale.

The basic developmental tasks at the cognitive level are, first, to distinguish between the affect and the idea of an instinct; and second, between the unconscious primary processes and the secondary processes, waking thought and judgement. A baby's awareness of the affect/emotion attending her awareness of hunger is modified by her learning to name and recognise the concept/idea 'hunger'. But the pressure of the affect can some-times mobilise unconscious processes which tend towards a hallucinatory fulfilment of the instincts. As Theseus observes in Shakespeare's *A Midsummer Night's Dream*:

> *Such tricks hath strong imagination,*
> *That, if it would but apprehend some joy,*
> *It comprehends some bringer of that joy.*
> (V, i, 18–20)

It is by the reality testing conducted by the secondary processes that the individual attains to real and predictable fulfilment; although, as Freud was at pains to emphasise, the requirements of civilisation, the embodiment of the collective's understanding of the secondary processes, are a neurosis-level inducing deferment of gratification. The sense of frustration at this deferment leads to intermittent hatred of the frustrator, be it the parent, the educators or the police – in fact, anyone who threatens the consolations of narcissism.

We now have enough forces, or concepts of them, to tell the developmental story at the macro/human rather than micro/endo level. At the heart of Freud's theoretical edifice is the Oedipus complex, so let us now look at this mighty story.

Unwittingly, King Oedipus kills his father and marries his mother. Before the songwriter Prince, he is the proto-'sexy mother-fucker'. From this sublime Sophoclean tragedy, and perhaps Jocasta's generalisation, 'Many a man before you, in his dreams, has shared his mother's bed' (*Oedipus Rex*, ll. 1074–5), Freud constructed a developmental psychodrama.

A boy-baby's first experiences are of his mother's absolute availability to him, to satisfy all his desires. Then comes the experience of the partial withdrawal of this availability. When he understands that his mother is dividing her attention between him and his father, he feels rage, and imagines removing or killing his father and once again having his mother all to himself. (Look at a kid at solitary play, punching and kicking the air – he seems to be forever fighting imaginary adversaries.) But when the boy sees clearly the disparity between himself and his father, their penis sizes and their strengths, he realises the futility of his wish. This despair is worsened by an anxiety that his father has discovered his wish and may annihilate him first. The resolution of these terrors comes with the awareness of his father's love for him, his understanding that one day he will be as strong as his father, and that by the eternal relinquishment of his desire for his mother he will be able to have some sort of unthreatened relationship with her and his father – and probably a mother-like woman of his own, eventually. The internalisation of the prohibition of the wish, and the attendant fear of punishment, is the instituting of the Superego, the community line of guilt.

What of girl-babies? Here is another story. A woman is forced by 'the Gods' to send away her husband, but is allowed to keep her child by him. In their household she brings up the girl, barely seeing her for the shadow she bears of her absent husband. The girl grows up into a beautiful young woman: talented, but deeply troubled by the burden of the pasts of others. One day, her father returns to visit them both. Though he now has a new wife in another town, he sleeps with his first wife. His daughter is puzzled – she doesn't know if she is upset. But she does know the moment he kisses her at their parting, as he parts her lips to bring his tongue into her mouth, that two things have suddenly happened: she has flamed into being, she is visible; and she can see herself burning.

They begin a secret, sexual relationship, meeting in the caves of the mountain deserts. Eventually her mother begins to suspect, and when the daughter seems to taunt her with a careless confidence, she drags her to the 'Oracle'. But such is the daughter's desire and cunning, even the 'Sybil' is fooled. The daughter sees her mother broken by this utter humiliation. For a moment she feels an absolute, god-like triumph – and in the next instant, utter desolation and bereavement.

> *My performance is so good that I'm frightened . . . The doctor* [psychiatrist] *looks at me sitting before him in my vulgar dress, and he believes me. I know it, and so does my mother. He's mine, not hers, and so I have what I wanted – what I thought I wanted. She is alone. I've taken her husband and now her only ally, the one person with whom she can share her troubles . . . And I, I begin to know the misery of wounding the person I love most.*[11]

This is a true story – hence 'doctor' and not 'Sybil' – from Kathryn Harrison's astonishing Elektral autobiography, *The Kiss* (1997). Perhaps *the* Oedipal story was also true. Either, and both, ought to be sufficient proof of the heuristic value Freud makes of it, but I guess anti-Freudians will still quibble. In Harrison's life, unlike the Greek, phantasy is intentionally made actual, and the reservoirs of anxiety and desire that feed the Oedipus complex would seem to have been alleviated and satiated by achievement. But of course they haven't. The sense of guilt has been made infinitely more intense and unmanageable, inducing almost suicidal desperation. Freud concluded that this ineluctable psychodrama forms the developmental trajectory of all mortals, and the residues of anxiety and desire – some billion shades of guilt – that are deposited by whatever inevitable misnegotiation of it an individual manages, are carried forward into adult life, being displaced on all future relationships. The 'drama' is further complicated by Freud's belief that human nature is inherently bisexual – the child wants to be and have BOTH parents – and thus 'the idea of regarding every sexual act as a process in which four persons are involved'.[12] This complex is the defining contribution of psychoanalysis to the account of guilt. Some may see this structural, developmental guilt as an atheistic correlate to the Fall, when sexuality, knowledge and death enter the world as the defining parameters of human consciousness.

In what way might this idea help us to make sense of the four stories, or rather case histories, above? Please turn back to pages 142–3 and refresh your memories!

The Running Wife

This poor woman, many years earlier, had had a disastrous wedding night. Her 'very much older' husband couldn't. He tried all night, 'many times . . . running from his room into hers', but failed all night. In the morning he said angrily, 'I should feel ashamed in front of the housemaid'; so he got some red ink and spilled it on the sheets. In his ignorance, or perhaps just pathetic nervousness, he spilled it in the wrong place![13]

In the 'ritual' of the present there is not the former triangle of husband-wife-maid, but only the wife 'showing' the maid the stain on the tablecloth. Freud interprets this gesture as arising from the wife's anxiety to reassure her husband that he wasn't (always) impotent. But not only is he not there; the couple have been separated for years. So his wife is attending to (or trying to manage), in the present, an affect attached to a very old experience. I would suggest that the obliqueness of the communication might also arise out of her sense of guilt at her disappointment, contempt, even rage at her inadequate ex-husband. Freud, the son of a much-younger wife, doesn't pick up on the age difference and whether Elektral tensions and guilts had inhibited their mutual desires. Who was the husband's angry 'should' for, really?

In a scenario where lust is mutual and allowable, the woman might want to preserve **her** reputation. When Ovid fails to make the idiot stand, his mistress Corinna splashes her face with water before leaving the bedroom, so that her maid will think she has had a steamy time.[14]

What did the maid symbolise for this class – the family's informal press-secretary to the neighbourhood, an embodied conscience, or the necessary conduit/sewer of other people's sexuality? One thinks of Kafka, at 33, still fascinated and revolted by the 'evidence' of his parents' sexuality:

> At home the sight of the double bed, of sheets that have been slept in, of nightshirts carefully laid out, can bring me to the point of retching, can turn my stomach inside out; it is as though my birth had not been final, as though from this fusty life I keep being born again and again in this fusty room; as though I had to return there for confirmation, being – if not quite, at least in part – indissolubly connected with these distasteful things . . . the primeval slime.[15]

He passed them thousands of times to get to his room, but in a sense he never got past them at all. There are few literary geniuses whose sexuality was as guiltily 'fucked up' as Kafka's. He only managed to leave the nest to starve and die. Out of his private hell of an irreparable sense of separation from and longing for the love of his parents, came his many masterpieces of the protean terrors of not-quite-placeable guilt.

The Stoned Man

The young man makes a random, unintended move – he kicks a stone into the road. He then imagines a coincidence – his fiancée's carriage hitting that stone. He further imagines a (near) fatal consequence of the impact of these two bodies, stone and coach wheel; and his beloved broken, even dead. This last may not have been pictured, but the thought induces in him a series of sensations – anxiety, guilt, shame and fear – to which we will return. In response to these, and in order to lessen the distress, the unpleasure, they have caused (Freud uses the word 'obliged' to describe the motive), he goes to the stone, picks it up, and places it 'out of the way'. One possibility is instantly obviated: an object connected with him coming into fatal contact with an object connected to his fiancée. But then the same feelings – anxiety, shame, guilt and fear – return. They are the same, but in some strangely different way. He decides to put the stone back. This brings greater relief, but unsurprisingly only for a while.[16]

Freud suggests that his decision to remove the stone, based as it is on an irrational interpretation of the possibility of an accident, discloses a barely conscious awareness of an impulse to commit violence upon his fiancée; so removing the stone protects her from this impulse of his. But in undoing that protection, by returning the stone, he is reclaiming, again in a barely conscious way, a right to that impulse. In the first gesture there is the perfect paradox of impotence: a tiny pebble is imagined as being capable of over-turning the coach. At the symbolic level, the man is obviously the stone: he, or his impulse to violence, is a knot of badness like a stone, which could be sufficiently destructive of the woman he also loves and needs. A woman in a coach is also a powerful symbol of wombs and children, and as Melanie Klein saw, in children's play, sex is sometimes imagined as a brutal collision. The other aspect of the man-as-stone is that of the crushed, perhaps emasculated, person's sense of omnipotence – I feel like a pebble, but I am really a monolith. The defence is strong enough to release some energy of concern for the fiancée, to protect her from himself, and so he removes the stone. But the inadequacy of this response is revealed by the distress which ceases only when he returns the stone. But what does this mean, this acceptance of the tentative irruption of malice towards his fiancée? Is this the price for the recovery of a sufficient sense of the Reality Principle to realise two facts, one from physics – that tiny pebbles can't overturn coaches – and one from grammar and logic – that might (possibility) doesn't entail must (necessity)? Or perhaps not so much 'price' as 'partial benefit'. He has arrived, on the road, at an awareness of seemingly intolerable ambivalence: he partly loves and partly hates his fiancée. In his therapy he learns how to tolerate such ambivalence as ordinary life.

The Good Criminal

With the tale of the patient who feels relief after committing a seemingly pointless crime, we have the experiential and theoretical limiting case. In a fragment entitled 'Criminals From a Sense of Guilt', Freud considers the burden of guilt which is felt to be so boundless, so timeless and enduring that it feels unnameable and thus unthinkable, that it can find palliation, albeit brief, only in a present, tangible, codable transgression that will bring certain guilt and possible punishment.[17] This Absolute-Guilt, Freud conjectures, is the legacy of the psychodrama of the Oedipus complex, its irresolution in childhood still pressing on the adult psyche. To some, this contribution to criminology or forensics – that an innocent person commits a crime because she feels guilty – might seem a typically wild psychoanalytic proposition. One can but reiterate that the emotions around the Oedipus complex are so protean, and feel so dangerous and potentially fatal to someone – if not everyone – in the triangle, that any displacement or discharge is attended by relief. Consider this story.

A man in flight from the police seeks sanctuary in a church. He enters the confessional and tells the priest he has just committed murder. The priest asks him when he was last in Confession, and what has led him to murder. He replies that one day, when he was a boy, he had torn apart a butterfly. He didn't know why he had done it, but as soon as he had, he felt so bad, so ashamed, so guilty, that he went to Confession. But the priest just said, 'Butterflies don't count.' He was so shocked and horrified by this doctrinal decriminalisation of his act of violence, that he felt he had no bearings; and his guilt was still knotted within him. He decided never to go to church again.[18]

It may be wondered, with scepticism or scorn, whether the kid was a Nietzschean 'pale criminal'. The crucial point is that even he knew he was destroying, for whatever conscious or unconscious reason, something he had identified as beautiful and perhaps also good: he hadn't chosen to destroy a cockroach or a petri dish of bacteria. Some Freudians would find here further confirmation of their belief that the sense of beauty is a transform of libido. It is the melding of beauty and desire and need and violence and fear that returns us to the Oedipal realm. Interestingly, having destroyed the butterfly (mother, or is it father?), the boy doesn't go to either of his parents but to the superfather, the priest, that agent of the Highest Father.

At the heart of the Freudian project is the seminal idea of the 'unconscious', a realm without time or negation or contradiction. The pressure of the unconscious upon the conscious does strange things to our conscious experience of intention and explanation. 'Inside the neurosis', writes Wollheim, 'desire, belief, and action are so concatenated that there is no interaction between the neurosis and reality: in that none of the outer manifestations of the neurosis are directed upon reality, nor are any of its internal constituents ever tested against reality'.[19] In the other case material brought by the Stoned Man, better known as the Rat Man, Freud showed that, contrary to the familiar Reality Principle understanding of the way belief and desire produce action (functionally/instrumentally), the Rat Man's almost ritualistic actions and desires – studying late to impress his father or examining his penis to defy him – were generated and constructed to sustain the false belief that his father, long-dead, was alive.[20]

The Unbecoming Mourning Girl

In 'Mourning and Melancholia', Freud distinguishes between the guilt of the bereaved and the shamelessness of the melancholic. The self-hating disposition 'induced' in the bereft woman is seen as a strategy to contain her unbearable guilt over her desperate rage at the lost person. The melancholic knows his wound is different from that of the bereft. A perfect expression of this disposition is given in Shakespeare's *The Merchant of Venice*:

> *In sooth I know not why I am so sad.*
> *It wearies me, you say it wearies you . . .*
> *. . . I have much ado to know myself.*
>   (I, i, 1–2, 7)

The sense of not knowing the cause allows the parading of the wound. It becomes one's dress, one's persona. Some commentators have made the interpretation – which others see as culturally or anthropologically perilous – that Antonio's melancholy is the discharge of his barely conscious, and culturally illegal, homosexual love for Bassanio. Less controversially, one might state Freud's distressing truth:

> *A man who doubts his own love may, or rather **must**, doubt every lesser thing.*[21]

(Freud's emphasis, but note the modal verbs!) The melancholic does not feel guilt or shame, because his sensations have not crystallised into desires and concepts that can be appraised. Perhaps he seeks a present rejection or attack to which he might give a more ordinary sensation-binding response, *viz.* an ordinary emotion. Despite his modish black dress, he is a very pale criminal.

We have seen Freud trace the presence of some varieties of guilt:

1. The partly personal, partly vicarious guilt of the Running Wife.
2. The guilt at the impulse of hate, within ordinary ambivalence, of the Rat Man.
3. The boundless guilt of the irresolved Oedipal complex, aching for the relief of present mundane transgression: the Pale Criminal.

4. The longing of the melancholic for unknowingness to ground as guilt.

To these varieties of individual guilt, Freud – in his anthropological/sociological mode – added the notion of collective guilt. Human society and so human history begins, it is conjectured, with a brutal, reactive murder. Feeling frustrated and individually thwarted by the strongest male's monopolisation of the females in the primal horde, the remaining males unite to kill him, after which they also eat him. But they are surprised to find that the moment this is achieved, they feel a sense of guilt, individual and collective. This emotion prompts the memory of other emotions for the 'Father', such as love. In response to these, they institute certain taboos and rules which will avoid the repetition of such a murder and facilitate equal and safe opportunities for the fulfilment of the desires of each and every one of them.[22]

Taking this narrative as one parameter, Freud took contemporary Vienna as another. In *Civilisation and Its Discontents* (1930), he observed that the human cost of (high) civilisation, in terms of instinctual repression, was great; and when it became neurosis and psychosis, it was too great. Unlike some social theorists, Freud felt that all political (and religious) doctrines and ideologies would fail to deliver the happy society of happy individuals: whatever the classes or the resolution of the class-struggle, even a Stateless civil society would exact from its citizens the burden of some neuroses. The principal distinction was, and is, that the economically exploited classes have least access to the pleasant fruits of civilisation – the arts and the conversation about the arts.

Putting aside the questions of the historical validity and the explanatory force of Freud's conjectures, but not forgetting that cannibalism, mild or extreme, is always in present history, one might make the less controversial observation that societies find it very hard to remember and talk about their origins. (Perhaps it is too neat to say that in this they are exactly like Freud's ordinary neurotic who can't remember his infantile sexuality and infantile rage.) On the one hand, there are the epic narratives of the heroic establishment of societies sanctioned by divinities, Aeneas and Abraham. On the other hand, one might examine the amoral, temporal realm of the film *McCabe and Mrs Miller*.[23] Here, the hopefully named American frontier town, Presbyterian Church, is in reality a place of Hobbesian struggle, degradation and murderous exploitation that its Minister must wink at. Progress is marked by a whore persuading an adventurer to relocate the other whores (which he provided for the labourers) from their tents on the plains

– not so very different plains from Troy or Sinai – to a purpose-built brothel. In the symbolic, climactic scene, the Minister is shot in his church and it catches fire. We are left to conjecture – on the basis of the familiar forgetting of our present societies – that by the time the church is rebuilt in stone, not only will the brothel have gone, but the memory of it also. This naïve historical rewriting is also transparent in that post-wartime consolation-narrative, *It's A Wonderful Life*, where, in a fantasy scene, a divine agent shows the good Everyman, James Stewart, the ugly city that his lifelong self-abnegating impulses have forestalled.[24]

See Melanie Play: Klein's Account of Guilt

Only sickness and age constrained Freud's desire to explore all the areas of the terrain he had marked out for his new paradigm. Melanie Klein is the first great theorist of the nursery. Her work stands on two pillars, both unsettling for the modern mind:

1. *All the sufferings of later life are for the most part repetitions of these early ones, and **every child in the first years of its life goes through an immeasurable degree of suffering**.*[25] [my emphasis]

2. ***I do not believe in the existence of a child in whom the capacity for love cannot be brought out.***[26] [Klein's emphasis]

This capacity, Klein believed, is tied to an intrinsic sense of guilt that prompts reparation. Though the depravities of the twentieth century have persuaded people to rethink their belief in the 'absolute innocence' of children, there is still the cherished hope that if external pressure on the family dyad or triad is lessened by societal and social provision, then children will be spared much unhappiness. In dissenting from this, and positing an ineluctable psychodrama between mother and child, Klein is accused of being ahistorical and pessimistic. We will return to this criticism. Given Klein's affirmation of the theoretical worth of the death-drive, the second quote above seems, surprisingly, to be a reinstitution of the Pelagian heresy which denies original sin and implies an inherent good that mortals – by free will alone, without divine grace – can manifest. Enlightenment liberals might find this reassuring still, but postmodernists and relativists are against any such *a priori* categorising.

We saw above that Freud believed in the resolution of the Oedipus complex by the establishment of the Superego, the guardian of the line of guilt, which happens at the ages of four to five. Klein suggested that this form of resolution marked the

152

'zenith' of a process that had begun much earlier, in the first year of life. Here is her version. She posits that the child is programmed to relate, but that its first relations are with parts-of-persons, *viz.* objects; and the very first is with the breast. The ego-less baby imagines that its desires create the warm-breast which nourishes her. When she has had a satisfying feed, she designates the breast as a Good Object; but when the feed is unsatisfying or absent, she designates it as a Bad Object, which is frustrating and attacking her. Sometimes this frustration at the breast intensifies to the point where the baby feels unmanageable rage, or worse still, the primal terror of a sense of total disintegration. She tries to manage these feelings by projecting them into the Bad Breast, by using the mouth and anus as means of evacuation or as weapons of attack. This strategy brings relief until the baby realises that the Bad Breast, with her rage imposed on it, may retaliate and annihilate her. Klein calls this splitting and fear of the Object the 'paranoid-schizoid position'.

Gradually, the baby realises that she didn't create the breast, and that the breast is a single entity which is part of a person – a not-me Other-person – who loves her because she gives her good feeds. When the baby remembers her rages, she feels guilty and desolate that these might have damaged this person who loves her. This sadness and pining Klein calls the 'depressive position'. It is when the baby sees her mother continuing to be well and to be concerned for her that she realises she hasn't hurt her mother irreparably, and that they can have a mutually healthy relationship.

Freud placed the process of the establishment of the Superego at a point where the child has some facility for verbal communication, a facility that can ameliorate the aggression that provides the energy for the process. Despite this, in some children it seemed that their Superego – their psychic parent – was more strict and punishing than their actual parents. In moving this developmental sequence to the first year of life, a significantly less verbal stage, Klein saw the child at the mercy of frustrations which released his aggressive and destructive instincts to the point where they became unmanageable, with little hope of these sensations being bound into emotion and thought by language. Thus the stakes seemed that much higher: the infant/child's need to evacuate or project his hatred, and his subsequent fear of the 'lost' projected hatred homing in on him, were all the more powerful.

> *They were dreading a cruel retaliation from their parents as a punishment for their aggressive phantasies directed against those parents . . . unconsciously, expecting to be cut to pieces, beheaded, devoured and so on . . .* [27]

We are now a long way from Wordsworth's uncomplicated, inno-cent child. But Klein was able to support these terrifying conjectures through her incredibly extensive observations and detailed case notes on the play of her young patients.

Unsurprisingly, she came to similar conclusions to Freud about the idea of criminality; that the persistently naughty child is perhaps trying to use conscious, present wrongdoing, with its predictable punishments, as a way of lessening a deeply uncon-scious sense of guilt and anxiety over barely remembered displays of aggression. Such children 'would feel compelled to be naughty and to get punished, because the real punishment, however severe, was reassuring in comparison with the murderous attacks which they were continually expecting from fantastically cruel parents'.[28]

These ideas, and those of Wilfred Bion, Klein's greatest disciple, seem on first acquaintance even wilder and more repellent than Freud's. And yet they provide a conceptual framework that can help one understand a variety of strange phenomena: the slide from emotional deprivation to moral depravity of torturers and murderers, as in Henry Dick's *Licensed Mass Murder*; the *frisson* of fear watching the gestation of the eponymous *Alien*; and also latency-period sexuality as portrayed in the Spanish film, *The Tit and the Moon*, in which a young boy responds to the advent of a baby brother with a generalised fascination with the breasts of his mother and of all the women in the town.[29]

It is important to remember that Klein talks of 'positions', not 'phases'. So one's lifelong psychodrama will consist of an ineluctable, and irrepressible, pendular movement between the paranoid-schizoid and the depressive positions. The intensity of one's first experiences at these positions will give one an internal reference point for later repetitions.

> *Any pain caused by unhappy experiences, whatever their nature, has something in common with mourning. It reacti-vates the infantile depressive position; the encountering and overcoming of adversity of any kind entails mental work similar to mourning.*[30]

In childhood, the depressive position had repaired, even 'brought back to life', the internal Good figures that the child felt she had almost fatally damaged. Though in later life the Other, whether kin or friend, is actually dead, the ordinary mourner still needs to establish the aliveness of her memories and the Other's presence in her ego. The melancholic is distinguished by his inability to do this: he just goes bleating on and on.

Psychoanalytic theory contains very few statements concerning health – the criteria for individual mental well-being and for mutually fulfilling social relations. One such is in Klein's great paper, 'Love, Guilt and Reparation'. Here, she reiterates her core beliefs:

> At the bottom our strongest hatred, however, is directed against the hatred within ourselves. Feelings of guilt are a fundamental incentive towards creativeness and work in general (even of the simplest kinds).[31]

Perhaps if Freud had had time to be in the nursery longer, he would have felt, like Klein, compelled to observe:

> I must say that the impression I get of the way in which even the quite small child fights his unsocial tendencies is rather touching and impressive.[32]

And perhaps it is only when women and men have children of their own, and experience the strangely puzzling phenomenon of the seemingly boundless rage and despair of little children, that they understand finally the necessary yet ordinary parental and human tasks of the containment and holding of human distress.

Stop Making Sense: Other Voices

Freud and Klein set the broad terrain of the psychoanalytic meaning of guilt. In this section I will introduce 'shame', the concept often connected with guilt. I will defend the idea of internalisation that both concepts require to explain their origin and abiding force, and I will describe how the five basic physical senses are attached to them.

Guilt is usually confused with shame, and both are sometimes subsumed under barely specific 'anxiety'. When one remembers that even animals (as well as infants) feel anxiety, one realises that some other experience or faculty must be present in guilt and shame. It is a moot point whether animals feel shame and guilt. Though their beloved beasts look shameful and guilty to pet owners and farmers, this seems more like a human social construct. After all, 'bad' pigs and dogs are no longer tried and hung as they were until a couple of centuries back. The human capacity for these emotions is based on the faculty of internalisation.

What is internalised may be something initially external, or it may be an introjection of something initially projected out; and the 'thing' is a force, or an object, a part-object, or a self. Old

English caught this idea perfectly in the phrase defining remorse, 'agenbite of inwit': 'remorse of conscience'.[33] 'In this cannibalistic encounter who is biting whom?', asks Aldous Huxley.

> The creditable aspects of the self bite the discreditable and are themselves bitten, receiving wounds that fester with incurable shame and despair.[34]

No one would question the experiential accuracy of the sensation of biting. Just as hunger seems to be an internal 'biting', so is remorse. Perhaps the objection is to the idea of 'selves' – that it is too sophisticated a concept for a young child.

We could say that psychoanalysis proposes three levels of mentation: plain thinking, daydreaming and unconscious phantasy. Some emotional affect is tied to each, but that attached to phantasy is the least accessible to consciousness. Consider this mother's story about a visit to the Body Zone at the Millennium Dome: 'Putting my three year old to bed that night, she asked me, "Mum, do I have escalators in my legs?"'[35] Now, at the level of actual (shared) reality, at the shopping mall and the tube station, the little girl can think, compare, how *big* escalators are and how *little* are her legs. From these and from the concept of 'toy', she might have daydreamed, even before visiting the Dome, about a big doll body, so big that one would need ladders or escalators to get to the top, inside or out. But her thought – and this is what connects it to *phantasy* – is that she *might* have escalators *inside* her legs. But in this phantasy the idea of *agency* is in suspense, for she *knows* she can't 'get on' her own legs. Nor can her own legs 'get on' her, for where is the 'her' that her legs could get on? The phantasy shows her trying to make sense of the puzzle of 'willed motion', and beyond this, the criteria for 'aliveness'. This child has negotiated the dangers of alexthymia – being or feeling unable to find or use words – and performed a very complex linguistic, conceptual and psychological operation. She has taken something in: it is, at its most rudimentary, an idea of a force over which she has no control, but which – crucially – she has given a shape and a name. It is possible that if this child had already done some work on this fundamental puzzle, what she was doing with her remark was being playful with her mum.

Here, we are back at the boundary that psychoanalysis has dared to claim and explore. What bridges the distance between the three year old (and there may be even more precocious two year olds minting such phantasies) and the 'unverbal' six-month infant, is precisely the unconscious – or, in a contemporary metamorphosis, 'the unthought known'.[36]

Most people would say that shame is both a more awful and a less awful experience than guilt. This, again, is because of the 'where' that it is experienced. 'Shame is the Cinderella of the unpleasant emotions, having received much less attention than anxiety, guilt and depression', writes Rycroft, prompting in me the trivial fantasy of what her magical glass slipper would symbolise.[37] Erikson explains this insufficient attention as arising from the fact that 'in our civilisation it [shame] is so early and easily absorbed by guilt'.[38] But at least he accords it a stage – the second, and taking place in infancy – in his developmental account of the eight dichotomies to be negotiated in a human life. He pairs it with 'doubt', and contrasts them both with 'autonomy', the attainment of a sense of integrity, skill and self-sufficient power with regard to primary bodily functions – eating and excretion. Shame is the sensation consequent upon the exposure of failed autonomy or hubris. The audience is one's mother/parent, one's status reference group, one's Superego, or one's Ego-Ideal. Imagine yourself at a posh dinner, eating pea and tarragon soup. If your hand slips, your bib will turn green and your face red – and red and green must never be seen! But what if a pea falls in your cleavage – oh, Princess, what colour then!

These shameful displays are visible to the fumbler and to the audience. There is a worse humiliation, captured by the common expression 'to have egg on one's face', when the fumbling eater can't see the debris of his clumsiness, and the shame is worse because the Egg Man must now relive all the possibilities of having been seen, from the breakfast table to the workplace. But the front of the body which *hasn't* been seen reminds one of the back of the body which *can't* be seen. It is the literal and metaphoric difficulty of the sense of a behind, to do with faeces, the past, and leaving the unseeable, which inspires Erikson's wonderful aphorism, 'Doubt is the brother of shame'.[39] A parent's ambivalence about having a child will take one form with respect to difficulties in feeding that child; but a different intensity will attend difficulties with anal training. From the child's point of view, writes Erikson, 'from a sense of loss of self-control and of foreign overcontrol comes a lasting propensity for doubt and shame'.[40]

It is at the next developmental stage that 'guilt' is introduced, forming the negative of the dichotomous pair with 'initiative'. The guilt here is once again the nameless residue of the Oedipal situation. What the child must relinquish is the desire to know its mother's body, transforming it into a desire to know the non-mother world. As Erikson says, 'Visual shame precedes auditory guilt, which is a sense of badness to be had all by oneself when nobody watches and when everything is quiet except the voice of the Superego'.[41] One's eyes can't see themselves without the mirror of another's eyes, and – tragically – one's lips can't kiss themselves; but one can hear, both with the 'inner' and 'outer' ears, the commands that one speaks to oneself. From this phenomenon, Isakower argued that the Superego derives from the auditory sphere.[42] It seems to be the defining quality of shame that it is brief, whereas guilt is enduring. For Sartre, Hell is a place where one can't turn out the light.[43]

Another fundamental point in connection with shame and guilt is an anthropological one – the distinction between 'shame cultures' and 'guilt cultures'. Examples of the former include Japan and Pakistan (about which Salman Rushdie wrote his novel *Shame*); and of the latter, any Western country – though within these there may be shame-bound subcultures like the military. These are human, social constructs, and the crucial factor is who is in the in-group. Perhaps guilt and shame are a zero-sum pair, so that in any given culture more shame means less guilt. Nina Colthart, an English analyst who converted to Buddhism, could declare in a tone more believable than Adrian Mole's, 'I do not feel guilt'.[44]

The sense that is least theorised is smell. Freud made the enlightening point that when *Homo sapiens* became upright, the now greater distance between the anus and genitalia and the nose altered the value of smell. Strict clinical practices and religious rituals were instituted to deal with the feared meaning of the smell of menses and smegma and faeces. Even contemporary cultures differ in where the line of an unacceptable smell is drawn. It is the least controllable and, perhaps because of this, the most power-fully affecting sense when it 'invades' consciousness – remember the smell of school soap, your pet's fur, your first kiss . . . ? But can one smell shame or guilt?

It is a commonplace that one can smell fear, and that animals can smell it better than humans. Human fear is at its most intense in a duel, the unsupported battle, and in a physical, hands-on duel-dyad such as boxing. Just before the climax of a boxing match, there is a strange homoerotic embrace, when the combatants can smell, feel and taste blood, sweat and perhaps even tears – but certainly fear. Perhaps the fear is prompted by a sudden awareness of a sense of puzzlement: 'What am I doing here? Whose fight is it? What is its meaning? What would victory mean?' The person who gets past this moment wins – he can effect the necessary separation with a consciousness-shattering blow to the other.

So what is the meaning of such fights, and the meaning of the hesitation before the killer blow? Perhaps humans sense in that hesitation the fear of unmanageable guilt at attaining the forbidden: a fear of the stench of sin poisoning the sweet scent of victory. It might seem another typically wild psychoanalytic conjecture to suggest that boxing contains a recrudescence of the primal horde. Given the theoretical primacy of the Oedipus complex, it is interesting that there are, in reality, very few narratives of fathers and sons fighting. There seems to be an asymmetry in the sense of a right to self-defence in the fight between fathers and sons. The son knows intuitively that he needs the father to be alive to give him a self he can defend and live with. So one might conjecture that in the stand-off between the unhappily named Gayes, the preacher-father felt he could shoot, while his song-writing son Marvin, even at 44, felt no equivalent permission. The latter's recent top-selling single had been 'Sexual Healing'! After the filiacide, Marvin's mother (whose own father had shot her mother), lamented: 'For some reason, my husband didn't love Marvin and, what's worse, he didn't want me to love Marvin either. Marvin wasn't very old before he understood that.' His sister added: 'I have no doubt that this is exactly how Marvin chose to die. He punished Father, by making certain that the rest of his life would be miserable.'[45]

The limiting case of reaction-formation, when a person manages a terrifying desire by acting out the opposite desire, is the troubled child's fantasy of saving his father's life. This is illustrated perfectly in the film *Back to the Future*. The young man of the 1980s is stranded in the 1950s, the time of his parents' youth. He sees his father as a dorky 'wuss' humiliated by the class neanderthals. At this point he hesitates about helping; but later, when his father falls in front of a car, he leaps forward – saving his dad's life and, with the impact of the car, losing consciousness.[46] Because the teenage boy (unlike the air-fighting kid) has arrived at moral consciousness, he would realise that even this action would not allow him a guiltless life.

Is such hesitation the last vestige of Oedipal rage? Several million readers and critics have tried to give the definitive explanation for that perfect narrative of hesitation, *Hamlet*. T.S. Eliot famously initiated the Copernican shift when he questioned its perfection, calling it 'an artistic failure' and introducing into the language that haunting phrase, '[absence of] objective correlative'.[47] At about this time, his co-writer of the Hogarth stable, Freud, was puzzling over exactly this – the fact that the child's Superego does not correlate with the objective level of kindness or threat from its parents. The child feels, of course, an absolute sense of objective, psychic reality: the awareness of an unmanageable burden of desire, guilt, shame and fear within him/her, even if no one else can see or confirm it. So it is that Hamlet can say to his uncomprehending 'friends', Rosencrantz and Guildenstern, in absolute truth:

> *O God, I could be bounded in a nutshell and count myself*
> *a king of infinite space, were it not that I have bad dreams.*
> (II, ii, 258–60)

It is because he sees those dreams/phantasies made flesh – and ugly, sex-smelling flesh – in his uncle, that he hesitates over killing him, for that would be more like suicide! Even when he says, 'Now could I drink hot blood' (III, ii, 398), he is still only a thought away from being paralysed by sophistry born of unconscious guilt. At the least, Freud's suggestion, unlike Eliot's theory, preserves one's absolute awe at the play.

Displacement is a key idea in psychoanalysis. Once his Oedipal hatred is displaced onto his uncle, Hamlet is stuck again. In this final example, I want to show how guilt can be so intense and protean that once the sense to which it is tied becomes manageable, it gets displaced onto a sense that is not manageable. A strange 'synaesthesia' happens in this realm, not merely like 'hearing' colours, but where one's anxiety about the uncertainty of one sense is heightened by the intense awareness of another sense.

Freud introduces Lady Macbeth as a perfect exemplar of the phenomenon he names as 'Wrecked By Success'.[48] (Today's adolescents, 18–30, would define success as having the financial means to be wrecked by drink, drugs and sex whenever one wanted. And yet even among their heroes, the appetites may pall, bringing the depression known as 'Paradise Syndrome' – a recent sufferer being Dave Stewart of The Eurythmics.) The attainment of Lady Macbeth's desires seems to release an unconscious and utterly unmanageable (Oedipal) guilt which not only casts a shadow over her enjoyment of the fruits of success – queenly power – but almost compels her to suicide as a form of atonement.

When, at the beginning, she reads the witches' prophecy and knows Duncan is coming, she 'prays':

> *Come, you spirits*
> *That tend on mortal thoughts, unsex me here . . .*
> *Come to my woman's breasts,*
> *And take my milk for gall, you murd'ring ministers.*
> (I, v, 40–1, 47–8)

This is a rare example of a person wishing for some external force to do the work of projection. She is certain that she can't see these beings, in their 'sightless substances'. At the murder scene, her bravado collapses at a perspective/gestalt, a shape-shift, of Duncan's face that she had not registered during the hours of feasting just ended. (It is said that the shapes one can't see immediately in some dual-perspective puzzles reveal one's anxieties.)

> Had he not resembled
> My father as he slept, I had done't.
> (II, ii, 12–13)

Despite being unsexed and half drunk, she can't use the (penile) daggers to penetrate Duncan's flesh: she daren't even touch the body of the father.

After the murder, Macbeth longs for blindness and can barely let go of the daggers – he stands paralysed. The deed done, Lady Macbeth has enough manic energy to see the dead Duncan and to 'refute' Macbeth's misperception that the blood he has spilled would stain oceans: 'I shame to wear a heart so white . . . A little water clears us of this deed.' (II, ii, 63–4, 66) Macbeth, however, has taken in the idea of an indelible stain. The fact of the absence of the stain in the real world leads to a synaesthesia: visual absence becomes a sense of an enduring silence always about to be shattered by sound, the sound of the external world, the sound of judgement. By the end of the play, Lady Macbeth is seeing something that isn't there: the spots of blood from seventeen years earlier. Before Bodyform towels gave women the 'power' to fly and swim, it was precisely spots of (menstrual) blood which revealed the womanliness of the woman trying to unsex herself, like Pope Joan or Teena Brandon.[49] For Macbeth, the synaesthesia is from sight to sound and touch; for Lady Macbeth, it is to smell:

> Yet who would have thought the old man to have had so much blood in him . . . Here's the smell of blood still. All the perfumes of Arabia will not sweeten this little hand. Oh, oh, oh!
> (V, i, 41–2, 52–4)

In her sleepwalking she is invisible to herself, and in this blindness she falls to her death, and release. We are to understand that her being stuck at smell is an index of her weaker moral capacity. Macbeth comes to understand his moral collapse in a way she never does. I don't know if this would have any diagnostic value – asking criminals which sense was ascendant at what age, and which during the crime?

The voice of guilt is like a maddening, trashy pop song – unstoppable, a loop, a Laingian Knot.[50]

Jill feels guilty
  that Jack feels guilty
    that Jill feels guilty
      that Jack feels guilty.

He *feels that he is unhappy because he is guilty*
to be happy when others are unhappy and that he
made a mistake to marry someone who can only
think of happiness.

It can be worse, as Laing knew, for a man with less than 'six degrees of separation' from the Thane of Glamis:

Jimmy McKenzie was a bloody pest at the mental hospital
because he went around shouting back at his voices. We could
only hear one end of the conversation, of course, but the other
end could be inferred in general terms at least from: 'Away tae
fuck, ye filthy-minded bastards . . .'[51]

What kind of physic, what kind of therapy would help poor Jimmy?

Speak Up Ye Buggers! Start Making Sense: Therapy

It was decided at one and the same time to alleviate his distress
and ours, by giving him the benefit of a leucotomy. An improve-
ment in his condition was noted. After the operation he went
around no longer shouting abuse at his voices, but: 'What's
that? Say that again! Speak up ye buggers, I cannae hear ye!'[52]

The advent of the leucotomy made actual what for Macbeth and Shakespeare, centuries earlier, had been a fantasy of healing. Like Laing's modern Everyman Jack, above, Macbeth as king feels guilty for having been part of the cause of the monumental burden of guilt that his wife carries. In one of his most tender speeches, Macbeth asks the doctor:

Canst thou not minister to a mind diseased,
Pluck from the memory a rooted sorrow,
Raze out the written troubles of the brain,
And with some sweet oblivious antidote
Cleanse the stuff'd bosom of that perilous stuff
Which weighs upon the heart?

(V, iii, 40–5)

This can stand as a prophetic misconception of the way psycho-analysis works. Interestingly, this is the most famous doctor of medicine in Shakespeare and, within this play, there is the powerful contrast between his inability and the almost mystical powers of healing of the English king. There is not space within this book for a detailed discussion of the way therapy works. The obvious can be restated: therapy provides the space for barely-remembered and unmanageable thoughts and feelings to find words and gestures and to be discussed in such a way that they can be transcended and forgotten healthily. And again, the therapist does not see her task as involving a quasi-priestly or quasi-warden role, as defined by contemporary paradigms, religious or political. These facets of guilt are attended to by the State and the Church. A person may go willingly to a confessor and religiously perform penitential tasks; and he may go willingly to prison and comply with the penitentiary requirements, stated and implied. But after these, he may still feel a residue of unconscious guilt.

Even seemingly ordinary, good people may feel troubled. I came home to find that my housemate, who is hardly ever in the house long enough to produce dirt, had cleaned the toilet and bathroom, even polished the taps. 'Oh, thank you so much', I said. 'I don't do enough', he said. 'You do more than enough', I replied. 'It doesn't help', he said, in a strangely tragic tone. I was surprised, and said with some hesitation: 'Is it guilt?' 'Yes', he said, and again in such a sad tone that I felt we should speak no more about it.

This is the realm of psychoanalysis. Its right to this realm is still challenged by religion and other paradigms – and specifically for a certain range of symptoms such as obsessive-compulsive disorder. The abbreviation OCD for this condition (which Freud had long dissected) was first popularised by Rapoport, the title of whose book used a typical symptom: *The Boy Who Couldn't Stop Washing*. Such a symptom isn't merely the product of better plumbing! The idea of an intense, ineluctable guilt was captured millennia past by the idea of 'scrupulosity'. Freud saw such symptoms of repetition as ways of managing unmanageable sensations/emotions like anxiety and guilt. Rapoport dissents from this explanation, citing research which shows the inadequacy of psychoanalysis to alleviate such symptoms. Her ethological conclusion is that the primal instinct for some ordinary activity such as cleanliness in nest-building and nest-living has gone chemically wrong, and that the best therapeutic strategy is drug-based.[53]

A sense of guilt is therefore not privileged, in terms of theory or technique, as the primary symptom to be attended to.

It was Freud's colleague Josef Breuer's inability to cope, as a man, with his patient's desire for him as a complex man, sexually and emotionally available now and to her, rather than a man defined by a single professional role predicated on an almost object-like abstinence, which prompted Freud to reconsider these emotional dynamics and to place at the heart of the psycho-analytic process the concepts of 'transference' and 'counter-transference'.[54] The past must come into the present, into the therapeutic space, as powerfully as it can – and that can only be by the 'misperceptions' of transference, if there is to be a new future, rather than endless, futile shadow-repetition. In the re-creation of powerful thoughts and feelings that transference facilitates, there is the hope that the patient might (be helped to) complete or at least continue the transition from what Klein calls the paranoid-schizoid position to the depressive position. These are the most painful sessions, whatever one's age. Klein held the analytic (if not the received motherly) line when she wrote: 'This is done in analysis only through purely analytic measures, not at all by advising or encouraging the child.'[55]

To remind the reader of the contrast, one might quote from the Hebrew ritual to relieve scrupulosity: 'May everything be permit-ted you, may everything be forgiven you, may everything be allowed you.'[56] This seems a curious tense – the intercessionary subjunctive – showing once more the complexities of the grammar of the human heart. A different reference point is the wonderfully cynical strapline in *House of Cards*, in which the devious Minister often leaks assent by replying: '*You* might think that: I couldn't *possibly* comment!'[57] Some may argue that the therapeutic emotional abstinence which intends to be non-directive and facilitating might become manipulative in this way.

The renewed interest in psychoanalysis during the 1960s was coincidental with the so-called 'permissive society', one of the howling misnomers of that century of language abuse. There was no genuine, intergenerational dialogue, closing with the benign granting of permission. No parental blessings were offered, just the implicit curses of sullen silence and resentment, or 'guilt-trips' as they were called.

The distinction between psychodynamic and non-psycho-dynamic therapies is of the same order as the difference in potential emotional charge between live theatre and the cinema. In his great paper, 'Hate In The Counter-Transference', Donald Winnicott examines the pressures, internal and external, that the therapist must manage and use.[58] This is not to deny the worth of non-psychodynamic therapies. And, of course, the patient in non-psychodynamic therapy isn't watching a film of a therapist – the simple point of difference is that he/she will be, on the basis of theory and technique, trying to abstract out, control, disinhibit, 'over'-contain, transferential dynamics. Psychodynamic therapists might suspect that in such other therapies, though seemingly guiltless knowledge and behaviour are arrived at, the heart or psyche may still feel fundamentally broken by guilt.

Roll Away the Stone: Final Thoughts

Where does the debate about guilt in psychoanalysis go from here? The disciplines of anthropology and sociology invite connection.

a) A Ruthless Computation of the Forces

The Homeric heroes knew nothing of that cumbersome word **responsibility**, *nor would they have believed in it if they had. For them, it was as if every crime were committed in a state of mental infirmity. But such infirmity meant that a god was present and at work . . . For [them] there was no guilty party, only guilt, immense guilt . . . With an intuition the moderns have jettisoned and have never recovered, the heroes did not distinguish between the evil of the mind and the evil of the deed, murder and death. Guilt for them is like a boulder blocking the road; it is palpable, it looms. Perhaps the guilty party is as much a sufferer as the victim. In confronting guilt, all we can do is make a ruthless computation of the forces involved.*[59]

How wonderful that the metaphor Calasso chooses for guilt, in his sublime meditation on Greek mythology, should be the same as that of Freud's Rat Man. And there is another perfect coincidence of these great Hellenists. The above quote displays the guilt attached to mighty political actions. But guilt is also lodged in something ordinary, diurnal and utterly essential.

The primordial crime is the action that makes something in existence disappear: the act of eating. Guilt is thus obligatory and inextinguishable . . . The gods aren't content to foist guilt on man. That wouldn't be enough, since guilt is part of life always. What the gods demand is an awareness of guilt. And this can only be achieved through sacrifice.[60]

There have been, and there remain, many different social formations. And one might ask questions like: Do arranged-marriage cultures privilege the mother–son relationship in such a way that the Oedipus complex is significantly attenuated? But despite the experiential fact of psychic bisexuality, each individual learns to live as one gender, with its allowed powers and attendant terrors. Perhaps it is male fear and womb-envy which provide the best explanation for the literary-anthropological puzzle: Why is Isaac saved, but not Iphigenia? Some argue that it is the male bias, even within psychoanalysis, which has led to the under-use of the term 'Elektra complex'. If the primary triangle is the source of psycho-analytic guilt, then the specificity of women's experience of this triangle must be honoured.

I am mindful, as a male, that the concepts 'female masochism', 'eroticisation of female self-hatred' and 'female violence' need to be theorised more subtly. The way in which a culture situates a woman's moral right to a violent impulse or a violent response will determine her psychological sense of this right, and the attendant guilt she is expected to feel. Any shift in this 'ideology' will affect, within three generations, the formation of the Superego of the children to come. In the West, if not yet in the East, there is a debate about whether there can be gender-blind definitions of 'provocation' and thus of legal responsibility and moral guilt. One cannot imagine, in any century before the twentieth, a woman publishing a book entitled *Eve was Framed*.[61] The Greek myths didn't blame Helen.

These recent conceptual revaluations, such as the delineation of 'date rape' and the redefinition of 'abuse' after Cleveland, throw their tragic light on past narratives, but also a more hopeful light upon the future. They also affect one's reading of texts: most recently the Sylvia Plath–Ted Hughes controversies. It is worth recalling that even *the* dramatist, writing when a queen was ascen-dant, did not write 'enough' on the mother–daughter relationship. There are no mothers in Shakespeare's great comedies, but many fathers and daughters. Why?

b) Taking the Group Seriously

Some, like Dalal, the title of whose book is taken as the heading for this subsection, would say that this is the next theoretical chal-lenge: 'to build bridges between psychoanalysis and sociology.'[62] He is inspired by the phrase in Freud's account of the resolution of the Oedipus complex: '*Ideologies* of the Superego' (his emphasis).[63] Though one might concur with his questioning of the theoretical and moral worth of a monolithic individualism, the question remains: In what way does a group *need* other groups? Freud observed an 'inclination to aggression' that humans 'do not feel comfortable without'; and also that despised subgroups, like Jews, 'rendered most useful services to their hosts'.[64] But as the internecine warfare among the Christian States (of 'universal love') shows us, one 'enemy' isn't enough.

Out of the unprecedented barbarities of the last century, both at the level of the hearth and the State, has come the idea of 'the impassability of the Other': to make disappear the hope and right to flourish of another individual or another culture is an action requiring a sense of absolute guilt.

Murder and war are justified by the belief of scarcity, whether born of reality, imagination or greed. The baby, believing the breast she needs may not be enough, or may disappear, takes it all in, makes it disappear. The baby cannot imagine that others may be hungry. Later, there is the perfect developmental moment when the baby being fed turns the spoon to feed her feeder: she believes there is enough for all. Nations perennially fail to attain this moment. At one end of the global village are the self-famishing; at the other, the politically famished. Starving saves the labours of the sacrificial knife, and also prolongs guilt. All the G8 or dinner-table talk about the 'problem' of famine is just an evasion. Yes, it is hard to talk about such things – for but two thoughts away from consciousness is the terrifying realm of fearful guilt. For many, there is something absolutely unbearable about the whining special pleading of an Albert Speer or a Myra Hindley. Their monstrous mountains of text and talk, decades of it, didn't and don't produce even a squeaking mouse of believable understanding of guilt, let alone remorse, that would begin the dialogue of reconciliation. Perhaps their abiding ignorance and moral deformity is the effluence of society's perennial, messy and fruitless engagement of these fundamental concepts.

Coda

The impassability of the Other. Who believes this? It is known that perverts, however defined, do not usually come to therapy, and when they do, they do not wish to be 'cured', only to have their nagging guilt allayed. They say, 'Don't I have the right to do this?' The only answer is: 'It also depends on the right of the Other! And what does it mean that you can't allay your own guilt?'

So how many Others? Could this not also be an index of civilisation: the increasing range of possible actions of infringement of the Other that the mentally healthy individual, Seinfeld's 'whole new animal', should feel guilty about? But this kind of guilt would be based neither on a sense of sin nor a fear of punishment, so it would neither cripple the bearer nor harm the Other, but rather facilitate their genuine intimacy. In that index is the hope of good hesitation, that will slowly leaven the community and attenuate, generation upon generation, the 'bad' guilt that the Superego demands. Perhaps I should feel guilty in concluding that what the world needs is more guilt!

Acknowledgements

I would like to thank: Ivan Ward of the Freud Museum, for his generosity of spirit and lavish editorial attentions; Duncan Heath and Jeremy Cox, of Icon, for their steadying hands; my colleagues at Cambridge University Counselling Service for splendid supervision and support; and the following, whose affection is between the lines: François Danis, Dan Jones, Matthew Jones, Alan MacDonald, Dieter Peetz, Corinna Russell, Maggie Smith, and Wendy Thurley.

Kalu Singh came to England from India, and to psychoanalysis via Chemistry, Philosophy, English and Education. He works as a Civil Servant and as a Sessional Counsellor in a University Service. He lives in Cambridge.

Notes

1. Townsend, S., *The Secret Diary of a Provincial Man: Adrian Mole*, in *The Guardian*, 15 January 2000.
2. Meade, M., *The Unruly Life of Woody Allen*, London: Weidenfeld and Nicolson, 2000.
3. Ibid.
4. The Bible: Exodus, 20:5.
5. Bruce, L., *The Essential Lenny Bruce*, London: Macmillan, 1972.
6. Goldhagen, D.J., *Hitler's Willing Executioners: Ordinary Germans and the Holocaust*, London: Little, Brown, 1996.
7. Seinfeld, J., *Seinfeld*, USA: Castle Rock Entertainment, 1998.
8. Apocryphal.
9. Linehan, G. and Mathews, A., *Hippies*, UK: BBC2, 1999.
10. Freud, S., *Inhibitions, Symptoms and Anxiety* (1925), London: Penguin Freud Library, vol. 10, 1979, p. 240.
11. Harrison, K., *The Kiss*, London: Fourth Estate, 1997, pp. 142–3.
12. Freud, S., letter to Fleiss (1899), quoted in Wollheim, R., *Freud*, London: Fontana, 1991, p. 120.
13. Freud, S., *Introductory Lectures on Psychoanalysis* (1916a), London: Penguin Freud Library, vol. 1, 1973, p. 301.
14. Ovid, *The Erotic Poems*, London: Penguin, 1982.
15. Kafka, F., *Letters to Felice*, London: Vintage, 1999, p. 547.
16. Freud, S., *Notes Upon a Case of Obsessional Neurosis* ('The Rat Man') (1909), London: Penguin Freud Library, vol. 9, 1979, p. 70.
17. Freud, S., *Some Character-Types Met With in Psychoanalytic Work* (1916b), London: Penguin Freud Library, vol. 14, 1985, p. 317.
18. *Butterflies Don't Count*, UK: BBC2, date uncertain.
19. Wollheim, R., *Freud*, London: Fontana, 1991, p. 137.
20. Freud (1909), op. cit., p. 84.
21. Ibid., p. 121.
22. Freud, S., *Totem and Taboo* (1912), London: Penguin Freud Library, vol. 13, 1985.
23. Altman, R., *McCabe and Mrs Miller*, USA: 1971.
24. Capra, F., *It's a Wonderful Life*, USA: 1946.
25. Klein, M., 'Criminal Tendencies in Normal Children' (1927), in *Love, Guilt and Reparation and Other Works: 1921–1945*, London: Vintage, 1988, p. 173.
26. Ibid., p. 184.
27. Klein, M., 'On Criminality' (1934), in Klein (1988), op. cit., p. 258.
28. Ibid.
29. Dick, H.V., *Licensed Mass Murder*, London: 1972; Scott, R., *Alien*, UK: 1979; Luna, B., *The Tit and the Moon*, Spain: 1994.
30. Klein, M., 'Mourning' (1940), in Klein (1988), op. cit., p. 360.
31. Klein, M., 'Love, Guilt and Reparation' (1937), in Klein (1988), op. cit., pp. 340, 335.
32. Klein, M., 'Criminal Tendencies in Normal Children' (1927), in Klein (1988), op. cit., p. 176.
33. Joyce, J., *Ulysses* (1922); Joyce is quoting an old text.

34. Huxley, A., *The Perennial Philosophy*, London: Flamingo, 1946, p. 309.
35. Engle, C., letter to *The Guardian*, 8 February 2000.
36. Bollas, C., *The Shadow of the Object: Psychoanalysis of the Unthought Known*, London: Free Association Books, 1987.
37. Rycroft, C., *Dictionary of Psychoanalysis*, London: Penguin, 1968, p. 152.
38. Erikson, E., *Childhood and Society*, London: Paladin, 1963, p. 227.
39. Ibid., p. 228.
40. Ibid., p. 228.
41. Ibid., p. 227.
42. Isakower, O., 'On the Exceptional Position of the Auditory Sphere', *International Journal of Psychoanalysis*, vol. 20, 1939.
43. Sartre, J.-P., *In Camera* (1944), London: Penguin, 1990.
44. Coltart, N., Freud Museum Conference, 1997, question time.
45. Ritz, D., *Divided Soul: Marvin Gaye*, London: Michael Joseph, 1985, pp. 7, 336.
46. Zemeckis, R., *Back to the Future*, USA: 1985.
47. Eliot, T.S., '*Hamlet*' (1919), in *Selected Prose*, London: Faber and Faber, 1975, p. 48.
48. Freud (1916b), op. cit., p. 299.
49. Apocryphal; Peirce, K., *Boys Don't Cry*, USA: 1999.
50. Laing, R.D., *Knots*, London: Penguin, 1970, pp. 26, 28.
51. Laing, R.D., *The Politics of Experience*, London: Penguin, 1967, p. 146.
52. Ibid.
53. Rapoport, J., *The Boy Who Couldn't Stop Washing*, London: Collins, 1990, p. 15.
54. Freud, S. and Breuer, J., *Studies on Hysteria* (1895), London: Penguin Freud Library, vol. 3.
55. Klein, M., 'Criminal Tendencies in Normal Children' (1927), in Klein, op. cit., 1988, pp. 176–7.
56. Rapoport, op. cit., p. 232.
57. Dobbs, M., *House of Cards*, London: Collins, 1989; BBC TV, 1990.
58. Winnicott, D., 'Hate In The Counter-Transference' (1947), in *Collected Papers*, London: Karnac, 1992.
59. Calasso, R., *The Marriage of Cadmus and Harmony* (1988), London: Vintage, 1994, p. 94.
60. Ibid., pp. 311–13.
61. Kennedy, H., *Eve Was Framed*, London: Vintage, 1993.
62. Dalal, F., *Taking the Group Seriously*, London: Jessica Kingsley, 1998, p. 121.
63. Ibid.
64. Freud, S., *Civilization and Its Discontents* (1930), London: Penguin Freud Library, vol. 12, 1985, p. 305.

Further Reading

Appignanesi, R. and Zarate, O., *Introducing Freud*, Cambridge: Icon Books, 1999.

Calasso, R., *The Marriage of Cadmus and Harmony*, London: Vintage, 1994.

Clendinnen, I., *Reading the Holocaust*, Cambridge: Cambridge University Press, 1999.

Cox, M. (ed.), *Remorse and Reparation*, London: Jessica Kingsley, 1999.

Dalal, F., *Taking the Group Seriously*, London: Jessica Kingsley, 1998.

Freud, S., *Some Character-Types Met With in Psychoanalytic Work* (1916), London: Penguin Freud Library, vol. 14, 1985.

Hinshelwood, R., Robinson, S. and Zarate, O., *Introducing Melanie Klein*, Cambridge: Icon Books, 1999.

Klein, M., 'Criminal Tendencies in Normal Children' (1927), in Klein, M., *Love, Guilt and Reparation and Other Works: 1921–1945*, London: Vintage, 1988.

Schimmel, S., *The Seven Deadly Sins: Jewish, Christian and Classical Reflections on Human Psychology*, Oxford: Oxford University Press, 1992.

Ward, I., *Introducing Psychoanalysis*, Cambridge: Icon Books, 2000.

6

Narcissism

Jeremy Holmes

Introduction

Narcissism starts from mirrors – from the mirroring mother, whose gleaming eye and responsive smile reflects delight in her child, through the seductive yet claustrophobic 'hall of mirrors' of overprotective parents, the suicidal patient confronting the cold lifeless mirror of the empty bathroom, to the watery surface that shatters into a thousand pieces as Narcissus vainly reaches out to embrace his own reflection.

We are all fascinated by mirrors. But who and what do we behold when we peer into them? Does what we see seem alien – a stranger whom we hardly recognise? Do we look 'alright' – do we say to ourselves 'you'll do' as we make ready for a party? Do we secretly admire what we see, or collapse in horror and loathing like the fairy-tale dwarf seeing his deformity for the first time? Do we preen ourselves in front of the mirror, pirouetting with backwards glance, flirting with our own image? Or do we, like Rembrandt, gaze squarely at the face that stares back at us, trying with every fibre to penetrate the mysteries of the self – a self that is at once so familiar and so strange?

Havelock Ellis, the late nineteenth-century sexologist, was the first to link the classical Narcissus myth with psychological difficulty, seeing homosexuality, then regarded as a sexual perversion, as a pathology of self-love; a man loves another man, a woman a woman, who is like (a reflection of) him or herself, rather than the supposedly appropriate opposing gender. Hence the Oxford English Dictionary definition of narcissism, a term coined by Wilhelm Nacke in reviewing Ellis' work, as 'morbid self-love or self-admiration'. Note the necessary qualifier, 'morbid' – self-love is not necessarily problematic, and indeed is generally seen as a mark of psychological health.

The term 'narcissism' can be used in a number of distinct ways. In a *lay* sense it tends to be synonymous with *self-centredness* or

173

self-preoccupation, and is appropriately used in describing people whose speech is littered with the pronoun 'I'; whose conversation tends to take the form of what one long-suffering spouse of a chronic narcissist dubbed 'Radio Me'. For Charles Rycroft, narcissism is a variant of

> *solipsism ... the tendency to use oneself as the point of reference round which experience is organised. In this sense the discovery that one is not the only pebble on the beach and that the world was not constructed solely for one's own benefit involves a loss of narcissism.*[1]

There is an implicit value judgement here which, as we shall see, psychoanalysis tries to theorise: to be self-centred is normal and acceptable in the young, but, if 'selfishness' persists into adult life, it is maladaptive and liable to be frowned upon. Here consideration for others and altruism are contrasted with the inability or refusal to see the world from anything other than one's own point of view, with consequent potential for trampling on other's feelings.

The idea of narcissism has been used *sociologically* by authors such as Christopher Lasch to describe a constellation of attitudes characterised by extreme individualism, lack of interest in the past or future, disregard for others, preoccupation with personal relationships at the expense of political activity, and lack of concern about social cohesion.[2] People so described (no doubt not without a streak of puritanical envy) might be the 'me generation' of today's young affluent middle class, or the decadent and *fin de siècle* hedonists of the late nineteenth-century European upper classes, so beautifully depicted by Oscar Wilde (of whom more below). Collective or group narcissism underlies such diverse phenomena as delusions of racial superiority, and various cults and messianic groupings in which individual narcissism may be either legitimised or submerged in devotion to a charismatic leader.

Psychoanalytic ideas about narcissism fall under three distinct headings: libidinal narcissism, destructive narcissism, and healthy narcissism. Sigmund Freud saw 'primary narcissism' as a normal developmental stage in which the infant thinks only, and blissfully, of itself. This is a precursor of *object relations*, the capacity to relate to – 'invest libido in' – others. Freud believed that people suffering from paranoia and schizophrenia, and to some extent hypochondriacal illnesses, regressed, often in the face of loss, to a 'secondary' narcissistic state in which 'libido' (here conceptualised as a kind of psychic fluid) is withdrawn from the external world and reinvested in themselves and their own bodies. Ronald Britton calls this state of psychic withdrawal into the self 'libidinal narcissism'.[3]

By contrast, Karl Abraham, and later the Kleinian school (especially Herbert Rosenfeld and Otto Kernberg), emphasise the destructive aspects of narcissism, in which the narcissist pathologically envies, hates, and actively seeks to destroy the object, that is *the other*. Only the self can be allowed to exist. Herbert Rosenfeld uses the powerful metaphor of the 'mafia gang' which is imagined taking over the mind, ruthlessly insisting that no external relationship is permissible. This triumphant 'thick-skinned' narcissism is contrasted with 'thin-skinned' libidinal narcissism, which is more defensive than destructive.[4]

A third psychoanalytic approach to narcissism is associated with the self-psychology school of Heinz Kohut.[5] Kohut saw narcissism, i.e. self-love, and object-love not as lying on a continuum, but as two distinct developmental lines which persist throughout life, each with its own characteristic features and pathologies. He emphasised the healthy aspect of narcissism, seeing such phenomena as parental adoration of their children, the child's excitement in itself and its world, and 'normal' hopes, aspirations, ambitions and ideals as all belonging to the sphere of positive narcissism. In this model, as development proceeds, narcissism is not replaced by object-love but, rather, is tempered by gradual disillusionment so that in maturity it continues to underlie good self-esteem and *realistic* goals. 'Secondary narcissism', and the inability to progress along the path of moderated self-love, result from 'narcissistic wounds', often arising out of parental neglect or abuse. Here, lacking external validation of their narcissism ('*We* do not find you loveable'), individuals fall back on self-love so that at least a modicum of hope and motivation may survive.

Many of these psychoanalytic ideas are brought together in the psychiatric sense of narcissism contained in Kernberg's notion of 'narcissistic personality disorder', in which the sufferer is self-centred and demanding, overestimates his or her own abilities and specialness, is envious, exploitative and unable to consider others' feelings – but underneath this bombastic self-importance, the sufferer is often deeply depressed and has profound feelings of emptiness. As we shall see, finding ways to help these individuals is a major challenge for psychotherapy.

Clinical Manifestations of Narcissism

In this section I shall consider aspects of narcissism as they might arise in a psychoanalytic situation, which I divide, somewhat artificially, into 'necessary narcissism', everyday 'clinical narcissism', and 'entrenched narcissism'.

The most obvious example of necessary narcissism is to be found in normal parental fascination and pride in their children, which, as we shall see, is a prerequisite if children are to develop good self-esteem. As Freud puts it:

> Parental love, which is so moving and at bottom so childish, is nothing but parent's narcissism born again, which, transformed into object-love, unmistakably reveals its former nature.[6]

Of course, most parents are able to temper their narcissistic over-investment with realism. They can also see their offspring as separate beings, with their own projects, whose purpose is not merely to fulfil their parents' hopes and ambitions. Also, as Neville Symington points out, effective parenting involves a huge sacrifice of narcissism, putting aside one's own self-centredness in order to concentrate on one's child, and allowing that child access to one's partner.

There are, however, those individuals who cannot *not* talk about their children, especially if successful, thereby inducing a certain envy and weariness in the listener. Similarly, those whose conversation consists mainly of boasting about their own achievements, wealth, and the important and powerful people with whom they are connected, are often compensating for feelings of insignificance and inferiority. Their conversation is peppered with the pronouns 'I' and 'me' and 'mine'; their primary need is to be centre stage, yet with little apparent interest in the lives and reactions of their audience. They may be entertaining and fascinating, or sometimes unbearable bores.

Again, they may excite envy, since most of us have a well of residual narcissism which our developmental process has helped keep in check, but which is never fully abandoned, only partially transcended in favour of the more palpable satisfactions of object relationships. The rich and famous, and their attendant publicity machines, provide necessary icons into which the majority of us who lead mundane lives can project our own secret narcissistic hopes and desires. The 'narcissistic bubble' with its brilliant reflections floats tantalisingly above our heads; when it bursts, the occupant is left naked and pitifully vulnerable.

The therapist's reactions to a client are an invaluable guide to the presence of narcissistic phenomena. Often, there is a feeling of a lack of real contact or dialogue with the client, who may superficially agree with the therapist's comments, but, with glazed and unresponsive eyes, return to his or her own preoccupations without showing any discernible impact once the therapist has had their say. As a therapist, one may feel bored or excluded, mad or importuning (as though the therapy is for one's own rather than the client's benefit), or even envious of the client, whose life seems so much more colourful and exciting than one's own.

One of the more seductive manifestations of narcissism is to be found in clients who idealise and overvalue therapy and their therapists. They insist on being treated by the top man or woman, the best that is going: nothing less will do. The therapist becomes a saviour, imbued with special powers that compensate for the patient's feelings of ordinariness and insignificance. One therapist, well known for outstanding writing in the field, decided never to take on clients who approached her after reading her work: she found they invariably had projected huge narcissistic longings into her that were often resistant to analysis, and which she was destined to disappoint, not being able to live up to the ideal of the 'perfect therapist' that they thrust upon her.

There are certain characteristic features of more severe narcissism to which we can now turn. In a paper first published in 1922, Abraham focused on 'negative narcissism', in which, paradoxically, sufferers are not so much irredeemably pleased with themselves but, rather, are in a constant state of anxious self-dissatisfaction.[7] What is 'narcissistic' about negative narcissists is that they are just as self-preoccupied as their grandiose cousins, but are locked into self-hatred rather than self-love.

Abraham quotes from Leo Tolstoy's *Boyhood and Youth*:

> [M]*y occupations . . . included . . . much looking at myself in the glass, from which, however, I always turned away with heavy feelings of depression and even disgust. My outward appearance, I was convinced, was unsightly, and I could not even comfort myself with the usual consolation in such cases – I could not say that my face was expressive, intelligent, or distinguished.*[8]

Freud saw the 'negative therapeutic reaction', in which patients deteriorate rather than get better when offered an apposite interpretation of their distressed state, as a manifestation of negative narcissism. For these patients, the 'ideal self' is so far removed from the 'real self' that striving towards it may seem futile – the ideal is too far away to even contemplate. As nothing less than perfection will satisfy, any attempt to change – to lessen the gulf between where one is and where one would like to be – is resisted in order to preserve the relative comfort of the status quo. People are often frightened to change, tending to cling to what they already have, however unsatisfactory it is: there can be a perverse satisfaction in being miserable, if it is familiar.

The origins of such negative narcissism are often to be found in a harsh superego, internalised from parental strictures. One patient described how she came home from school one day, delighted with having achieved 99 per cent in a maths exam, only to be roundly criticised by her father for not getting 100 per cent!

With his libidinal perspective, Freud saw narcissism as a staging post on the way from autoeroticism to object relationships. The unconscious sexual and masturbatory *phantasies* of narcissistic patients (as opposed to their conscious *fantasies*) are important clues to their pathology. In men, there may be a huge preoccupation with the penis, either their own or that of others. Sometimes the narcissist has abandoned hope of mutuality in relationships and relies instead on power and coercion to gain access to his objects, access that provides a sense of security and satisfaction. Sadomasochistic phantasies are common. In female narcissism, the whole body itself may become idealised, with terror and desperation whenever signs of imperfection appear. Fantasies of being made love to by rich and famous men in exotic locations are perhaps a harmless manifestation of normal female narcissism, but some women are in thrall to powerful men, and remain so, however much they suffer as a result. Those who feel powerless and empty, and view themselves as objects to be used, have to meet their narcissistic needs as best they can.

Grandiose phantasies are a normal aspect of adolescent narcissism, but may persist into adulthood, albeit in a highly concealed form. It is rare that a client will speak of such things until they feel they can fully trust the therapist, and, even then, may only do so with much embarrassment and hesitation. Such thoughts are deeply coloured with *shame*, which many, like Phil Mollon, view as the crucial 'narcissistic affect'.[9] The patient may dream of being a famous pop singer, football player, artist, academic, or politician, and of untold riches and power. The possibility of artistic success is particularly seductive to the narcissist because of the social construction of genius. The idea of 'genius' encapsulates the quintessence of narcissism – someone who is touched by the gods and who can effortlessly achieve great things.

'Narcissistic rage' is another important clinical phenomenon. The narcissist may have managed to construct a world that more or less meets their needs, and in which, to use Freud's famous phrase, 'his majesty the baby'[10] is waited on hand and foot by various courtiers, or at least has found ways to recreate momentary feelings of narcissistic bliss with the aid of drugs, alcohol or sex, or through the purchase of luxury goods. But sooner or later reality will intrude. The sufferer discovers that their needs have to be balanced with those of others, that helpers are motivated not just by devotion but by the necessity of earning a living, or simply that reality has its own logic and does not always bend to the dictates of human will. A therapist may be on holiday just when the patient needs them, or bring a session to an end when the patient is in full flow.

Such phenomena, great or small, may trigger an outburst of narcissistic rage. The patient will metaphorically, or sometimes literally, stamp his foot, smash or trash precious things, or shout the place down. One such patient, whenever he was thwarted, regularly had appalling rows with workmen or fellow drivers who got in his way on narrow lanes. In therapy he appeared compliant and accepting, but it gradually emerged how much he deeply resented and took personally the therapist's holiday breaks, which he felt were invariably calculated to come at a time when he was most in need of support and comfort. As a child he had hour-long outbursts in which he threw himself inconsolably to the ground and screamed himself sick. With unempathic parents and having spent long periods in hospital during his childhood, he was enormously insecure, and, like Fisher-Mamblona's gosling Feli,[11] appeared to be catapulted into fits of rage whenever he felt threatened, as a form of 'displacement activity'. (This term refers to an apparently irrelevant set of behaviours triggered by intense emotions that cannot be 'directly' discharged or dealt with at the time.) The rage itself seems to provide a measure of security for the narcissist who is fundamentally so lonely and deprived of a secure base.

Beneath narcissistic rage lies what Mollon terms 'narcissistic vulnerability' or, as Kohut calls it, the 'narcissistic wound'. The narcissist is caught in a bind whose limits are the universal need to feel special on the one hand, and the equally imperative need to adapt to reality on the other. An attempt is made to create a world which will boost their sense of specialness and importance, but underneath lurks despair and depression and feelings of insignificance. In these circumstances, the narcissist is vulnerable to even minor slights and rejections which disconfirm their specialness, as well as to the everyday, or sometimes extraordinary, mishaps and traumas which unrelenting fate decrees.

Two contrasting clinical patterns of narcissism have been described. Rosenfeld's 'thick-' and 'thin-skinned' narcissists become, in Glenn Gabbard's terminology, the 'oblivious' and the 'hypervigilant'.[12] *Oblivious* narcissists appear to have little understanding of others' feelings and ride roughshod with their arrogant and self-serving ruthlessness. They are grandiose and exhibitionistic in their manner. *Hypervigilant* types are shy, inhibited and self-centred in their sensitivity to rejection or criticism. They seem to have 'one skin missing', and are so easily emotionally bruised that their self intrudes in every encounter. Anthony Bateman argues that these stereotypes are not mutually exclusive and that the hypervigilant are far less fragile than they appear, with huge rage lying not far beneath their frailty, while seemingly oblivious people, once engaged in therapy, may ultimately reveal emptiness and despair.[13]

Literary Examples of Narcissism

Ovid's Version of the Narcissus Myth

Many contemporary ideas about narcissism can be found in embryonic form in the classical Narcissus myth which gave its name to the syndrome. Here, I follow Ted Hughes' powerful translation of the Ovid version.[14]

The story starts not with Narcissus but with Tiresias, the only person to have lived both as male and female, and whom Jove and Juno therefore called in to adjudicate their dispute over who derived the greater pleasure from the act of sex: man or woman. Tiresias' vote was for women. (Although in some versions he diplomatically replies that while women experience ten times the intensity of pleasure, men experience it ten times more often!) Juno, inexplicably angry, strikes him blind, while to compensate, Jove opens Tiresias' *inner* eye, giving him the gift of prophecy. Thus Ovid reveals the narcissistic themes of bodily pleasure, envy, and the difficulty in knowing how another truly feels, especially when one is oneself consumed with desire.

Narcissus was the product of his mother Liriope's rape by the river-god Cephisus. Narcissus was outstandingly beautiful from birth, so much so that envious gossips came to Tiresias questioning whether a creature so beautiful could live for long. Here the profound theme of the transience of beauty, and of the links between narcissism, envy and death is introduced.

Tiresias answers enigmatically: he can live long, '*unless he learns to know himself*'. The paradox turns on the fatal word 'unless'. The terrible dilemma of the narcissist is thus elegantly summarised: either the narcissist remains trapped forever in the shadow world of self-love, or he is released from the bondage of self-unknowing (and by implication being unable to know others), but on price of death. Although the narcissist thinks only of himself, ironically he can never really know himself, since he cannot take a position outside himself and see himself as he 'really' is. If he could accept that beauty fades then his loveliness would be something to celebrate; by grandiosely denying the reality of loss and change, this beauty is transformed into monstrosity.

Narcissus grows into a beautiful young man. Many fall in love with him, but he keeps his distance. Then the wood-nymph Echo sees him and is immediately stricken. Previously a chatterbox, she has lost her power of speech as punishment from her mother Juno who discovered that Echo was being used as a decoy by Jove to engage her in conversation while he was away chasing other women. All she can do is repeat the words she has just heard. How is she to declare her love? One day Narcissus is lost in the woods and calls out to his friends: 'Come to me.' Echo reveals herself: 'to me', 'to me', she calls. Narcissus turns and runs: 'I would rather be dead than let you touch me.' Echo is mortified, and slowly dies of lost love, until all that is left is her voice.

Narcissists break hearts. They cannot see the impact of their actions on others. They attract flatterers and fawners, themselves narcissistically traumatised, hoping for reflected glory. Echo's 'God-mother' (Juno) is so envious of her relationship with her 'God-father' (Jove) that she blights the father–daughter relationship so essential to healthy female narcissism – a relationship in which the adolescent daughter knows that her father sees her as beautiful, but where, at the same time, he is utterly respectful of her sexuality.

Echo, the hypervigilant, becomes the mirror image of the oblivious Narcissus. He is untouchable; she eternally longs to be in his arms. He thinks only of himself and is ruthlessly selfish; she can only think of him, and her damaged self-esteem remains fragile even unto her death. He cannot identify with others and so make their voices his own, thereby enlarging the range of his personality; she has no voice of her own, and is condemned to pale imitation. In attachment terms, both are anxiously attached: she clings insufferably to her object, he forever keeps his at a distance.

Many others fall unrequitedly in love with Narcissus. Eventually one, in a crucial therapeutic move, has the courage to confront his tormentor. (It is a 'his' – there is a suggestion of bisexuality throughout the myth, as though Narcissus cannot be content with the love of only one sex.)

> *Let Narcissus love and suffer*
> *As he has made us suffer*
> *Let him, like us, love and know it is hopeless . . .*[15]

One day, thirsty from hunting, Narcissus finds a 'pool of perfect water' and there, as he stretches out to drink:

A strange new thirst, a craving, unfamiliar,
Entered his body with the water,
And entered his eyes
With the reflection in the limpid mirror . . .
As the taste of water flooded him
So did love.[16]

He falls deeply in love with his own image. But the harder he tries
to embrace himself, to kiss the lips that 'seemed to be rising to kiss
his', the more frustrated and lovesick he becomes. He bemoans his
fate. Eternally separated from his love-object, he experiences loss
and grief for the first time. At last he comes to know himself:

You are me. Now I see that . . .
But it is too late.
I am in love with myself . . .
This is a new kind of lover's prayer
To wish himself apart from the one he loves.[17]

He realises that he must die: 'I am a cut flower', 'Let death come
quickly'. At last he feels compassion for another: 'The one I loved
should be let live. He should live on after me, blameless.' But he
knows this is impossible. When he dies, both he and his observing
self die – and even as he crosses the Styx he cannot resist a glimpse
of himself in the water. But at the moment of his death he is
transformed – metamorphosed – into a beautiful flower. To this
day, the narcissus, with its evanescent delicate trumpet and
seductive fragrance, is a tribute to Tiresias' prescience.

Tiresias, like a good psychotherapist, knew that if we are to
survive psychologically, we must outgrow our narcissism. If we
can accept our own transience and mortality, then we can be transformed – our self-esteem will be secure and we will be blessed
with an inner beauty. If not, we are condemned to a living or actual
death, perhaps at our own hands, as our narcissism grows ever
more demanding and insistent. We will grow a thick skin over the
vulnerability which has made us shy away from relationships.
Loving only ourselves we envy those who can relate to others, and
do our damnedest to destroy them, using our beauty as a weapon.

Shakespeare: Sonnet 62

For Shakespeare's protagonist, the act of writing is a process of
self-discovery:

Sin of self-love possesseth all mine eye,

And all my soul, and all my every part;
And for this sin there is no remedy,
It is so grounded inward in my heart.
                    (62: 1–4)

There is perhaps an ironic tone here. Is it really such a sin to love oneself? Well-founded healthy narcissism needs to be 'grounded in the heart' if it is to serve its purpose, and to keep us buoyant in the face of life's tribulations. And yet the narcissist who has eyes only for himself is lost. He is consumed with envy, constantly having to boost himself by comparing himself with others. Like Snow White's step-mother, he boasts:

Methinks no face so gracious is as mine . . .
As I all other in all worths surmount.
                    (62: 5, 8)

What is more – and here's the rub – when age creeps in, all is lost, as self-love turns to self-loathing:

But when my glass shows me myself indeed,
Beated and chapped with tanned antiquity,
Mine own self-love quite contrary I read;
Self so self-loving were iniquity.
                    (62: 9–12)

The resolution comes in the final couplet which, like Tiresias' paradox, depends on a metamorphosis:

'Tis thee, my self, that for myself I praise,
Painting my age with the beauty of thy days.
                    (62: 13–14)

The solution to narcissism is to love another. But, unlike Narcissus who longs for some separation between lover and beloved, Shakespeare highlights the merging aspect of love. 'Thee' and 'my self' form a unity in which there is no distinction between self and other, in which self-love and object-love come together, or as Freud put it:

[A] *real happy love corresponds to the primal condition* [i.e. of early infancy] *in which object-libido and ego-libido cannot be distinguished . . .*[18]

Being in love both destroys and preserves narcissism, in the practical sense that to love is to escape from oneself, but also helps one to feel good about oneself; and in the theoretical sense that self-love passes over, and so is lost, via projective identification, into the image of the beloved, where it is metamorphosed into a celebration of their existence. The 'paint' of the ageing, perhaps theatrical, narcissist – the makeup, rejuvenating creams and cosmetic surgery – is transformed by mutual happiness and the hue of the loved one.

This sonnet was probably written to Shakespeare's young and handsome noble patron. Thus while offering a partial solution to the inherent problem of narcissism – transience – it could be seen as narcissistic in that it is based on the love of a younger man by an older one, who projects all his own narcissism into youth.

In Freud's schema:

> A person may love according to the narcissistic type:
> (a) what he himself is (i.e. himself)
> (b) what he himself was
> (c) what he himself would like to be . . .[19]

Narcissus, and the poet at the start of the Sonnet are in category (a). The penultimate line of the poem suggests that all types of love – certainly all falling in love – contain an element of narcissism in that the beauty is as much in the eye of the beholder as in the separateness of the beloved. The last line suggests that movement from (a) to (b) or (c) may represent progress but still remains within the bounds of narcissism. Taken with Ovid, we can suggest that truly relational love depends on the capacity for both merging and separation. Unlike narcissistic and 'echoistic' love, such love is both eternal and transient, depending on the capacity simultaneously to trust and to cope with separation and loss.

Wilde: The Picture of Dorian Gray

All three of Freud's varieties of narcissism are amply illustrated in Wilde's novel The Picture of Dorian Gray (1891), which was doubtless stimulated by contemporary fascination with 'alters' and doppelgangers. It contains one of the classic images of narcissism – the diabolic pact in which the narcissist defeats ageing by presenting an eternally youthful face to the world, while the true horror of his inner self is depicted in a grotesque portrait, locked away in his innermost attic sanctum.

The novel starts with a series of epigrammatic statements about Art. These are essentially anti-puritanical celebrations of the 'uselessness' of art and the supreme importance of beauty as a

virtue in its own right. They represent another of the metamorphoses of narcissism. By transforming his narcissism into Art,
Wilde transcends its self-centredness, since 'artistic beauty' (as
opposed to 'real beauty') does not fade and is a form of communication. Even destructive narcissism finds justification: 'Vice and
virtue are to the artist materials for an art.'[20]

The novel centres on three main characters, each of whom
perhaps represents a facet of Wilde's personality. Dorian – the
golden boy – is an incredibly beautiful young man; Lord Henry
Wotton, a forerunner of Algernon in *The Importance of Being
Earnest*, is a witty and ruthless *roué* who takes Dorian under his
wing; Basil Hallward is the painter touched with dangerous
genius, whose portrait of Dorian has such magical properties.

Dorian gazes at his portrait, and imagines a Faustian pact:

> *How sad it is! I shall grow old, and horrible and dreadful. But
> this picture will always remain young. It will never be older
> than this particular day of June . . . If it were only the other
> way! For that I would give everything . . . I would give my soul
> for that!*[21]

The novel turns on the interplay of Wotton and Dorian's narcissism. Each is enormously excited by the other: Gray by Wotton's
intellect and social ease, Wotton by Gray's looks and innocence,
and by the fact that he is able to manipulate him at will. Dorian
falls in love with a pretty young actress, Sibyl Vane, but like a true
narcissist he has no real feelings for her, and is merely excited by
the idea of possessing someone who is so admired by everyone
else. In this way she vicariously enlarges the scope of his narcissism, and her love for him is flattering. But then, to his horror, he
realises that others find her ordinary and lacking in talent. The
mundane and socially inferior concerns of a real person begin to
intrude and he drops her. Mortified, she commits suicide, which
tips Gray into a life of debauchery and viciousness. Rosenfeld's
mafia gang has taken over his personality, and there is no escape.
While his looks remain unchanged, the secret portrait reveals the
cruelty and ugliness of his soul.

As the novel descends into Gothic horror, Hallward visits
Dorian in a vain attempt to get him to mend his ways. Gray reveals
the 'omnipotence' and grandiosity of the narcissist: 'I shall show
you my soul. You shall see the things you fancy only God can
see.'[22] Then Gray confronts Hallward with the despair of the
narcissist. Like Narcissus when he finally realises that his ever
elusive beloved is none other than himself, now Gray grasps how
his pursuit of eternal youth has condemned him to cause and to

suffer unutterable misery. Hallward offers him the chance to repent, but destructiveness takes over and Gray stabs the artist to death. Gray manages to escape the revenge of Sybil's brother, and shows some slight stirrings of redemption as he decides not to exploit another lovesick woman, Hetty Merton. He revisits the picture in the hope that this act of charity will show in a softening of his image, but it is too late: his sins cannot be wiped out so easily. His final act is to plunge the murder knife into the magical canvas. As he does this, he falls, stricken, so that in the morning his servants find an old and ugly man dead on the floor, with the portrait mysteriously intact, now depicting the bloom of youth from the moment it was painted twenty years before.

The narcissist is likely to become suicidal at the moment of narcissistic collapse. *Dorian Gray* is grotesque because in it the normal relationship between phantasy and reality is reversed. The seductiveness of Art lies in its capacity to create an artificial reality that is both an expression of narcissism and, through self-knowledge, a release from it. Thus in Seamus Heaney's poem 'Personal Helicon', he describes his fascination with wells as a child, into which, 'big-eyed Narcissus', he would stare endlessly. He compares this with his adult activity as a poet in which: 'I rhyme/To see myself, to set the darkness echoing.'[23]

Theorising Narcissism

Theories about narcissism have stimulated fierce debate within psychoanalysis and centre on two main issues. The first concerns the relationship between primary and secondary narcissism, the second about the healthiness, or otherwise, of narcissistic phenomena in general.

Primary and Secondary Narcissism

Freud differentiated *primary narcissism*, a normal developmental stage in early infancy en route to states of object relatedness, from *secondary narcissism* in which troubled individuals regressively take themselves as their primary love-object rather than another. Secondary narcissism is relatively uncontentious. It covers the range of different conditions described earlier in which people are pathologically self-preoccupied; unable to relate; approach others not as ends in themselves but as means to selfish ends; resort to 'self-soothing' behaviours such as drug addiction, deliberate self-harm or promiscuous sex; become self-defeatingly self-reliant, and so on.

The main debate has focused on the precise meaning of the term primary narcissism, and whether it refers to any real phenomenon. Freud's original idea was that the child – after the stage of auto-eroticism, but before becoming aware of his mother as a separate being, and therefore as someone to love (or 'libidinally cathect') in her own right – narcissistically invests himself with the love he had felt from his mother. Later, however, Freud used the term in a more general sense to denote an undifferentiated state of existence, occurring before the child has developed even a rudimentary ego or self.[24] In this state, the infant basks in maternal tenderness and care, and is suffused with blissful feelings of love and being loved that are neither object- or self-directed, or are perhaps both at the same time.

As psychoanalysis has moved from a libido-oriented to an inter-personal perspective this concept has been challenged. Michael Balint and Ronald Fairbairn argue that we are object related from the start of life,[25] and research by Stern on infant behaviour seems to support this view.[26] Infants interact intensively with their mothers from birth and can for example differentiate the smell of their own mother's milk from that of others in the first few hours of life. Melanie Klein argues that young babies have an ego that is actively involved in mental processes such as splitting, ideal-isation and denigration. In this schema there seems little room for the notion of primary narcissism. As Symmington roundly puts it, 'the only narcissism that exists . . . is secondary narcissism'.[27]

Even the original conceptualisation of secondary narcissism is questionable. Freud saw homosexuality, psychosis, and hypo-chondria as examples of secondary narcissism in which libido is directed inwardly to the self, rather than outwards to another. Today, few would argue that people suffering from schizophrenia do not form object relationships. They are, if anything, inter-personally over-sensitive. Similarly crude distinctions between homosexual and heterosexual types of loving are utterly outdated. Many homosexuals form mature loving relationships, and, con-versely, heterosexual object choice is not infrequently narcis-sistic, in the sense of choosing a glamorous 'trophy partner' whose main psychological role is to boost the subject's narcissism through stimulating envy in others.

Healthy versus Pathological Narcissism

In the late 1960s Kohut mounted an important challenge to the (then conventional) views on narcissism. Kohut argued that Freud's idea – of a single developmental line from narcissism to object relationship – should be abandoned. For him, the growth and shaping of normal healthy narcissism is a separate and necessary developmental process in its own right. Rather than seeing narcissism as a 'bad' thing, to be found in the mentally ill, immature and those not properly analysed, he argued that healthy narcissism is a precondition of successful living, including object relating, and that the phenomena of secondary narcissism should be considered as representing 'breakdown products' of the normal process of narcissistic maturation.

Kohut quotes Freud's famous statement that: 'a man who has been the undisputed favourite of his mother keeps for life the feeling of a conqueror; that confidence of success often induces real success', and from a chapter entitled 'Baby Worship' in Anthony Trollope's *Barchester Towers* in which a mother is looking at her little boy:

> 'Diddle, diddle . . . dum . . . hasn't he got lovely legs?' . . . Said the rapturous mother '. . . He's a little . . . darling, so he is; and he has the nicest little pink legs in all the world . . .'[28]

My own research shows how often this process appears to have gone wrong in the infancy of people destined later to suffer from narcissistic and Borderline personality disorders. Such sufferers believe either that they were unwanted, or an 'afterthought', or were adopted; that their mothers had 'terrible' labours which made them determined never to have another child; that they were responsible for their mothers' post-natal depression, or for causing their fathers to walk out. All this suggests a narcissistic self that has been blighted from birth.

When things go right, the child begins to build up a sense of himself as special and lovable, and is able to enjoy healthy exhibitionism, and grandiosity. A child aged three who jumps off a sofa onto a soft landing, shouting to his parents 'Look at me, I can fly!', will be admired with affectionate pride. When that child goes to school a year or two later, his parents will collect him from the school gate with a 'gleam' in their eye – seeing their own child standing out from the crowd as though suffused with a special light. If parents cannot love their children in this way, then the seeds of shame and self-disgust are sown.

Kohut coined the word 'selfobject' to describe this specialness of intimate relationships in which the other is neither fully part of the self, nor fully separate. A young child's parents are selfobjects, in that they are experienced as extensions of the self which the child can to some degree control. This selfobject relationship can be seen as purely illusory and defensive – a way of avoiding the traumatic realisation of the helplessness and vulnerability of childhood. For Kohut, however, selfobjecthood is an antidote to the excessive preoccupation with autonomy and separateness which he sees as pathologically endemic in Western culture.

As development proceeds, so infantile grandiosity (or 'omnipotence') and exhibitionism have to be tempered with reality and self-awareness. Kohut calls this 'optimal frustration', and states:

> *If the child is spoiled (not optimally frustrated), it retains an unusual amount of narcissism or omnipotence; and at the same time because it lacks actual skills, feels inferior. Similarly, overly frustrating experiences . . . lead to retention of omnipotence fantasies.*[29]

Getting the right balance between necessary frustration and a shameful awareness of helplessness is a skilful task, and one which, according to Kohut, is best done by more than one parent: from a classical oedipal perspective it is the father's role to frustrate the child's sense of exclusive possession of the mother. At the same time the father, or 'paternal principle' (which can equally be provided by the mother herself or a male relation), helps the child to metamorphose his grandiosity and exhibitionism into what Kohut calls the 'bipolar self', whose twin poles are the ideals to which we strive, and ambition – a word Kohut uses for the sense of real potency (as opposed to delusions of omnipotent control) in achieving those ideals. Again, it is noteworthy how frequently the childhood of Borderline patients is characterised by abusive, drunken or disappearing fathers – and often all three.

The ultimate blow to narcissism is the fact of our own death; coming to terms with death is a mark of maturity and wisdom. For Kohut, narcissism, successfully negotiated, leads to the capacity to accept mortality, to see oneself as one is without over- or underestimation, to develop a sense of creativity and humour and to trust one's intuition and empathy. The paradox of this process is that narcissism needs to be healthily established before it can be given up.

Donald Winnicott wrote famously about a child's use of a spoon during a consultation: holding it, sucking it, hitting with it.[30] Victoria Hamilton similarly emphasises the infant's acquisition of the ability to *grasp* an object as illustrating both healthy narcissism and its transcendence.[31] Grasping is a huge achievement for a small child and often seems to produce a sense of mastery and satisfaction – there is a triumphant look in the child's eye as he manages to wrest his cup from the high-chair table and bring it to his mouth for the first time. At the same time, grasping is an escape from the solipsism of infancy – an encounter with the real world that carries through into the metaphorical use of the word: to denote our ability to comprehend ideas. 'Spoiling' a child – help-ing too much, in a way that compromises autonomy – interferes with this process of discovery of the world.

In the Kohutian schema, defective narcissism is as problematic as excessive narcissism, and pathology arises when normal selfobject development is inhibited. A modicum of what Britton calls 'epistemic narcissism' – an unshakable belief in the rightness of one's own ideas – is the mark of a creative and assertive self. For Britton however, as a follower of Rosenfeld, such epistemic narcissism is essentially defensive. In 'destructive narcissism' the sufferer feels so threatened by the existence of people outside himself upon whom he depends, and feels so envious of them, that in order to maintain his omnipotent position as 'lord of all he surveys' he must eradicate the object forthwith. The pathological aspects of narcissism – treating others as a means to an end, ruthless self-centredness, lack of empathy – are all manifestations of this envious need to deny the importance of the object.

The mirror image of this thick-skinned narcissism is to be found in the utterly vulnerable patient who controls her object by remorselessly tugging at their heart strings. Leslie Sohn's metaphor of the Pied Piper who lures all the healthy children into the mountainside, leaving only the crippled boy behind, captures the way in which such patients may present only the wounded part of themselves to the therapist, while the healthy aspects are inaccessibly sequestered, emerging perhaps unwittingly in dreams and scraps of creativity.[32]

Kernberg similarly emphasises the pathological aspects of narcissism, in which he postulates a 'grandiose self comprising a fusion of real self, ideal self and ideal object, and resulting in an idealised self-sufficiency, making the subject impervious to inti-mate relationships, including analysis'. According to Kernberg, the narcissist is saying:

I do not need to fear that I will be rejected for not living up to the ideal of myself which alone makes it possible for me to be loved by the ideal person I imagine would love me. That ideal person and my ideal image of that person and my real self are all one and better than the ideal person whom I wanted to love me, so that I do not need anybody else any more.[33]

Or, as the nursery rhyme has it: 'I care for nobody, no not I, for nobody cares for me.'

The radical self-sufficiency of the narcissist is of course in direct denial of the inescapable fact of parental sex – the ultimate act to which we owe our existence and over which we have no control

('I did not ask to be born' is the despairing cry of depressed narcissism). The narcissist strives to think of himself as a 'self-made man', but may pay the price of inability to allow the 'free intercourse of unconscious parts of the mind – free association'.[34]

In sum, the narcissistic self comprises three layers of feelings: an outer denial of dependency and a consequent self-admiration; beneath which lies overwhelming oral rage and envy; and below that, a frustrated yearning for loving care.

Attachment Approaches to Narcissism

'Attachment theory' brings an empirical approach to bear on psychoanalysis.[35] It emphasises the importance of protection and security provided by the care-giver (usually the mother), for the child, who turns to a 'secure base' when threatened. Can attachment theory, with its emphasis on evidence and observation, help reconcile the Kernbergian and Kohutian perspectives? Attachment theory makes a clear distinction between healthy and sub-optimal developmental lines, which it sees as being established quite early in the course of psychological growth, so that by one year, children can be divided into those with secure and those with insecure attachment patterns. Insecure attachment is seen as a defensive response to sub-optimal parenting – a way of maintaining contact with a supposedly 'secure' base that is in fact rejecting, inconsistent or psychologically confused and unavailable. This produces the characteristic patterns of insecurity: avoidant, ambivalent (clinging), and disorganised.[36]

In secure attachment the mother is responsive and attuned. As Winnicott put it, her face is the mirror in which the infant begins to find and know itself.[37] Healthy narcissism starts from the warm responsive mirror-mother who is able accurately to reflect back the infant's feelings which form the core of the self. Through the presence of another we can come to know and accept ourselves. Where attachment is insecure, this mirroring process is compromised. The mirror may be blank and unresponsive (leading to the avoidant pattern); suffused with the parent's feelings rather than those of the infant (ambivalent pattern); or chaotic and confusing (disorganised pattern).

Narcissus and Echo could be seen as typifying the avoidant and ambivalent strategies. As her son was the product of a rape, Liriope may have had difficult feelings about Narcissus from the start. This 'ghost in the nursery'[38] meant that her helpless rage towards his father may have led to an aggressive care-giving pattern, in which Narcissus, seeking some sort of security, will have suppressed his loving feelings and tried to become emotionally self-sufficient. He may have denied the reality of parental sex that led to his existence, and in phantasy seen himself as self-generated. His beauty ensured that this relationship with himself would always be on offer, but his own suppressed rage about rejection by his mother meant that he could not trust an other and thereby establish a secure base, preferring to use people in a punishing and coercive way instead. At school or with his peers, Narcissus would have been a bully, picking on victims like Echo as his prey.

Echo, by contrast, illustrates ambivalent attachment: her self exists only in response to others, never as an active agent. Her narcissism is in this metamorphic sense anti-narcissistic. Her only hope is to cling to the object in order to achieve a modicum of security.

As development proceeds, so external attachment patterns with care-givers are internalised as representations of Self, Other, and their varying relationship (for example, the distressed self, and secure or insecure responses from the 'secure base'). These representations in turn colour relationships with significant others. This whole process depends in part on the care-giver's capacity to see the child as a separate sentient being. For all their difficulties, at least Narcissus and Echo have coherent selves, albeit based around insistent self-sufficiency or compulsive caring, respectively. For the avoidant Narcissus, this will feed into a grandiose self; for the ambivalent Echo, a depleted self. Insofar as Narcissus denies the importance of the secure base and takes himself as his object, he will demonstrate clinical features of narcissism. Echo will be vulnerable to dependency and negative narcissism; her only security, in the sense of an internal object to which she can cling, is a denigratory superego – derived from Juno's rage.

Avoidant and ambivalent strategies involve either the absorption of some of the functions of the necessary Other into the self, or the 'projection' of self-characteristics onto the clung-to object, attributing to the other one's own qualities. By contrast, without a consistent means to achieve even partial security, the 'disorganised' individual resorts to bizarre methods to approximate to a secure base. Disorganised people lack a coherent representation of the Other, and have to rely on various forms of self-splitting to create a secure base effect. In 'narcissistic' phenomena such as cutting the body with razor blades (for example, in Borderline Personality Disorder), or self-starvation (in anorexia nervosa), the body becomes an 'Other' to which the sufferer relates, albeit in a pathological way.

Psychological and to some extent physical survival depends on the ability to form a close attachment relationship and thereby to achieve an external secure base in reality, and an 'internal secure base' within the self.[39] The relationship with this secure base is healthily narcissistic, in the sense that the other is seen to be there for the benefit and security of the subject. The establishment of this base is a precondition for seeing the other as a separate being, and for having fun together and exploring the world in a companionable way – in short, for establishing an object relationship.

The clinical phenomena of narcissism can be seen as attempts to use the self as a secure base surrogate. For the hypervigilant, 'Echoic', person this means taking the body and/or the Self as the secure base, clinging to it in an escalating cycle, since the more it is clung to, the more questionable it seems as a source of security, and so the more insistent the clinging. The oblivious narcissist has taken a different route to partial security. Despairing of mutuality, he relies on coercion and power to maintain some sort of relationship with others. His own fundamental powerlessness creates unbearable envy, so, turning the tables, he evokes envy in others, and thus excites their attention, albeit from a distance.

An Integrative Perspective: The Emergence and Metamorphoses of Narcissism

Erik Erikson's model of the growth of the mind visualises a series of stages, each with its own positive or negative polarity: basic trust versus mistrust; autonomy versus shame and doubt; industry versus inferiority; generativity versus stagnation; integrity versus despair.[40] In concluding this section, I offer a similar model to integrate the various aspects of narcissism, both healthy and pathological. The stages described are necessarily artificial, and not superseded, merely added to, as development proceeds. Each can be activated at any time.

Stage 1, first year of life – secure sense of creative self in relation to a responsive other.
The crucial issue here is parental attunement: empathy, mirroring, and responsiveness. Treated with ordinary parental devotion, the child feels himself as 'special', unique, the centre of his own universe. He is a distinct sentient being, in relation to responsive others. Knowing that his word is his care-giver's command, he can begin to tolerate periods of frustration and separation. He is helped to reach out to the world and to trust that he will be met with acceptance and joy. Here the beginnings of good self-esteem, or healthy narcissism, are installed. Conversely, in the absence of parental attunement the child may experience feelings of inner emptiness, dread, insignificance, impotence and periods of

inconsolable rage. A temperamentally difficult or physically imperfect child may be at particular risk here.

Stage 2, second year of life – narcissistic investment in the body and its growing powers.
Healthy exhibitionism arises at this stage. Parents delight as their children reach developmental milestones, as they begin to walk, talk, gain sphincter control, and to explore the world. The secure base is not just a source of security but of encouragement and approbation. The child invests his body with the glow of healthy narcissism, and enjoys the gleam in the parental eye as he enters the society of kin and friends. The stressed, depressed, aggressive, rejecting, overwhelmed or resentful parent will denigrate or fail to notice her child's fumbling need to elicit gleam, leading to the beginnings of shame and self-disappointment that are so characteristic of the narcissistically wounded.

Stage 3, third year of life – beginnings of optimal frustration.
Healthy narcissism knows its limitations. A child who is narcissistically entangled with his mother cannot test his hopes and ambitions against reality. The American ideal (and illusion) of 'log cabin to White House' has to be tempered with the ability to distinguish castles in the air from real dwellings. In the Lacanian schema, the 'Nom (and 'Non') du Pere' – the name and 'no' of the father – both set limits to narcissism, but also help the child to feel that he is part of his parent's clan, and indeed the human race. Individual narcissism begins to be subsumed into social narcissism. Without this process, grandiosity and denial of reality threaten to persist.

Stage 4, adolescence – ideals and ambitions.
Healthy adolescents have their heroes, hopes, ambitions, fervent beliefs and secret dreams. The narcissistically wounded adolescent is in despair and depression, seeing the world as doomed, oppressed by death, and either defying it with risky behaviour or shrinking from it into regressive avoidance. The body becomes a source of pleasure and pride, or else a hated encumbrance that fails to measure up to impossible ideals. An outpouring of creative energy is a mark of healthy self-belief, at this stage not needing to be evaluated or measured up. Rage and destructiveness express narcissistic feelings of failure to find a mirroring ideal.

Stage 5, adulthood – transfer of narcissism to the next generation.
Omnipotence lessens as real potency takes over. The healthy adult begins to know his or her strengths and limitations. He feels good

about himself, his relationships, family and society. His narcissistic hopes are invested in his children. Projects are conceived
and brought to fruition. Frustrated ideals are replaced with love of
truth. Failure is met with acceptance. Meanwhile, the unhealthy
narcissist consolidates his self-centred world, either exciting envy
or enviously undermining the possibility of intimacy with others.
Sufficient unto himself, he becomes more and more self-absorbed
– either hyper-vulnerable to every slight, or brutally bullying his
way to a 'top' whose twin peaks are his own self-aggrandisement
and the denigration of others.

Stage 6, later life – the getting of wisdom.
For Kohut, the installation of healthy narcissism together with
optimal frustration sets an individual on a road that leads to the
ability to see their world as it is, to accept the reality of one's own
death, to trust one's intuition and empathy, find sources of creativity and humour, and ultimately to achieve a measure of wisdom. In
the absence of these metamorphoses, the onset of middle age and
beyond raises feelings of terror at one's own inevitable extinction.
Depression and hopelessness become ever present possibilities.
Narcissism may manifest itself in increasing hypochondria,
endless ruminating on past achievements or failures, or a coercive
tyranny in which power, rather than mutuality, dominates relationships.

In this health/pathology model, the task of therapy, whatever stage
is presented, is to find the seeds of healthy narcissistic strivings,
and to reduce the impact of pathological narcissism.

The Psychotherapeutic Treatment of
Narcissistic Difficulties

Critics of psychotherapy – perhaps motivated by the puritanism
that Wilde so outrageously flouted – accuse it of being self-
indulgent, a luxury occupation for those who have nothing better
to do with their lives: in other words, of fostering rather than
helping to overcome narcissism. Certainly, at its worst, psychotherapy can encourage aspects of psychological life that are
typical of narcissism itself: self-preoccupation and interminable
regression, an exaggerated sense of entitlement, unrealistic hopes
that all past wrongs can be put to rights given sufficient therapeutic love and empathy. This tendency within psychotherapy to
become the 'disease of which it purports to be the cure' is yet
another of narcissism's metamorphoses, the mirror image of
Wilde's self-conscious use of narcissism as an artistic device to

overcome narcissism. A more positive view, one which Carl Jung was fond of advocating when contrasting Western with Eastern paths to enlightenment, is that it is necessary to find one's Self before contemplating the possibility of transcending it, and, as the popular phrase has it, you must love yourself before you can begin to love others.

Working with narcissistic patients is difficult in many ways. Here are three vignettes illustrating some of the day-to-day dilemmas they raise for therapists.

Vignette 1:
Bill, a 40-year-old barrister, came into hospital following a near-fatal suicide attempt. His career had been hugely successful, but the pleasures of success never seemed to last, and his death-wish came out of a deep sense of dissatisfaction in his marriage, and the realisation of just how cut off he felt from his wife. This was a typical mid-life narcissistic crisis. A great sportsman, bon viveur, womaniser and money-maker, his life felt empty and meaningless. He was referred for psychoanalysis, but it was holiday time and no one could see him for several weeks. He was furious – filled with narcissistic rage. What right had the analysts to be away when he needed help *now*, not in a few weeks' time? If that was the way he was to be treated, let his suicide be on his carers' heads. His ward psychiatrist rang round again, spending quite a long time on the phone, but still to no avail. Bill insisted that he be seen. Why could not the psychiatrist see Bill himself? What was the psychiatrist to do? By agreeing to see Bill, would he be merely pandering to his own narcissism and, like all Bill's conquests, dancing to his self-serving tune? But by refusing to comply with his request, would he not be reinforcing Bill's deep-rooted feeling of not being listened to, throwing him back once more into alienated self-sufficiency?

Vignette 2:
Caroline was both hypervigilant and oblivious. Adopted, she had two older sisters who were her parents' obvious favourites. Her mother became bed-ridden when Caroline was thirteen and from then on she was expected to wait on her, and to satisfy her father's sexual needs. She had major depressive breakdowns in her thirties and forties, and eventually entered weekly supportive psycho-therapy which kept her out of hospital and brought some stability into her life. Ending treatment seemed difficult, as she idealised both therapist and therapy, and the compromise was to move to monthly sessions. One of Caroline's characteristic patterns was to 'bolt' when she felt anxious or rejected; on one occasion she took a major overdose and locked herself in the boot of her car, and was

only saved by a police helicopter search. Naturally these episodes, usually much milder, caused huge worry to her husband and children whenever she disappeared, and they would immediately start to look for her, not stopping until she was either found or reappeared of her own accord. In one session she was describing a recent example of these episodes, emphasising how unsympathetic her husband had been when eventually he found her. After many years of supportive work, the therapist was suddenly filled with boredom and weary irritation. Without much thought he suggested that perhaps her long-suffering husband was furious with her; he asked her to think about how it must feel for him when she disappeared. Caroline blanched, her lip trembled, she looked frightened and angry, as though she was about to walk out. There was five minutes' silence. Eventually, she decided to stay and the session ended without mishap. At the end she had to pay her bill, and asked to borrow the therapist's pen. She commented on what a nice pen it was – without thinking, the therapist found himself offering it to her as an unwitting present.

Here we see how the thin-skinned narcissist's anger is often projected into those around her; how difficult and dangerous confrontation can be, how important it is to maintain therapeutic potency, how often the 'father-principle' is discarded in favour of a regressive 'maternal' collusion, and how guilty it can make the therapist feel when he does confront such patients.

Vignette 3:
Peter, who had spent most of his childhood in children's homes, was a classic and extreme case of oblivious narcissism, who had lived a life of ruthless selfishness until his late forties. It was not his depression, violence, alcoholism, lawbreaking habits, loneliness, or declining physical attractiveness to women, but a thin-skinned hypochondria which had led his GP, who had exhausted every pill and physical specialist, to refer him for psychiatric help. As he walked down the corridor to the consulting room, he would invariably start each session by asking in a way that was at once challenging, aggressive, deferential and defensive: 'How are you, doctor?' Finding a way to interpret this apparent concern as another aspect of his narcissism – a need to control the therapeutic situation from the start, as a defence against the threat of relationship formation which being in therapy implied – without alienating and putting him down, was a tough technical challenge.

These examples illustrate some of the common themes of therapy with such people: seductive excitation of the therapist's narcissism; rage and demandingness that can easily stimulate rejection, thereby reinforcing the patient's sense of being let down by everyone but himself; and boredom, again leading to a rejecting neglect of the patient's underlying misery.

Kohut and Kernberg advocate very different ways of handling these issues. Kohut describes three characteristic patterns of transference in therapy with narcissistic patients: mirror transference, idealising transference, and 'twinship' transference. His advice to therapists is along the lines of acceptance and against premature interpretation. As W.B. Yeats put it:

> *I have spread my dreams under your feet;*
> *tread softly because you tread on my dreams.*[41]

The patient must feel able to invest the therapist and therapy with their hopes and dreams. 'Persecutory therapists' who interpret these phantasies as defensive too early and too crashingly, will merely reinforce the narcissistic wound which has led to the need for them in the first place.[42] Kernberg, however, sees dangers in collusion, and emphasises the denigration that is the accompanying shadow of idealisation.[43] He stresses the importance of dealing with negative transference and assisting the patient to develop appropriate concern and guilt for the objects that he uses so thoughtlessly. Patients must be helped to deal with their rage and disappointment, and should not be misled into thinking that therapy can in itself undo past wrongs. Being in therapy stirs up the basic conflicts and deficiencies that have already led to a narcissistic superstructure in the personality. This will arouse a measure of resistance at best, and at worst suicidal feelings. As Rosenfeld puts it:

> *When he is faced with the reality of being dependent on the analyst, standing for his parents, particularly the mother, he would prefer to die, to be non-existent, to deny the fact of his birth, and also to destroy his analytic progress and insight representing the child in himself, which he feels the analyst, representing the parents, has created.*[44]

Kernberg acknowledges, however, that for some patients this will prove too much and that in these cases, in order to maintain a therapeutic alliance, a more supportive approach may be necessary. I end this essay by listing some key principles that I have found can help in working with narcissism in its various manifestations.

• The therapist must be able to accept the idealisation of his relationship with the patient while at the same time not being afraid to challenge the patient's denial of his covert denigration of others' feelings and need for omnipotent control.

- In challenging narcissism, the therapist must guard against using his own position of power and narcissistic superiority to bully and reinforce the patient's low self-esteem.
- A collusive relationship of mutual admiration must also be eschewed.
- Supporting a patient's narcissism can be a legitimate therapeutic strategy, especially in counteracting compulsive negative narcissism and self-denigration. The therapist must find a positive 'spin' to counterbalance attempts by the patient to do himself down.
- Disillusionment in the therapist and therapy is healthy, but should be gradual rather than traumatic. In time-limited therapy, the ending should be discussed and interpreted right from the start.
- The therapist must be able to set limits both to the demandingness of the thin-skinned and the fury of the thick-skinned narcissist.
- Creativity, humour, playfulness and the use of dreams are all positive manifestations of transformed narcissism and are crucial ingredients of therapy.
- Curiosity about the therapist may be part of the omnipotent need to control or to enviously cut him down to size, but is also a potentially healthy escape from self-preoccupation into wishing to know about the world.
- Gratitude comes late in the therapy of narcissism.
- The gap between actual and ideal self is distorted in narcissism. In the ambivalent, 'Echoic', negative, hypervigilant type, the gap is too great. In the 'Narcissistic', thick-skinned, oblivious type, there is fusion of Ego and Ego-Ideal. The therapeutic task is to narrow the gap in the former, helping the sufferer to find and accept good things about himself; in the latter to open it up, helping the patient to come to terms with loss and failure.
- The two types are not mutually exclusive. Beneath the thick skin of the narcissist, there is huge vulnerability and longing for closeness; below the fragility and pitifulness of the hypervigilant type, there is often ruthless self-centredness.
- The narcissist seeks his object in the mirror, but is doomed to disappointment as the mirror is cold and lifeless and cannot rescue him from his loneliness. Therapy can transform narcissism through 'mirroring' – the playful, warm, responsive mirroring of the attuned Other.

In conclusion, Freud, narcissistically perhaps, saw psychoanalysis as the third of the three great blows that civilisation has dealt to man's narcissism: the Copernican revolution, which displaced the earth from the centre of the universe; the Darwinian revolution, which dethroned Man from his superiority over the rest of Nature; and the psychoanalytic, in which the conscious mind is demoted to a servant of the unconscious forces that rule our lives. To this, an attachment perspective might add a fourth blow: the understanding of how, at a very fundamental level, our prized individuality arises out of our relationships with others. In each case, the miracle of transformed narcissism leads to deeper understanding: we see the beauty and simplicity of the universe; realise the extent to which we are linked with, rather than excluded from, nature; understand how we are psychologically all of a piece; and that, rather than divided and isolated selves, we are inescapably interconnected.

Jeremy Holmes is Consultant Psychiatrist/Psychotherapist in North Devon, Senior Lecturer in Psychotherapy at Exeter University, and Chair of the Psychotherapy Faculty of the Royal College of Psychiatrists. His interests are in attachment theory, the integration of psychotherapy within psychiatry and the treatment of severe personality disorder.

Notes

1. Rycroft, C., *Critical Dictionary of Psychoanalysis*, London: Penguin, 1972.
2. See Lasch, C., *The Culture of Narcissism*, New York: Doubleday, 1979.
3. Britton, R., *Belief and Imagination*, London: Routledge, 1998.
4. Rosenfeld, H., *Psychotic States: A Psycho Analytic Approach*, New York: International Universities Press, 1965.
5. Kohut, H., *The Analysis of the Self*, New York: International Universities Press, 1971.
6. Freud, S., 'On Narcissism' (1914), in *Standard Edition of the Complete Psychological Works of Sigmund Freud*, vol. 14, trans. J. Strachey, London: Hogarth Press, 1953–73, p. 91.
7. Abraham, K., *Selected Papers of Karl Abraham*, London: Hogarth Press, 1973.
8. Tolstoy, L., quoted in Abraham, quoted in Hamilton, V., *Narcissus and Oedipus*, London: Routledge, 1982, pp. 122–3.
9. Mollon, P., *The Fragile Self*, London: Whurr, 1993.
10. Freud, S., op. cit., p. 91.
11. Fisher-Mamblona, H., 'On the Evolution of Attachment-disordered Behaviour', in *Attachment and Human Development*, vol. 2, 2000, pp. 8–21.
12. Gabbard, G., *Psychodynamic Psychiatry in Clinical Practice*, Washington: American Psychiatric Press, 1996.
13. Bateman, A., 'Thick- and Thin-skinned Organisations and Enactment in Borderline and Narcissistic Disorders', in *International Journal of Psycho-Analysis*, vol. 79, 1998, pp. 13–26.
14. Hughes, T., *Tales from Ovid*, London: Faber and Faber, 1997.
15. Ovid, in Hughes, T., op. cit.
16. Ibid.
17. Ibid.
18. Freud, S., op. cit., p. 100.
19. Ibid., p. 90.
20. Wilde, O., *The Picture of Dorian Gray* (1891), London: Penguin, 1985.
21. Ibid., p. 31.
22. Ibid., p. 168.
23. Heaney, S., *Opened Ground: Poems 1966–1996*, London: Faber and Faber, 1998, p. 15.
24. Laplanche, J. and Pontalis, J-B., *The Language of Psychoanalysis*, London: Hogarth Press, 1980.
25. Balint, M., *The Basic Fault*, London: Hogarth Press, 1968; Fairbairn, R., *Collected Papers*, London: Hogarth Press, 1952.
26. Stern, D., *The Interpersonal World of the Infant*, New York: Basic Books, 1985.
27. Symmington, N., *Emotion and Spirit*, London: Karnac, 1993, p. 120.
28. Both quotes taken from Kohut, H., in Morrison, A. (ed.), *Essential Papers on Narcissism*, New York: New York University Press, 1986, pp. 69–70.
29. Kohut, H. and Seitz, P., 'Three Self Psychologies – or One?', in Goldberg, A. (ed.), *The Evolution of Self Psychology: Progress in Self Psychology*, vol. 7, Hillsdale, NY: Analytic Press, 1963, p. 20.

30. Winnicott, D., *Playing and Reality,* London: Penguin, 1971.
31. Hamilton, V., op. cit.
32. Sohn, L., 'Narcissistic Organisation, Projective Identification, and the Formation of the "Identificate"', in *International Journal of Psycho-Analysis*, vol. 66, 1985, pp. 201–13.
33. Kernberg, O., in Morrison, op. cit., pp. 134–5.
34. Mollon, P., op. cit., p. 109.
35. See Bowlby, J., *A Secure Base*, London: Routledge, 1988.
36. Holmes, J. and Harrison-Hall, A., forthcoming, 2002.
37. Winnicott, D., *The Maturational Processes and the Facilitating Environment*, London: Hogarth Press, 1968.
38. Fraiberg, S., Adelson, E. and Shapiro, V., 'Ghosts in the Nursery: A Psychoanalytic Approach to Impaired Infant–Mother Relationships', *Journal of American Academy of Child Psychologists*, vol. 14, 1975, pp. 387–422.
39. Holmes, J., *The Search for a Secure Base*, London: Brunner–Routledge, 2001.
40. Erikson, E., *Identity, Youth and Crisis*, London: Faber and Faber, 1968.
41. Yeats, W.B. , 'He Wishes for the Cloths of Heaven', in *Collected Poems*, London: Macmillan, 1972.
42. Meares, R. and Hobson, R., 'The Persecutory Therapist', in *British Journal of Medical Psychology*, vol. 50, 1977, pp. 349–59.
43. Kernberg, O., *Borderline Conditions and Pathological Narcissism*, New York: New York Universities Press, 1975.
44. Rosenfeld, H., 'A Clinical Approach to the Psychoanalytic Theory of the Life and Death Instincts: An Investigation into the Aggressive Aspects of Narcissism', in Spillius, E. (ed.), *Melanie Klein Today*, vol. 1, London: Routledge, 1988, p. 247.

Further Reading

Abraham, K., *Selected Papers of Karl Abraham*, London: Hogarth Press, 1973.
Balint, M., *The Basic Fault*, London: Hogarth Press, 1968.
Britton, R., *Belief and Imagination*, London: Routledge, 1998.
Dawkins, R., *The Selfish Gene*, London: Butterworth, 1979.
Erikson, E., *Identity, Youth and Crisis*, London: Faber and Faber, 1968.
Fairbairn, R., *Collected Papers*, London: Hogarth Press, 1952.
Freud, S., *Three Essays on Sexuality* (1905), in *Standard Edition of the Complete Psychological Works of Sigmund Freud* (hereafter *SE*), vol. 7, trans. J. Strachey, London: Hogarth Press, 1953–73.
——*Leonardo Da Vinci and a Memory of his Childhood* (1910), in *SE*, vol. 9, 1953–73.
——'On Narcissism' (1914), in *SE*, vol. 14.
Gabbard, G., *Psychodynamic Psychiatry in Clinical Practice*, Washington: American Psychiatric Press, 1996.
Hamilton, V., *Narcissus and Oedipus*, London: Routledge, 1982.
Holmes, J., *The Search for a Secure Base*, London: Brunner–Routledge, 2001.
Kernberg, O., *Borderline Conditions and Pathological Narcissism*, New York: New York Universities Press, 1975.

Kohut, H., *The Analysis of the Self*, New York: International Universities Press, 1971.

——*How does Analysis Cure?*, Chicago: University of Chicago Press, 1984.

Lasch, C., *The Culture of Narcissism*, New York: Doubleday, 1979.

Mollon, P., *The Fragile Self*, London: Whurr, 1993.

Morrison, A. (ed.), *Essential Papers on Narcissism*, New York: New York University Press, 1986.

Rosenfeld, H., *Psychotic States: A Psycho Analytic Approach*, New York: International Universities Press, 1965.

Spillius, E. (ed.), *Melanie Klein Today*, vol. 1, London: Routledge, 1988.

Stern, D., *The Interpersonal World of the Infant*, New York: Basic Books, 1985.

Symmington, N., *Emotion and Spirit*, London: Karnac, 1993.

Winnicott, D., *Playing and Reality*, London: Penguin, 1971.

——*The Maturational Processes and the Facilitating Environment*, London: Hogarth Press, 1968.

7

Phobia

Ivan Ward

A Bridge Too Far: The Phobic Reaction

Suppose you are crossing Hungerford Bridge in London with someone who suffers from Gephyrophobia – a fear of crossing bridges. As you walk from Embankment underground station and ascend the stone steps which take you onto the bridge, your companion starts to talk nervously about the prospect of crossing it. You arrive on the bridge and his body begins to stiffen, his head held very still as he stares straight ahead. After a few steps he begins to sweat and holds onto your hand, clutching it tighter and tighter as you guide him across. You notice that he cannot help glancing downwards into the water, especially through the gap between the pedestrian bridge and the railway bridge to which it is attached. Unmistakable signs of panic are taking him over as you arrive at the centre of your crossing – profuse sweating, rapid breathing and heartbeat, clenched muscles and a wide-eyed look of fear. You try to say something to calm him down. 'Don't talk!', he says. All of his concentration is being mustered to take on the task in hand. Suddenly he exhales deeply and his body relaxes. He releases his grip on your hand and starts to walk more confidently forward. 'What's happened?', you ask. 'It's okay once I've got halfway over', he says, and you are left pondering the origin and development of such a phobia.

Helter Skelter: Science of the Irrational

Most people do not question why a child is scared of the dark, or why a person hates tomatoes. We slide the emotional response and the putative stimulus together. 'I hate tomatoes.' In the simple declarative we posit a causal relation between the psychological output 'hate' and the culinary input 'tomatoes'. If someone comes along and asks 'Why?', we feel uncomfortable, not wanting our likes and dislikes to be scrutinised too closely. Freud realised that the supposed chain of causality was little more than an illusion. Inputs and outputs did not really 'add up'. By questioning the equation between 'stimulus' and 'response' he announced the influence of unconscious factors in the mind.

Ernest Jones, Freud's disciple and biographer, listed three senses in which things did not add up in the physiology and psychology of anxiety reactions:

1. A 'disproportion between the external stimulus and the response'.
2. A 'disharmony between bodily and mental manifestations'.
3. An 'internal disharmony' within the body or mind itself.

The first of these is the most obvious. We find it in some of our greatest literary creations. Scholars have spent endless hours debating the reasons for Hamlet's excessive overreaction to, and preoccupation with, his father's death. Doesn't he realise that fathers die all the time? Hamlet's reaction is quite out of proportion to the stated facts as they are presented, and this, says T.S. Eliot, is the reason why *Hamlet* is not a great work of art. It doesn't add up. It's out of proportion. There is no 'objective correlative' that makes it make sense.[1] But what is a failure of art for Eliot is proof of the unconscious for Freud. The lack of proportion between the experiential input and the excessive reactive output is precisely what indicates the influence of another level of meaning and determination, both in the text and in the reader.

And the same is true of phobias. In stating the obvious – that crossing a bridge is not a death-defying endeavour – psychoanalysis justifies its concept of the unconscious and its mode of inquiry through free association. If it frightens you to death nevertheless, there must be something else going on.

But what if the danger were real? Suppose the bullets were flying, the bombs were dropping and the hand grenades exploding all around you? Writing between the wars, Ernest Jones was not very sympathetic. 'How much distress, for instance', he inquires,

> *should be allotted as normal for someone exposed to an air raid during the war, or still more for someone exposed to the appalling conditions of the actual front, without recourse being had to pathological factors?*

Warming to his theme, he continues:

> *Generosity is prone in such cases to make considerable allowances for the situation and to pass over responses of*

anxiety as natural and inevitable which perhaps a more critical mood would scrutinise more strictly.[2]

This might seem insensitive; it also points to a change of focus. Little more than a decade later, Anna Freud opened her residential nurseries for children who had been bombed out in the Blitz. She discovered that it was not the bombs and destruction of their homes that was traumatic for the children, but the separation from – and worries about – their parents.[3]

The second point is less easy to notice. There is something out of kilter between the mind and the body. They don't seem to be reading the same script. A politician may give a brilliantly controlled speech at his party conference, yet find himself drenched in sweat or suffering palpitations. In his mind there is no fear. Only in his body does fear ooze out from every pore. Or let's say you take a child to a theme park. She is anticipating a 'scary' ride that she has heard about or seen before. It's really scary. You realise that her excited talk is not relieving the tension, it is turning the screw of her anxious expectation. She is winding herself up. The signs of fear build to a crescendo while waiting in the inevitable queue. She doesn't want to go on the ride, she wants to go home. She is too scared. Taking the Ernest Jones approach, you ignore her protests and drag her onto the ride. But once on board you realise that, far from being consumed with fear, her screams and bodily reactions correspond to excitement and pleasure. 'Can we go again?', she says, as you disembark.

In his book *Affect and Emotion*, Graham Music recounts an experiment in which mothers leave their toddlers suddenly in a room. Some children cry and get upset, others seem hardly to notice the departure or return of their mothers.

Yet, when the pulse rate, adrenalin and cortisol levels of both groups are measured, we see that all have similar physiological reactions to their mothers' disappearance.[4]

The third disharmony identified by Jones is a kind of fragmentation of mental faculties. He calls it an 'inco-ordination' in the mind itself, and notices that when you are really frightened there is a curious mixture of over-excitation with paralysis. My friend walking across the bridge neither plays dead nor runs away. His body is at once stiff and unresponsive, yet agitated. He feels nauseous. His head is spinning. He is not ready for action, he is just ready to implode. He is frightened of something, yet his attention is not directed to any particular source of danger. He finds himself in a strange mental state that makes no sense as far as biological survival is concerned. It doesn't add up in the ledger of natural selection.

The phobic reaction contains elements of all the incompatibilities, disharmonies and inconsistencies that Jones describes. A phobia does not 'make sense'. It is an *irrational* fear. And that is the defining feature that opens it up to a science of the irrational – psychoanalysis.

Charles and Alfred: Theories of Phobia

It is not easy to say why, in a particular situation, a phobia is produced rather than an inhibition, or a somatic symptom, or a diffuse state of anxiety. Psychical events have many causes – 'overdetermined', Freud calls it. For any developmental outcome there is a complex play of forces clamouring to be expressed, and it is impossible to predict how the dice will eventually fall. Nevertheless, phobias and phobic phenomena are typical during certain periods of childhood, and adult phobias can often be traced back to earlier forms which preceded them. There are two common non-psychoanalytic theories of phobias which have achieved the status of 'common sense'. The first is a biological theory which assumes that phobias – such as the fear of spiders or snakes or high places – are leftovers from our evolutionary past and refer to real dangers faced by our ancestors.

> *Most of us have a sense of repulsion if we meet with a snake. Snake phobia, we might say, is a universal human characteristic; and Darwin has described most impressively how he could not avoid feeling fear of a snake that struck at him, even though he was protected by a thick sheet of glass.*[5]

Freud's sympathy with the argument should not blind us to the fact that jumping away from a striking snake is not the equivalent of a snake phobia. Genetic explanations are also limited in scope, unable to explain the multitude of phobias that actually exist. Further, since we succeed in passing on our genes if we respond to danger in an appropriate way, it is difficult to see how the genetic argument can account for the curious incapacity that overwhelms the person with a phobia when faced with the object of their fear.

The second non-psychoanalytic view is a simple 'trauma' theory, which has achieved the ultimate credibility of being the basis of a BBC television series.[6] A child is afraid of dogs because, when he was little, a dog jumped up to his push-chair and frightened him. Another is worried that Red Indians will attack her at home after she saw the film *Calamity Jane*. The phobia is a conditioned response to traumatic experience. In the post-Freudian films of Alfred Hitchcock, numerous characters exhibit phobias. The trauma theory is enlisted to explain their motivation or to effect narrative resolution. Thus the eponymous heroine of *Marnie* has a murderous childhood secret expressed in her fear of lightning and the colour red; the policeman who let his partner drop and suffers ever after from a fear of heights, falls for the wrong girl in *Vertigo*; the psychiatrist without a past unaccountably fears the white of a tablecloth in *Spellbound*. When Hitchcock himself was asked if he had ever been really frightened about anything, he would simply reply: 'Always.'[7] On other occasions he would tell a story from his childhood. He was always terrified of being alone, but at six years old, after committing some domestic misdemeanour, his stern father sent him to the police station with a note. The duty officer dutifully read the note and locked young Alfred in a cell for some minutes. He was scared of policemen after that, but the experience taught him an important lesson in life: don't get arrested.

The Birds: Representing the Inner World

The trauma idea seems a plausible explanation until it is discovered that, for instance, the phobia only develops some years after the alleged traumatic incident, or that the incident itself is only known through information given by parents. Tracing the phobia back to the traumatic scenario, we often find a more complex synthesis of factors. In one example, a paralysing fear of birds and feathers was linked to the moment when a bird flew into a room and could not get out. A child was with her grandmother, unable to cope as the terrified bird flew around the room bumping into things and shedding feathers across the floor. The child, too, became terrified, observing the frantic efforts of the bird to escape and her grandmother's flustered attempts to help it.[8] Psycho-analysts would unpack the elements of this story and give due weight to each: the factor of helplessness, the absence of the mother, the grandmother's fear, the loss of parts of the bird's body, the fear of attack, the sense of being trapped, the bird as embodiment of aggression, the association of birds (in some cultures and folklore) with death, and so on. The traumatic incident is not seen as an aberrant intrusion into the calm waters of a happy childhood, but as part of the wider story of the person's emotional life, with its inevitable storms and dangerous currents of feeling.

Birds fly around the room in Hitchcock's masterpiece, *The Birds*, based on a story by Daphne du Maurier.[9] It is a drama in which the principal male character is relegated to the margins of the narrative. Although the (dead) father is significant, it is relationships between women that pivot the story around the ineffectual lawyer 'Mitch' Brenner. If 'Hitch' himself was scared of policemen and the law, it was his mother and her surrogates who dominated his life. 'Even after his marriage, his mother often went along on vacation with him and his wife, and on those occasions he was more concerned with her than with his wife.'[10]

In the story, a younger woman and an older woman – a mother – struggle over possession of the son. When socialite Melanie Daniels follows Mitch to his home town of Bodega Bay with a gift of lovebirds for his younger sister Cathy, she brings with her a plague of biblical proportions. The aggressively attacking birds testify to something within the emotional dynamics of the story. Most often this is interpreted as the mother's aggression unleashed in response to a threat that the sexually expressive Melanie represents. However, with all due respect to Oedipus, this is not a simple Oedipal drama. Struggles within the dyadic relationship between mother and daughter take centre stage, as well as the mother's vulnerability and fear of abandonment.

In the following scene, Melanie and Annie, the local teacher and an ex-girlfriend of Mitch, are discussing his mother Lydia:

Annie: *You know, her attitude nearly drove me crazy. I simply couldn't understand it. When I got back to San Francisco I spent days trying to figure out just what I'd done to displease her.*

Melanie: *And what had you done?*

Annie: *Nothing! I simply existed. So what was the answer? A jealous woman, right? A clinging possessive mother.* (She shakes her head.) *Wrong. With all due respect to Oedipus, I don't think that was the case at all.*

Melanie: *Then what was it?*

Annie: *Lydia liked me you see. That was the strange part of it. In fact, now that I am no longer a threat, we're very good friends.*

Melanie: *Then why did she object to you?*

Annie: *Because she was afraid.*

Melanie: *Afraid you'd take Mitch? ...*

Annie: *No, I don't think so. She's not afraid of losing her son, you see. She's only afraid of being abandoned.*

But it's not hard to see the consequences of defiance of the mother. Later in the same scene, Melanie asks Annie if she should go to Cathy's party.

Melanie: *Do you think I should go?*

Annie: *That's up to you.*

Melanie: *It's really up to Lydia, isn't it?*

Annie: *Never mind Lydia. Do you want to go?*

Melanie (firmly): *Yes.*

Annie: *Then go.*

The room is silent. Melanie nods, slowly, and then smiles . . .

Suddenly into the silence, comes a THUMP outside, startling them both. The thump is made by a seagull that has smashed itself into the door.

The four central female figures form a complex network of attachments – Melanie, Lydia, Annie and Cathy. Each of them could be responsible for the birds. There is rage against mothers (from Melanie), against daughters (from Lydia) or siblings (from Annie), and fear of abandonment in all of them. In the birds, there are more than birds: they represent a dimension of unconscious female experience. They demonstrate the underlying conflict in the mother–daughter bond, and potential dangers to negotiate in the process of growing up. Similar themes are found in *Snow White*, *Cinderella* and many other mythic confrontations between mothers and daughters.

Psychoanalytic explanations of phobia are thus concerned with the inner world. In particular they assign a determining influence to 'phantasy', 'anxiety' and 'psychic conflict', especially the conflict between love and aggression (ambivalence). A woman with a 'worm phobia' did not report any traumatic experience. But she did report a tormenting phantasy from her sixth year – that she was buried alive and exposed to worms.

The Lion, the Witch and the Wardrobe: Imaginary Dangers

The description of my friend crossing Hungerford Bridge clearly shows a phobia in its capacity as an 'irrational fear'. The phobic person does not really know why he is afraid, any more than a person who laughs at a joke knows why he is laughing. It seems silly to say: 'I am afraid of crossing bridges.' Recognition of the 'irrationality', however, makes little difference to its psychical reality for the phobic person. In the grip of the phobic reaction, the phobic individual exists in a peculiar state of knowing something and not knowing it at the same time. The phobic object exists in two mental registers at once, both equally real to the person. Discussing the common phobias of childhood, Anna Freud recounts the story of a little girl with a fear of lions:

> *This child countered the well-meant assurances of her father that lions could not climb up to her bedroom by saying plaintively that, of course, her father talked of real lions who could not climb, but her own lions were more than capable . . .*[11]

In phobias, as with all neuroses, we move in 'the no-man's land between reality and fantasy'.[12] The child believes avidly in the reality of the phobic symbol, despite the strength of his intellectual assessment. Children, too, can be stupid. Such premature debility of the child's intellect led Freud to assume that a phobia was not a simple fear of an external object or situation which could be escaped through avoidance, but a response to a threat located within the mind. A child who avoids school because of bullying is in a different situation from one who avoids school because some inchoate panic overwhelms him at the school gates. He just hates school. Both are 'school-phobic' in the descriptive sense – they both avoid school – but only the latter is school-phobic in what Freud calls the 'dynamic' sense, in which the fear is fuelled from within. In the case of the school-phobic child, we might find an intolerable fear that the mother will disappear or die when he leaves her. Hard and fast distinctions are difficult to make in practice, but from a theoretical point of view it is useful to regard phobias as responses to the demands of the inner world.

Having taken this step from the outer world to the inner, we are no longer surprised to find inconsistencies in the matter of knowing and not knowing, or questions of belief. Dreams are a nightly reminder that we can believe in almost anything. Have you ever, while dreaming, said to yourself, 'It's only a dream'? Or woken yourself up and started again? We know we are dreaming when we are dreaming, yet inside the dream its contents carry conviction. We know and do not know at the same time. We believe in a world populated by objects and experiences that have not, will not and cannot happen in reality. Philosophers discuss the truth conditions attached to the King of France's beard (there is no King of France), but in our dream we may be more concerned with the pea soup that he has inadvertently spilled down it.

If our mind harbours kings and princes that do not exist, it also harbours demons and goblins. In the dreams of children we see fears embodied, given private form in a manner that resonates with the more public representations of myth and fairy tale. Consider these dreams of a normal seven-year-old girl:

Dream 1

I was in a room in the dark; it was pitch black, but I could still see. The room was guarded by monsters and I escaped with other people (I was the leader), but all the other people got caught. I ran into an alley, there were lots of doors and monsters all around. In the alley was an old witch. In my head I heard the words, 'No one who goes down this alley ever comes out . . . Ha, ha, ha . . .', then I saw a flash of light that lighted up the old witch's face that was really frightening.

Dream 2

I went through a door. It was an old house that looked like a museum. When I went in, everything was yellow and there were men in yellow suits swinging on trapezes and they were laughing (in a malevolent way). On the floor there were all these spiders and there were dips in the floor that the spiders were crawling about in. I kept running but I tripped over and landed to see a really big spider – like the queen spider – right by my face, and I screamed.

Dream 3

I was being chased by something and I came to a cliff. I thought I was going to fall off it, but I jumped off and flew away. I flew for hours. It was really fun and a really good dream.

We are not surprised to hear of dreams populated by witches and spiders and devouring monsters. Few of us are so detached from our childhood selves that this strikes us as an alien experience. Psychoanalysts would see in the witch figure a representation of the mother – the 'bad mother' as we created her in phantasy.[13] Just as the goddesses of antiquity were both deities of creation and destruction,[14] so the mother may be an object of both love and fear. Mothers change all the time. We would like to imagine that nothing could be more stable than the figure of the mother on whom we base our sense of security. Yet they frustrate us and torment us as well as relieve and protect us. Children love them, fear them and fear *for* them.

In Donald Winnicott's famous case of 'The Piggle', the frightening figures of the dream world spill over into the waking world of a two-and-a-half-year-old girl. After her mother's confinement and the birth of her sister Susan, Gabrielle's personality began to change, displaying considerable anxiety and a lack of freedom in her play. She called to her parents till late at night, tormented by elaborate fantasies, unable to go to sleep. 'She has a black mummy and daddy', explained her parents:

> The black mummy comes in after her at night and says: 'Where are my yams?' . . . Sometimes she is put into the toilet by the black mummy. The black mummy, who lives in her tummy, and who can be talked to on the telephone, is often ill and difficult to make better.[15]

In a subsequent letter, her father said: 'Going to bed created a major scene – as happens quite often now. She says she is frightened of the black mummy coming after her.'[16] But if the 'black mummy' only exists in the realm of the imagination, if it only has reality from the inside, then the question arises: of what is she really frightened? 'She seems to be suffering greatly from what was once called "a sense of sin"', wrote her father.[17]

The Naked Diner: Psychical Mechanisms for Phobia Formation

It should not have taken so long to establish the obvious: that it is not the phobic object which is really frightening; and that the source of fear is inside the mind. Such a conclusion could have been predicted on logical grounds alone when one considers the multiplicity of phobias. Here is a selected list:

Allodoxaphobia – fear of opinions.
Anemophobia – fear of air drafts or wind.
Ataxophobia – fear of disorder or untidiness.
Automatonophobia – fear of ventriloquists' dummies, animatronic creatures, wax statues: anything that falsely represents a sentient being.
Bufonophobia – fear of toads.
Ergophobia – fear of work.
Eurotophobia – fear of female genitalia.
Gephyrophobia, Gephydrophobia, or Gephysrophobia – fear of crossing bridges.
Hellenologophobia – fear of Greek terms or complex scientific terminology.

Mastigophobia – fear of punishment.
Misophobia – fear of being contaminated with dirt or germs.
  (Also Verminophobia – fear of germs.)
Neophobia – fear of anything new.
Nyctophobia – fear of the dark or of night.
Octophobia – fear of the figure 8.
Ophthalmophobia – fear of being stared at.
Oneirophobia – fear of dreams.
Ornithophobia – fear of birds.
Papyrophobia – fear of paper.
Paraphobia – fear of sexual perversion.
Phobophobia – fear of phobias.
Phonophobia – fear of noises or voices or one's own voice.
Scatophobia – fear of faecal matter.
Scelerophobia – fear of bad men, burglars.
Siderodromophobia – fear of trains, railways or train travel.
Social Phobia – fear of being evaluated negatively in social
  situations.
Sociophobia – fear of society or people in general.
Telephonophobia – fear of telephones.
Thanatophobia or Thantophobia – fear of death or dying.
Xenophobia – fear of strangers or foreigners.
Zoophobia – fear of animals.

At least we can be sure that Stanley Hall, who devised this nomen-clature, did not suffer from Hellenologophobia. 'It sounds like a list of the ten plagues of Egypt', Freud remarked drily, 'though their number goes far beyond ten'.[18] But how is the phobic object imbued with the qualities which cause panic or anxiety? Where do these qualities come from, and how do they then rebound on the phobic person?

Consider the last of the three dreams above. The optimistic and grandiose transcendence of fear in the dream fails to obscure the ultimate indeterminacy of the danger: 'I was being chased by . . . something.' This nebulous apprehension transforms into a specific object: 'I came to a cliff.' And in defining the fear – objectifying it – the subject finds a means of escape: 'I jumped off and flew away.' The narrative of the dream mirrors the psychological process by which a phobia might be created. Unnameable fears within the mind are externalised and given form.

But what is the source of fear? What lurks inside, threatening, ever ready to attack? How can it be that part of our selves should be traitor to ourselves? It took no genius to see that human passions may undermine the integrity of our rational self. Poets, artists and philosophers before Freud told of the horrors and dangers that human passions could provoke. Our emotional lives, forged in a cauldron of dependency which is our biological fate, must be moderated and controlled if they are not to torment us with their demands. In *The Interpretation of Dreams*, Freud says the following about dreams of wild animals (one of the commonest forms of childhood phobia):

> *Wild beasts are as a rule employed by the dream work to represent passionate impulses of which the dreamer is afraid, whether they are his own or other people's . . .*[19]

With the awakening of the repressed impulse, emotion becomes flesh.

What happens next? Freud's account would lead us to suggest three different sources for the construction of the phobic object. Firstly, a *splitting* of disavowed parts of the child's self: 'I do not hate daddy, I love daddy'; secondly, a *projection* of the repressed 'passionate impulses': 'I do not want to hurt daddy; daddy wants to hurt me'; thirdly, a *displacement* from the real object of fear: 'It is not daddy who wants to attack me, it is the horse, the dog, the tiger.' Freud continues:

> *We have not far to go from here to cases in which a dreaded father is represented by a beast of prey or a dog or a wild horse – a form of representation recalling totemism.*[20]

In Freud's world, emotions are dangerous. It's as simple as that. It seems such an old-fashioned view that we are surprised when we realise it's true. I can love too much, be too greedy, plague myself with envy and hate. But it's all part of 'me'. In projecting the emotion, I am attempting to rid myself of bits of myself – dangerous bits that might be attacked if I kept them inside and recognised them as my own. A middle-aged woman refuses to accept that she has ever in her life wanted to cheat. The cheating part of her – the little girl on her third birthday playing pass-the-parcel, for instance – became so 'bad' and persecuted that it was expunged from her consciousness, and now exists independently. She cannot, even as a thought experiment, acknowledge it inside herself. 'It often happens', says Freud, 'that the dreamer separates off his neurosis, his "sick personality" from himself and depicts it as an independent person'.[21]

In waking life as in dreams, parts of the self can be separated off and appear to achieve independent existence away from us. Unfortunately, from that other place they can come back to haunt us. In an analysis of a restaurant phobia, the Kleinian psychoanalyst Hanna Segal suggests that unwanted aggressive, greedy, dirty and 'persecuted' parts of the self are thrown into the other people who may be encountered at the restaurant.[22] Colloquially, we would say that she is 'putting her shit into other people', and psychoanalysts take this in an almost literal sense. They do not take the metaphor literally because of some theoretical prejudice or personal predilection, but because of what patients say to them in analysis. Hanna Segal's patient remembered that as a child she loved the pink sugary pills she was given by her mother:

> *Till one day she was given one and to her horror found that inside they were full of a disgusting brown stuff . . . She then remembered two bits of dreams from the following night: the first one had to do with a bunged up lavatory and in the second one she saw a child peeing into the soup.*[23]

(Freud would probably point out that the onset of menstruation, regarded with horror in many cultures, may reactivate these earlier traumas and feelings of disgust.) However, the metaphor of 'dumping' onto other people does not capture the fundamental sense of disintegration or the mental pain that this particular patient was suffering from. She often felt depersonalised and unreal. She could form no relationship except on the basis of totally controlling her objects. Various hypochondriacal symptoms had led to numerous surgical interventions. Her phobias of crowds and food had led to severe anorexia. It was as if everywhere she went she was under attack from dangerous faecal bullets – of criticism, hatred, disdain, anger, rejection – being shot at her from other people. 'In phobically avoiding crowds she was avoiding the come-back of her projected disintegration.'[24]

Social Panics and Phobic Objects

These mechanisms – splitting, projection, displacement – are instrumental in the construction of a phobic object both for the individual and for social groups. In *Totem and Taboo*, Freud describes the way in which malevolent demons are created in 'primitive' societies. Someone dies – perhaps an important chief or a big man of the tribe. There is emotional ambivalence in the survivors, leading to an internal conflict and splitting between the affectionate and hateful currents of feeling. The hostile part of their attitude (which is unconscious) is projected outwards onto the dead person, and the dead person is turned into a demon. As Freud puts it:

It is no longer true that they are rejoicing to be rid of the dead man; on the contrary, they are mourning for him; but strange to say, he *has turned into a wicked demon ready to gloat over their misfortunes and eager to kill them.*[25]

In scapegoating, too, a similar process occurs. The hatred and blame felt towards authority figures – the collective 'fathers' – may be disavowed and displaced onto others less powerful. There they can embody all the badness that has caused us misfortune, and can relieve us of the strain of our ambivalence. Thus, the deep-seated sense of national humiliation which traumatised Germany between the wars could be transformed, through ritual slaughter, into an ideology of national redemption. In blaming the Jews, we redeem the father; in forcing the Jews to take on our sins – the dirty, humiliated and greedy parts of ourselves – we redeem ourselves; and in eliminating the Jews, we cleanse the fatherland and become reconciled to our forgotten past.

It may be surprising to find that so much psychological energy can be taken up in maintaining the integrity of father figures. Historians have written of the panic that sweeps through a battlefield when the cry goes up that 'the king has lost his head', and we can see the effects in opinion polls when a population perceives weakness in political leaders. Nevertheless, how can a threat to the stability of the father – a largely symbolic construct after all – function in the same way as a failure in the function of the mother? If the breast is not there to feed you, your whole world is destroyed. No wonder it's scary. The mother is the environment in which you have your being. But if your father slips on a banana skin, it's not the end of the world, is it?

In that seminal work of cultural interrogation, *The Simpsons*, Marge Simpson goes to a psychoanalyst to cure her of a phobia of flying. It turns out that as a child Marge was told her father was a pilot – until one day she discovered that he was really a cabin steward. This was a devastating trauma to Marge. She had run onto the plane, eager to see daddy off, and there he was *in an apron* serving drinks. The subsequent phobia served to obliterate the scene from her mind, and the humiliation – perhaps horror – it no doubt aroused. At this moment of disappointment, which happens to each of us in some form or other, there appears a kind of rent in the fabric of reality itself, a kind of anxious intimation that the world we know, or think we know, could fall apart; as if the collapse of the symbolic world is indeed equivalent to the collapse of the physical world. 'What am I even at the best but an infant sucking the milk Thou givest, and feeding upon Thee, the food that perisheth not', asserts St Augustine, directly linking the symbolic world with the feeding relation.[26] Now imagine a crisis of faith.

The history of social panics shows how phobic objects can be created to deal with threats to the body politic. Periods of social transition or fragmentation are ideal conditions for the spewing forth of phobic objects. Witches cavorting with the Devil and bringing every misfortune into their communities; Jews killing innocent children and drinking their blood; Reds under the bed plotting to brainwash your neighbours: the language of disgust and horror is used for political ends to subjugate, disenfranchise, incarcerate and destroy. Closer to our own time, single mothers, beggars, homosexuals and foreigners have all been used by governments to help maintain the status quo or provide a convenient scapegoat in times of crisis.

Stuart Hall and his colleagues described the social processes whereby the 'mugger' came to represent and crystallise threats to the social order in Britain in the early 1970s.[27] In tracing the subtle shifts of meaning which transformed the traditional white working-class crime of 'bag snatching' into the spectre of the black 'mugger', they described a complex tapestry of psychological and sociological threads. Fears of being violated, robbed and beaten were related to fears about the stability and intactness of the outside world, and were projected into the construction of the phobic object. Once the panic was localised, the mechanisms of the state apparatus – the police and legal system – could be mobilised to deal with it. Thus, it seemed perfectly appropriate to the general public that a black man should be sent to prison for twelve years for snatching someone's bag. One would hardly have realised from newspaper reports that, according to Home Office statistics at the time, young black men were many times more likely to be assaulted than other sections of the population. But the image of the rapacious black man was appropriate for the service it was required to perform. It spoke directly to unconscious hopes and fears which had been present for centuries:

> The symbolism of the race-immigrant theme was resonant in its subliminal force, its capacity to set in motion the daemons which haunt the collective subconscious of a 'superior' race: it triggered off images of sex, rape, primitivism, violence and excrement.[28]

Inchoate fears could conveniently coalesce around the main templates of racism: black people as children, animals, monsters, faeces. Remember Gabrielle and her frightening 'black mummy'.

Thus it was no accident that the black man became the 'phobogenic object'.[29] It was because he could encapsulate, contain and condense a panoply of fears and forbidden urges – sexualised phantasies of alien conquest, archaic fears of the evil demon, troubling intimations of the savage within. When one talks to a naïve racist (one whose hostility and aversion is not rationalised by a political conviction, but is a fearful visceral response), the (xeno)phobic quality of their reaction is evident. Immigrants bring disease, immorality, dirt, 'germs', bad smells, economic threat and an amorphous 'difference' that is hard to define but definitely bad.

In some cases, the phobogenic object becomes a cornerstone of the cultural system.[30] The 'untouchables' in India not only clean the toilets of the wealthy but also signify the inherent attributes of dirt themselves in order to maintain supernatural legitimation of the caste system. In a million small ways, communities regulate access to resources and relations between racial groups through phobic belief systems. When I was at school in North-East London, I was reliably informed that black people ate dog food. That is to say, we appreciated and deserved nothing better. Comedian Arnold Brown, growing up in Glasgow, was told by a classmate that all Jewish people were rich (xenophobic code for 'greedy', and so equally undeserving). 'You know, I remember that day even now – running home excitedly to break the news to my mother and father', he recounts. 'We spent that weekend taking up the floorboards.'[31]

They Shoot Horses, Don't They? Phobia as Symbol

In the classic cases of phobia there is a remarkable degree of *condensation*. Condensation is an obvious characteristic of a phobia, yet it calls into question some of the psychological ideas we have been discussing so far. If the phobic person is projecting *fragmented* aspects of a disintegrated personality, why should these *coalesce* into a phobia?

Freud considered the issue in his infamous case of Little Hans.[32] Hans suffered from a fear of horses so intense that it left him at times unable to leave the house. I call the case 'infamous' because Freud treated it, and the observations upon which it was based, as a means to confirm the sexual theories he had elaborated in *Three Essays on the Theory of Sexuality*. In this earlier book, Freud asserted the existence of childhood sexuality; with Little Hans he gave the abstract theories a personality. 'I already knew the funny little fellow', says Freud, 'and with all his self-assurance he was yet so amiable that I had always been glad to see him'.[33] Many students who first come across this case assume that Freud and the child's father (who is recording the observations) are putting words into Hans's mouth. We find it distasteful to contemplate the possibility that children may have sexual feelings or phantasies, and this produces a seemingly unbridgeable gulf between the psychoanalyst and the general public.

What both sides might agree is that a child's wishes are different from an adult's. When a child says 'I wish you were dead', we know that this is said with a child's understanding of what 'death' means, and does not contradict the tender feelings of love and the need for protection that the child also feels. When a child says 'I wish I could marry mummy', we know that this is said with the child's understanding of what 'marriage' entails, despite the childish passion with which the wish is articulated. Apart from the jokes among mothers at the school gates about the embarrassing comments little Johnny comes out with, it is rare that the child's passions and ideas are taken seriously. Children have sensual bodily experience and emotional relationships; they are curious about the riddles of existence – Where do I come from? What is the difference between boys and girls? – which they interpret according to their own theories and bodily feelings; they fall in love and experience jealousy; they have obscure urges and strange ideas hidden from their parents. In the collective denial of children's sexuality and phantasy life, we abandon them to solve these momentous problems on their own – and we fail to relieve the anxieties which lie at the heart of the child's sexual life.

That's how Freud thought about it. If the child wants to know where babies come from, he says, it's because he wants to know where this particular baby comes from – the one who may take away his mother's love and threaten his whole existence. If he wants to know the difference between boys and girls, it's because he feels a threat to the precarious identity that defines him as one or the other. In adolescence, the childhood fears may return. An adolescent boy may worry that he is growing breasts; a girl may be horrified by the hairs appearing on her body and for a fleeting moment imagine that she is turning into a man. The paedophilic representation of the child's sexuality as a sphere of pleasurable quasi-adult experience is a million miles away from the psychoanalytic understanding which sees sexuality as troubling to the child, and which places psychic pain at the centre of the human condition. In the latter case, the adult's role is to help the child through the inevitable anxieties, frustrations and disappointments that his or her sexual constitution and sensuous emotional experience will bring.

So Little Hans found himself in the Oedipal maelstrom. Nobody is surprised when we see the dramas played out nightly on our TV screens. Frank loves Pat but he's married to Peggy; Robbie loves the girl next door but he fears rejection; Sandra is torn between her child and her lover. For children, too, the configuration of family life creates an inevitable psychodrama. Love and hate, jealousy and dependence, fear and yearning are all mixed up together. Ambivalence is at its height. It must seem that whichever way the child turns, there will be a danger. If he goes towards one parent, he may upset the other; if he detaches from one parent, that parent may not love him any more. If he feels angry, he fears retaliation; if he feels love, he conjures up the spectre of rejection. Parents who love and protect you may also attack you, abandon you, die, collapse, blow up, try to control you, and so on. Imagine this precarious state of affairs with all these possible dangers, real and imaginary, linked as they are to your own ambivalent feelings, intense urges and dependencies. This emotional cataclysm is the normal state of affairs for anyone growing up, and it is hardly surprising that childhood phobias during this period may be regarded as 'normal'.

For Little Hans, the phobic object, 'horse', was the repository of many fears. The horse may bite, it may fall down, it may die, it may run out of control, it may knock you down, and so on. One characteristic of the horse was particularly frightening: the fear that it would bite him. 'The idea of being devoured by the father is typical age-old childhood material', says Freud:

> It has familiar parallels in mythology (e.g. the myth of Kronos) and in the animal kingdom. Yet in spite of this confirmation the idea is so strange to us that we can hardly credit its existence in a child.[34]

We are even less likely to credit the specific fear which, for Freud, provides the motive for the phobia in this case:

> His fear that a horse would bite him can, without any forcing, be given the full sense of a fear that a horse would bite off his genitals, would castrate him.[35]

Freud first used the term 'castration complex' in a paper, 'On the Sexual Theories of Children' (1908). It is one of the strange theories that children make up to explain the difference between boys and girls. What Freud saw in Hans was a little boy full of many fears, dominated by the huge shadow of castration anxiety. Castration anxiety was evoked as a result of his dangerous libidinal urges to have his mother to himself, and the observation that his mother and sister, long thought to be the same as him, were different in one crucial respect. Other characteristics of the horse pointed to the source of the castration threat. At one point, Hans became particularly fearful of what horses wear before their eyes, and by the black around their mouths. Freud suggested that these were visual references to his father's eyeglasses and moustache.[36]

Under investigation, then, Hans's phobic object or situation revealed itself as a complex amalgam of anxieties and impulses, and the result of numerous psychical mechanisms. There was the fear of being eaten (related to 'oral' conflicts and frequently depicted or alluded to in fairy tales), anxieties around 'pooh' and defecation (another 'weird idea' that nearly every parent has experienced with their young children), fear of losing his mother (separation anxiety), worries about his little sister Hanna and where she came from, and finally the dominant castration anxiety. Reviewing the case, Anna Freud remarks:

> [F]ears and anxieties . . . are compressed by the child into one encompassing symbol which represents the dangers left over from preoedipal phases as well as the dominant ones due to phallic–oedipal conflicts.[37]

Transformations

A man goes to analysis with a spider phobia – the spider might crawl into his mouth and kill him, or he may be pulled up into the web and eaten. In his 'real life' he feels trapped in a relationship of hate and dependency with his mother and the rest of his natal family. He remembers a childhood experience from the age of five.

> He was playing under the kitchen table when his mother announced she had something new to show him. She pushed her face close to his and smiled, revealing for the first time her new dentures. He became terrified and screamed, for he was suddenly overwhelmed by a fear that she would devour him, immediately leading to a phantasy of his mother as a dangerous orally incorporating spider, which subsequently became the nucleus of the phobia.[38]

Leaving aside the specific meaning of the phobia, this story illustrates the cardinal theme of transformation of the benign into the malevolent, of seduction and betrayal, commonly found in children's fiction. Grandma turns into a wolf, the kindly old woman turns into a witch, the trusted teacher turns into a killer. The stories oscillate between fear and fascination, temptation and repulsion. On seeing the hideous and ghastly face of the Grand

High Witch herself, the boy-hero of Roald Dahl's *The Witches* identifies the feeling precisely:

> *There are times when something is so frightful you become mesmerised by it and can't look away. I was like that now. I was transfixed. I was numbed. I was magnetised by the sheer horror of this woman's features.*[39]

'Children who suffer from phobias', observed Anna Freud, 'not only flee from the object of their anxiety but are also fascinated and compulsively drawn toward it'.[40]

Adolescent horror films articulate some of the dangerous consequences of developing sexuality: hairs sprouting in unexpected places, putrid matter erupting on the skin, sexual 'pollutants' escaping from the body, swellings appearing as if from nowhere and, most significantly, intense emotional tangles with parents, teachers and peers. The films serve as a gory rite of passage, a defile to pass through from one state of being to the next. You probably know the kind of stories I have in mind: a group of students at a co-ed college visit the empty house on the hill for an illicit party, only to discover that the Dean of Faculty is a devil-worshipper ready to slice them up.

Younger children, too, worry about the integrity of their bodies and the protective nature of the world in which they find themselves. There is a frightening indeterminacy in the child's categorisation of the world: the distinction between imagination and reality, between animate and inanimate, living and dead; trust in other people; ambivalence to parental figures; concerns about the vulnerability of the body. Feelings of psychological safety are evidently not as secure as we like to imagine. We carry around inside us, says Freud, an infantile morbid anxiety 'from which the majority of human beings have never become quite free'[41] – a precondition for the construction of phobias.

The Horror, the Horror: Edgar Allan Poe

A mother can turn into a witch, or a father can turn into a monster. But many phobias have an abstract quality that seems distinct from a relationship with living human beings, even if the relationships are distorted by phantasy. My own father, as a child and young man, suffered from a recurring nightmare: a nebulous shape was bearing down on him, two spherical objects like huge dumb-bells, threatening to crush him. Yet the real terror was reserved for the thought that if the two parts of the object came together, something terrible would happen. He had to keep the spheres separated and immobile, straining in the dream to keep them apart. Similarly, Freud's 'Wolf Man', as a child, dreamed of seven wolves sitting impassively in the tree outside his window. What terrified him was not the wolves, but their immobility. As Freud tells it, the passivity of the wolves was a reversal of the reality on which the dream was based. It represented the child's perception of his parents' love-making – the 'primal scene' interpreted by children as something violent and disturbing – and the passivity of the little boy, transfixed at the spectacle. A perception of violent agitation is erased in the wishful presentation of quiescence.

Thus, despite the fearful apprehension in the dream, it circumvents the anxiety which lies at its root. There is something uncanny about the primal scene, says Freud. The child does not understand what is going on, he does not know 'where to put himself'; he has obscure intimations and confused feelings, often of an aggressive nature; his world is turned upside down. He witnesses an act which speaks of a time before his own existence and threatens to create his rival, and in which his parents are monstrously transformed into a single beast. The perception squeezes him out of the family equation, yet draws him further in. Fascinated and repelled in equal measure, is it any wonder that apprehension of the primal scene may be something traumatic? If the dumb-bells come too close together, something dreadful will happen; but if they slip too far apart, you are left high and dry.

Considering the work of Edgar Allan Poe, the theme of betrayal is made horrifying and explicit. In so many of his works, a safe world suddenly becomes dangerous because somebody runs amok, or because impersonal forces of evil are mysteriously unleashed. The refined and considerate host becomes the evil torturer, refined only in the art of hideous death. You fall asleep and wake up in a coffin, buried alive with no one to hear your cries. The box which contained a work of art is revealed to contain a decaying body, and so on. Attachment theorists might argue that Poe's evident uncertainty, his lack of trust in the world and indeed his descent into alcoholism and gambling addiction all point to an early relationship marked by ambivalence and disruption. And indeed the facts of Poe's life support such a view.

Born in Boston on 19 January 1809, it seems that little Edgar had the great psychological boon of a happy mother. On the back of a miniature portrait of herself, Elizabeth Poe wrote: 'For my little son Edgar, who should ever love Boston, the place of his birth, and where his mother found her best, and most sympathetic friends.' This early idyll was not to last, however. By 1810, the family had moved to Norfolk, Virginia. His father, David Poe Jr., a travelling actor, had died or deserted the family and Elizabeth was left destitute. She died on 8 December 1811 in Richmond, Virginia, shortly before Edgar's second birthday. He was later adopted by the Allan family and sent to school in England when he was six. From the bare lineaments of this tragic story, one will hardly be surprised that the themes of betrayal, misplaced trust, helplessness and physical suffering are so evident in Poe's work. But there are other aspects of his writing that the vicissitudes of his early relationships cannot so easily explain. (The fact that Poe borrowed many of these themes from the numerous 'penny dreadfuls' and stories of the macabre that were fashionable at the time should not dissuade us from making psychological conjectures.)

Why should the themes of burial or immurement be so prominent in Poe's work? In 'The Cask of Amontillado', a man gets walled up alive in the cellar; in 'The Pit and the Pendulum', the walls of the cell begin to close in on the victim, threatening to crush him or push him into the dreaded pit; in 'The Black Cat', the cat that will not die is walled up with the dead wife; in 'The Murders in the Rue Morgue', one of the victims is stuffed up the chimney; while 'The Premature Burial' speaks for itself. A person suffering from the common phobia of travelling in lifts or being in confined spaces would sympathise with the horror that these depictions attempt to arouse. There is also a kind of unnameable horror that can only be hinted at. The prospect of being crushed by the walls of the dungeon, cut to pieces by the pendulum or eaten by rats is as nothing compared to the horrors of the pit which cannot be described:

> *I rushed to its deadly brink. I threw my straining vision below. The glare from the enkindled roof illumined its inmost recesses. Yet, for a wild moment, did my spirit refuse to comprehend the meaning of what I saw. At length it forced – it wrestled its way into my soul – it burned itself in upon my shuddering reason. O for a voice to speak! – oh, horror! – oh, any horror but this! With a shriek I rushed from the margin and buried my face in my hands – weeping bitterly.*[42]

Perhaps little Edgar wept bitterly when the other momentous event of his first two years took place – the birth of his sister Rosalie when he was less than a year old. It seems inconceivable to many that such small children can intellectually register the events in their environment, or be affected by happenings which they cannot yet understand. Freud assumed – and modern research supports his hunch – that children know more and notice more than we give them credit for. What might the child scarcely old enough for thinking have made of the new arrival and the problem of where it came from? Or how might the experience have accrued meaning retrospectively as the child acquired new knowledge and emotional complexity?

Psychoanalysts have asserted that the contents of the mother's body are of supreme interest to the child. The phantasy of intra-uterine existence, the aggressive wish to rip out the contents of the body, and the body as the first object of philosophical inquiry, have been described by both Freud and Klein.[43] In another paper, Freud recounts a childhood recollection of Goethe's. Goethe is less than two years old, and throwing pots and pans out of the kitchen window, followed by the best china. Freud surmises that the memory serves as a screen for the desire of the young Goethe to throw out the baby that had recently arrived and usurped his favoured position in the home. In a flash, the great bedrock of his life had become the great betrayer. Freud tells of a similar experience in his own life.[44]

Imagine the turmoil of emotions as the child's stable world threatens to turn upside down. For Klein, the fear of retribution for the phantasied attacks on the mother may make the body 'a place of horrors'. If I want to attack your insides and scoop out the contents, you may want to do the same to me. In similar vein, Ricky Emanuel interprets the childhood fear of burglars and intruders.[45] In phantasy, the child invades the mother's body in order to damage or steal its contents; the impulse rebounds on the child as the phobic fear of intruders coming into the house to 'get' him. Such ideas might be reanimated during adolescence. We find the 'return of the repressed'[46] in the common themes of teenage horror films. 'What do you want?', asks the terrified victim trapped in her house. 'I want to see what your insides look like', replies the disembodied voice from the other end of the telephone.[47] The idea that such phantasies may exist at the deepest levels of our personalities seems abhorrent and unbelievable. It is when we see them enacted by normal people under stress that we wonder where this dark side of human nature comes from. The deranged high-school students carrying out the disembowellings in *Scream* would have been joined by their normal classmates had they found themselves together at the massacre of My Lai during the Vietnam War.[48]

But the mother's body as a 'place of horrors' is also our first home and our first place of safety. The subliminal evocation of intra-uterine existence can create the feeling of the 'uncanny', as Freud calls it, because we have experienced it before. Something from a previous existence is coming back to entice us, desired and feared as a place of dreadful pleasures and exquisite anguish.

If wombs are like tombs, it is possible to link the theme of betrayal in Poe's stories with the specific fear of being boxed in or walled up. It represents the horror and fascination of intra-uterine life. Or does it? At the risk of alienating even the most open-minded readers, I feel compelled to point out (as Freud did nearly a hundred years ago) that young children may imagine that babies are born from the anus. Understandably, they base their idea of birth on the template of their own bodily experiences. (The next time you're chatting with a three-year-old, just ask!) Sedimented in the unconscious, this strange idea can persist in the adult mind, and find subtle means of expression. The horror of the pit may be the horror of being trapped in the rectal canal, a place which, once valued, soon becomes the repository of everything disgusting and 'bad'.[49] So to explain this particular constellation of themes we have to take into account not only the history of attachment to the mother, but the phantasy life and unconscious desires of the small child as they reverberate in his developing mind. Perhaps, in the end, Poe's secure early attachment asserts itself: the victim about to fall into the pit is rescued in the nick of time; the poor soul who is prematurely buried lives to tell the tale; the descent into the maelstrom is ended by a miraculous escape; and in 'The Cask of Amontillado', the narrator, after all, is the one with the trowel.

A Classification of Phobias?

Psychoanalysts have explored a number of specific anxieties, and made anxiety itself a cornerstone of their theory and practice.[50] It would be convenient if the multiplicity of phobias could be classified in relation to a limited number of infantile situations which give rise to anxiety, but the complexity of the phobic object would suggest otherwise. The phobia does indeed *evoke* these situations – birth, helplessness, separation and abandonment, loss of love, primal scene, threats to bodily integrity (castration), death of self and others. It also *symbolises* some of our most frightening phantasies and sadistic urges. And it *represents* – stands in for – some of the people closest to us: mum and dad, brother, sister, and that shadowy critical figure which Freud calls 'the parental agency' and Klein 'the combined parent figure'. In 'evoking', 'symbolising' and 'representing', a developed phobia will have contributions from many sources. Nevertheless, in a particular case, one or other anxiety situation and phantasy content may predominate.

Freud himself confessed to a fear of trains, telephones and death, which might be classified as mildly 'phobic'. If we recall that journeys often involve separation from home, that death is frequently represented as a journey, and that disembodied voices may have something deathly about them, it would not take us long to find some unity in these phenomena around the common childhood anxiety of separation.

But how would we classify the bridge phobia? My friend crossing the bridge was, like Little Hans, fearful of a number of possibilities. The bridge itself, of course, which joins one side of the river to the other. The fear of falling, or being submerged, or drowning. Then there was the middle of the bridge, which seemed to be the point of greatest fearful anticipation. The edge of the bridge was terrifying, as was the gap between the two bridges. It is easy to find in all this a multitude of basic anxieties: separation (the middle of the bridge is furthest away from the safety of either side); the primal scene (if we assume that the bridge symbolically joins the two parental 'banks'); castration (the edge of the bridge as a cut, or the gap between the two bridges representing 'something that has been taken away'); and the primitive anxiety of falling into the 'void'.[51] Analytic investigation might enable us to find a dominant anxiety, but I suspect it is more likely we would find that anxieties from all phases of development can happily coexist. Moreover, a phobia is constructed from private meanings and unique experiences. Each element weaves itself into a story of everyday life that reveals long-forgotten passions and underlying anxiety. Perhaps, as a little boy, my friend was frightened by dangerous thoughts and excitements when his parents left him alone with the babysitter each week while they went to play Bridge. To be aware of the possible anxieties gives us a handle on phobic phenomena, but not a single key. There is no simple dictionary to tell us what they mean.

Confronting the Monster: The Function of Phobias

Phobias function as part of the psychic economy of the subject. They are, in effect, bits of the mind which have been placed into the outside world. And they have been placed there for a reason – or at least there are consequences to them being so placed. Phobias have both intra-psychic and inter-personal functions. Intra-psychically:

- They are a vehicle for hateful and aggressive feelings.
- They help temporarily to circumvent the problem of ambivalence.
- They condense anxieties into a 'knowable' form and give some measure of control over them.

● They help stabilise phantasy activity and legitimate it.

One could even say that phobias have a progressive aspect as well; they offer the child and adult an image of the future – this is what you have to overcome in order to grow up.[52]

The central feature of *avoidance* in phobic phenomena hints at a connection to obsessional rituals. Freud saw the repetitive 'undoing' of obsessional rituals as a defence against 'temptation' – that is to say, the enactment of an unconscious phantasy – and against the impulses that lead to temptation. Thus, agoraphobia may be a defence against a dangerous exhibitionistic phantasy, claustrophobia may be a defence against a wish to go back to the womb, a fear of heights may be a defence against an uncontrollable impulse to jump, a terror of spiders may be keeping at bay the phantasy of ripping off their legs, and so on.

Anne-Marie Sandler has considered the role of phantasy in a more sophisticated way.[53] She posits two types of phobia: the classic 'extrusive' type, in which an internal danger is extruded onto an external object (through splitting, projection and displacement); and 'intrusive' phobias, in which the anxiety is aroused by the situation. In the first case, the fear performs an ongoing function in maintaining the internal equilibrium of the person; in the second case, the equilibrium is disturbed by the external reality. The phobic object or situation upsets the delicate psychic balance the child has achieved through phantasy activity. Children (and adults!) often develop phantasies in which there are attackers, robbers, wild animals, devouring monsters and the like. In imagination, the child triumphs over these figures or finds some other way to reassure himself that he is in control.[54] The phobic object is one which reinforces the frightening figures created in phantasy and creates a state of panic. It puts too great a demand on the person – they can no longer control the disturbing urges and impulses through phantasy. A child who was able to control threatening homosexual feelings through games and phantasies of foreign soldiers attacking him with bayonets, found his coping mechanisms broke down when he was required to go swimming. The phobic object or situation lines itself up with the (projected) hostile forces which are ranged against the child, and tips the balance. 'Intrusive' phobias are therefore not generally seen as part of the personality. The phobia only 'kicks in' during specific situations or when specific demands are made – for example, a fear of flying or swimming – while for the rest of the time the person seems free of any debilitating anxiety. Sandler further specifies the particular role of traumatic experiences in the causation of intrusive phobias:

*[A]n overwhelming frightening experience can act as an impor-
tant organising agent for the child's subsequent fantasies.*[55]

In similar vein, the French psychoanalyst André Green has recently
developed the concept of 'central phobic position' to describe the
organisation of a central defensive core to the personality (defending against intense feelings or intimacy with others) caused by the
impact of traumatic experiences.[56]

Childhood phobias occur typically during the Oedipal period,
as in the case of Little Hans, at a time when the nascent (or, for
Kleinians, not-so-nascent) superego begins to exert its influence.
The free expression of libidinal and aggressive urges is no longer
acceptable and, moreover, the child begins to fear the consequences of his emotional expression. In this scenario, the phobia
may function as a kind of detached, surrogate superego controlling
the child's chaotic and fragmented Oedipal impulses through
threats of punishment. Just as a child's toy may function as an
outlet for forbidden emotions and obscure urges, or its play be
used to repeat traumatic events in its life, so the phobic object or
situation both expresses the emotion and holds it in place. It joins
the inner world with the outer, connecting the torrent of repressed
urges and ideas with the 'parental agency'. The phobia is a kind of
insurance: the parents don't turn into monsters; your ambivalent
feelings don't tear you apart. The twin threats get drawn into the
gravitational pull of the phobia. Paradoxically, it makes the real
world safe again.

Finally, there is a conflict between what we might loosely call
'developmental forces' and forces which attempt to hold the
subject back. Growing up not only offers opportunities and
rewards, it also entails significant losses which the subject is not
likely to contemplate without some degree of trepidation. The
phobia can be seen as the result of an *impasse* between these
competing tendencies, which may have the effect of blocking
development. Just as a stomach-ache, headache or some other
physical symptom may be used to justify a day off school, so the
construction of a phobia may be a more permanent way to avoid
the unwanted demands of reality. In other words, it keeps reality at
bay and gives you a bit of space to grow up at your own pace.

In their interpersonal functions, phobias keep the parental
figures 'good' (bad frightening wolf as opposed to good protective
daddy), encourage idealisations, and also regulate 'distance' with
parental figures. The child afraid of wild animals climbing
through her bedroom window, or the possibility of spiders crawling into her mouth, will find herself in the parents' bed, a little girl
safely protected from the traumatic awareness of Oedipal desires.

In entering the parents' bed, however, the child is simultaneously experiencing these desires in their most intimate location while continuing to deny their existence. The phobia allows the child to maintain a dependent relationship, refusing the doubtful promises of Oedipal awakening and separation. In growing up, children are required to step off the Oedipal cliff into the unknown – but some stand petrified at the edge. And when you think about it, who can blame them? A phobia may be a child's way of keeping things in place while cognitive, emotional and libidinal developments realign themselves. If the child is unable to achieve separation, however, and early idealisations remain intact, the phobia may indicate a more serious split in the mind.[57]

Once again, Hitchcock's film *The Birds* offers a telling illustration. From one perspective, the film is a story of sexual awakening. It begins with (much older) brother Mitch buying a pair of lovebirds for Cathy's eleventh birthday. He wants them 'not too demonstrative' and 'not too aloof'. Just 'friendly'. The misnamed lovebirds are required to acknowledge sexuality and deny it at the same time, occupying a middle space of Oedipal safety. But to no avail. Faced with the impending eruption of sexual life, and the spectre of incestuous longings from the past, the violently repressed returns. Remarkable as it may seem (Annie is killed by the birds, while Melanie becomes catatonic), Cathy gets through the attacks unscathed. 'Can I bring the lovebirds?', she asks at the end, as the family walk precariously to the car through the carpet of squawking birds.

Treatment

Perhaps the relation to dependence and sexual awakening is one reason why, above all other neuroses, phobias seem susceptible to a cure by 'love'. An agoraphobic woman may suddenly find herself cured after she enters a fulfilling sexual relationship, a man petrified of heights may show a remarkable ability at rock-climbing while in the throes of a first love affair, a hypnotist may get sensational results with suggestion. It is also why childhood phobias may gradually lose meaning, like a 'transitional object'.[58] A child who was terrified of spiders suddenly finds she can pick them up – 'at least the small ones' – and put them out of the house.

As for the treatment of phobias, psychoanalysts have questioned the efficacy of a behavioural approach which gradually habituates the person to the object of their fear. They argue that although results seem impressive at first sight, the fact that the underlying anxieties are not articulated and worked through means that they will simply attach themselves to some other object or another symptom altogether. I think this undervalues the direct approach. Freud advocated that in the analysis of a phobia there comes a time when you simply have to tell the patient to go out and face it. After the 'unfolding' of the phobia through the analytic process, uncovering the layers of phantasy and anxiety, the object of fear must be confronted and overcome, just as it must in the process of growing up.

> One can hardly master a phobia if one waits till the patient lets the analysis influence him to give it up. He will never in that case bring into the analysis the material indispensable for a convincing resolution of the phobia.[59]

In the case of agoraphobia, for instance, one must encourage the patient 'to go into the street and to struggle with their anxiety while they make the attempt'.[60] If nothing else, it gives the analysis something 'real' to work with.

Freud doubted whether phobias could be classified as independent pathological processes, since phobic phenomena can be found in schizophrenia, obsessional neuroses and other conditions. Charles Brenner is even more doubtful of the diagnostic value of the category:

> If all phobias . . . were dynamically or genetically similar in many important ways, calling a symptom a phobia would be useful. In fact, however, the reverse is the case. The only thing all phobias have in common is the defensive use of avoidance. They share nothing else, either dynamically or genetically, which distinguishes them from any other class of symptoms.[61]

Similar symptoms can have different causes. Nevertheless, phobia – or 'anxiety hysteria' as it was originally called – has a right to be considered one of the 'founding symptomologies' of psychoanalysis, illuminating some of the essential aspects of its theory.

Ivan Ward is director of education at the Freud Museum and a part-time lecturer at London Guildhall University. He is the series editor for *Ideas in Psychoanalysis* and author of *Introducing Psychoanalysis*, also published by Icon–Totem.

Notes

1. The 'objective correlative' is described by Eliot as 'a set of objects, a situation, a chain of events which shall be the formula of that *particular* emotion'. Eliot, T.S., 'Hamlet and his Problems' (1919), in Kermode, F. (ed.), *Selected Prose of T.S. Eliot*, London: Faber and Faber, 1975, p. 48.
2. Jones, E., 'The Psychopathology of Anxiety' (1929), in *Papers on Psychoanalysis*, London: Bailliere, Tindall and Cox, 1948, p. 294.
3. Ward, I. (ed.), *The Psychology of Nursery Education*, London: Karnac Books–The Freud Museum, 1997.
4. Music, G., *Affect and Emotion*, Ideas in Psychoanalysis series, Cambridge: Icon Books, 2001, p. 38.
5. Freud, S., *Introductory Lectures on Psychoanalysis: Anxiety* (1917), in *Standard Edition of the Complete Psychological Works of Sigmund Freud*, London: Hogarth Press, 1953–73 (hereafter *SE*), vol. 16, p. 398.
6. Bondy, N. and Cable, S. (producers), *Phobias*, BBC1, July 2000.
7. Spoto, D., *The Dark Side of Genius: The Life of Alfred Hitchcock*, Boston: Little, Brown, 1983, quoted in Almansi, R., 'Alfred Hitchcock's Disappearing Women', in *International Review of Psychoanalysis*, vol. 19 (1), 1992, pp. 81–90 (p. 87).
8. Bondy and Cable, op. cit.
9. Evan Hunter, *The Birds*, directed by Alfred Hitchcock, 1963.
10. Almansi (1992), op. cit.
11. Freud, A., 'Fears, Anxieties and Phobic Phenomena', in *Psychoanalytic Study of the Child*, vol. 32, New Haven: Yale University Press, 1977, p. 88 (slightly amended).
12. Ibid.
13. See 'Phantasy' on pp. 71–99 of *On a Darkling Plain*. This essay is also available as a separate book: Segal, J., *Phantasy*, Ideas in Psychoanalysis series, Cambridge: Icon Books, 2000.
14. Freud, S., 'The Theme of the Three Caskets' (1913), in *SE*, vol. 12.
15. Winnicott, D., *The Piggle: An Account of the Psychoanalytic Treatment of a Little Girl*, ed. I. Ramzy, London: Penguin Books, 1977, p. 6.
16. Ibid., p. 37.
17. Ibid., p. 36.
18. Freud, S. (1917), op. cit., p. 398.
19. Freud, S., *The Interpretation of Dreams* (1900), in *SE*, vol. 5, p. 410.
20. Ibid.
21. Ibid.
22. Segal, H., 'A Note on Schizoid Mechanisms Underlying Phobia Formation', in *International Journal of Psychoanalysis*, vol. 35 (2), 1954, pp. 238–41.
23. Ibid., p. 239.
24. Ibid., p. 240.
25. Freud, S., *Totem and Taboo* (1913), in *SE*, vol. 13, p. 63.
26. Kristeva, J., *In the Beginning was Love: Psychoanalysis and Faith*, trans. A. Goldhammer, New York: Columbia University Press, 1987, p. 24.
27. Hall, S., Critcher, C., Jefferson, T., Clark, J. and Roberts, B., *Policing the Crisis*, London: Macmillan, 1978.

28. Ibid., p. 224.
29. Fanon, F., *Black Skin, White Masks* (1952), trans. C.L. Markmann, London: Paladin, 1970.
30. In his compelling psychohistory of racism in the United States, Joel Kovel shows how economic forms are related to patterns of racism and the particular phobic meanings attached to racial groups (see Kovel, J., *White Racism: A Psychohistory* (1965), London: Free Association Books, 1988). He describes three forms or historical phases of racism: 'dominative', 'aversive', and 'meta-racism'. In the first case, characteristic of slave society, the rapacious savagery of the black man threatening the purity of the white woman is controlled through domination and violence. In the second case the infectious dirt of the black person has to be controlled through avoidance. While in the third case, characteristic of late capitalist democracies with their equal-opportunities policies and the like, awareness of difference is avoided through denial that racism exists. In each case the spectre of the black person threatens the cultural illusions and power structures of the status quo. Thus other people or whole groups become the repositories of the unwelcome parts of the self which can then function as phobic objects.
31. Wilmut, R. and Rosengard, P., *Didn't You Kill my Mother-in-law?*, London: Methuen, 1989, p. 223.
32. Freud, S., 'Analysis of a Phobia in a Five-Year-Old Boy' (1909), in *SE*, vol. 10, pp. 3–149.
33. Ibid., p. 41.
34. Freud, S., *Inhibitions, Symptoms and Anxiety* (1926), in *SE*, vol. 20, p. 105.
35. Ibid., p. 108.
36. Freud, S. (1909), op. cit., p. 41.
37. Freud, A. (1977), op. cit., pp. 87–8.
38. Little, R., 'The Resolution of Oral Conflicts in a Spider Phobia', in *International Journal of Psychoanalysis*, vol. 49 (2–3), 1968, p. 492.
39. Dahl, R., *The Witches*, London: Jonathan Cape, 1983, p. 70.
40. Freud, A. (1977), op. cit., p. 88.
41. Freud, S., 'The Uncanny' (1919a), in *SE*, vol. 17, p. 252.
42. Poe, E.A., 'The Pit and the Pendulum' (1842), from 'The Complete Works of Edgar Allan Poe', www.eserver.org/books/poe/.
43. Freud, S., 'On the Sexual Theories of Children' (1908), in *SE*, vol. 9; Klein, M., 'The Theory of Intellectual Inhibition' (1931), in *Love, Guilt and Reparation*, London: Delta, 1975.
44. Freud, S., *The Psychopathology of Everyday Life* (1901), in *SE*, vol. 6, p. 51.
45. See pp. 52–3 of 'Anxiety' in this volume. 'Anxiety' is also available as a separate book: Emanuel, R., *Anxiety*, Ideas in Psychoanalysis series, Cambridge: Icon Books, 2000 (see pp. 36–7).
46. Freud, S. (1919a), op. cit., p. 249.
47. *Scream*, directed by W. Craven, 1997.
48. Sim, K. and Bilton, M. (producers), *Four Hours in My Lai*, Thames Television, First Tuesday series, date unknown, 1988.
49. Meltzer, D., *The Claustrum: An Investigation into Claustrophobic Phenomena*, Strathclyde: Clunie Press, 1992.

50. Emanuel (2000), op. cit.
51. Emanuel, R., 'A-Void: An Exploration of Defences Against Sensing Nothingness', in *International Journal of Psychoanalysis*, vol. 82 (6), 2001.
52. Campbell, D., 'Discovering, Explaining and Confronting the Monster', unpublished paper, 1995.
53. Sandler, A.-M., 'Comments on Phobic Mechanisms in Childhood', in *Psychoanalytic Study of the Child*, 44, New Haven: Yale University Press, 1989, p. 101.
54. Ibid., p. 109.
55. Ibid., p. 107.
56. Green, A., 'The Central Phobic Position: A New Formulation of the Free Association Method', in *International Journal of Psychoanalysis*, vol. 81 (3), 2000, pp. 429–51. See also Gillman, R., 'The Oedipal Organization of Shame: The Analysis of a Phobia', in *Psychoanalytic Study of the Child*, vol. 45, New Haven: Yale University Press, 1990, pp. 357–76.
57. Kahn, M.M.R., 'Role of Phobic and Counterphobic Mechanisms and Separation Anxiety in Schizoid Character Formation', in *International Journal of Psychoanalysis*, vol. 47 (2–3), 1966, pp. 306–13.
58. Winnicott, D., 'Transitional Objects and Transitional Phenomena', in *International Journal of Psychoanalysis*, vol. 34 (2), 1953, pp. 89–97.
59. Freud, S., 'Lines of Advance in Psychoanalytic Therapy' (1919b), in *SE*, vol. 17, pp. 165–6.
60. Ibid., p. 166.
61. Brenner, C., quoted in Compton, A., 'The Psychoanalytic View of Phobias: Part IV: General Theory of Phobias and Anxiety', in *Psychoanalytic Quarterly*, vol. 61 (4), 1992, pp. 426–46. (Parts I–III of this article can be found in the same volume.)

Further Reading

Almansi, R., 'Alfred Hitchcock's Disappearing Women', in *International Review of Psychoanalysis*, vol. 19 (1), 1992, pp. 81–90.
Compton, A., 'The Psychoanalytic View of Phobias: General Theory of Phobias and Anxiety', in *Psychoanalytic Quarterly*, vol. 61 (4), 1992.
Emanuel, R., 'A-Void: An Exploration of Defences Against Sensing Nothingness', in *International Journal of Psychoanalysis*, vol. 82 (6), 2001.
Fanon, F., *Black Skin, White Masks* (1952), trans. C.L. Markmann, London: Paladin, 1970.
Freud, A., 'Fears, Anxieties and Phobic Phenomena', in *Psychoanalytic Study of the Child*, vol. 32, New Haven: Yale University Press, 1977.
Freud, S., *The Interpretation of Dreams* (1900), in *The Standard Edition of the Complete Psychological Works of Sigmund Freud*, London: Hogarth Press, 1953–73 (hereafter *SE*), vols. 4 and 5.
——*The Psychopathology of Everyday Life* (1901), in *SE*, vol. 6.
——'On the Sexual Theories of Children' (1908), in *SE*, vol. 9.
——'Analysis of a Phobia in a Five-Year-Old Boy' (1909), in *SE*, vol. 10, pp. 3–149.

——*Totem and Taboo* (1913), in *SE*, vol. 13.

——'The Theme of the Three Caskets' (1913), in *SE*, vol. 12.

——*Introductory Lectures on Psychoanalysis: Anxiety* (1917), in *SE*, vol. 16, p. 398.

——'The Uncanny' (1919), in *SE*, vol. 17.

——'Lines of Advance in Psychoanalytic Therapy' (1919), in *SE*, vol. 17.

——*Inhibitions, Symptoms and Anxiety* (1926), in *SE*, vol. 20.

——'The Oedipal Organization of Shame: The Analysis of a Phobia', in *Psychoanalytic Study of the Child*, vol. 45, New Haven: Yale University Press, 1990, pp. 357–76.

Green, A., 'The Central Phobic Position: A New Formulation of the Free Association Method', in *International Journal of Psychoanalysis*, vol. 81 (3), 2000, pp. 429–51.

Hall, S., Critcher, C., Jefferson, T., Clark, J. and Roberts, B., *Policing the Crisis*, London: Macmillan, 1978.

Jones, E., 'The Psychopathology of Anxiety' (1929), in *Papers on Psychoanalysis*, London: Bailliere, Tindall and Cox, 1948.

Kahn, M.M.R., 'Role of Phobic and Counterphobic Mechanisms and Separation Anxiety in Schizoid Character Formation', in *International Journal of Psychoanalysis*, vol. 47 (2–3), 1966, pp. 306–13.

Klein, M., 'The Theory of Intellectual Inhibition' (1931), in *Love, Guilt and Reparation*, London: Delta, 1975.

Kovel, J., *White Racism: A Psychohistory* (1965), London: Free Association Books, 1988.

Kristeva, J., *In the Beginning was Love: Psychoanalysis and Faith*, trans. A. Goldhammer, New York: Columbia University Press, 1987.

Little, R., 'The Resolution of Oral Conflicts in a Spider Phobia', in *International Journal of Psychoanalysis*, vol. 49 (2–3), 1968.

Meltzer, D., *The Claustrum: An Investigation into Claustrophobic Phenomena*, Strathclyde: Clunie Press, 1992.

Music, G., *Affect and Emotion*, Ideas in Psychoanalysis series, Cambridge: Icon Books, 2001.

Sandler, A.-M., 'Comments on Phobic Mechanisms in Childhood', in *Psychoanalytic Study of the Child*, vol. 44, New Haven: Yale University Press, 1989.

Segal, H., 'A Note on Schizoid Mechanisms Underlying Phobia Formation', in *International Journal of Psychoanalysis*, vol. 35 (2), 1954.

Ward, I. (ed.), *The Psychology of Nursery Education*, London: Karnac Books–The Freud Museum, 1997.

Wilmut, R. and Rosengard, P., *Didn't You Kill my Mother-in-law?*, London: Methuen, 1989.

Winnicott, D., *The Piggle: An Account of the Psychoanalytic Treatment of a Little Girl*, ed. I. Ramzy, London: Penguin Books, 1977.

——'Transitional Objects and Transitional Phenomena', in *International Journal of Psychoanalysis*, vol. 34 (2), 1953, pp. 89–97.

8

Eros

Nicola Abel-Hirsch

Eros: 'A Principle of Attraction'[1]

Eros is the idea of a force which 'binds together' the elements of human existence – physically through sex, emotionally through love and mentally through imagination.

In Freud's time, talk of sex, particularly the sexual wishes and phantasies of children, was shocking to many of his contemporaries. But what would shock us today? An idea explored here is that one cannot have the binding of intercourse (sexual, emotional or intellectual intercourse) without a form of love. You can of course have sexual penetration without love – paedophilia is a reminder of that – but this is not the same as an intercourse. The form of love necessary for intercourse is understood to be the two-way recognition of the difference of the other, separate from the subject, existing in his or her own life and each an object of concern to the other. Without this, there is no 'two' to be bound in intercourse with each other.[2]

I take my starting point from Freud's concept of 'life instinct', which he calls 'Eros'. Prior to his introduction of Eros, Freud placed a key emphasis on sexuality as the source of motivation and energy in many activities, whether overtly sexual or not. When he introduced the concept of Eros, he included sexuality in it, but also added the notion of a general principle of attraction. Eros, he said, is what binds things together – and, one could add, binds them together in a way that leads to something alive or new.

Beyond the Pleasure Principle

In the middle years of his life, and against a backdrop of war and the death of his daughter Sophie, Freud wrote what he describes as a highly speculative paper. 'Beyond the Pleasure Principle' (1920) is an exploration of life and death, conceptualised by Freud in terms of 'instincts'. Freud has interesting questions to ask, such as: What brings things to life? Has death been there from the beginning of life? He turns to biology and makes use of his findings in thinking about the dynamics of the mind. He reaches the view that 'life instinct', or Eros, 'holds all living things together'.[3] In later works, he further comments that it 'form[s] living substance into ever greater unities, so that life may be prolonged and brought to higher development'[4] and, again, that it 'aims at complicating life and at the same time, of course, at preserving it'.[5]

One piece of biological research that caught his attention was work on 'vital differences'. The research studied cells which come together and then separate again. The cells are rejuvenated by this process. Freud suggests that whilst organisms generally aim for a release of tension, which leads eventually to death (see 'A Note on Thanatos' below), at the same time:

> [U]nion with the living substance of a different individual increases those tensions, introducing what may be described as fresh 'vital differences' which must then be lived off.[6]

Freud saw this conjugation of cells as the forerunner of sexual reproduction in higher creatures involving, as we now know, the recombination of genetic material. Freud's view is of a live process in which 'bringing together' has a disruptive but rejuvenating effect on the elements or parties involved. Eros is a *tension* in the organism.

There is an interesting contemporary question in this context to do with the difference between cloning and reproduction. Both processes result in a life. Cloning, however, leads to a repetition of something that is already there. By contrast, in sexual reproductive activity, although foreign bodies are generally taken by the immune system to be a threat to life, the body has to encounter – and be host to – first the sperm and then the developing embryo.

In his or her emotional/mental life, a person can react like an immune system repelling foreign experience or ideas. In order for sexual, emotional or mental intercourse to be possible, the 'foreignness' or difference of the other person or idea has to be entertained. Part of the difficulty in doing this is that difference involves the recognition that the other person has things one does not have oneself. The other sex, for example, has a body with different sexual characteristics. At the same time, difference holds the promise of something new and is the necessary condition for intercourse (between different parties) – be this sexual, emotional or intellectual.

Sex and Love

With his concept of Eros, Freud introduces new ground to his overriding interest in the sexual instincts. Eros provides the potential for a unified theory of sex and love in which neither is secondary to the other and both are forms of a 'binding together' or intercourse between different elements. Freud does not develop his ideas on Eros himself, and is perhaps more interested in the idea of 'death instinct'. Nevertheless, Freud's Eros can be developed today, particularly in relation to Melanie Klein's innovative work on love, and the work of Wilfred Bion and others on imagination. However, to go back a step, first I want to illustrate the problems that arise if sex and love are kept separate from each other. This happens in a curious way in psychoanalytic theory itself when a rather simplistic opposition is set up between the theory of Freud (Instinct Theory) and that of Klein and others (Object Relations Theory).

'Instincts' and 'Relations'

Firstly: **Instinct Theory** – a caricature of this can be seen in the view that men only want sex. In this view, the appetite for sex arises within the person. The person then looks for someone to satisfy their need. What matters is the sex rather than the person who offers it.

Secondly: **Object Relations Theory** – a caricature of this can be seen in the view that women only want love. In this view, all that matters is the emotional relationship. There appear to be no sexual desires arising in the woman.

In both these caricatures, there is a split between sex and love. In the first, the relationship with the other person is a means to get sex. In the second, sex for the woman is a means to get love.

In fact, if one splits sex and love like this, it could be argued that what one gets is neither sex nor love. Sex without recognition of, and concern for, the other person cannot be an intimacy between *two* people. Likewise, the love in the caricature above of Object Relations Theory seems more like a wish for security or flattery than a desire to be with the other person. This is not to say that the quantity and quality of love in an affair would be the same as, say, that in a long-standing marriage, but that a concern for the other as other (cf. love) makes intercourse between two different people possible. In the same way, in relation to love, the way sex is expressed is very different between lovers or, say, mothers and babies, but something is arguably missing if the mother–baby relationship is devoid of anything sensual.

With this in mind, it seems better to try to hold the two theories together (Instinct and Object Relations) and draw on both. In contrast to Klein and other object-relations analysts, Freud places greater emphasis on sex than on love, but his concept of Eros can encompass their understanding of love, as well as more recent work by Bion and others on the imagination.

A Note on Thanatos[7]

From the time of his 'speculative paper' 'Beyond the Pleasure Principle', Freud held to the view that conflict between life and death instinct lay at the heart of life. In his view, death instinct, which he called 'Thanatos', is the opposite to Eros. It aims at death either through reducing differentiation and silently pulling the organism back into an inorganic state, or through active destruction. Innate, the instinct is initially turned on the self; it is then deflected onto the outside world as aggression.

Freud conceived of Eros and Thanatos as having a multitude of differing relations with each other. He thought, for example, that eating involves both instincts, one in the destruction of the object eaten and the other in the intent through eating to live. Another example is sexual intercourse, in which aggression is put together with the most intimate unity.

A great deal has been written about Freud's concept of death instinct. One question in particular relates to whether aggression is always to do with the death instinct. In contemporary psychoanalysis, a convincing view is to see 'life instinct' and 'death instinct' as two masters. The question then ceases to be, 'Is aggression death instinct?' and becomes, 'Is aggression being used, in this particular instance, to serve life or to serve death?'

Eros in the Body: What is Sexuality?

Much has been written on sexuality. My focus here is going to be on sexuality from the point of view of Eros.

Eros 'Form[s] Living Substance into Ever Greater Unities'[8]

In Freud's model of sexuality,[9] we start off at the level of the infant with what he calls 'polymorphous perverse' sexuality. By this, he means that infantile sexuality, whilst it may involve excitement felt in the genitals, is more like the sexuality seen in adult foreplay (for which it is the precursor). All kinds of parts of the body can become sexually stimulated. In particular, as a part of the body becomes a general focus for the infant and child, it also becomes a focus of sexual excitement. Initially, the infant concentrates on feeding – involving the mouth and the nipple and the act of sucking. This, Freud delineates as the 'Oral phase' in the development of the child's sexuality. The second phase is the 'Anal phase' and is connected with the child's focus on its bowels and toilet-training. Freud thought that this was followed by what he termed the 'Phallic phase'. This phase in particular has been controversial, as some think that it does not give a picture of the development of the girl's sexuality and that it is an attack on women to define their sexuality in relation to their absence of a penis. It does seem that there are real problems with this phase, but perhaps what can be said here is that the Phallic phase has in it the idea of the hatred (as well as attraction) of difference. The other sex has what one does not.

Freud argues that in adolescence and adulthood the diverse strands of sexuality (for example, from different erotogenous zones like the mouth, anus, skin and genitals) become united and focused on genitality.

Although Freud does not explicitly liken this model of 'binding diverse strands into a complex whole' to the same factor in his model of Eros, they are very much alike, and it may be that the sexual model informed his emphasis on this in Eros.

The binding together of 'diverse strands' of sexuality is dependent on the recognition of vital differences, particularly the difference between the sexes and that between the generations (between parents and children).

Eros, Sexuality and 'Vital Difference': Two Children's Phantasies

One seven-year-old girl, after spending many weeks experimenting with weeing like a boy (standing up over the toilet), asked her mother if sex was people weeing on each other. She seemed content at that point with the answer 'no' and did not ask what, if not weeing, sex then was. The impression she gave was that accurate information about sex (information to which she had access) was not what mattered at this point, she would work it out in her own time. She may also have been feeling anxious about the idea of penetration in intercourse.

It would not be right, I think, to say that the little girl wanted to be a boy. It seemed more that she wanted to be both a boy and a girl, and in her model of intercourse both can do the same thing – wee on each other. Her model of sexual intercourse – weeing – is also something she was physically capable of doing herself in 'intercourse' with her father, or 'as a boy' with her mother.

At this point in the young girl's development, the difference between the sexes and the difference between the generations is held at bay.

By contrast, in a dream from her sister who is two years older, we do see a differentiation, and an excited one at that, between boys and girls. In the dream, the girl was with her friend in the girls' toilet at school. Each was in a neighbouring toilet-booth and each had the door open. Two boys from their class came in. The girl quickly closed her door. She allayed her own worries about having been seen with the thought that the other girl's door was still open and she would certainly have been seen.

Then the girl was in the seaside resort she visited every year with her family. The resort is on the Atlantic and has the large rolling waves of a surfing beach. There are seals in the water. In the dream, the girl is out in deep water waiting for a wave she can surf on. She cannot see her family, but they are around her in the sea. She is then 'picked up' by the wave and flung across the water. It was, she said on telling the dream, like flying.

If the child were in analysis, then one would have her thoughts about the dream and other analytic material to help in understanding it. Without this, what follows is more speculative.

In the child's mind, it is possible that 'seeing' genitals is to do with having sex, and that toilets appear in the dream not just because that is actually where the children might 'see' each other at school, but because the child connects defecation with sex and babies.

Faeces are the first thing a child produces. Faecal material is his or hers and it can be either given as a gift or withheld by the child. To give up the equation of faeces and baby – to realise that they are not produced in the same way – can be hard for the child, because it involves an admission to herself that she is small, and not able to have father's babies as mother can. The child is of a *different* generation to the parents.

What of the ocean in the dream? It would seem to be a sense of an exciting and expansive force that can take her over and support her at the same time. Anyone who has ridden a wave to shore, had an orgasm, fallen in love or felt an idea coming to life knows that all four are the same kind of experience. In each case, a moment of mobility is granted – to body, feelings or mind.

The dream conveys something of the conflicts the child might feel in relation to her emerging sexuality, and may itself be a way of trying to work on these. In particular, the conflict between wanting to be 'seen' by a boy (and eventually 'entered' by a man) and the anxiety or shame felt about this.

In the Oedipal situation, to which I now turn, it is in phantasy that the child can put sex and love together in the desired relationship with mother or father. In adulthood, if one's sexual partner can be known to be different from one's infantile phantasy world, then the kind of complexity of wishes and feelings seen in the child's dream can add depth to the new adult relationship.

Oedipus: Incestuous Desire and its Resolution

Many people will have come across the story of Oedipus, and numerous papers have been written on it in psychoanalysis and other disciplines. Freud commented on the capacity of this story to fascinate, and it has continued to do so even when more of its unconscious content (the wish to kill one parent and marry the other) is consciously known by today's post-Freud audience.

A brief sketch of the myth, portrayed in the plays of Sophocles, is as follows. Laius, the father of Oedipus, is warned by an oracle that his son will kill him and marry his wife. In the film *Edipo Re* (1960), directed by Pier Paolo Pasolini, one sees a young father jealous of his baby, Oedipus. The baby has mother's attention, and the breast is for milk and therefore not sexually available to the father. Whether or not jealousy of the child is involved, the oracle is believed and the baby is pierced by a brooch in the ankles and left to die on a desolate hillside. Oedipus (the name means 'swollen feet') is, however, saved and grows up believing himself to be the son of a neighbouring king. He then hears of the prophecy himself and leaves the people he believes to be his parents in order to protect them from the threatened murderous violence towards his father and seduction of his mother. On his travels, he comes to a crossroads where he has to jump for his life out of the way of a fast-moving carriage. His rage boils over and he kills the man in the carriage, who in fact is his natural father. He arrives in Thebes (his birth home, although he does not know it), where he encounters the Sphinx, who sets him the following riddle:

What is that which has one voice and yet becomes four-footed and two-footed and three-footed?[10]

(Apollodorus, *The Library*, 3.5.7–9)

The answer to the riddle is man, who in the course of his life first crawls, then walks and ends up with a walking-stick. Oedipus answers correctly. The Sphinx, as a consequence of his correct answer, kills itself.

Creon, the current king of Thebes, has offered the kingdom and the hand of Jocasta, Laius's widow, to whoever can solve the riddle. Oedipus, apparently unwittingly, marries his mother and they have children. Oedipus then discovers that he is the murderer of the previous King and further, that it is his birth-father that he has murdered. He has murdered his father and married his mother as the oracle predicted. When Jocasta discovers the truth, she kills herself; Oedipus blinds himself. The corruption of relations between parents and children is repeated when Oedipus himself is unable to take care of his own children. He puts on one of his sons a 'curse of strife' which he describes as a continuation of the curse on Laius.

Freud thought that the play portrayed a dynamic that is every child's wish: namely, to marry one parent and murder the other. He gave as an example the Freud family nanny's dream that his wife (her mistress) had died and she then married Freud. Through his self-analysis, he found the same constellation in himself.[11] Freud emphasised the child's wish to marry the parent of the opposite sex, but both Freud and psychoanalysts since have thought that the child experiences a heterosexual and a homosexual version of the same wish, with the parent of the opposite sex and the parent of the same sex respectively. The young girl above, who asked if sex was people weeing on each other, seems to want the possibility of both versions. She wanted to be like her father, and wee on mother, and at other times was very intent on 'marrying' father.

What might lead the child to give up these incestuous phantasies? Freud thought that little boys feared a retaliatory castration by the excluded father. The story he gives for the little girl is less clear. Klein thought that the equivalent fear for the girl was that her phantasied attacks on mother will lead to a reprisal by mother.

The violence of the feared castration or retaliation echoes the violence in the myth of Oedipus which is strikingly lacking in love. Parents abandon their baby to die. There is no possibility of repairing violent acts or even 'mistakes'. Instead, people kill or blind themselves. As an adult man, Oedipus is unable to love his son.

Recent work in psychoanalysis, however, has looked more closely at the place of love in the Oedipal situation and, in particular, love for the one who is 'left out'. This is love for the parent the child wishes to exclude, in order to have a passionate relationship with the other parent. Love for the excluded one can become a sympathetic love of the child for itself too, excluded from the parental relationship. Freud (and this was much developed by Klein after him) suggests that this form of love is a factor in children giving up or repressing incestuous desires.

Parents, of course, can help or hinder in these things. In particular, sexual intrusion by a parent can inhibit and damage a child's sexual and general development. It may also be that the parents are not together and that one or other is not available to the child. This would clearly affect the child, but internal processes are also strong and a child can have a concept of a parental couple even if the external reality is different from this.

If the child is able to leave the parents alone – literally and in the child's mind – the parental relationship becomes a template for allowing 'intercourse' to occur. The child may, for example, be enabled to allow ideas to come together in his or her own mind, instead of having to rigidly control what he or she thinks.

To be excluded from the 'exciting' and 'mysterious' relationship of the parents and feel small and unknowing as a child might, are, however, difficult experiences. In some people, there is a great wish to avoid the experience of generational difference and continue in the illusion that one is really the erotic partner of the parent. The price paid for this, however, is that one loses the chance for real physical or psychic intercourse with a new partner. This was the case for Anna O.

Anna O: The Avoidance of 'Vital Difference'[12]

Anna O's real name was Bertha Pappenheim. She was a friend of Freud's wife and was in treatment with Joseph Breuer, Freud's early mentor and colleague.

The psychoanalyst Ronald Britton argues that Anna O was unable to give up the illusion of her father as her partner, and enacted this relation with Breuer. Britton comments that Freud heard two versions of the story of Anna O's treatment with Breuer. One was the official version, the other was told one summer evening when the two men dined alone.

When she entered treatment with Breuer, Anna O was twenty-one. On the surface of things, she was very eligible, but according to Breuer had never had a romantic attachment or any sexual thoughts. During the time she had nursed her dying father, Anna became progressively weaker and developed anorexia. She acquired a severe cough, a squint, various paralyses and suffered a loss of normal speech. At the same time, two distinct states of consciousness established themselves. In one, she was melancholy and anxious but relatively normal. In the other, she hallucinated and misbehaved.

Breuer gave an attentive interest to her symptoms and states of mind. He became the only person she would recognise and he also became the only person who could feed her. When he was there, she became euphoric; when he was away, she became much worse. Britton notes that Breuer did not seem to connect her states of mind to her attachment to him.

Britton takes up the story himself on the basis of new evidence provided more recently by the historian of psychoanalysis Henri Ellenberger.[13] Breuer's wife appears to have been angry and impatient with his involvement with Anna O. Britton suggests that Anna O was hospitalised for a few days from 7 June 1881 as a consequence of Frau Breuer's insistence that her husband spend more time with her. The Breuers left for a few days, and during that month their daughter was conceived.

Exactly one year later, Anna O's treatment ended with her enactment of two extraordinary scenes. The first scene was reported in the official story, the second scene was not. The first scene involves a hallucination Anna O had suffered whilst nursing her father. She and Breuer appeared to believe this to be the key to her illness, now expiated through the enactment and cured. The second scene happened shortly afterwards:

> *After leaving Anna O for the last time Breuer was called back to find her confused and writhing with abdominal cramps. Asked what was the matter, she replied, 'Now comes Dr Breuer's child'. Freud commented 'at that moment Breuer held the key in his hand but he dropped it'. In conventional horror he took flight and left the patient to a colleague.*[14]

Britton argues that Anna O had the (unconscious) belief that she was in her father's bedroom not as a daughter/nurse, but as his partner. The union is a deadly one, as she starves herself to death with him, but it is nonetheless a union. Anna O then repeated her belief with her new doctor. Instead of being Breuer's patient, she is his partner – and an exciting and interesting partner at that. In phantasy, she has his child. It seems that Breuer could not let himself see this – perhaps he felt he was implicated in her feelings for him; he certainly did not know what to do with them. Freud, by contrast, was able to be curious about what had happened.

A Concluding Note on Sexuality

Freud's concept of Eros as 'binding' into more complex wholes focuses attention on how diverse strands are drawn together in the development of a person's sexuality. It is a complex model of sexuality, and can accommodate individuals' different sexual development. Further to this, whilst Freud's emphasis on genitality may contain elements of moral judgement, it is firmly based on his recognition of the link between intercourse and new life. This is self-evident when it comes to human procreation, but the importance of intercourse as a model goes much further than this.

Even in relation to sexuality, intercourse may not be literal and could be an alive intimacy between two people. What would not be intercourse from the point of view of Eros, even if it involved penetration, would be those situations where another person's body is just used for sex (this is really a form of masturbation) or where a rigid, sadistic or dismissive control is exerted over the other person and their separateness and difference denied. This is not to say, of course, that sexuality does not have aggression in it. The distinction is between aggression as part of an intercourse and aggression used to avoid or destroy an alive interchange.

Eros in the Emotions: What is Love?

In relation to sexuality, love and thought, there is a difference between seeing the relationship between oneself and the other as one would wish it to be, and on the other hand discovering what *it* really is. In 'love', this is broadly the difference between idealised love and a more complex and generous love. Idealised love is the way love often starts, and it tends towards a partial and wish-fulfilling picture of both the other and oneself. There may be little awareness of difference or the idealisation of it. As with assumptions in thought (which I move on to later), idealised love is notorious for ignoring evidence that contradicts it. At the same time, unless it has to be held onto in a rigid way, idealisation can 'melt' as one begins to find out about the other person. One's love can then become something more complex and generous: complex because it involves a recognition of more aspects of the personality, including uncomfortable or unpleasant ones; generous because it involves a recognition of the other person in his or her own right, and a concern about them.

Idealised Love

My face in thine eye, thine in mine appeares,
And true plaine hearts doe in the faces rest,
Where can we finde two better hemispheares
Without sharpe North, without declining West?
What ever dyes, was not mixt equally;
If our two loves be one, or, thou and I
Love so alike, that none doe slacken, none can die.[15]
(John Donne, 'The Good-Morrow')

Freud thought it part of the essential nature of falling in love to idealise the loved person. People, he suggests, would not be so foolish as to fall in love if they had their eyes properly open to the strengths and weaknesses of the loved one. Love is an everyday madness – a point recognised by the seventeenth-century play-wright William Congreve, when he wrote:

> *If this be not love, then it is madness, and then it is pardon-able.*[16]

> (William Congreve, *The Old Bachelor*)

Along with the idealisation of the loved person, Freud thought that people saw an idealised view of themselves in the love partner. When people tell another their 'life story', it is an account that has within it the way they wish to be seen, as well (perhaps) as a real desire to be known by the other person.

Associated with being at one's best, idealised love is an unstable structure, since the worst (one's 'sharpe North' and 'declining West') has been left out of the picture – but has not in fact gone away.

When there is an idealisation, it means that criticisms, doubts and hostilities are kept at bay and are often taken to belong to someone else. A male patient, for example, told me that *all* was well between his wife and himself, the problem was just that their child was so unpleasant and obstructive. The fact that destructiveness and anger are kept at bay, and in this case located in the child, can result in paranoid feelings and beliefs that something is going to come in from outside the relationship and spoil or destroy things, as the patient's child was felt to do.

Idealisation is a part of the state of mind that Klein called the Paranoid Schizoid Position.[17] She thought this was the earliest state of mind in the infant, and one that can recur throughout life, particularly when one is faced with a new situation. In this state of mind, Klein argues, love and hate are kept separate from each other. The split which occurs between love and hate gives some order to the baby's chaos of feelings and protects what is good, enabling it to grow.

An example of such a split between love and hate is given by Meg Harris Williams and Donald Meltzer,[18] who suggest that an infant may locate opposite feelings in different places in relation to mother's body. The loving feelings may be located in mother's skin – which can be touched, stroked and experienced as beautiful. The hateful feelings may be located in her insides, which become an ugly place of violence and damage. Perhaps Ted Hughes had such feelings in mind when he drafted the following:

> *. . . Those are not dogs*
> *That seem to be dogs*

Pulling at her. Remember the lean hound
Running up the lane holding high
The dangling raw windpipe and lungs
Of a fox? Now see who
Will drop on all fours at the end of the street
And come romping towards your mother,
Pulling her remains, with their lips . . .[19]

(Ted Hughes, 'The Dogs Are Eating Your Mother')

The fear that one cannot manage hostile feelings or put right damage done can prevent a person from being free to know about their hostile or destructive feelings at all. If, however, a person has the belief that good will prevail, it makes him or her better able to face the destructiveness that may also be present.

A Complex and Generous Love

One of Melanie Klein's papers, written in the 1920s, begins with a description of the opera *The Magic Word*.[20] The stage opens on a child of six sitting with his homework. He does not want to do it and is rude to his mother. She responds that he will have dry bread and no sugar in his tea as punishment. At this added frustration, the child flies into a rage and smashes things in the room. There is a squirrel in a cage and he tries to stab it with his pen. The squirrel escapes through the window. He opens the grandfather clock and pulls out the copper pendulum. Then the objects he has mistreated come to life and attack him back. The chair refuses to let him sit down, the stove spits sparks at him. A sad tune is played by the shepherd on the wallpaper who was separated from his loved one when the child ripped the piece down between them.

The child collapses and flees out of doors. There he finds more terror. The insects fight and a tree-trunk bleeds sap. In a dispute about who should get to attack the child first, a squirrel is wounded and falls to the floor. This time, instead of fighting or running away, the child stops and binds the squirrel's paw. As he does so, he whispers 'Mama'. All the animals then stop fighting and whisper 'Mama' too.

When Klein read an account of the opera, she saw more than an explosion of frustration and anger from the child. What, she asks, is being attacked by the child? She concludes that it is the parents in their relationship to each other: the shepherd and the shepherdess are torn apart from each other, the squirrel in the cage is attacked, the pendulum torn from the clock. There is to be nothing inside something else – no penis inside mother's body.

Klein argues that the retaliation from the damaged objects portrays the anxiety that one's attacks will be returned upon oneself in a magnified and terrifying way. This can lead to more violence or a flight from the scene, but the child does neither. What is it that allows the child to break the vicious cycle by caring for the squirrel? The child seems to have found within himself a capacity for concern and a belief that he can put things right. The child 'has learnt to love and believes in love'.[21]

The child's concern for the squirrel is the complex and generous love that belongs to what Klein calls the Depressive Position.[22] By 'position', Klein means the way that the whole of a person's personality is orientated at a particular moment in time, including their anxieties and defences against these. Klein thought that the Depressive Position emerges from the Paranoid Schizoid Position when infants become able to realise that the mother they love and idealise is the same person as the mother they hate and fear. The infant's concern is then that the loved person will have been damaged, perhaps irrevocably, by his or her attacks – the anxiety that mother's insides really have gone to the dogs.

In the earliest Paranoid Schizoid Position, the main anxiety is the survival of the self. Destructiveness is turned outwards to protect the self. In the Depressive Position, the main worry is for the other, the child's worry for the injured squirrel. At first sight, depression would not seem to have much to do with love. Klein, however, thought that *love has to take destructiveness into account*. The capacity to tolerate guilt, without getting too paranoid or overwhelmed by the guilt, is the basis of concern – without which, the notion of enduring love is meaningless. Segal,[23] for example, argues that sustainable peace can follow war only if winner and loser alike can take seriously the amount of damage done and feel guilt at the waste of life and resources. If not, one enemy is replaced by another in a repetitive cycle.

If the child is so frightened by the possibility of irrevocable damage that damage cannot be thought about at all, the child loses the opportunity to check his or her fear of damage against mother's actual state, or to discover a capacity to make reparation. Instead, one might see a rigid denial and idealisation in which everything *has* to be alright or, for example, a 'manic' reparation in which the person rushes around blindly doing good without knowing what is feared to be damaged.

Eros as Putting Something (Back) Together

In his concept of Eros, Freud's interest and attention is in the binding of different elements together; Klein's is in putting some-thing damaged back together (reparation). One important form of reparation is the putting together of a picture about what has happened. Even if the damage (i.e. to the mother or father, represented by the squirrel above) has been done in phantasy, it is real psychically, although not necessarily materially. Reassurance that it is not real does not work on such fears. It may give a temporary relief, but the fear remains. For the person concerned, the wish to destroy has paradoxically to be accepted in all its awfulness (as if mother is actually destroyed) before reparation can be meaningful. Reparation can also involve the recognition that in external reality the damage cannot be put right.

A Concluding Note on Love

Love can feel simple. From a psychoanalytic view, this simplicity is seen as the outcome of a complex intercourse that is going well. By contrast, idealistic love (or denigratory hate) of the other person can, if rigid, result in a simplistic and repetitive kind of relationship.

Something similar can be seen in relation to Eros in the mind, where the capacity to grasp the complexity of a situation can issue in a simple end-idea, whilst the use of rigid, simplistic assumptions can mean that views get repeated without an openness to discovering anything new.

Eros in the Mind: What is Imagination?

Imaginative work is an intercourse between one's internal life and the world around us.

One view of imagination is that it is an activity in which one can think anything one likes, where there is limitless freedom but at the same time inconsequential freedom – inconsequential because it is not connected to reality and therefore not able to make any real difference. Another view, and my view, is that imagination is connected both to a person's inner world and to external reality. From a psychoanalytic point of view, the capacity to be imaginative is to do with the capacity to let oneself be affected. This involves a willingness to be in touch with one's psychic reality and to be affected through an interchange with the world around one, with external reality. One often does not choose what one is going to be affected by and cannot prejudge the outcome.

Imaginative activity may be more obviously linked to artistic work, but it is also integral to making logical hypotheses of the kind, 'If X happens, then Y will happen.' Segal[24] illustrates this point with examples from science-fiction writing and contrasts the 'as if' quality of 'space opera' (an escapist world of heroes and heroines, like daydreams) with science-fiction stories that imagine what would happen if a current parameter were to be changed, such as 'what if' there were no gravity.

In what follows, I am going to look at two points in people's lives that seem of particular importance to the development of the capacity to be imaginative. One is very early in life. The second is what has been called 'the mid-life crisis'.

In the depths of one's mind, one probably never gives up being omnipotent. Somewhere in one's mind, that is, one never gives up believing that one knows everything or is capable of knowing everything, that one is the best and will live forever. In contrast to this, imagination is perhaps most liberated at those moments when one becomes aware of what one does not know or does not have. This is the case in my two examples. Firstly, the baby . . .

The Origins of Imagination

Imagination is necessary to our thinking about things when they are not there and our thought about them when they are.[25]
(Mary Warnock, philosopher)

A baby starts to get hungry and becomes fretful. It then begins to make sucking movements with its mouth and seems to settle down into a contented state. After a few minutes, it breaks down into cries. What happened in the few minutes of contentment? The baby was probably hallucinating the breast. It believed it was feeding – until hunger pangs broke through the hallucination.

Hallucination is an ancestor of daydreams. In both, people try to give themselves what they want and, in particular, try to gratify and soothe themselves. When this breaks down, what happens? The baby may not realise he or she has been hallucinating. The hunger pains may instead be experienced as a 'bad' hallucination of being attacked by a cruel presence.

In hallucination, the baby manufactures its own world; as it gets more in touch with reality, the two are put together. Imagination is where the capacity to manufacture our own world meets up with reality. In particular, as the psychoanalyst Wilfred Bion suggests, it is the discovery of absence which enables the first imaginative thought – the baby who can endure and know the reality of mother's absence can also imagine her in her absence.[26]

Imaginative Creativity and the Mid-life Crisis

Whoever does not, sometime or other, give his full consent . . . to the dreadfulness of life, can never take possession of the unutterable abundance and power of our existence: can only walk on its edge, and one day, when the judgement is given, will have been neither alive nor dead.[27]

In his paper 'Death and the Mid-life Crisis', Jaques suggests that a critical phase in the development of the individual occurs around the age of 35. Jaques took a random sample of some 310 painters, composers, poets, writers and sculptors of greatness. He found that, in comparison to the rest of the population, more of them died in their mid-thirties. He makes a link to 'the mid-life crisis', implying that some of these creative people were not able to find a way through it. With less intensity perhaps, it is a crisis that assails everyone when faced with the limitation of what they have achieved and the now visible end of their life. If a person arrives in mid-life without having been able to face some complexity of feeling (including destructive feelings), he or she has limited tools with which to face the mid-life crisis. This, Jaques suggests, can lead to an increased emphasis on appearance, and insistence that all is fine and nothing is changing:

> *The compulsive attempts, in many men and women reaching middle age, to remain young, the hypochondriacal concern over health and appearance, the emergence of sexual promis-cuity in order to prove youth and potency, the hollowness and lack of genuine enjoyment of life, and the frequency of religious concern, are familiar patterns.*[28]

If, however, one can entertain thoughts about the limits of life, it can deepen one's own experience and respect for other people's lives.

Jaques suggests that when hate, destruction and death are found in youthful art, they tend to take the form of the satanic or the macabre. Whilst in those artists who have been able to endure the crisis, the elements of hate, destruction and death have a more tragic and integrated place in their work. If, by contrast, the artist is not able to get through the crisis, one can see an impoverishment of imaginative activity and its replacement by something more conservative and repetitive.

Wordsworth went through a change in mid-life, both politically and poetically, from being a revolutionary and an innovator to becoming the established and conformist Poet Laureate. Ronald Britton notes that Wordsworth had an unusual capacity in youth to represent loss in his work.[29] In mid-life, Wordsworth took up a more conventional lifestyle. At this point, Britton argues, he seems to have lost the capacity to embrace the periods of upheaval and uncertainty needed if new thought is to be possible. A sense of loss and new realisation is replaced by assertion, coherent belief and moral certainty. Wordsworth, in this view, went on to do good work in his long later life, but his great work was written in his youth.

By contrast to Wordsworth, the work of the contemporary painter Howard Hodgkin is generally accepted to have come to life when he entered his forties. During this period, Hodgkin left his marriage of twenty years and declared his homosexuality. Andrew Graham-Dixon comments:

> If many of the pictures of the first part of his career seem to betray a desire to be elsewhere, the pictures of his later career see that desire fulfilled. They become new and vivid worlds, no longer so sketched around with irony or so often deflected into satire. They are more naked: their colours are raw and the skin of paint that they present to the world becomes increasingly vulnerable, liquid and membranous. They speak of more (more pleasures and predicaments) and they do so more urgently and eloquently.[30]

In a recent article, Hodgkin conveys that the change which occurred in mid-life has continued to the present day. He comments that, although he finds the work more difficult, 'the results are getting ever nearer to what I want'.[31] Hodgkin will be 70 years old in August 2002.

Phantasy and Imagination

He loved her and she loved him
His kisses sucked out her whole past and future or tried to
He had no other appetite
She bit him she gnawed him she sucked
She wanted him complete inside her
Safe and Sure forever and ever . . .

His smiles were the garrets of a fairy palace
Where the real world would never come
Her smiles were spider bites
So he would lie still till she felt hungry
His words were occupying armies
Her laughs were an assassin's attempts
His looks were bullets daggers of revenge
Her glances were ghosts in the corner with horrible secrets
His whispers were whips and jackboots
Her kisses were lawyers steadily writing . . .

Her vows put his eyes in formalin
At the back of her secret drawer
Their screams stuck in the wall
Their heads fell apart into sleep like the two halves
Of a lopped melon, but love is hard to stop

In their entwined sleep they exchanged arms and legs
In their dreams their brains took each other hostage

In the morning they wore each other's face[32]

(Ted Hughes, 'Lovesong')

Hughes' striking poem is the outcome of imaginative work – imaginative work which has a considerable access to phantasy. The poem portrays an intense intercourse on the edge of something sadistic, and one in which the difference between the two people does not return to them in the same form in the morning. On reading it, one has the sense that it is a true picture of such a relationship. It is the imaginative activity which gives a truthful portrait of the relationship – whether the relationship itself is truthful is a different kind of question. By 'truthful portrait' is meant more than accuracy. From a psychoanalytic point of view, it involves other factors too – such as the psychological depth and resonance of what is described.

Phantasy is rather different. I illustrate imaginative work above by Hughes' poem *as a poem* – a composed structure in verse. But phantasy, by contrast, is in the poem and, for example, in the young girl's dream. What then is phantasy?

The psychoanalyst Elizabeth Bott Spillius makes the following point about phantasy:

> *The word conveys contrasting implications . . . It has a connotation of the imagination and creativity that underlie all thought and feeling, but it also has a connotation of make-believe, a daydream, something that is untrue by the standards of material reality.*[33]

An example of the first connotation of the word 'phantasy' (something that underlies all thought and feeling) is the point made earlier that access to infantile phantasies can deepen involvement in an adult relationship and offer some gratification (although unconsciously and not completely) of early desires. Hughes' lovers, for example, know about infantile possessive longings for the other. The second connotation of phantasy – to the fore in daydreams and idealised relations – is more to do with seeing ourselves as we would wish to be. In the world of daydreams and idealised relations, unwelcome qualities or conflicts are located elsewhere. Such 'make-believe' phantasy tends to be fleeting – unless it becomes too addictive *a* – as Hughes says – *fairy palace / Where the real world would never come.*

Although work is done in phantasy – as the young girl works on conflicting feelings in her dream – it is not the same kind of work as happens in imaginative activity. Imaginative thought is more sustained work than phantasy. Whilst it has its roots in phantasy, imaginative thought is where the capacity to manufacture or represent our world meets up with reality. Imaginative work is an intercourse between one's internal and external worlds.

Intercourse in the Mind and Defences Against It

Many psychoanalysts, including Freud and Klein, posit that people are born with what Bion calls 'pre-conceptions'.[34] A pre-conception is a template, enabling us to recognise certain relations when we come across them in our experiences in life. The baby, for example, is born with the expectation of the breast. People are also thought to be born with a template of intercourse; that is, with a kind of pre-knowledge of parental intercourse – the primal scene. Intrinsic to this template is a model of bringing two different things together and Bion, for example, thought a model of intercourse was unconsciously invoked every time we bring things together – in bodies, feelings and ideas. From this point of view, intercourse as a model runs through our lives from birth and is not confined to maturity.

If one's unconscious view is that it is disastrous to let two things come together, then a good deal of energy may go into rigidly ensuring that no thought should interact spontaneously with another. An example of this is a patient who told me, after some time in analysis, that he listened only to the things he thought I was not aware of saying. Anything he felt I wanted to make a point of or showed the slightest pleasure or interest in, he would ignore. He did not give me any 'feedback' about which of my thoughts he had listened to and would not respond to, or elaborate on anything I said. He and I were never to interact in a spontaneous way with one another. His view of intercourse was that of a battleground in which only one of us would prevail. He feared that if he let down his guard, I would take over.

Perverse relations are also a way of avoiding intercourse and difference (separateness). An example of this occurs in the work of the psychoanalyst Betty Joseph. Joseph noted that her patient

*was doing something with his fingers . . . He touches the tips of
the fingers of one hand against the fingers of the other very
softly and almost unceasingly . . . This masturbatory activity
seems to have something in common with the mental chunter-
ing, the going over and over things in his mind.*[35]

The patient probably would not realise that there was anything
sexual in his finger movements. In the analytic exploration of this,
however, he and Joseph worked out how the touching of the
fingers was an action that repeated something about all his
relationships. The picture they discovered over time was one in
which he could 'touch' a relationship but not consummate it. In
his conscious mind, he knew he was detached from his wife and
his analyst, but had not been conscious that this detachment
expressed a fear of closeness. In the touching of skin to skin,
Joseph and her patient saw a picture in which there was no real
separation from the other person – and no real intercourse either.

It may seem odd to derive a sexual meaning from such an
innocuous, apparently trivial, action – the touching of the fingers.
However, we are familiar with hand gestures that have a sexual
meaning. We know about the socially shared, common ones, such
as the single-fingered 'up-yours'. Joseph's example is of an action
that is more subtle and private.

Simplistic Assumption or Imaginative Simplicity

Freud thought that 'life instinct', or Eros, united different elements
to produce ever more complex forms. Imagination is interesting in
this context because its relation to complexity is often as a starting
point rather than necessarily a complex end-product. I cannot
speak for the experience of an artist, but certainly in the psychoanalytic world the most impressive clinicians and theoreticians
are those who can take in the complexity of a patient or a problem
and then, as a consequence of this, make what can be a simple
point. The simple point is the outcome of a capacity to entertain a
complicated situation, without 'grasping after certainties'. Bion,
who wrote on this subject, was very taken by a letter that Keats
wrote to his brother in 1817. In the letter, Keats speaks of his
admiration for writers, particularly Shakespeare, in terms of
'negative capability'. By this, he meant a capacity to stay with
what is unknown until new understanding emerges, rather than
quickly assume that the new situation is a familiar one.[36]

By contrast, an assumption is a simplistic starting point which is
then applied to the data. I need to make a differentiation here
between an assumption and a 'pre-conception'. Some of Freud's

contemporaries and many others since, for example, have made arguments that imply Freud's theory of sexuality operates like an assumption: i.e., he thought (or assumed) sex was everywhere and so he saw sex everywhere. Psychoanalysts, as well as philosophers, have worked on the problem of circular arguments. The work of Bion on 'pre-conceptions' is particularly useful in this context. Bion argued that theory should be held in the analyst's mind as a 'pre-conception'. By this, he meant the use of a theory to help recognise what material might be, rather than a theory used to impose a premature meaning on it. A pre-conception would, for example, be what a psychoanalyst knows about rivalry. This could help the analyst recognise rivalry in the patient's material and draw on psychoanalytic theory to understand it. (It is always messier than this in practice.) An assumption would occur if it was presumed that whenever the analyst heard about brothers and sisters, for example, the material would necessarily be to do with rivalry. It is a constant struggle for the psychoanalyst to try to minimise the number of assumptions being made.

Assumptions are interesting things in their own right, particularly in the context of Eros. Assumptions can look like the binding activity of Eros, but if rigidly held are actually a deadening force when it comes to thinking. One reason for this, mentioned earlier, is that assumptions ignore any evidence that does not fit, and, because of this, can only be repetitive rather than explorative.

Conclusion

I have suggested that the idea of Eros can illuminate some aspects of sexual intimacy, love and imaginative activity. We can now draw out some of the qualities that the three areas have in common.

- Relations between people and within oneself can have greater fluidity and complexity if destructive impulses are taken into account. From this point of view, feeling alive (Eros) involves one's love and hate.
- Pivotal to having a life of one's own is the recognition of difference and sometimes absence and exclusion.
- Once difference is recognised, there arises the possibility of intercourse. Sexual, emotional and imaginative intercourse are key vehicles of Eros. Procreation preserves the species. Intercourse is also a model for the interaction between two 'foreign' elements (people, ideas, etc.) that can lead to something new.
- In some circumstances at least, the more complex a grasp one has of a situation, the more alive the outcome. This has been

contrasted with the application of assumptions which either limit or exclude genuine imagination.

- One way of seeing whether something is on the side of Eros (life instinct) or Thanatos (death instinct) is by looking at what it does or does not lead to. Does an understanding, for example, lead to further thought or does it close it down? In love, does one want to know more about the other person, or is the relationship to be ended when the other steps outside one's preferred view of them? In sexual relationships, is there a developing intimacy between two people, or is there the absence of interest and concern?

In this essay, we have seen how the force of Eros 'binds together' the strands of our human existence – physically through sex, emotionally through love and mentally through imagination. The 'paradox' of Eros is that this 'aliveness' is not a settled state or a drive to homogeneity, but involves the disruption of an intercourse between 'vitally different' aspects of oneself, other people, experiences or ideas.

Acknowledgements

My thanks to my patients. I also want to thank Elizabeth Bott Spillius, Betty Joseph, Maggie Mills, Ivan Ward and Penny Woolcock for their support and insight.

Nicola Abel-Hirsch is a psychoanalyst with the British Psychoanalytical Society. She studied Social Policy and Social Work Studies at the LSE and now works in private practice in West London.

Notes

1. 'The analogy of our two basic instincts extends from the sphere of living things to the pair of opposing forces – attraction and repulsion – which rule in the inorganic world.' Freud, S., 'An Outline of Psycho-Analysis' (1940 [1938]) in *Standard Edition of the Complete Psychological Works of Sigmund Freud* (hereafter *SE*), vol. 23, London: Hogarth Press, 1953–73, p. 149.

2. Elizabeth Bott Spillius's thought on the nature of difference is drawn on throughout the book.

3. Freud, S., 'Beyond the Pleasure Principle' (1920), in *SE*, vol. 18, p. 50.

4. Freud, S., 'The Libido Theory' (1923a [1922]), in *SE*, vol. 18, p. 258.

5. Freud, S., 'The Ego and the Id' (1923b), in *SE*, vol. 19, p. 40.

6. Freud (1920), op. cit., p. 55 (my emphasis).

7. See ibid.

8. Freud (1923), op. cit., p. 258.

9. Freud, S., 'Three Essays on the Theory of Sexuality' (1905), in *SE*, vol. 7.

10. Frazer, J.G. (trans.), *Apollodorus: The Library*, 3.5.7–9 (Loeb Classical Library), Cambridge, MA: Harvard University Press, 1921, pp. 343–51. Quoted in Edmunds, L., *Oedipus: The Ancient Legend and Its Later Analogues*, Baltimore, MD: Johns Hopkins University Press, 1985, p. 52.

11. For texts in which Freud explores this issue in relation to himself, see: Freud, S., *The Interpretation of Dreams* (1900), *SE*, vol. 4; and Masson, J. (ed.), *The Complete Letters of Sigmund Freud to Wilhelm Fliess: 1887–1904*, Cambridge, MA: Harvard University Press, 1985.

12. Britton, R., 'Getting in on the Act: The Hysterical Solution', in *International Journal of Psycho-Analysis*, vol. 80 (1), February 1999, pp. 1–15.

13. Ellenberger, H., 'The Story of "Anna O": A Critical Review with New Data' (1993), in *Beyond the Unconscious: Essays of Henri F. Ellenberger in the History of Psychiatry*, ed. M.S. Micale, trans. F. Dubor, Princeton, NJ: Princeton University Press, 1993, pp. 254–72.

14. Gay, P., *Freud: A Life for Our Time*, London and Melbourne: J.M. Dent, 1988, pp. 66–7. Quoted by Britton, op. cit., p. 7.

15. Donne, J. (1572–1631), 'The Good-Morrow', in *The Nation's Favourite Love Poems*, ed. D. Goodwin, London: Penguin, 1997, p. 73.

16. Congreve, W., *The Old Bachelor* (1693), act 4, sc. 7, in *The Oxford Dictionary of Quotations: New Edition*, ed. A. Partington, London: BCA–Oxford University Press, 1992, p. 215.

17. Klein, M., 'Notes on Some Schizoid Mechanisms' (1946), in *The Selected Melanie Klein*, ed. J. Mitchell, London: Penguin Books, 1986.

18. Meltzer, D. and Williams, M.H., *The Apprehension of Beauty: The Role of Aesthetic Conflict in Development, Art and Violence*, Old Ballechin, Strath Tay: Clunie, 1988.

19. Hughes, T., 'The Dogs Are Eating Your Mother', in *Birthday Letters*, London: Faber and Faber, 1998, p. 195, reproduced by kind permission of the Ted Hughes Estate and Faber and Faber. This poem, addressed to Frieda and Nicholas – Ted Hughes' and Sylvia Plath's children – concerns their mother's suicide and is intended to explore how the children can recover both themselves and their mother's spirit.

20. Klein, M., 'Infantile Anxiety Situations Reflected in a Work of Art and in the Creative Impulse' (1929), in Mitchell, op. cit.
21. Ibid., p. 89.
22. Klein, M., 'Mourning and Its Relation to Manic-Depressive States' (1940), in Mitchell, op. cit.
23. Segal, H., 'From Hiroshima to the Gulf War and After: Socio-political Expressions of Ambivalence', in Steiner, J. (ed.), *Psychoanalysis, Literature and War: Papers 1972–95*, London: Routledge, 1997, pp. 157–69.
24. Segal, H., *Dream, Phantasy and Art*, London: Routledge, 1991. See Chapter 8, 'Imagination, Play and Art'.
25. Warnock, M., *Imagination*, London: Faber and Faber, 1976, p. 12.
26. Bion, W., 'A Theory of Thinking', *International Journal of Psycho-Analysis*, 43 (4–5), 1962; reprinted in Bion, W., *Second Thoughts: Selected Papers on Psychoanalysis*, London: Karnac, 1984, pp. 110–20.
27. Rilke, R.M., 'Letter to Countess Margot Sizzo-Noris-Crouy' (12 April 1923), concerning her poem 'Duino Elegies', in *The Selected Poetry of Rainer Maria Rilke*, ed. and trans. S. Mitchell, London: Pan Books, 1987, p. 317. Quoted by Britton, R., *Belief and Imagination*, London: Routledge, 1998, p. 165.
28. Jaques, E., 'Death and the Mid-life Crisis' (1965), in Spillius, E.B. (ed.), *Melanie Klein Today: Volume 2: Mainly Practice*, London: Routledge, 1988, pp. 226–49.
29. Britton, R., *Belief and Imagination*, London: Routledge, 1998. See Chapter 11, 'Wordsworth: The Loss of Presence and the Presence of Loss'.
30. Graham-Dixon, A., *Howard Hodgkin*, London: Thames and Hudson, 1994, p. 21.
31. Hodgkin, H., quoted by Adams, T., 'It's the Vision Thing', *The Observer Review*, 10 June 2001.
32. Hughes, T., 'Lovesong', in *Crow: From the Life and Songs of the Crow*, London: Faber and Faber, 1970, reproduced by kind permission of the Ted Hughes Estate and Faber and Faber. 'Lovesong' is part of a longer story – 'The Story of Crow'. Crow reaches a river he needs to cross if he is to reach Happy Land, where he believes his bride awaits him. At the river, a hag demands that he carry her across. As he does so, she gets heavier and heavier, pushing him down into the gravel on the river bed, until only his head is above water. She questions him and demands he sing the answer. When he gets part of it right she gets lighter, when wrong she gets heavier. She asks him seven questions: 'The questions change. They begin at the negative extreme and end at the positive. The first question expects the darkest answer. "Who paid most, him or her?" Crow's answer is "Lovesong".' (Keith Sagar, 'The Story of Crow', in *The Laughter of Foxes: A Study of Ted Hughes*, Liverpool: Liverpool University Press, 2000, p. 179.)
33. Spillius, E.B., 'Freud and Klein on the Concept of Phantasy', *International Journal of Psycho-Analysis*, vol. 82, part 2, April 2001, pp. 361–75 (p. 362).
34. Bion, op. cit.

35. Joseph, B., 'Addiction to Near-death' (1982), in *Psychic Equilibrium and Psychic Change*, ed. E.B. Spillius and M. Feldman, London: Routledge, 1989, pp. 127–39.
36. Bion, W., *Attention and Interpretation*, London: Tavistock, 1970; reprinted London: Karnac, 1984, p. 125.

Further Reading

Freud's concept of Eros has not been much explored in a direct way. There is a widely held misconception that Freud's Eros was exclusively sexual, but in fact it is a more general principle about a life-giving drive towards intercourse and complexity. In this essay, I have included Freud's work and recent developments in psychoanalytic thought.

The Beginning of Eros in Psychoanalytic Thought
'Beyond the Pleasure Principle' is the key text in relation to Eros and psychoanalytic thought. It is a rather uncharacteristic work for Freud, full as it is of biology, but it is far-reaching and seminal to his thinking about what it is to be alive.

In 'The Ego and the Id', Freud develops the ideas started in what he calls his *Beyond*. This is written without the biology and may be easier to read.

Freud, S., 'Beyond the Pleasure Principle' (1920), in *Standard Edition of the Complete Psychological Works of Sigmund Freud* (hereafter *SE*), vol. 18, London: Hogarth Press, 1953–73.
——'The Ego and the Id' (1923), in *SE*, vol. 19.

Of Eros in the Body: Sexuality
I read quite widely the English language texts on Sexuality when writing *Eros* and found, perhaps unsurprisingly, that the most open-minded, comprehensive and insightful text was Freud's 'Three Essays'. If it has been bettered, I have not found it.

A belief in the contemporary psychoanalytic world is that British psychoanalysts, and in particular British Kleinian psychoanalysts, do not pay attention to sexuality, whilst French psychoanalysts do. There is certainly less published work about adult sexuality in British psychoanalysis, although this may not reflect clinical practice. French psychoanalyst André Green has written evocatively on Eros for those who wish to pursue the topic further.

Texts that refer specifically to the Oedipus complex include Freud's *Interpretation of Dreams* and Ronald Britton's contemporary *Belief and Imagination*.

Freud, S., 'Three Essays on the Theory of Sexuality' (1905), in *SE*, vol. 7.
——*The Interpretation of Dreams* (1900), in *SE*, vols. 4 and 5.
Green, A., *Chains of Eros* (1997), London: Rebus Press, 2000.
Britton, R., *Belief and Imagination*, London: Routledge, 1998.

Of Eros in the Emotions: Love
Melanie Klein is perhaps particularly known for her work on the death

instinct and aggression, but she is also responsible for some of the most innovative work on love. She does not link her work directly to Freud's concept of Eros but it fits well with it. A good place to start is Klein's papers in the *Selected Melanie Klein*, ed. by Mitchell. If one wants to go on from there, Klein's work is collected in four volumes.

Hanna Segal is an eminent contemporary psychoanalyst and the author of a lucid and profound account of Klein's work. Her collection of essays, *Psychoanalysis, Literature and War*, contains a paper on war and peace which builds on Klein's work on love.

Klein, M., *The Selected Melanie Klein*, ed. Juliet Mitchell, London: Penguin Books, 1986.
——*Collected Works of Melanie Klein*, London: Hogarth Press and Institute of Psychoanalysis, 1975. Vol. I: *Love, Guilt and Reparation, and Other Works*; Vol. II: *The Psycho-Analysis of Children*; Vol. III: *Envy and Gratitude, and Other Works*; Vol. IV: *Narrative of a Child Analysis*.
Segal, H., *Klein*, London: Karnac, 1989.
——*Psychoanalysis, Literature and War*, ed. John Steiner, London: Routledge, 1997.

Of Eros in the Mind: Imagination

Wilfred Bion is a central figure in this area. My suggestion would be to start with *Second Thoughts*, although a colleague, David Bell, suggests *Learning from Experience*. I give both references below. The work of Bion specifically referred to in the text includes the last of a group of four books: *Learning from Experience*, *Elements of Psychoanalysis*, *Transformations* and *Attention and Interpretation*. *Attention and Interpretation* has had a considerable effect on psychoanalysis but would not, I think, be the best place to start.

Ronald Britton's book is a clear and thought-provoking contemporary Kleinian exposition of psychoanalytic ways of thinking about the mind.

Betty Joseph's writing is intensely clinical and her approach gives us an innovative development of Bion's work.

Elizabeth Bott Spillius's paper on phantasy explores complex ideas relevant to imaginative thought in an accessible way.

Bion, W., *Second Thoughts: Selected Papers on Psychoanalysis* (1967), London: Karnac, 1984.
——*Learning from Experience* (1962), London: Karnac, 1984.
——*Attention and Interpretation* (1970), London: Karnac, 1984.
Britton, R., *Belief and Imagination*, London: Routledge, 1998.
Joseph, B., *Psychic Equilibrium and Psychic Change*, ed. Elizabeth Bott Spillius and Michael Feldman, London: Routledge, 1989.
Spillius, E., 'Freud and Klein on the Concept of Phantasy', *International Journal of Psycho-Analysis*, vol. 82, part 2, April 2001, pp. 361–75.

The references I have given are not exhaustive. The majority of authors in the list are from the Kleinian tradition. In privileging textual coherence, I am aware that I have not dealt with much interesting work from the Independent and Contemporary Freudian analytic traditions in Britain.

Literary References

Adams, T., 'It's the Vision Thing', *The Observer Review*, 10 June 2001.

Donne, J. (1572–1631), 'The Good-Morrow', in *The Nation's Favourite Love Poems*, ed. D. Goodwin, London: Penguin, 1997, p. 73.

Graham-Dixon, A., *Howard Hodgkin*, London: Thames and Hudson, 1994.

Hughes, T., 'Lovesong', in *Crow: From the Life and Songs of the Crow*, London: Faber and Faber, 1970.

——'The Dogs are Eating Your Mother', in *Birthday Letters*, London: Faber and Faber, 1998.

Rilke, R.M., 'Duino Elegies', in *The Selected Poetry of Rainer Maria Rilke*, ed. and trans. S. Mitchell, London: Pan Books, 1987.

9

Libido

Roger Kennedy

Introduction: Libido as a Theoretical Concept

Libido is Sigmund Freud's concept of the mental aspect of sexual energy underlying the various transformations of the sexual drives. It is a theoretical concept which, as we shall see, was put forward originally in order to account for pathological clinical observations from neurotic patients, where sexual tensions associated with sexual ideas were seen to have a key role in producing anxiety and other symptoms. Libido came increasingly to have an important place in Freud's theory of the mind and its development. As time went on, he began to include observations from more psychotic illnesses, such as manic depression, hypochondriasis and paranoia. Eventually, libido was to be replaced by Eros, into which it was incorporated, when Freud introduced a theory of sexuality which became both broader in scope and linked to Ancient philosophy. We can see Freud's shifts in theory as a journey from the investigation of the minutiae of his patients' sexual lives to the consideration of the fundamental place of life and death in the human condition.

Libido in Freud's theory of the sexual drives is both a 'quantitative' concept, referring to hypothetical amounts of sexual energy motivating the sexual drives, and a 'qualitative' notion, which means that libido is about specifically sexual drives; it is not to be confused with mental energy in the general sense. In Freud's words, libido is a

> *quantitatively variable force which could serve as a measure of processes and transformations occurring in the field of sexual excitation. We distinguish this libido in respect of its special origin from the energy which must be supposed to underlie mental processes in general, and we thus also attribute a qualitative character to it ... [Its] production, increase or diminution and displacement should afford us possibilities*

for explaining the psychosexual phenomena observed.[1]
(Freud, 1905)

Libido is thus a hypothetical way of measuring the sexual processes, an imagined unit of quantitative measurement; it is a concept. It is what Jacques Lacan,[2] the French psychoanalyst, described as:

> *A quantity which you don't know how to measure, whose nature you don't know, but which you always assume to be there. This quantitative notion allows you to unify the variation in qualitative effects, and gives some coherence to the manner in which they succeed one another . . . [T]he notion of libido is a form of unification for the domain of psychoanalytical effects . . . [I]ts use falls within the traditional scope of any and every theory, tending to end up with a world, the terminus ad quem [end-point] of classical physics, or a unitary domain, the ideal of Einsteinian physics. We aren't in a position to align our poor little domain with the universal domain of physics, but the libido partakes of the same ideal.*[3]
> (Lacan, 1978)

Thus we have the notion of libido as a theoretical quantity, which aims to help to explain and give coherence to the field of psychoanalytical effects, in particular those involved with sexuality, or, to be more specific, what Freud called 'Psychosexuality', laying stress on the mental factor in human sexual life (Freud, 1910).[4] It may be difficult to define, and it may be imaginary and unmeasurable, and yet it is a necessary hypothetical concept, just like gravity and mass and space-time are hypothetical concepts, without which physics could not be elaborated.

Freud discusses the nature of libido and other hypothetical concepts in his theoretical framework in his paper on 'Instincts and their Vicissitudes' (1915). He makes the point that, although there is often an assumption that the sciences should be built upon clear and sharply defined basic concepts, in reality the sciences usually start with fairly indefinite concepts in order to grasp observable phenomena. These concepts, such as drives and libido, are more in the nature of conventions, although

> *everything depends on their not being arbitrarily chosen but determined by their having significant relations to the empirical material, relations that we seem to sense before we can clearly recognise and demonstrate them. It is only after more thorough investigation of the field of observation that we are able to formulate its basic scientific concepts with*

increased precision, and progressively so to modify them that they become serviceable and consistent over a wide area.[5]

(Freud, 1915)

Thus libido is a theoretical concept, or 'convention', which aims to help make sense of the psychosexual field, however vague and unmeasurable it may be; it represents one aspect of Freud's thought, his wish to make psychoanalysis an organised and even 'scientific' study of psychosexual phenomena. Like the notion of a drive, libido is a scientific concept on the 'frontier' between the mental and the somatic; it is a psychical entity, and yet it refers to bodily phenomena.

Libido in Freud is also concerned with the nature of love and desire, or with lust and sexual appetite, which is what *libido* means in Latin; and here Freud moves away from purely scientific considerations into the precarious field of human emotions. As he wrote:

Libido is an expression taken from the theory of the emotions. We call by that name the energy, regarded as a quantitative magnitude (though not at present actually measurable), of those drives which have to deal with all that may be comprised under the word 'love'.[6]

(Freud, 1921)

In ordinary language, we talk of the 'hunger' of the nutritive drive, and so with the sexual drives, we can talk about libido or 'sexual hunger'. People talk about their libido being raised or diminished, when referring to their sexual interest and drive, their wish to have sex, the accumulation of sexual hunger and tension pressing to be satisfied. It may or may not be connected to love for the other person. Indeed, in some people with problems about commitment, their libido may only increase when in a brief relationship; while with others, it is only in the context of a committed relationship that their libido can be raised enough to establish a successful sexual relationship.

On the other hand, as can be seen throughout Ancient Greek literature, the sexual drives can 'drive' people mad, making them blind to their own and other people's interests. Thus the action of Sophocles' play, *Women of Trachis*, reveals the power of sex in determining the fate of the main characters. Deianira, a hitherto faithful and devoted wife, becomes a murderess by mistake, when she attempts to give her unfaithful husband, Heracles, a love-charm to win him back. There is a whole choral ode celebrating the invincible power of love or lust, before which even the Kings of heaven, the underworld and the ocean must bow down.[7] In Sophocles' *Antigone*, one of the main themes is the power of Eros. The chorus sings of Eros that he who has it is mad;[8] it causes several deaths in the play, and makes the king of Thebes, Creon, a broken man, as his son and wife end up killing themselves as a result of its power.

We have seen, then, that Freud's notions about sexuality encompass both an attempt to create a scientific study of psycho-sexuality, and also more general aspects of the complex emotion of love, which reach back to Ancient literature. Freud's libido, like that of the Greek Eros, can be a blind force driving humans beyond ordinary reason.

No Libido Please, We're British!

In the early years of psychoanalysis, libido was used by Freud in a general sense to cover the hypothetical energy of the sexual drives in much the same way as it is now used in ordinary language, though with various modifications. But with the introduction of the concept of 'narcissism' in 1914, Freud began increasingly to elaborate a complicated theory of libido and its development, which became essential to his whole conceptual framework. By 1920, this libido theory had become assimilated into an even more general theory of the interaction between two basic drives in the life of the mind – Eros, or the life drives, and Thanatos, or the death drives. In due course, I shall discuss aspects of these various psychoanalytic theories, and how they may be related to clinical work. But before that, I will make some general points about the place of libido theory in contemporary psychoanalysis, particu-larly in Britain, where it seems to have virtually disappeared. I shall ask throughout this essay whether or not this act of exclusion misses out vital elements of Freud's thinking, leaving psycho-analysis impoverished as a result, or whether this is just a sign of psychoanalysis having moved on from an outdated theory, more appropriate to the world of nineteenth-century physics.

The issue of the current relevance, or not, of the term 'libido' has to be seen in the context of the current state of psychoanalytic theory, where sexuality as the central issue for psychoanalysis has been replaced by object relations theory, with its emphasis on early development before the child becomes recognisably sexual. Its great advance on classical Freudian theory was to emphasise the importance of the *relationship* between the subject and his environment, particularly the mother–infant relationship, rather than focus only on the inner world of the individual. This theory describes the *subject's mode of relation to the world; this relation is the entire outcome of a particular organisation of the personality, of an apprehension of objects that is to some extent or other fantasied, and of certain special types of defence.*[9]

(Laplanche and Pontalis, 1967)

Object relations theory is concerned with both the inner world of the subject and the world of others. It concerns itself with the relation of the subject to his or her objects. However, as Gregorio Kohon points out:

It is not only the real relationship with others that determines the subject's individual life, but the specific way in which the subject apprehends his relationships with his objects (both internal and external). It is always an unconscious relationship to these objects.[10]

(Kohon, 1986)

While object relations theory extends the scope of psychoanalysis – by, for example, pointing towards the vast field of infant and child observation and research, which can provide new data and even confirmation of psychoanalytic ideas – the central importance of sexuality in the theory and practice of psychoanalysis seems to have been displaced. In 1995, André Green even wrote a paper asking if sexuality had anything to do with psychoanalysis these days,[11] as it seems to have virtually disappeared in so many ways. He makes the point that direct discussions of sexuality seem to have declined in ordinary clinical presentations, and sexuality itself seems to have become marginalised as a central analytic concept, even though Freud placed it at the centre of psychic development, analytic theory and clinical work. Green argues that the current fashionable focus on object relations, on early development, borderline pathology and techniques drawn from baby observation, obscures the meaning and importance of sexuality in psychoanalytic theory and practice. But he argues that without, for example, the Freudian notion of libido, we cannot account for the variations, extensions, fixations, regressions, time-lags, enmeshings and unravellings of psychic functioning and development.

For Jacques Lacan, libido is an essential element of sexuality and of his own approach to the study of the unconscious. In his view, what Freud intended to make present in the function of this libido was not some generalised primitive mode of thought, 'like some shade of an ancient world surviving in ours'. Rather:

The libido is the effective presence, as such, of desire. It is what now remains to indicate desire – which is not substance, but which is there at the level of the primary process, and which governs the very mode of our approach.[12]

(Lacan, 1973)

Lacan maintains that the libido is the essential element of the 'primary process', the basic way that the unconscious functions. Freud divided the functioning of the psychical apparatus into the *primary* and *secondary* processes. In the former, psychical energy flows freely from one idea to another, as can be seen in dreams, where one idea may surrender all its energy to another idea by the process of 'displacement', or appropriate the energy of several other ideas by the process of 'condensation'. In the case of the secondary process, psychical energy is more bound, less freely mobile; it coincides with waking thought, judgement and reasoning.[13] Like the primary process, the libido for Lacan is a free current which gets tied down in various ways, organised and tamed by the secondary process.

The playing down of the role of sexuality in favour of early object relations does not only have theoretical consequences but may also deeply influence what psychoanalysts do or do not see in their patients. For example, instead of seeing hysteria as a condition involving a fundamental conflict concerned with sexual impulses, it is often now seen as a condition involving defence mechanisms to keep primitive, psychotic anxieties at bay or under control. As Kohon (1986, 1999) has described,[14] we can understand why psychoanalysts claim not to find hysterics in their consulting rooms. Their patients may be hysterics, but since the theory looks for something else, it can also find something else. Thus the desexualisation of psychoanalytic theory has potentially serious consequences for day-to-day practice.

One could add that current psychoanalytic theory and practice not only often lack the theoretical concept of libido in the technical sense, but also lack it in the ordinary sense of the word; it has become a sexless theory. It is perhaps only French psychoanalysis, with the all-pervasive influence of Jacques Lacan on French thinking, not to mention the role of French culture, that has preserved the central place of sexuality. For the British in particular, 'No libido, please' could be taken as the slogan for much psychoanalytic work.

This is not to deny the importance of the place of early relationships in the life of the individual, but we could ask if psychoanalysis has gone too far in eliminating drives and sexuality, forgetting that people in the real world fuck, or want to fuck, or can't fuck when they want to! My own position with regard to the status of a term like libido is that I am not wholeheartedly for its retention, certainly not without modifications and extensions in its place in psycho-analytic theory, which I will propose in due course. There is a problem, however, about trying to find terms which capture the animal nature of our sexual drives and at the same time incorporate the human element, involving sexual feelings and desires, as well as the many transformations and complexities of the sexual drives. Somehow, we need to include aspects of force, need, urgency, the urge to obtain gratification which can come to dominate some people's lives. While libido may be too much linked to a 'fluid' and energetic model, more appropriate for the science of hydraulics, it does nonetheless manage to capture the quality of sexual hunger rather well, and how this hunger has many variations, a multiplicity of aims, with the capacity to be diverted and divided up in various ways. I would also maintain that Freud's theory of libido raises many fundamental issues concerned with the nature of our sexual life – and our mental life in general – that have been too often ignored and that would be worth revisiting. At the very least, we can understand libido historically as an integral element of Freud's theory of the mind.

What follows is a historical exposition of Freud's libido theory, with various interpretations of its meaning and significance based on subsequent analytic thinkers. This will lead to some suggestions for modifying the theory in the light of subsequent developments, without, hopefully, depriving it of its core elements.

Freud's Early Theory of Libido/The Missing Link

We can follow the first steps towards a theory of libido in the Freud/Fliess correspondence – a fascinating series of letters, including some theoretical sketches, between Freud and his close friend Wilhelm Fliess, which date from 1887 to 1904, spanning the birth and early development of psychoanalysis.

The first recorded mention of libido comes in 'Draft E', a theoretical sketch probably from June 1894, concerning how anxiety originates in 'anxiety neurosis', a type of illness where the patient suffers from chronic and excessive anxiety, with accompanying somatic symptoms such as breathlessness, indigestion, cardiac pains and some phobic features. Freud distinguished anxiety neurosis from hysteria and *neurasthenia*, or what we probably now call 'chronic fatigue syndrome'. The theory is concerned with how psychical sexual tension is transformed into anxiety due to a failure to discharge sexual tension along psychical paths, and how something blocks the psychical elaboration of the sexual excitation.

Freud collects together a number of cases in this draft, with a variety of roots for their anxiety. These include those people suffering from anxiety due to their virginal status, those who are intentionally sexually abstinent who regard everything sexual as abhorrent, those women who are neglected by their husbands or are not satisfied due to lack of potency, women who do not obtain satisfaction due to the practice of coitus interruptus or whose husbands suffer from premature ejaculation, as well as men who practice withdrawal or who turn excessively to masturbation, men whose potency is diminishing but force themselves to have intercourse, and men who have to abstain from sex for neurotic reasons. He asks how all these cases may be brought together, and suggests that:

> *What recurs in them all is abstinence. Informed by the fact that even* [sexually] *anaesthetic women are subject to anxiety after coitus interruptus, one is inclined to say that it is a question of a psychical accumulation of excitation – that is, an accumulation of psychical sexual tension. The accumulation is the consequence of prevented discharge. Thus anxiety neurosis is a neurosis of damming up . . . And since no anxiety at all is contained in what is accumulated, the fact can also be accounted for by saying that anxiety has arisen by transformation out of the accumulated sexual tension.*[15]

> (Freud, 1985)

But, Freud asks, why and how does this transformation into anxiety occur? This question preoccupied him throughout his life, and he gave various explanations for it depending on the stage his theorising had reached, although the key issues and much of the explanation remained constant. At this early point in his thinking, he considers it a question of how tension originating inside the body ('endogenous' tension), such as that arising from hunger, thirst and the sexual drive, is dealt with by means of specific reactions, which prevent the further occurrence of the excitation in the bodily organs concerned. We may picture this tension as growing either continuously or discontinuously, but only being noticed when it has reached a certain threshold. Above this threshold, Freud postulates that it is deployed psychically, that

> *. . . it enters into relation with certain groups of ideas, which then set about producing the specific remedies. Thus psychical sexual tension above a certain value arouses psychic libido, which then leads to coitus, and so forth.*[16]

So far, this fits with the ordinary understanding of libido as an accumulation of tension that presses for release in a specific reaction – for example, intercourse or masturbation. But if the action fails to ensue, the sexual tension and emotion, or *affect*, increases quickly and urgently:

> [It] *becomes disturbing, but there is still no ground for its transformation. In anxiety neurosis, however, such a transformation does occur, and this suggests the idea that there things go wrong in the following way. The psychical tension increases, reaches the threshold value at which it can arouse psychic affect; but for several reasons the psychic linkage offered to it remains insufficient: a sexual affect cannot be found, because there is something lacking in the psychic determinants. Accordingly, the physical tension, not being psychically bound, is transformed into anxiety. If one accepts the theory so far, one has to insist that in anxiety neurosis there must be a deficit to be noted in sexual affect, in psychic libido. And this is confirmed by observation. If this contention is put before women patients, they are always indignant and declare that on the contrary they now have no desire whatever, and similar statements. Men often confirm the observation that since suffering from anxiety they have felt no sexual desire.*[17]

Thus the problem in anxiety neurosis is one of an insufficient or missing psychic linkage, which can be turned into affect by what Freud calls at this point 'psychic working over'. In ordinary life, sexual tension finds an outlet in action such as intercourse. But if there is constantly no outlet for the release of tension, anxiety will occur in those patients who have problems in *working over* sexual tension. Such psychic work can ordinarily deal with the tension appropriately and without causing bodily symptoms. But when such working over cannot occur, then bodily symptoms will arise instead.

Although at this point in his thinking, Freud's concepts are still developing, much of his approach to how sexual psychic tension becomes transformed into anxiety, due to a lack of the ordinary linking processes in the mind, will be retained in various ways. The basic technique of psychoanalysis, involving trying to find words for disturbing feelings, can be seen as offering links where they are missing. From this point on, the theory behind the practice will become increasingly elaborate and reworked, but the clinical basis for it will remain.

Elaboration of Libido Theory/Dammed Libido

Freud's book 'Three Essays on the Theory of Sexuality' (1905) stands with the *Interpretation of Dreams* (1900) as his most original contribution to human knowledge. Yet the essays are somewhat difficult to digest because, in the form in which they are now read, there are many additions and revisions, a whole series of different layers added to the original text. Nonetheless, the basic tenets of psychoanalytic theory are there to be seen, and, in particular, the cardinal role of the investigation of sexuality in the life of the human subject, and libido theory, have a key place in this investigation. Years later, in his fourth edition of the book, written in 1920, Freud states that despite the changes to psycho-analytic thinking, the basic findings from the three essays remain intact, despite attempts by some to

abandon it and to adopt fresh views which were intended to restrict once more the part played by the factor of sexuality in normal and pathological sexual life.[18]

His first essay is concerned with observations from the sexual 'aberrations', mainly perversions of various kinds, as well as observations from homosexual and neurotic patients. The second essay deals with infantile sexuality, and the third essay covers the transformations of puberty. Because of the complexity of the text, I can pick out only a few relevant themes.

Overall, what comes through from the book is an attempt to capture the great variety of sexual life, the place of biological elements in the subject's sexual life, the many aims of the sexual drives, the plasticity, fluidity and complexity of sexual feelings, and the precarious way in which the sexual organisation is united at puberty out of various fragmentary elements. Normal sexual life is shown to consist of many potentially perverse elements, perver-sion occurring when one of these elements begins to dominate over the others.

Libido, which was introduced as a term to indicate a kind of sexual hunger, is shown to flow in many different ways, to change from one object to another with apparent ease, like, we could add, the primary process. It is shown to have its sources in many different parts of the body, and to be a major source of anxiety and symptoms in neurotic patients. Libido is shown to pass through a long course of development, with many breaks, and hence many possibilities for that development to be interfered with.

But, when libido fails to find satisfaction, it can behave

*like a stream whose main bed had become blocked. It proceeds
to fill up collateral channels which hitherto had been empty.*[19]

These 'collateral channels' become the source of various perverse
tendencies in neurotic patients. It is notable that Internet porn
sites are categorised more or less according to these collateral
channels. Sexual practices which in limited amounts are a normal
part of sexual life – such as the use of the mouth, the anus, touching and looking, and some elements of sadism and masochism –
may come to dominate sexual life to the exclusion of everything
else, as if the collateral channel takes over from the main stream
and dominates the subject in a tyrannical way, overwhelming his
or her sexual life so that ordinary intercourse may not be possible.
It is as if one 'site' (on the Internet or the body) comes to dominate
the subject's sexual life. The subject's libido is said to be 'fixated'
at a particular stage of development – the moment, as it were,
when the diversion from the main stream of libido took place.
    Elsewhere, Freud gives a vivid example of such a fixation as the
cause of foot fetishism. The patient was a man who

> *is to-day quite indifferent to the genitals and other attractions
> of women, but who can be plunged into irresistible sexual
> excitement only by a foot of a particular form wearing a shoe.
> He can recall an event from his sixth year which was decisive
> for the fixation of his libido. He was sitting on a stool beside the
> governess who was to give him lessons in English. The govern-
> ess, who was an elderly, dried-up, plain-looking spinster, with
> pale-blue eyes and a snub nose, had something wrong with her
> foot that day, and on that account kept it, wearing a velvet
> slipper, stretched out on a cushion. Her leg itself was most
> decently concealed. A thin, scraggy foot, like the one he had
> then seen belonging to this governess, thereupon became (after
> a timid attempt at normal sexual activity at puberty) his only
> sexual object; and the man was irresistibly attracted if a foot of
> this kind was associated with other features besides which
> recalled the type of the English governess.*[20]

The fixation of his libido was the cause of his foot fetishism. One
could add here that the fixation of this patient was in the context of
a particular form of object relationship, the 'type' of the English
governess, someone who obviously took the place of a parent.
There may well have been traumatic issues related to his parenting
that were projected onto the governess at that particular moment,
making his libido particularly susceptible to fixation.
    Such fixations due to childhood scenes of various kinds are not

uncommon in these and other perversions, though one should add that it is not generally so easy to locate one scene as the main factor behind the perversion. There is usually a whole set of complex factors – in both the family and the individual – at work in perversion and neurosis, many of them obscure, and often involving one or more traumatic episodes. There is a complex interaction between the subject's personality or constitution and the external environment, an interaction which forms their history.

In Freud's 1912 paper on types of onset of neurosis, he attempts to clarify some of these obscurities by outlining the changes relating to the subject's libido which bring about the outbreak of neurotic illness. His aim in the paper is to

> *show that neurotic disposition lies in the history of the development of the libido, and to trace back the operative factors in that development to innate varieties of sexual constitution and to influences of the external world experienced in early childhood.*[21]

Various factors are cited as the precipitating causes of the onset of a neurosis. The first is 'frustration', from an external obstacle and/ or an internal obstacle. With the external obstacle, the subject is healthy so long as their need for love is satisfied by a real object in the external world. But when the object is lost or withdrawn, illness may take place if there is no substitute. With this type, to which, Freud adds, the majority of people belong, the possibility of falling ill only arises when there is abstinence. Frustration has a pathogenic effect because it 'dams up' libido, increasing sexual tension. The subject can remain healthy if he can transform this tension into active energy and find a way of satisfying his libido again, for example by finding a replacement for the lost love-object. Or else, like Alberich in Wagner's *Ring Cycle,* who renounced love in order to steal the Rhinemaidens' gold, he can renounce libidinal satisfaction, 'sublimating the dammed-up libido and turning it to the attainment of aims which are no longer erotic and which escape frustration'.[22]

Frustration, if persistent, can bring into play factors in the personality which hitherto had lain dormant. The person may begin to turn away from reality and become absorbed by the world of phantasy, creating new wishful structures which revive the traces of earlier, particularly infantile elements. Excessive phantasying may cause the libido to move on a backward path, causing 'regression' along infantile lines. A conflict between the subject's present-day way of functioning and these infantile elements may precipitate a neurotic illness.

Frustration due to internal factors arises from elements of previous development: in particular, previous fixations of the libido, which cause at some point in his life a difficulty for the subject in adapting to the demands of reality. Freud gives examples to illustrate the types of situation to which he is referring. These include:

> *A young man who has hitherto satisfied his libido by means of phantasies ending in masturbation, and who now seeks to replace a régime approximating to auto-erotism by the choice of a real object – or a girl who has given her whole affection to her father or brother and who must now, for the sake of a man who is courting her, allow her hitherto unconscious incestuous libidinal wishes to become conscious – or a married woman who would like to renounce her polygamous inclinations and phantasies of prostitution so as to become a faithful consort to her husband and a perfect mother to her child.*[23]

All of these people can fall ill if the earlier fixations of their libido are powerful enough to dominate their lives, particularly if, as with the first kind of frustration, they meet with an external obstacle such as a loss of various kinds. Furthermore, some people remain permanently 'inhibited' in their development; their libido has never left these earlier infantile fixations.

Freud adds a final example of people who appear to fall ill spontaneously, having been hitherto healthy. A closer consideration of these cases does, however, reveal that a change has indeed taken place in them, and this change is related to them having reached a particular period of life, such as puberty or the menopause, where biological processes come into play. Then, the

> quantity *of libido in their mental economy has experienced an increase which is in itself enough to upset the equilibrium of their health and to set up the necessary conditions for a neurosis.*[24]

Such a situation is fairly typical of those adolescents who break down at or near to puberty, or first show signs of disturbance at this time. Their earlier life may appear to have been relatively normal, or at least there has been no overt disturbance; but it is the powerful emergence of sexual feelings, and the attempts to deal with them, that become the driving force for adolescent turmoil. Eros can drive the adolescent mad, to recall the theme from Greek literature.

To give a brief example from an analysis of an adolescent boy.

'Simon' came into analysis at the age of seventeen following a suicide attempt. While feeling hopeless and depressed, he had gone to a park and cut his wrists with a razor blade, with the intention of severing an artery. He reported later that the pain of the cut stopped him. He had made a previous attempt to cut an artery a year previously. The first overt sign of disturbance had been at puberty at the age of thirteen, when he had probably attempted suicide by suffocation with a plastic bag.

The analysis subsequently pieced together that prior to the cutting he had been feeling depressed, and sexually and physically inadequate following a rejection by a girl he liked. He was also, from puberty onwards, greatly troubled by sexual feelings and fantasies. Related to his sexual anxieties, Simon described intense self-hatred, particularly a hatred of and wish to disown his body, which he felt was not masculine enough. He wished at times that he could have another body. His childhood was not marked by any particular disturbance, though his mother always tended to infantilise him, calling him her 'cute little boy'; while his father remained a rather distant and cut-off figure, depressed and unavailable.

One of the main themes of his analysis was how he became threatened by the emergence of sexual feelings at puberty, which precipitated the first outbreak of symptoms. He subsequently began to attack his maturing body through cutting, in part as a way of trying to cling onto the old immature body image. Important therapeutic work was done by focusing on the dynamic interplay between Simon's wish to avoid growing up and his need to accept the reality of his maturing body, as well as beginning to deal better with his sexual desires, or the quantity of libido driving him.

The damming-up of libido is for Freud a basic factor in the production of a neurosis, which can open up paths to regression, causing conflict and neurosis. In Simon's case, the damming up could be seen to open up his regressive wishes to remain a child and to attack his maturing body. Freud adds that we are reminded here that the quantitative factor should not be left out in any consideration of the precipitating causes of illness, and that all the other factors – frustration, fixation and developmental inhibition – remain ineffectual unless

> they affect a certain amount of libido and bring about a damming-up of libido of a certain height. It is true that we are unable to measure this amount of libido which seems to us indispensable for a pathogenic effect; we can only postulate it after the resulting illness has started.[25]

Once more, we can see how crucial to Freud is his emphasis on the role of the quantity of libido in creating conditions for the outbreak of a neurosis; the damming-up of libido leads to collateral channels being opened up in the mind, particularly channels which had been basically closed up in childhood.

While this is a vivid description of what may take place when a neurosis breaks out, one may ask whether it is to be taken literally, or how much it can be seen as metaphor. Clearly, Freud is very much of his time, when the general principles of physics were considered to be at the basis of psychology; in order to claim respectability and credibility for a theory of mental functioning, one had to make some link with basic scientific concepts, such as that of quantities of energy. Indeed, to a great extent, this demand for scientific credibility remains with us today. However, one can also ask whether the use of the concept of hypothetical amounts of libido as anything other than a metaphor may be stretching the claims for scientific credibility too far, particularly as Freud admits that it is unmeasurable. Why use libido at all when it is only a hypothetical quantitative concept? Would we lose anything by dropping its use?

Because of the uncertainties about the status of libido, we can easily appreciate why it has now fallen into disuse, at a time when psychoanalysis is often under attack for being either unscientific or, worse, pseudo-scientific. However, a main point to make is that libido has a crucial role in Freud's theory, at least in the early and middle phases of his thought. It has a place as a key term, or signifier, in the network of other signifiers. Removing it means shifting the meaning of all the other terms he uses; it would also, as we shall see, make unintelligible the understanding of the place of narcissism in the development of his theory. But, we can still ask, is that a good enough reason to retain the term? Is its use only of historical interest? Or perhaps it is best seen as a useful, even metaphorical, way of capturing the experience of sexual life in terms which make sense, and which also link up with its use in the ordinary language of everyday life.

Development of the Libido/Stages in Life's Way

We have alluded to the fact that the libido develops, and that there may be regressions backwards to earlier developmental stages in the outbreak of neurotic illness. In the early editions of the 'Three Essays', Freud emphasises his discovery of infantile sexuality. This concept arose because memories and associations arising from the analysis of adults regularly led back to the early years of childhood. Later, for example in his case study on Little Hans in

1909, and then from direct observations by child analysts, there was some confirmation of his theory. Infantile sexuality is to be seen long before the genital organs come to dominate sexual life; that is, it is an important element of the 'pregenital organisation' of the libido. Such sexuality involves parts of the body, or what Freud called 'erotogenic zones', which can become the seat of pleasurable excitations. Such zones can be any part of the skin or mucous membrane capable of being the source of pleasure. The child passes through overlapping stages, where one after the other an erotogenic zone first dominates and then is overtaken by another leading zone.

At the oral stage, thumb-sucking is one of the earliest sexual manifestations of childhood, in which the child is searching for pleasure and comfort. It is a kind of substitute for the earlier intense pleasure of sucking at the mother's breast. Freud thus describes an oral sexuality at this stage of development. He also then describes the activity of the anal zone as providing pleasure. Thus:

> *Children who are making use of the susceptibility to erotogenic stimulation of the anal zone betray themselves by holding back their stool till its accumulation brings about violent muscular contractions and, as it passes through the anus, is able to produce powerful stimulation of the mucous membrane. In so doing, it must no doubt cause not only painful but also highly pleasurable sensations.*[26]

(Freud, 1905)

However, it was only gradually in Freud's theory that the libido's development was to be described as a series of successive, if over-lapping, stages: the famous oral, anal, phallic and genital stages. In the original 1905 edition of 'Three Essays', Freud merely described an 'auto-erotic' stage before object-choice has taken place, and when the infant obtains pleasure solely from parts of its own body, through for example sucking or masturbation.

It is worth making the point here that in Freud the issue of development is complex – something which is often ignored. It is not merely a question of a sequence of stages. Development in Freud is not a simple linear model, with one stage clearly following another, but a complex model, with constant interaction between the past and the present, and with the mind constantly reordering past experiences in the light of present circumstances. There are present in this model what one could call two kinds of history – the history of events and the history of layers. The history of events is the traditional kind of history as a linear narrative, with one event following another in linear time. The history of layers involves looking at history as a succession of shifting layers, as fragments of living reality, where, as in the unconscious, distinctions between the past and the present may be merged. During an analysis, associations from many different layers of the mind may emerge. Putting the associations into some kind of understandable linear narrative – the history of events – is also an important part of the clinical work, and involves the secondary process. But it is the history of layers which is the main generator of new connections and meanings, with some layers of the mind following directly from one another in time, while others merge, and yet others stand out in apparent isolation. The human subject can retrieve elements from many different layers.

An example of this can be seen in a session from a patient of mine near to the ending of her analysis. She had come because of anxiety symptoms, and had difficulties with being emotionally in touch with herself and her children. A mid-week session began with two dreams. In the first dream, Monday and Friday were rolled into one, with no gap between them. There was food around but she felt it was not good enough. Her immediate associations were that this was indicative of her attitude of avoiding what was on offer, and forgetting what was on offer when there were breaks in the analysis. In the second dream, I appeared and said that she should be grateful that I was so tolerant of her. Then I gave her something, a key or a bill. She then held onto my finger. Her associations were to her feelings about the difficulty she had in dealing with break-ups, and her fear that, with the impending ending of the analysis, *everything* would come to an end.

In the session, we explored her early oral level of development, corresponding to her needy, dependent side, an area with which she had had considerable difficulty. She replied that she often felt that things were slipping away from her; her mind felt like a sieve, so that everything of value passed through it; but she now suddenly saw the damage that came from pulling herself and others to pieces. She recalled some memories from childhood where she had constantly been self-destructive in this way. This led to some acknowledgement about the anger she felt about being left by me. She was then able to admit that there were positive things she got from the analysis, that is that there were other levels involved in what we were doing, not just the early needy oral level. For example, she free-associated that my index finger in the dream felt like something she was trying to hold on to; she was holding my finger for fear of being dropped, but also as something helpful. At this level, she was thus able to see me as separate from her, rather than muddled up with her fantasy of me as before. She added that it was also like the Michelangelo picture of the creation of Adam, with God touching Adam's finger, so that there was the possibility of something creative happening between us.

Overall, one could say with her that there were themes from a number of different layers of her mind; the problem for her was that she tended to want them to be perfectly ordered and indexed, rather than allow them to emerge spontaneously. The work of the analysis, right to the end, was very much about trying to challenge the rigidity of her selective processes.

Marcel Proust gives a description of the human personality which captures rather well what we mean about retrieving layers of the past:

> *A thing which we saw, a book which we read at a certain period does not merely remain for ever conjoined to what existed then around us; it remains also faithfully united to what we ourselves then were and thereafter it can be handled only by the sensibility, the personality that were then ours . . . So that my personality of today may be compared to an abandoned quarry, which supposes everything it contains to be uniform and monotonous, but from which memory, selecting here and there, can, like some Greek sculptor, extract innumerable statues.*[27]

The basis for Freud's complex view of human development can be seen already in the Freud/Fliess correspondence, where, in 1896, Freud described how memory traces are constantly being rearranged in accordance with fresh circumstances, a process which he called 'retranscription'.[28]

A year later, he describes the role of 'deferred action', *Nachträglichkeit*, in which early memories and experiences are revised and rearranged at a later date in order to fit in with fresh experiences, or with new developmental stages. In his 1899 paper on 'Screen Memories', Freud questions whether we

> *have any memories at all from our childhood: memories relating to our childhood may be all that we possess. Our childhood memories show us our earliest years not as they were but as they appeared at the later periods when the memories were aroused. In these periods of arousal, the childhood memories did not . . . emerge; they were formed at that time.*[29]

It was only some years later in the 'Wolf Man' case that Freud returned to this notion, where he emphasised how a scene from early life can become traumatic later, and how *Nachträglichkeit* has the effect of making the patient disregard time. Thus Freud writes of the Wolf Man:

At the age of one and a half the child receives an impression to which he is unable to react adequately; he is only able to understand it and to be moved by it when the impression is revived in him at the age of four; and only twenty years later, during the analysis, is he able to grasp with his conscious mental processes what was then going on in him. The patient justifiably disregards the three periods of time, and puts his present ego into the situation which is so long past.[30]

(Freud, 1918)

Thus the psychoanalytic concept of development does not merely refer to processes involving linear time, but, in addition, to a different kind of time – psychical time – where past and present are constantly being reorganised by the human subject. Furthermore, we can say that sexual life is bound up with a special kind of temporality, because the sexual drives go through what Freud called a 'diphasic' development.[31] That is, the onset of sexual development in humans occurs in two phases – the childhood period, followed by the so-called 'period of latency', in which sexual urges die down, before re-emerging at puberty. Childhood sexual issues can thus be reorganised in the light of the subsequent period of puberty, involving a reworking of what has gone before. Such reworking at adolescence may enable earlier conflicts to be potentially resolved, making adolescence a period where the subject may have a 'second chance' to deal with the past.

Lacan emphasised that the stages of libido development are tied to the subject's history. The so-called stages are to be seen within the context of the developing child's attempt to place themselves within a family and societal structure, and are also to be seen in the context of the adult's subsequent reorganisation of memory. The stages can be seen as nodes or turning points in the subject's attempts to recognise their history.

Thus, every fixation at a so-called instinctual stage is above all a historical scar: a page of shame that is forgotten or undone, or a page of glory that compels.[32]

(Lacan, 1966)

Furthermore, Lacan writes that these stages are already organised in subjectivity, that is within a symbolic structure involving relations between subjects; even before it is born, the child has a place in the parents' minds, possibly even a name. There is a family history, an organisation into which he will have to fit, or not.

And, to put it clearly, the subjectivity of the child who registers as victories and defeats the heroic chronicle of the training of his sphincters, enjoying the imaginary sexualization of his cloacal orifices, turning his excremental expulsions into aggressions, his retentions into seductions, and his movements of release into symbols – this subjectivity is not fundamentally different from the subjectivity of the psychoanalyst who, in order to understand them, tries to reconstitute the forms of love he calls pregenital . . . In other words, the anal stage is no less purely historical when it is actually experienced than when it is reconstituted in thought, nor is it less purely grounded in intersubjectivity. On the other hand, seeing it as a mere stage in some instinctual maturation leads even the best minds off the track.[33]

Melanie Klein added to the complexity of how these stages can be viewed when she reworked the concept of 'developmental stage' into the concept of 'position'.[34] A position, such as the paranoid-schizoid or the depressive position, is an organisation of defences, phantasies, object relationships, anxieties; it is a mental space in which the subject can be located at any time in their life. The subject can go in and out of positions throughout their life. There remains, for example, the potential to re-experience psychotic anxieties from early development; these anxieties are not simply overcome in the course of development, but remain potentially available, and liable to be re-experienced whenever the subject comes against certain critical situations, such as loss, frustration and the demands of being in psychoanalytical treatment.

To return specifically to the nature of libido development, it was in his 1913 paper, 'The Disposition to Obsessional Neurosis', that Freud delineated a separate anal-sadistic stage of the pregenital organisation, as a result of observations from obsessional neurotic patients. He highlights in these patients the extraordinary part played by impulses of hatred and anal erotism. He gives a fairly sketchy and rather unusual clinical example to illustrate his theme. This was of a woman patient who began, after some traumatic experience, to develop an anxiety hysteria, but who, one day, suddenly developed an obsessional neurosis which displaced the hysteria. The new neurosis was a reaction to a new problem relating to her current sexual life.

Freud describes how the patient

had been a happy and almost completely contented wife. She wanted to have children, from motives based on an infantile fixation of her wishes, and she fell ill [with anxiety attacks] *when she learned that it was impossible for her to have any by her husband who was the only object of her love ... Her husband understood, without any admission or explanation on her part, what his wife's anxiety meant; he felt hurt, without showing it, and in his turn reacted neurotically by – for the first time – failing in sexual intercourse with her. Immediately afterwards he started on a journey. His wife believed that he had become permanently impotent, and produced her first obsessional symptoms on the day before his expected return.*[35]

Her obsessional symptoms involved scrupulous washing and cleanliness, and protective measures against severe injuries which she thought others should fear from her – which Freud suggested were reaction formations against her own anal-erotic and sadistic impulses. That is, the wanting to be clean was a reaction to the anal impulses, and the fear of retaliation a reaction to her own sadistic impulses.

As Freud describes:

Her sexual need was obliged to find expression in these shapes after her genital life had lost all its value owing to the impotence of the only man of whom there could be any question for her.[36]

He then adds to the clinical picture the fact that the patient's sexual life began in early childhood with beating phantasies. Then:

After they were suppressed, an unusually long period of latency set in, during which the girl passed through a period of exalted moral growth, without any awakening of female sexual feelings. Her marriage, which took place at an early age, opened a time of normal sexual activity. This period, during which she was a happy wife, continued for a number of years, until her first great frustration [of not having children] brought on the hysterical neurosis. When this was followed by her genital life losing all its value, her sexual life ... returned to the infantile stage of sadism.[37]

Once more, we can see how Freud's theory is intimately related to concrete issues of people's daily sexual lives, something which is too often ignored these days.

Abraham, one of Klein's analysts, wrote two key papers on the development of the libido. The first, in 1916, gives evidence for the oral stage from the analysis of psychotic patients, while the second, in 1924, to which we shall return later, is a comprehensive account of the stages of libido development in relation to the various stages of object-love. The latter paper particularly influenced Klein and laid the basis for her own theory of object relations.

In his earlier paper on 'The First Pregenital Stage', Abraham makes observations on the oral stage of development, based on the psychoanalysis of ill patients, in whom such early experiences seem particularly available. It is worthwhile giving some details from this paper as it also reveals particularly clearly the clinical basis both for libido theory and for psychoanalytical theory in general.

Abraham first gives clinical material from the analysis of a schizophrenic patient with a family history of schizophrenia. This patient is described as preoccupied with himself in a markedly narcissistic manner in that the slightest fancy, a pun on a word, etc., could occupy him intensely and for long periods of time, while his own physical condition absorbed his interest more than anything else. His genital and anal sensations were of the highest importance to him. Moreover, he was addicted to anal as well as genital masturbation. During the period of puberty he derived pleasure from playing with faeces, and later on he occupied himself with his bodily excretions. For instance, he took pleasure in eating his own semen.

But it was his oral preoccupations that were of primary interest to the patient. He would wake up from exciting dreams with what the patient called 'oral pollutions', with saliva dribbling from his mouth. He was preoccupied with the love of milk, sucking fluid and his own tongue. He often used to wake at night with intense sexual desires, which could often be assuaged by drinking milk. He felt that his longing to suck milk was his deepest and most primitive need, to which genital masturbation, however pleasurable, was secondary (Abraham, 1916).[38]

Abraham further describes the presence in the patient of what he himself called 'cannibalistic ideas', which went back to early childhood when he had associated loving somebody with eating something good. It seemed to him that he wanted a substitute for human flesh – unlike Hannibal Lecter who actually wanted the real thing – and his associations led to the phantasy of biting into the breast. Abraham adds that the period during which he was nursed at the breast had been unusually full of important occurrences, with constant changes of wet-nurses, and the prolonging of the period of breast-feeding:

> These events were bound to have an effect on a child in whose sexual constitution the mouth zone was so strongly accentuated. They must have facilitated the fixation of the libido on an earlier stage or its regression to such a stage.[39]

Thus the characteristics of this case – the predominant importance of the oral zone, the intimate connection between the sexual and nutritive functions, and the strong presence of desires to incorporate the love-object – can be seen to be the same characteristics which Freud attributed to the earliest stages of libidinal development in infancy. While clearly this patient is highly abnormal, the extreme nature of his symptoms renders intelligible phenomena which we can see in other people in a less marked or a more disguised form – for example, in the patient I described who was coming to the end of her analysis, and who brought up issues around orality, as well as other areas. Abraham also discusses the presence of oral fixations in more neurotic patients, such as those preoccupied with eating and food, persistent thumb-suckers, and patients in whom the sucking habit may become abnormally dominant. One could obviously add smokers to his list, including of course Freud himself, who was a persistent cigar smoker.

In summary, Abraham gives a vivid clinical paper illustrating, through the use of remarkable clinical examples, the existence of the oral stage in the development of the libido, and, in particular, the existence of an early cannibalistic stage in this development.

Freud's 1911 paper on paranoia – his commentary on the Schreber case – and Judge Schreber's own memoirs of his psychotic illness also provide examples of how libido theory can help to explain adult symptoms. For example, Schreber describes how he is attached to God by means of divine rays. Freud makes the point that these rays can be seen as the concrete representation and projection outwards of libidinal connections. At the beginning of his illness, Schreber spent nearly two years in a catatonic state, in which the world, for him, had catastrophically 'disappeared'. Then came the gradual, delusional, reconnection to the world as a 're-libidinisation'.[40]

The Schreber case is also important for Lacan's theory of psychosis. Among other things, he focuses on the fact that Schreber's rays have a law that they must speak, while much of his delusional content refers to issues of language, such as the existence in God of a 'basic language', as well as the importance of various names. The Schreber case proves, for Lacan, that libido is not to be conceived as just an amorphous and unstructured kind of energy, but that it is articulated in some way through the language structure. Hence any theory of libido has to take account of the nature of the human subject. Lacan himself in his papers on psychosis offers a highly complex picture of how the subject's structure is distorted in psychosis, with various alterations in the relations with reality and in the language structure (Lacan, 1966).[41]

These various issues concerned with the nature of psychosis

lead us on to Freud's complex revision of his earlier libido theory with the full introduction of the concept of narcissism in 1914.

Narcissism and Libido/Self and Love

Prior to the narcissism paper, Freud divided the drives into two basic kinds – ego drives and sexual drives. Ego drives were the drives of self-preservation, such as hunger; while the sexual drives referred to sexual impulses. All mental occurrences were to be seen as involving a dynamic interplay between these two sorts of drives. Thus neurotic symptoms were a result of sexual impulses being repressed by the subject's ego, whose function was to protect the mind from excessive mental pain; they were a result of the conflict between the self-preservative function of the ego and the sexual drives pressing to be expressed.

The distinction between the drives of self-preservation and those involving sexuality can be seen already with the infant sucking at the breast. This sucking is first of all associated with the satisfaction of the need for nourishment. But the child's lips also behave like an erotogenic zone, with the flow of warm milk causing pleasurable sensations, the prototype of sexual satisfaction. Freud describes how sexual activity thus attaches itself at the beginning to functions serving the purpose of self-preservation, and does not become independent until later.

> No one who has seen a baby sinking back satiated from the breast and falling asleep with flushed cheeks and a blissful smile can escape the reflection that this picture persists as a prototype of the sexual satisfaction in later life.[42]
>
> (Freud, 1905)

While feeding requires an object, the breast, to satisfy hunger, sexual feelings are satisfied by a part of the subject's own body, such as the mouth; that is, sexual feelings at this stage are auto-erotic. The need for repeating sexual satisfaction becomes detached from the need to feed, so that sexuality, originally 'leaning on' the self-preservative functions, becomes independent of them at a later stage. Thus sexuality arises from body functioning, yet then becomes detached from its bodily origins.

Whether or not we accept Freud's theory of drives and their origins, the point is that the theory is designed to provide a basic duality for mental functioning. Without this duality it would be hard to explain mental conflict. Ego drives, based on self-preservation, are to be seen as more based on reality – on the need and ability to obtain food and supplies, and to avoid pain. While the sexual drives are more under the dominance of the pleasure principle – they are less susceptible to reality, more intent on seeking gratification. The libido remains under the dominance of the pleasure principle so long because of its ability to escape frustration through auto-erotism; satisfaction can be prolonged, in phantasy, by means of the repetition of auto-erotic activity, originally by sucking, and then later by masturbation.

Freud then describes how a major advance in understanding the nature of the psyche took place with observations from the analysis of psychotic disorders and the introduction of the term 'narcissism', and, with it, the definition of a new and complex duality – between ego-libido and object-libido.

The analysis of psychotic disorders revealed that the ego was not merely an agency of repression and avoidance of pain, but that libido was also attached to it. Thus, as could be seen in the schizophrenic patient described above, who had withdrawn libido from his objects, from other people, and was almost totally preoccupied with himself, it is possible to pathologically transfer onto oneself virtually the whole of the libido which in normal people is directed outwards towards the world and others. That is, the libido can be attached or 'invested' in various ways, either onto the self or onto others. The libido that has been withdrawn from the external world and has been directed towards the ego gives rise to the attitude of narcissism, or 'self-love' in ordinary language. Thus the self-preservative drives are, like the sexual drives, of a libidinal nature; they are sexual drives which, instead of external objects, take the subject's own ego as an object. This libido of the self-preservative drives is now described as 'narcissistic libido'. However, the ego usually does also retain a certain amount of purely self-preservative drives which are unattached to sexual drives; without this, hunger, for example, would always be sexualised. One can see in anorexics how there is a real confusion between food and sexuality. For example, by not eating, in a sense they do not wish to mature sexually; their periods stop, and occasionally in severe cases they may even delay sexual maturation in early adolescence. This is a real, contemporary issue, in that the fashion industry seems obsessed with images of thinness, putting considerable pressure on adolescent girls to keep thin by excessive dieting. One can see here how individual pathology and the social environment are in constant interaction. It is uncertain how much the existence of anorexia is a function of society's expectations about the look of the female body, and how much it would be a problem regardless of advertising pressure.

As for the origin of narcissism, Freud adds that the megalomania of the narcissistic patient is itself no new creation: it is a magnification of a situation that existed early in life, when the young child was at a stage when they overestimated the power of their wishes, and felt that they were the centre of the universe; that is, Freud postulates a stage of 'primary' narcissism, when auto-erotism was at its height. Thus the narcissism which has resulted from the withdrawal of libido from objects onto the ego is a secondary one imposed upon a primary narcissism.

We can now see that there was an original amount of libido attached to the ego, that the ego is a great 'reservoir' of libido, from which some is later given off to objects, forming object-libido. Freud pictures the relation of ego-libido to object-libido through an analogy taken from zoology:

> *Think of those simplest of living organisms* [the amoebas] *which consist of a little-differentiated globule of protoplasmic substance. They put out protrusions, known as pseudopodia, into which they cause the substance of their body to flow over. They are able, however, to withdraw the protrusions once more and form themselves again into a globule. We compare the putting-out of these protrusions, then, to the emission of libido on to objects while the main mass of libido can remain in the ego; and we suppose that in normal circumstances ego-libido can be transformed unhindered into object-libido and that this can once more be taken back into the ego.*[43]

Thus, instead of the existence of a conflict between ego drives and sexual drives, we now have a conflict between ego-libido and object-libido, with a constant see-saw between the two. With this new duality, Freud can explain both abnormal states – as seen in psychosis, with an extreme withdrawal of libido from objects, and hypochondriasis, when libido becomes attached to the subject's body or a part of the body – and also some normal ones, such as falling asleep, when the subject turns away from the world, withdrawing libido from objects and back into the ego. Being in love consists of an intense flowing-over of ego-libido on to the loved object. Indeed, the megalomania of the psychotic patient is, in Freud's words,

> *in every way comparable to the familiar sexual overvaluation of the object in* [normal] *erotic life. In this way for the first time we learnt to understand a trait in a psychotic illness by relating it to normal erotic life.*[44]

While Freud postulates a state of primary narcissism, when the infant's libido is virtually unattached to objects, subsequent thinkers have emphasised that it is impossible to view the infant as unattached to an object; that the infant is always related to some extent. Only in the uterus could one conceive of the possibility of a primary narcissism, and, even there, there may be the possibility of an awareness of the mother – if only through the loud presence of the maternal heart-beat.

Thus, Donald Winnicott emphasises that it is impossible to think of an infant without bringing in its mother; that it is more accurate to picture the mother–infant dyad as primary, rather than the infant themselves unattached to an object.[45] Most analysts since then have also added the notion of a relationship between the subject and the other to any consideration of sexual development – something which is there in Freud and Abraham, but which had been relatively undeveloped by other theorists.

The Human Subject and the Drives/
The Transformational Pathway

In the 'Three Essays', we have seen how, for Freud, the subject can gradually, through development, organise the drives. What is proposed in this final section is a way of understanding more about the subject as a 'libidinal subject', or as organiser of the drives.

Freud describes how the drives in childhood are not unified but consist of a number of different components, or 'partial' drives, each with a special libidinal connection to an erotogenic zone, a part of the body giving rise to a form of sexual excitation. Using evidence from, for example, the perversions where the partial drives fall apart, Freud describes how usually the sexual drive is put together from the various partial drives into what he calls a 'firm organisation'. This happens only at puberty, when the primacy of the genitals is finally beginning to be established, and sexual maturity, the capacity to impregnate and to be impregnated, occurs. The erotogenic zones then fit themselves into this new arrangement, with the genital zone as the leading zone. The new organisation is a result of the combination of the partial drives into a unity by the adolescent subject.

Freud's drive theory thus points towards the way that the subject may become organised, or disorganised if things do not go well, at adolescence. As Laufer and Laufer (1984) have pointed out, the unity of the mature body image at this time has a crucial role in creating the final sexual organisation.[46] What usually takes place is the integration of the old and the new, coming to terms with the loss of the old immature body image and accepting the libidinal investment of the new maturing body image. However, there may occur a breakdown in the process of integrating the

mature body image into the subject, with an accompanying fragmentation of the mind and the production of various symptoms,
including suicidal feelings, anorexia, and overt psychotic breakdown, as was outlined in the case of Simon above.

While the task of integrating the body image is important in
synthesising the partial drives, Freud, in his paper 'Instincts and
their Vicissitudes', reveals other ways in which the subject relates
to others, and shows how the subject is transformed in various
ways by the drive. He seems to describe an elaborate relationship
between the subject and the drives, where the subject appears and
disappears at various points in the complicated route or circuit of
the drive. Although the ultimate aim of each drive is to seek
satisfaction, there may be different paths leading to the same aim,
and various aims may be combined and interchanged with one
another, reflecting once more the fluidity of the libido.

To tie down some of these routes with regard to the sexual drives,
Freud examines – in detail – perversions such as sadomasochism.
He traces how the sexual drive, experienced as sexual enjoyment,
weaves its way through the relations between two subjects, such as
the sadist and the masochist. The position each subject takes in
relation to the other subject, that of the sadist to the masochist and
vice versa, will direct the drive and transform it in various ways.
Sexual enjoyment is different if one takes up the sadistic position
as opposed to the masochistic one, though there is also overlap.

Such situations reveal the presence of what we could call
a 'transformational pathway' between subjects.[47] The subject
appears and disappears at various points in a complicated drive
circuit; the drive can transform the subject, and the subject can
transform the drive. In this sense, we can see that libido as the
'driving force' behind the drive can find a place in contemporary
psychoanalytic theory, but as one element of a pathway leading
back and forth from an essentially libidinal human subject.

The philosopher Herbert Marcuse develops Freud's theory of
libido, with a mixture of his own brand of Marxism, for an attack
on the way that modern civilisation has become too repressive.[48]
Freud described how civilisation required that the sexual drives
be repressed so that humans could work effectively. Marcuse
argued that this may have been necessary so long as basic com-
modities were scarce, but became unnecessary once modern
technology could satisfy our needs without repression. Unpleasant
work could now be kept to a minimum, and so we no longer have to
thwart our sexuality. His revolutionary vision of a new society is
one in which the libido is liberated, no longer having to conform to
the excessive demands of a repressive civilisation. Instead, we
would have a 'libidinous' civilisation, which would dissolve

repressive institutions, allow more time for pleasure and enjoyment, and eliminate alienated labour.

Though Marcuse is not too clear about how such a society could be maintained, his vision of a new relation to sexuality has been influential; it was one of the guiding principles of the sixties' student movements. While such a vision may now seem hopelessly Utopian in our materialistic 'market' culture, perhaps we need to give more room to the notion of libido. Without it, we run the risk of losing our subjectivity in the quest for material gain.

Roger Kennedy is a consultant psychotherapist at Cassel Hospital, honorary senior lecturer in Psychiatry at Imperial College, training analyst of the British Psychoanalytical Society and the author of several books and many papers on psychoanalysis.

Notes

1. Freud, S., 'Three Essays on the Theory of Sexuality' (1905), *Standard Edition of the Complete Psychological Works of Sigmund Freud*, London: Hogarth Press, 1953–73 (hereafter *SE*), VII, p. 217.
2. Jacques Lacan (1901–81) was an influential and controversial French psychoanalyst. His main aim was to restore psychoanalysis to life by a radical re-interpretation of Freud's thought, and by putting psycho-analysis in touch with contemporary thought. Though forming his own school of psychoanalysis, he has had considerable influence on analysts in France and elsewhere. See Benvenuto, B. and Kennedy, R., *The Works of Jacques Lacan* (London: Free Association Books, 1986), for an introduction to his thought.
3. Lacan, J., *The Seminar of Jacques Lacan*, Book 2, ed. J.-A. Miller, trans. S. Tomaselli, Cambridge: Cambridge University Press, 1978, pp. 221–2.
4. Freud, S., 'Wild Psychoanalysis' (1910), *SE*, vol. 11, p. 223.
5. Freud, S., 'Instincts and their Vicissitudes' (1915), *SE*, vol. 14, p. 117. Although the German word *Triebe* is translated in the official title as 'Instincts', a more accurate translation would be 'Drives'.
6. Freud, S., 'Group Psychology and the Analysis of the Ego' (1921), *SE*, vol. 18, p. 90.
7. Sophocles, *Women of Trachis*, trans. E. Watling, Harmondsworth: Penguin, 1953, p. 136.
8. Sophocles, *Antigone*, trans. E. Watling, Harmondsworth: Penguin, 1947, p. 148.
9. Laplanche, J. and Pontalis, J.-B., *The Language of Psychoanalysis*, trans. D. Nicholson-Smith, London: Hogarth Press, 1967, p. 277.
10. Kohon, G., *The British School of Psychoanalysis: The Independent Tradition*, London: Free Association Books, 1986, p. 20.
11. Green, A., 'Has Sexuality Anything to Do with Psychoanalysis?', *International Journal of Psychoanalysis*, vol. 76 (5), 1995, pp. 871–83.
12. Lacan, J., *The Four Fundamental Concepts of Psychoanalysis*, Harmondsworth: Penguin Books, 1973, p. 153.
13. Mollon, P., *The Unconscious*, Ideas in Psychoanalysis series, Cambridge: Icon Books, 2000, pp. 62–4. Reprinted in *On a Darkling Plain*, pp. 1–38 (pp. 30–1).
14. Kohon, op. cit.; Kohon, G., *No lost certainties to be found*, London: Karnac Books, 1999.
15. Freud, S., *The Complete Letters of Sigmund Freud to Wilhelm Fliess*, trans. and ed. J. Masson, London and Cambridge, MA: Harvard University Press, 1985, p. 80.
16. Ibid., p. 80.
17. Ibid., pp. 80–1.
18. Freud (1905), op. cit., p. 133.
19. Ibid., p. 170.
20. Freud, S., 'Introductory Lectures on Psychoanalysis' (1916–17), *SE*, vol. 16, p. 348.
21. Freud, S., 'Types of Onset of Neurosis' (1912), *SE*, XII, p. 231.
22. Ibid., p. 232.

23. Ibid., pp. 233–4.
24. Ibid., p. 236.
25. Ibid., p. 236.
26. Freud (1905), op. cit., p. 186.
27. Proust, M., *Time Regained* (1927), trans. A. Meyer, London: Chatto and Windus, 1972, p. 267.
28. Freud (1985), op. cit., p. 207.
29. Freud, S., 'Screen Memories' (1899), *SE*, vol. 3, p. 322.
30. Freud, S., 'From the History of an Infantile Neurosis' (1918), *SE*, vol. 17, p. 45n.
31. Freud (1905), op. cit., p. 234.
32. Lacan, J., *Écrits* (1966), trans. A. Sheridan, London: Tavistock, 1977, p. 52.
33. Ibid., pp. 52–3.
34. See Klein, M., 'Notes on Some Schizoid Mechanisms' (1946), in Klein, M., *Envy and Gratitude and Other Works: 1946–63*, London: Hogarth Press, 1980.
35. Freud. S., 'The Disposition to Obsessional Neurosis' (1913), *SE*, vol. 12, p. 320.
36. Ibid., p. 320.
37. Ibid., pp. 321–2.
38. Abraham, K., 'The First Pregenital Stage of the Libido' (1916), *Selected Papers of Karl Abraham,* trans. D. Bryan and A. Strachey, London: Hogarth Press, 1927, pp. 254–5.
39. Ibid., p. 257.
40. Freud, S., 'Psychoanalytical Notes on an Autobiographical Account of a Case of Paranoia' (1912), *SE*, vol. 12, p. 70.
41. Lacan (1966), op. cit., p. 199ff.
42. Freud (1905), op. cit., p. 182.
43. Freud (1916–17), op. cit., p. 416.
44. Ibid., p. 415.
45. See, for example, Winnicott, D., *The Maturational Processes and the Facilitating Environment*, London: Hogarth Press, 1968.
46. Laufer, M. and Laufer, E., *Adolescence and Developmental Breakdown*, New Haven and London: Yale University Press, 1984.
47. See Kennedy, R., *The Elusive Human Subject*, London: Free Association Books, 1998, pp. 84–90.
48. Marcuse, H., *Eros and Civilization*, London: Allen Lane, 1955, p. 161ff.

Further Reading

Abraham, K., 'The First Pregenital Stage of the Libido' (1916), *Selected Papers of Karl Abraham,* trans. D. Bryan and A. Strachey, London: Hogarth Press, 1927.
Benvenuto, B. and Kennedy, R., *The Works of Jacques Lacan*, London: Free Association Books, 1986.
Freud, S., 'Screen Memories' (1899), *Standard Edition of the Complete Psychological Works of Sigmund Freud*, London: Hogarth Press, 1953–73 (hereafter *SE*), vol. 3.

——'Three Essays on the Theory of Sexuality' (1905), *SE*, vol. 7, p. 217.

——'Wild Psychoanalysis' (1910), *SE*, vol. 11.

——'Psychoanalytical Notes on an Autobiographical Account of a Case of Paranoia' (1912), *SE*, vol. 7.

——'Types of Onset of Neurosis' (1912), *SE*, vol. 12.

——'The Disposition to Obsessional Neurosis' (1913), *SE*, vol. 12, p. 320.

——'Instincts and their Vicissitudes' (1915), *SE*, vol. 14.

——'Introductory Lectures on Psychoanalysis' (1916–17), *SE*, vol. 16.

——'From the History of an Infantile Neurosis' (1918), *SE*, vol. 17.

——'Group Psychology and the Analysis of the Ego' (1921), *SE*, vol. 18.

——*The Complete Letters of Sigmund Freud to Wilhelm Fliess*, trans. and ed. J. Masson, London and Cambridge, MA: Harvard University Press, 1985.

Green, A., 'Has Sexuality Anything to Do with Psychoanalysis?', *International Journal of Psychoanalysis*, vol. 76 (5), 1995, pp. 871–83.

Kennedy, R., *The Elusive Human Subject*, London: Free Association Books, 1998.

Klein, M., 'Notes on Some Schizoid Mechanisms' (1946), in Klein, M., *Envy and Gratitude and Other Works, 1946–63*, London: Hogarth Press, 1980.

Kohon, G., *The British School of Psychoanalysis: The Independent Tradition*, London: Free Association Books, 1986.

——*No Lost Certainties to be Found*, London: Karnac Books, 1999.

Lacan, J., *Écrits* (1966), trans. A. Sheridan, London: Tavistock, 1977.

——*The Four Fundamental Concepts of Psychoanalysis*, Harmondsworth: Penguin Books, 1973.

——*The Seminar of Jacques Lacan*, Book 2, ed. J.-A. Miller, trans. S. Tomaselli, Cambridge: Cambridge University Press, 1978.

Laplanche, J. and Pontalis, J.-B., *The Language of Psychoanalysis*, trans. D. Nicholson-Smith, London: Hogarth Press, 1967.

Laufer, M. and Laufer, E., *Adolescence and Developmental Breakdown*, New Haven and London: Yale University Press, 1984.

Marcuse, H., *Eros and Civilization*, London: Allen Lane, 1955.

Proust, M., *Time Regained* (1927), trans. A. Meyer, London: Chatto and Windus, 1972.

Sophocles, *Antigone*, trans. E. Watling, Harmondsworth: Penguin, 1947.

——*Women of Trachis*, trans. E. Watling, Harmondsworth: Penguin, 1953.

Winnicott, D., *The Maturational Processes and the Facilitating Environment*, London: Hogarth Press, 1968.

10

Sublimation

Kalu Singh

Introduction: Better Mind the Bollocks

If the head's sublime, then what the fuck? Here is a working-class poet-painter's answer:

> *The head Sublime, the heart Pathos, the genitals Beauty, the hands & feet Proportion.*[1]

It is a riddle to tease the Sphinx. But is it a riddle or a reminder? For when one first reads Blake's 'Proverb (of Hell)' in adolescence, everything fits – except the third phrase. Yes, the high, mind-holding head must be Sublime; and the bleeding heart, Pathos; and Leonardo's 'Vitruvian Man' of outstretched limbs, that ancient puzzle of squaring the circle, is all about Proportion. But how to see Beauty in the genitals? Wouldn't the more obvious noun be 'danger', or – in the anti-sexual Christian dispensation – 'sin', or even 'Eve's sin', or 'corruption'? Or, in the mundane efflorescence of puberty, simply 'urgency'? Yes, the narcissist thinks of Beauty – but what of the Other's genitals? So does the pervert – but what of the Self's? Isn't the strongest sensation that of puzzlement which, as it gropes towards clarity, becomes anxiety? Looking at or thinking about the genital flesh-lock, something does seem to fit, literally, and yet there is a residue of sensation and thought. Sigmund Freud called this 'the uncanny', and stated more boldly that 'the genitals are hardly ever judged to be beautiful'.[2] But when we can see how Beauty comes in, are we also saying that the Sublime must be excluded from the genitals? And what are 'Beauty' and the 'Sublime' anyway – and aren't all these terms from art and not anatomy?

Somehow, at some point, one learns how to use the sentence, 'This is beautiful.' It is rare to remember this as a specific experience. It is lost among the experiences of learning how to say 'This is tasty/nice/lovely.' Virginia Woolf's 'hero-ine' Orlando is

299

startled to find that his Turkish gypsy hosts have no such word as 'beautiful'. Their equivalent phrase translates as 'How good to eat!'[3] Nor did the English have such a word until Tyndale minted it for his new Bible.[4] But he didn't mint the obvious pairing for it – 'uglyful'. Orsino's lament, 'If music be the food of love',[5] expresses how different modalities of appetite – aesthetic, sexual and plain hunger – can both substitute for each other and also fuse: but why do they?

It seems that all human societies develop such terms as 'beauty' and 'sublime' to mark out some specific experiences. The other puzzle about these terms is that they carry an ethical evaluation: to say that some thing or some relationship is beautiful or ugly carries a moral charge. There are three approaches to their use:

1. Aesthetics – this states the conditions of ascription of such terms to:
   a) the objects out there, whether of Nature or made by men and women.
   b) the inner experience, individual or shared, occasioned by the making or attention to these objects. It delineates the intellectual faculties and the range of emotions involved.

2. Developmental Psychology and Sociology – this describes how individuals learn to make such ascriptions, and the cultural values they embody. It is explanation at the inter-personal level.

3. Psychoanalytic Theory – this proposes an explanation at the intra-personal level: what is happening inside the individual to facilitate such experiences. Its core concept is *sublimation*. I will argue that this psychoanalytic concept offers a genuine contribution to the understanding of what is going on in these experiences and the use of these terms which was opened up by ethics and aesthetics.

Let us return to ordinary usage and see how desire, aggression and anxiety are inscribed in these terms. The limiting experience of anxiety is the sense of annihilation of the integrity of the Self. One might say that there are two poles here: before birth, the anxiety is pure physical emotion; before death, it is pure intellection – 'When I have fears that I may cease to be.'[6] These would seem two obvious candidates for the sublime, but in fact ordinary life treats them as enigmas to avoid wasting energy upon. The more insistent diurnal anxiety is about frustration of desire and managing the consequential aggression. Thinking again of Blake's mirror, anatomically the head and the genitals are well separated: perhaps the heart is at the mediating midpoint. But (male) slang shows an anxiety about the impossibility of separation: 'penis-brain' and 'dickhead' are terms of abuse only marginally less scornful than 'wanker'. There are no female equivalents such as 'vagina-brain' or 'twat-head'; and nor does 'prick' resonate with as much aggression as 'cunt', whether spoken by straight or gay men. For some men, the ultimate terror is to be *marked* as a woman. Even Queen Noel Coward appropriated heterosexual anxiety when he called Kenneth Tynan 'a cunt'.[7]

Women, in their turn, appropriate male definitions. Voltaire doubted a woman's ability to imagine the highest themes, because he believed that 'The composition of a tragedy requires testicles'.[8] Two centuries on, actress Helen Mirren, asked why she liked her female lead in David Hare's new play about a rock-chick, *Teeth 'N' Smiles*, replied: 'It's got balls!' 'And', teased the interviewer, 'that's good for a woman?'[9] A colleague, who aspired to be a writer, reported an adult dream of castration, which included the additional distress that he couldn't write with his newly cut member – pen-as-envy or writer's cock-block!

Again, some kind of experience of exchange or fusion between the physical and the intellect is being adumbrated here, as is the age-old anxiety of insufficiency of balls or even castration. The reader might already be annoyed at this familiar psychoanalytic melding. Here is a clever and scrumptious refutation of such scepticism. Knowing that the Germans had executed 15,000 of their own soldiers during the Second World War for an indiscipline which the Allies were recognising as post-traumatic stress disorder, Anthony Storr was interested to meet, in 1948, one of their psychiatrists who was visiting the Maudsley Hospital. He remembers the latter 'boasting that war neurosis was virtually non-existent in the German forces, and affirming that Freud's theories were nonsense. We asked him how they managed cases of incipient breakdown. "We threatened them with castration: that soon got them back in line", he replied.'[10]

How perfectly this echoes the British Tommy's fantasy about the defeatable enemy.

> Hitler has only got one ball:
> The other is in the Albert Hall.
> His mother, the dirty bugger,
> She chopped it off when he was small.[11]

If envy, greed and fear of the Other's possessions are the ordinary shadows of broken desire, what is ordinary health but sharing and gratitude or, in Joan Riviere's phrase, 'welcome by gratification'?[12]

It took Hollywood almost the entire first century of cinema to attain the courage to show this: in *Boogie Nights,* a young woman says to her lover, 'Your cock is so beautiful'.[13] I've yet to see a parallel celebration of the vagina. The nearest was in the TV sitcom *Third Rock from the Sun*, in which the alien Sally misunderstands a reference to Mesopotamia as to her own 'fertile crescent'.[14]

Let us begin by seeing how far aesthetics takes us.

Kunstry Matters: the Philosophical Sublime

Pretty-boy David defeated the Gentile giant, but the war between aesthetes and philistines is perennial – creating anxiety, resentment and anger on both sides. The philistines, with the wrath of the excluded and indolent, swear: 'We don't care if you ponces don't call it Art – we like it!' Like Humpty Dumpty, they assume the right to name and define at will. The space they find for the sublime seems to treat it as a synonym for '*very* beautiful'. From their elegant temples, the aesthetes insist on rites of passage requiring considerable learning and humility. Aesthetics begins by separating the 'useful/functional' from the 'beautiful', and the latter from the 'sublime'.

Hamlet's teasing pun to Ophelia, 'Do you think I meant country matters?',[15] is the nearest Shakespeare came to the most fearful word in the vernacular. The euphonious virgin-philosopher Kant was famously more interested in *Kunst* (Art). His masterly aesthetics argues that the faculties of Imagination, Understanding and Reason which process (sense) data from the external physical world and the internal mental world can – and in fact must – be used not only to gain conceptual knowledge and to inform practical action but also in what he calls 'harmonious free play'.[16] The aesthetic delight in, say, a tulip is disinterested and purposeless, and so is distinguishable from any interested pursuit of agreeable sensations of the tulip as Good – worthy or perfect. 'Delight in the beautiful must depend upon the reflection on an object precursory to some (not definitely determined) concept.'[17] This notion of being able to live with and enjoy a pre-conceptual or conceptually uncertain state anticipates Keats's brilliant idea of 'negative capability' ('when man is capable of being in uncertainties, Mysteries, doubts, without any irritable reaching after fact & reason'[18]) as an aspirational moral as well as aesthetic developmental marker. It also looks forward to Bion's recommendation that the therapist enter the therapeutic space 'without memory and desire . . . and with a capacity for reverie'.[19]

For Kant, the perception of form and limitation which characterises experiences of the beautiful, whether of the tulip or the abstract painting, induces in the mind a sense of being 'in *restful* contemplation'.[20] On the other hand, the Sublime experience is of the mind 'set in motion', beginning as 'a rapidly alternating repulsion and attraction produced by one and the same Object' of seemingly limitless (mathematical) magnitude or seemingly formless (dynamic) might – for example, the starry cosmos or the volcanic storm or high tragedy; and moving from humiliating terror to an invigorating awareness of the power of Reason, the faculty of ideas which can explain, contain and help to transcend that initial emotional disarray.[21] Kant introduces the concept of 'subreption' for this 'substitution of a respect for the Object in place of one for the idea of humanity in our own self – the Subject'.[22] The theme of substitution is germane to our project.

Though he further highlights the difference from the beautiful by calling the sublime 'a negative pleasure', it is through the latter concept, and its grounding in ideas, that Kant delineates the worth of human-made art. 'We say of a man who remains unaffected in the presence of what we consider sublime that he has no (moral) feeling.'[23] The task of the artist – and here Kant means 'original artist' and not merely 'imitator' or 'hack' – is to generate aesthetic ideas. These products of the free play of her imagination and understanding are what he calls 'inexponible': though there is an intuitive sense of a fit between the ideas and the work made, the concepts of understanding cannot explain it.[24] From the spectator's side, the inadequacy of concepts in relation to aesthetic pleasure is familiar: one runs out of worthwhile things to say about the final meaning of Virgil or Mozart.

For Kant, the presence 'proximately or remotely' of moral ideas, rather than 'sensation (charm or emotion)', is what makes a man-made object aesthetically worthwhile. His absolute belief in this can be seen in his aphorism: 'The beautiful is the symbol of the morally good.'[25] In the following two remarks he is making a developmental as well as moral point. 'Hunger is the best sauce... [but] ... Only when men have got all they want can we tell who among the crowd has taste or not ... The beauties of nature are in general the most beneficial, if one is early habituated to observe, estimate and admire them.'[26]

Disinterested attention presupposes the satisfaction of desire; and desire presupposes the satisfaction of need. Some people never make the transition. It is a real question and not merely an urban aesthete's jibe to ask: 'How much of one's humanity is perverted or lost if one doesn't frequently commune aesthetically with nature?' It's common enough to feel tired of every piece of art – CD, video, painting, book – one has; and also to meet precious, vicious aesthetes. Or to ask it another way, what did Blake get when he imagined the meaning of the creation of the tiger; or today, what has my friend's eight-year-old daughter, Marika, got from her introduction to the beauty of the cockroach? It is worth remembering that one's first early habituations are so intensely to people (and nature) that one must slowly learn that not everything is as alive as oneself. Most philosophers and mystics have consistently argued for the worth of experiences of beauty, and particularly the sublime. Such a motion of the imagination is felt to be intrinsically good. But there is a sceptical strand from Plato. He famously banished poets from his ideal Republic, believing that any genuine proto-socialist realism, by depicting human weakness and depravity, would fail to be educative and inspiring.[27] We laugh nervously at anyone who banishes artists or burns books. But more astutely, and perhaps humanely, he did question our ability to contain our imagination. In speaking of *theios phobos*, sacred fear, he reminds us that this faculty of the imagination is so protean and powerful that we would do well to limit our engagement of its forces.[28] More art per day doesn't always mean more good. Music only sometimes soothes the troubled breast, and, as clinicians have pointed out, some schizophrenics have been further deranged by attempts to heal them with art.[29]

The etymology of 'sublime' includes the ideas of boundary/limit/threshold; the traverse beams in a doorframe, a lintel; a process of approach to, crossing over or emerging from the boundary; reservoir, conduit and valve. We will see below that these ideas of container and change across a boundary connect with sublimation. The physiology of the sublime, or certainly of one of the defining examples – the Cortez-like view from the mountain – tells us that during this experience we don't actually focus our eyes on the scene, and we thereby facilitate the production of alpha waves which are typically related to relaxation. It could be said that this doesn't so much reduce the sublime to the merely gratifying, but frees the energy for the associative thinking which leads to a conceptual recognition of the sublime.[30] Chiming with these descriptions are the basic prescriptions to therapists of mental unfocusing – free-floating, evenly suspended attention, the third ear, etc. So we come to psychoanalysis.

Sexual Annealing: Freud's Account of Sublimation

Freud's theoretical paper on 'Sublimation' was lost – disappeared into thin air! All that remain are scattered remarks in various other papers. The best way into any psychoanalytic concept is through the Oedipus complex. Between the cosy fantasy of a man and woman simply having sex and then nurturing the resultant baby until it is old enough to have sex and make its own babies, and the lived experience – marked in countless narratives – of profound puzzlement and distress in the nuclear nest, Freud and Melanie Klein saw a cauldron of terrifying desires, thoughts and emotions that ordinary conceptions didn't dare approach. It feels strange arguing for the heuristic worth of the complex. But if I must, I ask the reader to try to understand, let alone explain, the following vignettes *without* recourse to psychoanalytic concepts. What kind of person, what kind of artist, is being described? What did their creative impulse mean?

1. Hank is the chat-show sidekick to Larry in the TV parody-sitcom *The Larry Sanders Show*. He is obsequious and inept, a dull foil of a fool, but still desperate to be as media-cool as Larry's producer Arthur. Eventually he thinks he has something impressive: a very young beautiful woman agrees to marry him – on TV. Her father shows up for the first time at the reception. When Larry and Arthur look up to greet him they see the spitting image of Hank. They are speechless with embarassment.[31]
2. Stephen Sondheim's parents were in the fashion trade. His father left when he was ten. His mother 'Foxy' became 'creepy ... She would sit across from me with her legs aspread ... would lower her blouse'. His father wanted him to 'get a proper job and not become a feckless artist'. On what she thought was her death-bed, Foxy wrote to her middle-aged son: 'The only regret I have in life is giving you birth.'[32]
3. European trash-TV viewers and Guinness Book of Records anoraks would have been introduced to Lolo Ferrari as 'the woman with the largest breasts in the world'. She also had huge bee-stung lips. In her TV cameos with Antoine de Caunes, the vicarious stud, and Jean-Paul Gaultier, the gay designer, and also in her live stage/bar shows where she invited men to touch the peaks of fantasy, she seemed to be enjoying the limitless power to fascinate and seduce accorded to those who inhabit superlatives. Even allowing for the shallow mask of celebrity, it felt reasonable to assume she got *some* sexual pleasure from these sexualised displays. But in her TV obituary, her photographer said: 'You can touch her, every part, but as soon as you touch her lips she becomes completely mad.' She confessed: 'During sex, I can't stand it when someone touches my breasts.' For her ageing mother, Lolo's androgynous husband/manager was the villain: 'The best revenge on Eric would be to pour acid on his face ... I'm going to do it.' Her father didn't speak to the camera.[33]

4. Some men, especially those who generate a public image of pork-sword wizardry, such as John Lennon, ask to call their wife 'Mother'. Why?[34]
5. At the age of twenty-five, Salvador Dalí exhibited two paintings: 'Sometimes I Spit For Pleasure On The Portrait Of My Mother', and 'The Great Masturbator'. Because of the former, his father banished him from the family home.[35]

So, here we have some 'artists':

1. Sondheim – transforming word and sound into the beauty of song and theatre.
2. Lolo – transforming *herself* into a thing of sexualised beauty.
3. Hank's wife – who *found* a lost, inaccessible object of beauty and desire in a simulacrum.
4. Lennon – *projecting* an old role onto the new Other.
5. Dalí – an unbridled imagination broken by envy, ingratitude and rage, getting himself removed from what his friend Lorca called 'the jungle of blood', heterosexual intercourse.

Psychoanalysis didn't merely add adverbs and intensifiers to common concepts and narratives: 'he *really* loved his mother'. It tried to provide a correlate for the sense of mighty, almost uncontainable and unthinkable, emotions and thoughts which attend ordinary development. Perhaps, given the way aesthetic narratives work – and here again is the crucial Kantian concept of inexponible ideas – the theorists chose received narratives to present the theory. The stories of Oedipus, Elektra, Hamlet and Faust induce a sense of inexhaustible wonder which seems to fit the puzzling taste for the dark side of family life.

Hank's wife is doomed to find that the physical simulacrum of her father can only be an unsatisfying shadow of the figure in ancient fantasy. And poor Hank is doomed to learn that he can have no real existence with her. The marriage does indeed collapse within a year.

It was Sondheim's poor revenge to be famously scruffy. It was a different revenge to be a successful artist. And perhaps another different revenge to be gay. Just think of him knowing for decades, perhaps only unconsciously until the letter, that his mother wished him dead – and yet still being able to write love songs like 'Maria' and 'Tonight'.

Lolo, child slang meaning 'big tits', had a real name, Eve – the proto-mother. Eric remembered Eve saying that 'Her mother refused to breast-feed her. Lolo thought her mother wouldn't breast-feed her because her mouth wasn't pretty enough or big enough.' Her mother admitted: 'When she was born, I had an impression that I'd been reborn. She had my face, madonna features . . . but I always hated my face . . . And I think she could feel this . . . inherited my sense of self-loathing.'[36]

As Ferrari is now dead, we can't ask when she first sensed her mother's absence of desire to offer a loving breast, and how consciously informed were her decisions to undergo plastic surgery. Twenty-two operations in five years – more than on Freud's mouth! At a trite, naïve realist level, she could now suck her own breasts, displacing her mother's. But more symbolically, she displaced them absolutely, and all women/mothers, by having the largest – and in the fantasy equation, most-wanted – breasts in the world.

What seemed missing from her understanding was her rage at, and despair of, her father. For of course she invited all the men of the world – except her father – to touch and imagine sucking. It was her revenge on his failure to be a father, whose principal psychoanalytic tasks are:

1. To protect the mother from the world, so she can breast-feed their child in peace.
2. To protect their child from her mother, so she can develop into a woman/mother.
3. To protect the child from herself, her unmanageable thoughts and emotions.
4. To protect the child from himself, his rage at being displaced by the child, and his desire that the child be his *pleasure-object*.

Lolo's avowed absence of desire to be seen and touched shows the terrifying levels of ambivalence that the Oedipal drama produces. Her mother, broken by *her own* mother, felt so humiliated by the public display and by her daughter's Monroesque drug-death that she displaced all her own sense of envy and guilt into a 'maternal' revenge-rage at her son-in-law.

Apart from the relational longings, there are of course the ordinary developmental tasks for the baby/child of attaining control of appetite and excretion – the mouth and the anal and urethral valves. Attending these are experiences of fullness, sometimes satisfying and sometimes unbearable, and experiences of evacuation which waver between a sense of expulsion, escape and grief over loss. But from early on, there is another dimension to the baby/child's life: its ability to be concerned with neither food nor desire, but to concentrate on tasks that seem without purpose or meaning for survival or connection – play and art. Later, some teenagers and adults would rather spend all their free (required-work free) energy in play and making than in fucking or even eating.

Freud believed that there must be some mechanism at work which facilitates the ordinary management of these inchoate instincts and energies and also directs them into the channels of play and art. One of these is sublimation. The theory of instincts and their transformations underpins all psychoanalytic theory. In a common perception of instinctual forces, there are just two simple modalities – attraction and repulsion or, in the human realm, love and hate. Freud's major contribution was to suggest that the instincts of sexuality and aggression are far more protean and subtle than they appear even to the cold eye of adult misanthropy. It is not too fanciful to say that Freud wavered between a perception of himself as a poet of high metaphorical abstraction and as a hard-scientist, like Mendeleyev, who would present a complete periodic table of the elemental instincts which, in their connections and transformations, would account for human development. Perhaps he was also struck by the scientific meaning of sublimation: to pass from solid to gas without an intervening liquid state.

Let us begin with the more familiar and definitive kind of instinct.

1. My partner, out of curiosity and sorority, asked her brother-in-law to bring his doe rabbit to 'visit' our middle-aged buck, who had not seen another rabbit since we got him at birth. The moment the doe entered the room, he attempted to mount her. Alas, she was not receptive. (What, no dinner and small talk?) After she left, our poor lover was distressed for hours.
2. Place food in front of a hungry dog which is neither afraid nor being pleasantly distracted, and it will not defer troughing in order to play or make pretty patterns in the soil.
3. A friend once kept three dogs from birth. She observed that two would not eat until the 'top dog' had begun to eat. But when this dog was passed on to another friend, the remaining two became 'neurotic' about beginning to eat: they seemed to have no cue. They didn't outgrow this anxiety.[37]

It is an anthropomorphic fallacy to say that those two dogs were paralysed by some kind of introjected superego. But it is a different kind of species-fallacy to deny special meaning and consequence to the greater period of developmental dependency and the latency period in humans.

In addition to the long-known characteristics of urgency and latency, Freud broadened the conception of the sexual instinct by positing the characteristic of plasticity. The 'obvious' species aim of the sexual instinct is genital docking. But the copulating human couple's experience is significantly different from that of dogs and bunnies. It involves the excitation of non-genital parts of the body: the lips, tongue, anus, skin, the eyes (scopophilia, the desire to look), and the mind (epistemophilia, the desire to know). In normal development, the point of non-genital excitation is to provide a forepleasure which, though it might be pleasurable in itself, gets its value from providing the gathering of energy for the genital connection and its associated discharge of tension – physical and mental. The less obvious aim is asexual:

> It [the sexual instinct] *places extraordinarily large amounts of force at the disposal of civilized activity, and it does this in virtue of its especially marked characteristic of being able to displace its aim without materially diminishing in intensity. This capacity to exchange its originally sexual aim for another one, which is no longer sexual but which is psychically related to the first aim, is called the capacity for* sublimation.[38]

Freud inferred from the non-genital aspects of adult sexuality the following developmental schema. The infant becomes aware of forms of excitation, tension and pleasurable relief, located in certain parts of the body. Unsurprisingly, these locii of superlative excitation are associated with the primary functions of feeding and excretion – the mouth and the anus/urethra. Both good and bad feeds and good and bad excretions provide the child with a sense of the range of pleasure and unpleasure. Interestingly, Freud suggested a third pre-genital stage after the oral and the anal: the phallic. This is a stage of mental/conceptual excitation based on the infant/child's curiosity about its own body and the bodies of its carers. (It is not a mere envy or glorification of the penis.) This desire to see and to know meets the frustrations of two boundaries. Neither the inside of its own body nor that of its mother is visible. And, gradually, even parts of the external body of the mother are denied to sight. Accompanying this is the relinquishing by the child of its absolute and exclusive desire for its mother in favour of new forms of identity and relatedness; namely, the resolution of the Oedipus complex.

As well as achieving the mighty developmental tasks of weaning and excretion control, the child learns how to learn, work, play and be alone and with others. Manifestations by children of latency-period sexuality have an aim of stimulation of the child's own body, and the consequential pleasure, but do not yet have a sexual object, an Other. Thus the crucial distinction that children have sexual phantasies but not sexual fantasies: the former, mostly unconscious, are of their nature more relational and conceptually explorative than grossly physical.

Freud took these two data – the fact of this seemingly boundless yet unusable sexual instinctual energy, and the fact of the developmental tasks of learning to play, relate and work – and posited various mechanisms to connect them.

It is important to remember that Freud saw sublimation as a normal element in the development towards the adult goals of the ability to love and to work (including genital love and creative intelligence). Inadequate discharge, control and sublimation of the instinct leads to various pathologies:

1. Sexual perversion: fixation at varieties of pre-genital, namely non-genital, sexual fascination and discharge.
2. Sexual neuroses: non-sexual bodily discharge as physical symptoms/ailments. (In a brilliant aphorism, Freud connected these two pathologies – 'neuroses are the "negative" of the perversions' – and made the observation that in some 'civilized' families these pathologies are distributed by gender.[39])
3. Emotional disaffection: an inability to form and negotiate human relationships, not just as a lover or parent, but also as a friend or even a colleague.
4. Philistinism: the refusal of or abstinence from the creative impulse – not simply refusing to listen to opera or scorning museums. It also denies the worth of artistic criticism.

Freud's theory is a dynamic, economic and some would say typically nineteenth-century mechanical paradigm. But how else to describe the progress of a process? Let us ask ten basic questions:

1. WHICH instincts are involved in sublimation?
When Freud stated in a twilight lecture, 'The theory of the instincts is so to say our mythology',[40] he was not questioning their explanatory value, any more than Homer was when grappling with the fundamental concepts of humanity and divinity. Freud dissented from the common reflex to propose *ad hoc* instincts for any human experience or activity, e.g., assertion, gardening, macramé. He began with two instincts, sexuality and aggression, and moved towards the complementary pair, the life/self-preservative and death instincts – Eros and Thanatos. He rejected the existence of a social instinct, seeing self-identity and social-identity as developmental markers generated by the basic instincts. If these mythological entities are the conceptual sentinels for Freud, they play themselves out on the terrain of bodily sensation. The defining characteristics of an instinct, in this sense, are that it has a source, an aim and an object. The source is internal and inescapable bodily excitation, the aim is the discharge of

excitation which is uncontainable, and the object is what facilitates, or is perceived to facilitate, the aim.

2. What can HAPPEN to instincts?

In order to present his fundamental belief in a permanent dynamic tension in and between human beings, Freud posited a permanent tension between the instincts. When the interactions between the instincts produce unbearable tensions, namely anxiety, then certain defence mechanisms come into play and the instincts undergo various transformations of aim and object. When attempting to describe the frustrations, renunciations, discharges, transformations and vicissitudes of instincts, he spoke of:

a) exchange
b) psychically related
c) mastering and deflecting
d) shifting
e) changed in the course of their growth
f) induced to displace
g) suppression, repression, reaction formation
h) reversal into its opposite
i) turning round upon the subject's own self
j) fusion and defusion
k) sublimation[41]

There is not space to give an account of all of these. The important point is that sublimation is a part of ordinary development and not a pathological defence.

3. What is the HEALTHY instinctual development?

Freud's account of development is invitingly simple and troublingly complex at the same time. The psychoanalytic terms for the agencies – *id*, *ego* and *superego* – and for the stages – 'oral', 'anal', 'phallic' and 'genital' – are as often used in ordinary conversation as rocket science's 'electrons' and 'black holes'. The complexity lies in his passing between these levels of explanation and in his change of emphasis and metaphor as he developed his theory. He suggests the metaphor of the id as a horse managed by the ego – but by using the 'borrowed forces' of the id, as if developmentally the rider grew out of the horse, like a centaur![42] The first axiom of the instinctual theory is that there is a great reservoir of undifferentiated instinctual energy, 'libido'; but this is variously called both the id and the ego. In restricting, for simplicity's sake, my account to the 1923 paper, *The Ego and the Id*, I am not denying the place of the variations.

311

The going-out or investment of a portion of that energy in an Object, Freud called 'cathexis'. For some thing, some Object, some person, to become knowable to consciousness, the mental presentation of that thing, the thing-presentation, has to be attached/connected to a word-presentation – an externally spoken but internally heard sensation. The puzzle is: could one express/articulate one's experience of the desire for, or satisfaction in, the Object *before* the connection was made – the pure affect?; or afterwards, the residue of affect that the word can't capture? This is a logical as well as developmental impossibility. Who can possibly *say* how much he, as a baby, wanted the breast or the sight of mummy?

When the sexual/libidinal instinct meets frustration, by the external object or internal anxiety, the cathexis is abandoned: the outgoing energy is drawn back by the id. It is desexualised and becomes the basis of the ego. 'The character of the ego is a precipitate of abandoned object-cathexes and it contains the history of those object-choices.'[43] Because the first interactions with the Object (carer) introduce the baby to the sense of the physical surface of its body as a boundary between it and the world, Freud spoke of the ego as 'first and foremost a bodily ego: it is not merely a surface entity, but is itself the projection of a surface'.[44]

There is a transitional phase, in which the inchoate ego presents itself as an Object for the id, that Freud termed (secondary) narcissism. And here he made only a conjecture: 'The question arises, and deserves careful consideration, whether this is not *the universal road to sublimation*, whether all sublimation does not take place through the mediation of the ego, which begins by changing sexual object-libido into narcissistic libido and then, perhaps, goes on *to give it another aim.*'[45]

The resolution of the Oedipus complex, for baby boys, consists in the withdrawal of libidinal cathexis from the mother and an identification with the father. The introjection of paternal prohibition becomes the psychic entity, the superego. But the other consequence of 'the ego's work of sublimation' is 'a defusion of the instincts and a liberation of the aggressive instincts in the super-ego'.[46] In a chilling phrase, Freud describes the superego as 'a pure culture of the death instinct'.[47] When we consider that it is also the site of evaluation – ethics and aesthetics – we can understand why Freud thought of healthy development as merely a theoretical ideal.

The story is further complicated by the fact of the child's 'homosexual tendencies'. After the anaclitic (non-narcissistic) heterosexual object-choice, these 'combine with portions of the ego-instincts . . . and help to constitute the social instincts, thus contributing an erotic factor to friendship and comradeship, to *esprit de corps* and to the love of mankind in general'.[48] Friendship can be seen as a crucial mid-term of human connectivity between kinship and citizenship. But though we all have experiences of the subtle varieties of friendship, why are there so few terms for them? What is unthinkable here about the gradations of obligation and gratitude? Why is it so hard for this muted Eros to speak its many names?

Freud then makes the observation that it is chaste homosexuals, who have performed what I would call a secondary-level sublimation, who 'are distinguished by taking a particularly active share in the general interests of humanity'.[49] In his account of the life of the greatest chaste homosexual, Leonardo da Vinci, Freud conjectured that 'he succeeded in sublimating the greater part of his libido into an urge for research'.[50] It is more common for the instinct for research to be repressed along with the sexual instinct, or for thinking to become sexualised. But Freud still concluded that he had not explained this.

4. What is the DEFINING MECHANISM of sublimation?

The concise formula as given by Rycroft is: 'All sublimations depend on symbolization and all ego development depends on sublimation.'[51] And symbolisation itself depends on the mechanisms of displacement and substitution (and condensation). There is the familiar reference point of symbolisation as a result of intrapsychic conflict, in which something bearable is made to stand for something still unbearable. This is an idea most easily understood in dream symbols, but still resisted with respect to physiological symptoms. But it still seems *a bridge too far*, or *a seventh degree of separation*, between the nipple and Nobel. And yet such bridges are being made all the time, from infancy.

Think of Freud's baby playing with his wooden reel and string. While his mother is away, invisible, he casts out and hauls back the reel, saying '*fort* [gone] . . . *da* [there]': the 'toy' *as* mother.[52] It was a lovely coincidence to find that when Elizabeth Gaskell's motherless heroine, Molly, is nine years old, she tells her father about her fantasy of having him on an unbreakable thread.[53] In the early case history, 'Dora', Freud saw transference as including 'revised editions' of earlier sublimations.[54] Think of the typically human propensity to seek similes and metaphors to communicate meaning – 'O, my love's like a red, red rose'[55] – and do not forget the long tradition of seeing the vagina as a rose, or even 'the mystic rose'. Think of Picasso showing bicycle handlebars *as* a bull's head. Psychoanalysts distinguish psychotics from neurotics by their lack of precisely this ability. Think of the childhood

313

word-puzzles in which one word is to be turned into another, by changing one letter at a time. This strengthens the faculty of displacement even without symbolisation. Think of the uncanniness of some words having two opposite meanings, as Freud did with 'uncanny'![56] The therapeutic rule of free-association facilitates these incremental shifts, these tiny stepping stones across the roaring waters of the unconscious. Perhaps the analyst's task is to help the client make a Venice of her mind.

5. HOW MUCH sublimation is possible?

The original strength of the sexual instinct probably varies in each individual: certainly the proportion of it which is suitable for sublimation varies. It seems to us that it is the innate constitution of each individual which decides in the first instance how large a part of his sexual instinct it will be possible to sublimate and make use of. In addition to this, the effects of experience and the intellectual influences on his mental apparatus succeed in bringing about the sublimation of a further portion of it. To extend this process of displacement indefinitely is, however, certainly not possible, any more than is the case with the transformation of heat into mechanical energy in our machines. A certain amount of direct sexual satisfaction seems to be indispensable [to avoid neurotic illness].[57]

This suggests that there is what might be called 'innate primary sublimation' and a 'secondary sublimation' which rides on the benefits of the former. At the societal level, if there is too much 'civilised' sexual morality – namely, excessive legal and institutional constraint on forms and occasions of sexual expression – then citizens will not only not be able to love well and happily, but will also be unable to think and create the very inventions and objects that the community takes as indices of its civilisation: 'Neuroses, whatever their extent and wherever they occur, always succeed in frustrating the purposes of civilization.'[58]

6. WHEN is sublimation most possible?
'Sublimation . . . can be achieved only intermittently, and least easily during the period of ardent and vigorous youth.'[59] This negative definition suggests that an individual's capacity for sublimation is shaped in latency. As Anna Freud observed, some ardent youths display an extraordinary relish for asceticism.[60] After that, even when desire outstrips ardent and vigorous ability, the pressure of mental desire – sex in the head – can be debilitating.

7. By WHOM is sublimation most possible?

'Sublimation can be achieved by a minority . . . Most of the rest become neurotic or are harmed in one way or another.'[61] Most people today would agree with Freud's scepticism about adolescent sublimation and his excoriation of the '"double" sexual morality for men', but they would be hesitant about the validity of the following observation: 'Experience shows as well that women, who, as being the actual vehicle of the sexual interests of mankind, are only endowed in a small measure with the gift of sublimating their instincts.'[62] We will pick up this theme later. When Freud states, 'An abstinent artist is hardly conceivable: but an abstinent young *savant* is certainly no rarity',[63] this seems to fit in with all of one's clichés of randy artists or 'sex and drugs and rock 'n' roll'. Apart from hypocrites like Stendhal's Julien Sorel, most adolescents would prefer to be Hesse's sensual Goldmund than the ascetic Narziss. Interestingly, Freud himself was to provide, two years later in 1910, a stunning counter example of the abstinent creative genius (for he was as much a scientist as he was an artist) in his study of Leonardo.[64]

There seems to be an initial paradox. If artists experience the zenith of the capacity for sublimation, the perfect equilibrium between sexual instincts and creative expression, why do they seem to want so much sex, and often unsatisfying and cruel sex? Perhaps because even artists rarely experience equilibrium – in fact, the other cliché of the artist or scientist is that of one who is 'mad'. What disturbs their balance are other instincts, which we examine below.

8. Is sublimation possible in WORK, the day job?

Humans must sublimate in order to enjoy art or to be artists. This is the loosest summary of the theory. But where does this leave all of the other non-sexual activities, also facilitated by sublimation – all of the thinking and doing and making of things which are not intended to be art-objects? What happens at work, the nine-to-five? A discussion of 'the significance of work for the economics of the libido' was among the topics Freud left undeveloped.[65] When he writes that:

> *Professional activity is a source of special satisfaction if it is a freely chosen one – if, that is to say, by means of sublimation, it makes possible the use of existing inclinations, of persisting or constitutionally reinforced instinctual impulses . . .*[66]

. . . he is really only redefining work as art. For most people, their limited creativity as well as external necessity and obligation

mean that they endure rather than enjoy their jobs. One consequence of this is that their leisure time and their non-work
relationships become the site of their more successful sublimations – or of the even more urgent expression of their sexual and
other instincts.

9. Is sublimation SUFFICIENTLY CONVULSING?

For Freud, physical relief and physical pleasure are the prototype:
'the sating of crude and primary instinctual impulses [which]
convulse our physical being'.[67] In his earlier paper of 1908 he even
emphasises his point: 'The sexual behaviour of a human being
often *lays down the pattern* for all his other modes of reacting to
life.'[68] So the act of creation (artistic or scientific) and the aesthetic
experience may be called 'finer and higher', but they are merely
'mildly intoxicating', inducing a 'mild narcosis'.[69] Similarly,
Freud was sceptical of the comforting illusions of religion and the
worth of spiritual/meditative bliss. This seems to be the realm of
impossible comparison. Freud never advocated using another
person as a kind of sexual toilet, and found it 'ethically objectionable' when sex became 'a convenient game'.[70] The Other is to be
shared, not merely had, and only in the context of one offering
oneself to be shared and not merely had. This is because our
attainment of the reality principle is defined by our ability not
merely to recognise the other, but also when necessary to wait for
the other to recognise himself as himself and not simply as our
construct. The possibly greater convulsions of careless sex would
be of lower value because too much hatred of the Self and the
Other remained unsublimated.

It is an ordinary experience to have shed more convulsive tears
at a high tragedy on the stage than at the death of a dearkin – but
still to feel the difference in value. One might imagine uniting two
intensities, as did my philosophy tutor when he said: 'For me, the
supreme pleasure would be to have sex and do higher maths at the
same time.'[71] But first one must have a sense of their separate
intensities. Being reminded of this, one soon realises the impossibility. Yet it is a developmental crux to arrive at that thought. It is
fitting that a poet, Yeats, adumbrated the idea more elliptically:

> *The fascination of what's difficult*
> *Has dried the sap out of my veins, and rent*
> *Spontaneous joy and natural content*
> *Out of my heart.*[72]

Instinctual vein-coursing satisfaction is displaced by the mind's
fascination with a puzzle. Some see this as one of the highest gifts

that a teacher can induce in, or impart to, a pupil. Unlike Sting or Hindu adepts, I can't comment on the uniting of two other intensities, sex and spirituality, in Tantric practices. But I am struck by the way in which the experience of the force of creation has led, in many cultures, to the force being named and personified: *Muses* in Greek and European literature, *Ras* in Hinduism, *Duende* in Spanish, and *Mojo* (fetish?) in voodoo and rock culture. Is this force to be seen as the residue of sublimation, somehow out there now but still accessible? And are these the non-sexual correlates of the projections of incubi and succubi?

10. What is the EVIDENCE for sublimation?

Psychoanalysis has been endlessly taunted for its lack of scientific proof. Even when it is stated that it provides explanation without prediction, this is still mocked as being insufficiently scientific. It is charged with committing the fallacy of affirming the consequent, and generally ignoring too much that it doesn't know. Freud's remark above about the vast energies of the sexual instinct, and the tendencies of all intense human emotions to find sexual expression, would probably be cited by his opponents as proof of his indefensible pan-sexualism. But consider these two stories, from playwrights:

1. A middle-aged woman, broken by grief at her father's death earlier that day, finds comfort and release in almost animalistically urgent, yet weeping, sex with her unreliable lover.[73]
2. A young English soldier gets an erection during a tour of a German death-camp.[74]

Here are two ordinary examples of absolute terror and absolute dismay finding sexual expression. Explain that without Freud! Even Kant would say that here was simply a lack of emotional resources to take comfort in the conceptual sublime itself – and the person therefore thrown back upon a bodily solution.

For sublimation, there are two basic types of evidence from therapeutic practice:

1. The client is enabled by analysis to discover the proper or deeper way to love and work, to relate to people and express her creativity. An analysis of her childhood inhibitions of sexual curiosity allows the belated completion of the necessary sublimations, which free up adult intellectual curiosity and expression.
2. The corollary is when someone who used to be able to love and work 'reasonably' well breaks down, after which he can barely

do either. Again, the factor of an earlier imperfect sublimation can be seen when someone who had an inquiring mind regresses to the point of voyeurism and overeating.[75]

Freud's rare incursion into child analysis also provides support for his thesis. After the five-year-old Hans had given up masturbation and looking at others on the toilet, his father observed that 'simultaneously with this repression a certain amount of sublimation set in':

> From the time of the beginning of his anxiety Hans began to show an increased interest in music and to develop his inherited musical gift.[76]

'Hans' grew up to be Herbert Graf, the opera singer and visually innovative director at the New York Met.[77]

Finally, it is important to state Freud's hesitation:

> Instincts and their transformations are at the limit of what is discernible by psychoanalysis. From that point it gives place to biological research.[78]

Mindin' i&i Own Business: Other Psychoanalytic Contributions

It was Freud's children, literal and metaphorical, who undertook the analysis of children. Unsurprisingly, he believed that their research would confirm his theories. So now we move across the teens. Puberty is fundamentally a biological reorganisation. For some boys, this sudden explosion of hormones seems to deprive them of the ability even to walk properly; they slope or even stumble, not quite knowing the extremities of their own body – Harry Enfield's comic adolescent character, Kevin, shows this perfectly. I am reminded again of Freud's remark about the ego as a bodily ego. All teenagers like their music played loud. Many boys like a kind of noise which is barely music – heavy metal – played uncomfortably loud. Interestingly, this musically aggressive genre is known as 'cock-rock'. (I hope it's obvious why.) My conjecture about the predilection for loud music is that it is a way of meeting and defeating the 'voices' of the superego.

Before latency, the child knew that its Oedipal desires were frustrated by incapacity – a tiny penis, no breasts. But now that ability can put desire into effect, the only inhibitions are morality and the traces or echoes of former terror of parental revenge. Does throwing oneself into the mosh-pit symbolically re-enact the adolescent desire to re-enter the womb? It was said that the predominance of nappy-pins in punk dress showed an ambivalence about being grown-up. Their inclusion of the swastika was the most pitifully puerile and apolitical element in their rage against the parental love-generation. In *The Buddha of Suburbia*, the mother pleads with her son: 'Please take off the swastika. I don't care about anything else.'[79]

There is also the ordinary cross-cultural fact that first love makes poets of all adolescents. Why should there be such a new aesthetic sensitivity to nature and a compulsion to fashion words into form? It is usually bad poetry, but this equation of sexual urgency, emotional longing and aesthetic fascination indicates a second flowering of sublimation.

I will look at two great theorists of childhood.

1. Melanie Klein

Klein took Freudian theory into the nursery, across the realm of words into the gestures and toys that are the symbolic pre-verbal language of children. From her observations of children at play, she concluded that Oedipal conflicts trouble the child long before the age at which Freud placed them. And of course at that age the child is at the mercy of instincts and emotions he can barely manage, let alone name. Klein is equal to Freud in producing 'shocking' aphorisms: 'the *school*-task signifies coitus or masturbation'; 'athletic games of every sort have a libidinal cathexis and genital symbolism'.[80] Consider this case material:

> For [almost seven-year-old] *Fritz, when he was writing, the lines meant roads and the letters rode on motorcycles – on the pen – upon them. For instance 'i' and 'e' ride together on a motorbicycle that is usually driven by the 'i' and they love one another with a tenderness quite unknown in the real world . . . The 'l's' are represented as stupid, clumsy, lazy and dirty. They live in caves under the earth.*[81]

Klein arrives, via the child's associations, at the interpretation that 'i' is the penis and 'l' faeces. But even if one baulked at that, there is something to be explained about the child's expenditure of energy in the narrative construction, classification and evaluation of the letters – things are being connected, displaced, symbolised. (One of the things I remember most clearly about the trip in my youth, when I passed chemically through the doors of perception, was a 'brief' episode in which the visible manifold seemed to have a transparent veneer of hundreds of brightly coloured capital letters.) It is hard for an adult to remember the impact of written letters on the construction and meaning of reality. When it comes to remembering the impact of the first words heard, we are lost. Perhaps it is an attempt to recapture these first sensations which prompts my friend's eight-year-old daughter Lisa to insist that the words her father reads to her at bedtime are words she *can't* understand.

Klein refers to H. Sperber, who had argued that 'sexual impulses have played an important part in the evolution of speech'; mating calls developed 'as a rhythmic accompaniment to work, which thus became associated with sexual pleasure'.[82] And she followed Sándor Ferenczi in positing a stage of identification before the stage of symbolisation. He had observed that 'at an early stage of its development the child tries to rediscover its bodily organs and their activities in every object which it encounters. Since it institutes a similar comparison with its own body as well, it probably sees in the upper part of its body an equivalent for each *affectively important* detail of the lower part.'[83] It is this limiting case of comparison which facilitates the beginning of symbolisation and future sublimation.

The Oedipal conflict in which the child, formed of masculine and feminine components, has both heterosexual and homosexual longings, is resolved differently by boys than by girls. Klein went on to assert that:

> The contribution which the feminine component makes to sublimation will probably always prove to be receptivity and understanding, which are an important part of all activities: the driving executive part, however, which really constitutes the character of any activity, originates in the sublimation of masculine potency.[84]

She used this to explain the fact that in her generation (and all previous ones) girls did better than boys at school, but not later on. This very year, research is published that shows girls continuing to do better than boys at university. So, even political solutions such as better access to college can attenuate a girl's castration complex – *her* version of *every* child's anxiety about an insufficiency of means – and facilitate sublimation and creativity.

We saw above how children can expend considerable amounts of (libidinal) energy on the minutest elements of literacy and oracy. Unsurprisingly, this barely bounded energy continues to be a part of the process of learning. Ordinary conversation reveals multifarious metaphors connecting food and digestion with reading and writing – the *voracious* reader, the *stodgy* book. In a brilliant paper, 'Some Unconscious Factors in Reading', James Strachey suggests that the way in which a person negotiates the two oral phases – sucking and biting – influences their later emotional tone towards reading and writing. The equally ordinary fact of many people enjoying reading while shitting, he suggests, contains a 'symbolic act of coprophagy'.[85] If this strikes the reader as too wild, he would do well to ponder, like Strachey, on the Word of God through Ezekiel:

> And thou shalt eat [thy meat] as barley cakes and thou shalt bake it with dung that cometh out of man, in their sight. Therefore the fathers shall eat the sons in the midst of thee and the sons shall eat their fathers.[86]

A more benign equation of reading and eating can be seen in a medieval Jewish ritual. Scriptural extracts would be written on eggs or cakes or a slate, then covered with honey. The young initiate would be asked to read to the teacher, and then be invited to lick and eat.[87] This appetitive connection is maintained in Proverbs: 'The lips of a strange woman drop as an honeycomb'[88] – which of course translates in male fantasy, bloke-speak, as the stunner on the train suddenly saying: 'Eat me, big boy!'

As the child moves from mere letters and words to intentional meaning, some of his slips in reading and writing and speaking assume the pathology of unconscious meaning. In their On Learning to Read, Bruno Bettelheim and Karen Zelan show how a child's 'academic' difficulties with literacy might have their roots in unconscious conflict.[89] Bettelheim alone, in the wonderfully entitled The Uses of Enchantment, had described the way in which children use fairy stories, with their themes of monsters and mutability, to process the conflicts of ordinary development.[90] Why do children ask for a particular fairy story to be read again and again, without alteration? By this point, any kind of narrative surprise has long been exhausted. The reason is that elements of the story resonate with, and thereby rearrange, material in the child's unconscious. The story becomes a temporary container for that unmanageable material. It is as if the child waits for an emotional Gestalt switch which will indicate that the material has become manageable. That the process is sub-rational is shown by the very use of the word 'enchantment'. Perhaps the quality of the sublimation achieved is gauged by the child's ability to become the teller of that story to someone else – in other words, a young dramatic artist herself.

Klein believed that the creative impulse is grounded in the reparative impulse which marks the attainment of the depressive position – the stage when the child's anxiety that its aggressive thoughts and feelings towards its carer might have damaged her/ him, prompt it to act to help, heal and attempt reconciliation.

2. Donald Winnicott

While accepting the received account of the sublimation of instinct, Winnicott felt that the theory needed developing in order to explain the phenomena revealed in his staggeringly large number of clinical observations of babies and children. 'Playing', he felt, 'needs to be studied as a subject on its own, supplementary to the concept of the sublimation of instinct'.[91] He proposed that in the maturational process facilitated by the 'good-enough mother', which takes a baby from a sense of me-as-the-whole-world to me-relating-to-a-not-me – that is, (my) mother, other people, objects – there is an intermediate position, an experiential space, a 'potential space', a third reality separable from inner reality and external reality. This is the realm of play and culture, and the 'objects' created/experienced here he calls 'transitional objects'. In trying to delineate this realm he is, perhaps, like Freud attempting his topography, drawn into paradoxical descriptions. For neither the baby's thumb nor its actual teddy bear is a transitional object. And yet, the transitional object is 'the child's first use of a symbol and the first experience of play'[92] – the beginning of language and culture.

Winnicott's greatest difference from Freud can be seen in his assertion that:

> If when a child is playing the physical excitement of instinctual involvement becomes evident, then the playing stops, or is at any rate spoiled ... Play is immensely exciting, not primarily because the instincts are involved [but because of] the precariousness of the interplay of personal psychic reality and the experience of control of actual objects ... There are significant mechanisms for object relating that are not drive-determined.[93]

It is difficult to gauge here the way in which the instinctual forces which might provide the energy for play are held in abeyance to facilitate it.

Winnicott gives an example which bears an uncanny resemblance to the heroic *fort–da* baby. One of his young patients was a seven-year-old boy who was obsessed with string, playing with it, drawing it, even tying furniture together. This behaviour stopped when his mother articulated for him his memories and anxieties about separation. But even this could be called 'unpure' playing, laden as it is with a solution to a problem. Winnicott makes an important distinction between daydream-fantasising, which has no poetic value, and ordinary dreaming, which does. He refers to the look of a child playing – in its 'preoccupation . . . it inhabits an area that cannot be easily left, nor can it easily admit intrusions'.[94]

The inability to play is for Winnicott a diagnostic marker – both for adults and children. He was sceptical of the worth of intellectual interpretations, even for adults. The reparative experience that the psychoanalyst hopes to facilitate is 'of a non-purposive state . . . a sort of ticking over of the unintegrated personality',[95] a necessary experience of *being* if subsequent *doing* is to be genuinely creative and not merely compliant. I am reminded of Kant's description of the aesthetic state. The baby with the good-enough mother seems to have the aesthetic experience before it has attained to recognising aesthetic objects. This is also the conclusion of Christopher Bollas:

> *The aesthetic experience is not something learned by the adult, it is an existential recollection of an experience where being handled by the maternal aesthetic made thinking seemingly irrelevant to survival.*[96]

Lipstick as Your Collar: Do Women Sublimate Differently?

[Suddenly, a surprise delivery of lipsticks.] *There were not enough of them to go round and here they were kicking and pummelling each other in order to possess one stick or even one of the right colour. It made me feel sick to see them fighting . . .*[97]

If you were told that this group was a bunch of fourth-formers, you might think: 'Ahh! the raging seriousness of maiden-youth.' If it wasn't them, but a bunch of ravers at Studio 54, you might think: 'Spoilt bitches!' But if it was, and it was, Auschwitz, how would you begin to explain and even theorise this aggression? Who could say, who would be allowed to say? Only women, or even a man? In this section I will look at this puzzle and what it tells us about female sublimation.

It seems that there is a force almost as strong as the instinct for food and self-preservation, a force that can even ride the aggressive instinct in order to be satisfied. But what force or instinct – for protection, sexual signalling, for adornment or beauty? Some ethologists would remind us of the exposed, saturation-pink genitalia of chimps – so in-your-face that they obviously don't need Colour Endure – and conclude that the lipstick highlights the connection between the visible and the hidden orifices of pleasure and procreation. Does this mean that lipstick's verbal correlate is a kind of Jungle-Jane bush-telegraphese – 'Me cunt. You want?' Is this a self-objectification or a self-instantiation, or only the false Self of false-consciousness? If the object that a person makes into a thing of beauty and a joy for six hedonistic hours is oneself, is that sublimation? Even after three generations of feminism, a troubled mother can write to *The Times* Parent Forum: 'Is eight too young for make-up?'[98]

This is the realm of perilous controversy where sociology and politics cross swords with biology and psychoanalysis. How is a woman *marked* as a woman; how by herself and how by others? What does lipstick signify; what kind of alphabet do young girls find in their mother's make-up bags? In so brief a text, I can only point to some female perspectives.

The received generalisations of feminism begin with a castigation of the patriarchal legacy. 'Beauty is permanent injustice ... The man issues the law which will lock the woman away ... Freud figures as Public Enemy No. 1 ... analytic vocabulary more or less leaves out women altogether'.[99] Women interiorise these 'truths' and within a few generations there is 'misogyny – a crop sown by one woman and reaped by another'.[100] (cf. 'A bayonet is a weapon with a worker at each end.'[101]). These quotations come from Christiane Olivier's polemic *Jocasta's Children*. She, too, begins with the mighty Sophoclean tale of Oedipus, but asks why 'it never seems to occur to them [women] to think to themselves, even for a moment, "I'm going through my Jocasta stage"'.[102]

In foregrounding Jocasta, Olivier reminds us of the fact of the mother's sexual desire for her baby. This spectrum of desire has at one pole the absolute perversion of actually fucking the baby, and at the other the semi-mystical 'primary maternal preoccupation' of Winnicott. In the middle band, there is mostly unconscious sexual desire resonating with the more accessible oral desire – the ordinary experience of finding one's dimpled baby nice enough to eat. But 'it is in her son', writes Olivier, 'that the mother has her only chance of seeing herself in male form'.[103] They form a mutually fascinated couple, and the problem for the boy is one of degrees of fusion and abandonment. In Olivier's formulation, the girl-child never attains to such libidinous mutuality.

> *The stark fact* [is] *that the girl has no primary love-object ... daughters come through a relationship with their mother that had no desire in it, and then, more or less belatedly, switched to their father.*[104]

324

A boy sees his anatomy writ large in his father. Whereas 'it is not uncommon to see a little girl first touching her mother's breasts and then her own chest and saying "Katie no boobs"',[105] few if any mothers point to the similarity of the possession of a clitoris. So 'the mother cannot be a locus of identification for the girl'.[106]

This early awareness of her insufficiency as a woman and as a desired object gives a girl a lifelong burden of proof of womanliness and desirability, a legacy of forever making-up to look other than the naked Self. The reparative paternal gaze is usually insufficient, because the father must be at work or is still trying to escape his own mother, seen behind the façade of his wife. So the absence of a sufficient gaze from both mother and father leaves the girl doomed to feeling unseen. If the solution is 'I attract, therefore I am', then is the struggle 'Am I or am I not to put on the colour "woman"?'[107] (cf. Jean Genet's dramatic premise that in a racist society, non-whites must put on and play the colour 'black'.[108]) To please is the default-setting learned by girls.

If the datum of vast libidinal energy in children is gender blind, the obvious question is: what are the consequences for the girl-child whose libido is not discharged by maternal desire, nor by the paternal gaze? Freud argued for a weaker capacity for sublimation in women. Perhaps because his client base was different, he failed to see that 'sublimation is *incredibly present and active* in the life of little girls: girls draw better, write better poems, make up far livelier plays than boys'.[109] At puberty, this development is thwarted by sociology, not biology. The structure that men make in order to facilitate adult sexuality, maternity and child rearing, results in her potential for sublimation being vitiated. In Olivier's rhetorical flourish: 'Man snatches sublimation away from woman by loading children onto her ... they are shut away in their bodies.'[110] Men do this 'so as not to have to meet [women] in the ground of sublimation'.[111]

Anorexics defend against the need for the male gaze by stalling the development of their bodies, and they often remain absorbed by high intellectual attainment – thus asserting the right to continuing sublimation. Another strategy of the sublimating woman who attains Parnassus (or Yale) is, as first-generation analyst Joan Riviere observed, to 'put on a mask of womanliness to avert anxiety and retribution feared from men'.[112] The most tragic choice is that taken by Claire Marsh, whose aspiration to gain male notice by appropriating masculinity – to be a 'ladette' or 'geezer girl' – sank to its nadir in 2001 when she became, at eighteen, the youngest woman ever to be convicted of rape.[113]

And in married life, the disparity grinds on. The home that a 'virtuous wife' creates allows the man – who has been fighting the world outside – to regress, to be a child, to eat and to read and to play in his den. But who creates such a space for her? How many women can trust their partners to be a good-enough parent for their young kids for a few hours? 'Once regression has been lost to them they find themselves without sublimation. [This] is the missing sector in the lives of women and mothers.'[114] I will return to these psycho-political themes below.

Francette Pacteau takes up a similar position: 'No man escapes castration anxiety . . . no woman escapes "beauty".'[115] From the male point of view, 'formulations of feminine beauty by men appear to be largely unconscious, indeed unconsciously motivated. They correspond to a variety of (mainly) masculine symptoms.'[116] In her study, *The Symptom of Beauty*, Pacteau focuses on the way in which beauty is attributed to women, the way the fantasy stages – creates the *mise-en-scène* for – this symptom. From the female side, 'there is, always, the image to which the question of her beauty must be referred. As beautiful as . . .'.[117] Madonna wanted to be a 'better' Monroe than Blondie managed. But what did Marilyn's model want . . .? Interestingly, the pervasiveness of their images means that none of these photo and film idols attains the aura of the *concept*, the *structural ideal*, that takes the imagination to the limit, e.g., 'The face that launched a thousand ships', or 'The love of the man of seven hundred wives', as in Helen of Troy and the Shulamite of Jerusalem.[118]

Pacteau takes from Anzieu his idea of 'skin ego', a development of Freud's basic idea of the bodily ego.[119] Initially, the infant has no sense of separation of skin or the direction of touch. Weaning and socialisation are defined by the incremental prohibitions on touching, at first the mother's body and then one's own. For the boy, it is the line against incest; for the girl, the line of ambivalent rejection – for although girls are weaned earlier, yet they may touch the mother for longer. Touching is sublimated into looking: contact-perception is replaced by distance-perception. The child copes with the seduction and aggression inherent in the prohibitions by creating the fantasy of a second skin as impenetrable and protective as the mother's skin. This thought induces the anxiety that the mother could and might tear off and repossess one's own skin. It is the girl's greater anxiety to *inhabit* visibility and to attract desire (or at least gazing) that leads to her greater fascination with the permutations of second skin – clothes, fabrics and furs, and the panoply of make-up. Men are of course fascinated by the revelation of skin, from ankles to cleavage to tights-tops . . . Yet when a man finally gets to the skin, he first meets his anxiety about the surface of his mother.

Sublimation was defined above as a substitution of non-sexual aims and objects for sexual ones, allowing for a mastery of both sexual and non-sexual objects. But, interestingly, in the cultural domain of fine art – painting and sculpture – the sublimating artist is preoccupied with the body as sexual object. 'The self-portrait of the artist at work', writes Pacteau, 'we may now read as a *mise-en-scène* of sublimation'.[120] So how to read the painting, 'The Origin of Drawing'? This is based on the legend in which a young woman draws the outline of the shadow cast on a wall by her beloved. One thinks of the possible refractions of the Freudian phrase, 'the shadow of the object fell upon the ego',[121] and wonders about this legend choosing a female artist. Pacteau continues by arguing that one of the ways of mastering the excess sexual energy in this creating experience, and of the body in general, is to intellect-ualise it – the rules of proportion for the body and for perspective in the artwork. 'The mathematization of the "well-proportioned" body offers a privileged instance of sublimation.'[122] Another way to master is by *fragment* and *concept* – for example, the medieval 'blasons', poems on bits of the body, or Courbet offering a headless, footless woman with the vagina at vanishing point, and not calling it 'Con' but 'The Origin of the World'.

In the work of the conceptual artist Orlan we see a more literal destruction of perspective. She films herself directing others (doctors) tearing off her face to demonstrate the emptiness of the image. This strikes me as jejune and mad naïve realism, differently tragic from Lolo. Early socialists hoped for the withering away of state in the ideal of perfect civil society. If lipstick is an impression only for the Object, do feminists dream of the withering away of that second skin of make-up? But if it also carries a woman's potential for impressing/painting on the Object, the lover's lips or collar, what then? Will a feminist ever write a Milneresque tract: 'On Not Being Able to Not-paint One's Lips'?[123]

Foundationed Deep, Somehow:
Psycho-Political Sublimation

We saw above how aesthetics places the emotions of desire, fear and anxiety within the framework of the conceptualisation of the ideas of form and limit, and how psychoanalysis argues for a transformation of desire and aggression, as well as anxiety, through sublimation. Our discussion has been focused on the individual and the family. In this closing section I want to look at the broader human connectivity – the *polis* – through two con-cepts, and ask what it means that the attempt to think about them seems to take us to the limit of our capacity for sublimation.

1. Genocide

Winnicott believed that it was possible to describe the conditions of good-enough parenting that might take the infant from kinship to democratic citizenship, and that might avoid the formation of a personality that needed the compensations of structural inequality or dictatorial and inegalitarian regimes, whether as master or slave.[124]

We might say that genocide is the (negative) political sublime, not merely disenfranchising a portion of the citizenry but 'deleting' it, by murder, from the register. How much imagination and perspective must one have to understand the fact of genocide? Even a scholar like Inga Clendinnen, with a deep knowledge of Aztec bloodlust, felt her imagination faint at the German Holocaust[125] – as did mine when I visited Auschwitz, and again on reading Tadeusz Borowski's *This Way for the Gas, Ladies and Gentlemen*.[126] Claude Lanzmann, the documentary artist of *Shoah*, asserts the

> *absolute obscenity in the very project of understanding. Not to understand was my iron law during all the eleven years of the production of* Shoah. *I clung to this refusal of understanding as the only possible ethical and at the same time the only possible operative attitude. This blindness was for me the vital condition of creation.*[127]

Was Lanzmann attempting a rare fusion of sublimation and repression? The category of 'obscenity' reflects an abiding puzzlement of the fusion of sexuality and art. Herbert Marcuse coined the phrase 'repressive desublimation' for the use by the State of a relaxation of legal constraints on censorship and sexual expression that would be politically pacifying.[128] It might be thought that apostasy is merely benign unrepressive desublimation, but the State-faith readily interprets such psychologically freed-up 'new thinking' as fatal heresy. Interestingly, Jacques Lacan, working at the limits of understanding in the psychoanalytic domain, also took it as a rule 'that it is on the basis of a certain refusal of understanding that we open the door onto psychoanalytic understanding'.[129]

By instituting National Holocaust Memorial Day, the present UK government set down an indication of the line of understanding for future children. But where was the space for scepticism about the project? For, tragically, the State understanding of genocide seems to include too much splitting: 'It was *them*, long ago. It couldn't happen *here*.' For me, the absolute filter is Walter Benjamin's eighth essay in his *Theses on the Philosophy of*

History, written shortly before his suicide in 1940: 'The current amazement that the things we are experiencing are "still" possible in the twentieth century is not philosophical. This amazement is not the beginning of knowledge – unless it is the knowledge that the view of history which gives rise to it is untenable.'[130]

Of course, political history must reveal economic history. Interestingly, Freud's instinct-theory is often criticised for relying on a supposedly untenable analogy with economics, as well as mechanics. Perhaps this reveals an anxiety about placing the 'hidden hand' of economics. One can't run an empire – Roman, British, Nazi or American – without murder, extortion and neglect, nor without the co-operation of opportunist businessmen *far away* who want to *look* as if their hands are clean. The German Holocaust was unprecedented because the combination of State command economy and industrial possibility was unprecedented. As Edwin Black, author of the newly published *IBM and the Holocaust*, puts it: 'For the first time in history, an anti-Semite had automation on his side.'[131] We are left with the grim conclusion that human genocidal intention and the inertia of bystanders are a constant. How ought one to live with this thought? Is this the limit of psycho-political sublimation – transmuting hate into bureaucracy?

2. Maternity

Do not rush this next puzzle. Why can't you name one country or group of human beings, in ten millennia, that has taken as its *primary* criterion of civilisation, maternity – the absolute, unconditional, (free) provision of support for mother and child from conception to age five, and the mother's right to choose abortion, midwifery, maternity hospitals, childcare? It is shocking to read in *A History of Women's Bodies* by Edward Shorter that it is only in the past three generations, and then only in the West, that there has been sufficient care for the first year[132] – and not even that really: there remains a shortage of midwives and nurseries in the UK.

If '*Arbeit macht frei*'[133] is the sick joke of the twentieth century, then Genesis 3:16 is the nadir of five millennia of misogyny: 'Unto the woman He said, I will greatly multiply thy sorrow and thy conception: in sorrow thou shalt bring forth children.' If God was going to punish mortals with a pain in the gonads, then why not both sexes? Some say that this verse is the primary justification for the absence of sufficient maternity provision. The fact that non-Judaeo-Christian cultures have been equally careless – consider Indian society, where opportunist medics with mobile scanners help women to abort girls – reminds one that the problem is more to do with men and women as such: male rage at abandonment by the mother and male fear of fusion with the mother. The Nazi *Freikorps* who saw themselves as the peak of new German manhood positioned their own women as cold angels and the newly politicised Soviet women as hot demonic whores: both fantasies expressing fear and rage at frustrated desire. Their primary love-object was often their boyhood horse![134]

Two defining human characteristics are the absolute vulnerability of the child (and mother) at birth, and the ability to plan. Whatever economic or religious reasons there are and have been, the point is to think of the psychological reasons for this abiding indifference to mothers and children. Imagine *Mrs* Thatcher seeing the particularity of women. Imagine the Tories freeing mothers from *Miss* Widdecombe's chains. Imagine Tony Blair valorising 'maternity, maternity, maternity'. Imagine the Queen insisting to a cross-party committee that the millennium be marked by the creation, at Greenwich, in a bellied dome, of the best 'Museum and Research Centre of Maternity' in the world. And think why it remains so unthinkable. Two millennia of patriarchal Mariolatry do not atone for the billions of hours that women have spent with the terrifying thought: 'Am I late?' Is this another limit of psycho-political sublimation – transmuting biology into art, the poor revenge of men who can make rockets, icons and symphonies but who cannot *create* the ultimate object – a new human being?

Thinking's Gonna Change My World: Coda

The Greek word *metanoia* means 'change' and also 'redemption'. In the art of being human, the only sublimation worth talking about is that towards the moral sublime. The rest is mere *Sensation*. That which we *can't* think about – be it genocide, maternity, friendship – diminishes our humanity. We do well to recall that Primo Levi's poem *If This Is A Man* carries a conditional curse upon the unthinking reader: 'May your children turn their faces from you.'[135] Right now, a child is falling in the rye. Who is to catch it? If you try, then you will be among the sublimating élite – not drowning, but saving.[136]

Acknowledgements

Ivan Ward's supererogatory care. Duncan Heath and Jeremy Cox for reality checks. The benign guidance of Michael Briant, Lucy King, Mark Phippen, Carole Robinson, and Glenys Scott. The steadying friend's bias of Jim Douglas, Dan Jones, Matthew Jones, Dieter Peetz, Corinna Russell, Wendy Thurley, and Janice Western. Gurnam Iqbal Nanner – the altered ego.

Kalu Singh came to England from India, and to psychoanalysis via Chemistry, Philosophy, English and Education. He works as a Civil Servant and as a Sessional Counsellor in a University Service. He lives in Cambridge.

Notes

References to Freud are given by paper title and date, and then: PFL = Penguin Freud Library (London: Penguin Books) with vol. no. and page ref.; *SE = The Standard Edition of the Complete Psychological Works of Sigmund Freud* (London: Hogarth Press) with vol. no. and page ref.

1. Blake, W., *Selected Poems*, London: Penguin, 1988, p. 70.
2. Freud, S., 'The Uncanny' (1919), PFL 14, p. 368; *SE* 17, p. 245; *Civilization and Its Discontents* (1930), PFL 12, p. 271; *SE* 21, p. 83.
3. Woolf, V., *Orlando* (1928), London: Penguin, 1993, p. 100.
4. Manguel, A., *A History of Reading*, Canada: Vintage, 1996, p. 272.
5. Shakespeare, W., *Twelfth Night* (1601–2), I.i.1.
6. Keats, J., *Selected Poems*, London: Penguin, 1988, p. 89.
7. Tynan, K., *Profiles*, London: Nick Hern, 1990, p. 220.
8. Christiansen, R., *Romantic Affinities*, London: Vintage, 1994, p. 231.
9. Hare, D., *Teeth 'N' Smiles*, London: Faber and Faber, 1976; BBC2 Arts Night, September 1975.
10. Storr, A., book review of Shephard, B., *A War of Nerves*, London: Jonathan Cape, 2000, in *The Times*, London: 8 November 2000.
11. Apocryphal – various versions exist.
12. Riviere, J., 'Womanliness as a Masquerade', *International Journal of Psycho-Analysis*, vol. 10, 1929, p. 307.
13. Anderson, P.T., *Boogie Nights*, USA: 1999.
14. Turner, B. and Turner, T., *Third Rock from the Sun*, USA: 1997.
15. Shakespeare, W., *Hamlet* (1600–1), III.ii.117.
16. Kant, I., *The Critique of Judgement* (1790), trans. J. Meredith, Oxford: Oxford University Press, 1952, pp. 39, 58.
17. Ibid., p. 46.
18. Keats, J., letter (21 December 1817), in Gittings, R. (ed.), *Letters*, Oxford: Oxford University Press, 1970.
19. Bion, W., 'Notes on Memory and Desire', in Bott Spillius, E. (ed.), *Melanie Klein Today*, London: Routledge, 1988, pp. 17–21.
20. Kant (1952), op. cit., p. 107.
21. Ibid., p. 107.
22. Ibid., p. 106.
23. Ibid., pp. 91, 116.
24. Ibid., pp. 179, 210, 212.
25. Ibid., p. 223.
26. Ibid., pp. 49, 50, 191.
27. Plato, *The Republic* (c. 375 BC), London: Penguin, 1955.
28. Plato, *The Laws* (before 347 BC), London: Penguin, 1970.
29. Wind, E., *Art and Anarchy*, London: Duckworth, 1985, p. 94.
30. Lap-Chuen, T., *The Sublime*, Rochester, NY: University of Rochester Press, 1998.
31. Shandling, G., *The Larry Sanders Show,* USA: 1993.
32. Sondheim, S., *Profile* interview, *The Guardian*, London: 9 December 2000.
33. *Look at Lolo*, Channel 4 TV broadcast, London: 9 December 2000.
34. Goldman, A., *The Lives of John Lennon*, London: Bantam, 1988, pp. 246, 376, 470.

35. Gibson, I., *The Shameful Life of Salvador Dalí*, London: Faber and Faber, 1998, p. 165.
36. *Look at Lolo*, ibid.
37. Haynes, J. and Western, J., private conversation.
38. Freud, S., 'Civilized Sexual Morality' (1908), PFL 12, p. 39; *SE* 9, p. 187.
39. Ibid., PFL 12, p. 43; *SE* 9, p. 191.
40. Freud, S., *New Introductory Lectures* (1933), PFL 2, p. 127; *SE* 22, p. 95.
41. a)–c): Freud (1908), op. cit., PFL 12, pp. 39, 46; *SE* 9, p. 195; d)–g): Freud (1930), op. cit., PFL 12, pp. 267, 286; *SE* 21, p. 97; h)–k): Freud, S., *Instincts and Their Vicissitudes* (1915), PFL 11, p. 123; *SE* 14, p. 126.
42. Freud, S., *The Ego and the Id* (1923), PFL 11, p. 364; *SE* 19, p. 25.
43. Ibid., PFL 11, p. 368; *SE* 19, p. 29.
44. Ibid., PFL 11, p. 364; *SE* 19, p. 26.
45. Ibid., PFL 11, p. 369; *SE* 19, p. 30 (my emphasis).
46. Ibid., PFL 11, p. 398; *SE* 19, p. 56.
47. Ibid., PFL 11, p. 394; *SE* 19, p. 53.
48. Freud, S., *Schreber* (1911), PFL 9, pp. 198–9; *SE* 12, p. 61.
49. Ibid., PFL 9, p. 199; *SE* 12, p. 61.
50. Freud, S., *Leonardo* (1910), PFL 14, pp. 170–1; *SE* 11, p. 80.
51. Rycroft, C., *Dictionary of Psychoanalysis*, London: Penguin, 1968, p. 159.
52. Freud, S., *Beyond the Pleasure Principle* (1920), PFL 11, p. 284; *SE* 18, p. 15.
53. Gaskell, E., *Wives and Daughters* (1866), London: Penguin, 1996.
54. Freud, S., *Dora* (1905), PFL 8, p. 158; *SE* 7, p. 116.
55. Burns, R., *Selected Poems*, London: Penguin, 1996, p. 252.
56. Freud (1919), op. cit., PFL 14, p. 347; *SE* 17, p. 224.
57. Freud (1908), op. cit., PFL 12, pp. 39–40; *SE* 9, p. 188.
58. Ibid., PFL 12, p. 54; *SE* 9, p. 202.
59. Ibid., PFL 12, p. 45; *SE* 9, p. 193.
60. Freud, A., 'Adolescence' (1958), in *Anna Freud: Writings*, vol. 5, Madison, CT: International Universities Press, 1969.
61. Freud (1908), op. cit., PFL 12, p. 45; *SE* 9, p. 193.
62. Ibid., PFL 12, p. 47; *SE* 9, p. 195.
63. Ibid., PFL 12, p. 48; *SE* 9, p. 197.
64. Freud (1910), op. cit., PFL 14; *SE* 11.
65. Freud (1930), op. cit., PFL 12, p. 268fn; *SE* 21, p. 80fn.
66. Ibid., PFL 12, p. 268fn; *SE* 21, p. 80fn.
67. Ibid., PFL 12, p. 267; *SE* 21, p. 79.
68. Freud (1908), op. cit., PFL 12, p. 50; *SE* 9, p. 198.
69. Freud (1930), op. cit., PFL 12, pp. 267, 269, 271; *SE* 21, p. 81.
70. Freud (1908), op. cit., PFL 12, p. 52; *SE* 9, p. 200.
71. Black, B., private conversation.
72. Yeats, W.B., *Selected Poems*, London: Penguin, 2000, p. 66.
73. Hare, D., *The Secret Rapture*, London: Faber and Faber, 1997.
74. Griffiths, T., *Comedians*, London: Faber and Faber, 1976, p. 65.
75. Rycroft (1968), op. cit., p. 159.
76. Freud, S., *Little Hans* (1909), PFL 8, p. 295; *SE* 10, p. 138fn.
77. Norman, J., 'Little Hans', in Matthis, I. (ed.), *On Freud's Couch*, London: Jason Aronson, 1998, p. 94.

78. Freud (1910), op. cit., PFL 14, p. 229; *SE* 11, p. 136.
79. Kureishi, H., *The Buddha of Suburbia*, London: Faber and Faber, 1990.
80. Klein, M., *The School in Libidinal Development* (1923a), and *Early Analysis* (1923b), in *Love, Guilt and Reparation and Other Works 1921–45*, London: Vintage, 1988, pp. 63, 77.
81. Klein (1923a), op. cit., p. 64.
82. Klein (1923b), op. cit., p. 85.
83. Ibid., p. 85 (my emphasis).
84. Klein (1923a), op. cit., p. 74 (my emphasis).
85. Strachey, J., 'Some Unconscious Factors in Reading', in *International Journal of Psycho-Analysis*, vol. 11, 1930, pp. 328–30.
86. Ibid., pp. 328–30.
87. Manguel (1996), op. cit., p. 71.
88. The Bible, Proverbs, 5:3.
89. Bettelheim, B. and Zelan, K., *On Learning to Read*, London: Penguin, 1981.
90. Bettelheim, B., *The Uses of Enchantment*, London: Penguin, 1976.
91. Winnicott, D., *Playing and Reality*, London: Penguin, 1971, p. 45.
92. Ibid., p. 113.
93. Ibid., pp. 45, 55, 161.
94. Ibid., p. 60.
95. Ibid., p. 64.
96. Bollas, C., *The Shadow of the Object*, London: Free Association Books, 1987, pp. 34–5.
96. Levi, T., *A Cat Called Adolf*, London: Valentine Mitchell, 1995, p. 11 (first sentence mine).
98. *The Times*, London: 29 January 2001.
99. Olivier, C., *Jocasta's Children*, London: Routledge, 1989, pp. 70, 142, 6–7.
100. Ibid., p. 43.
101. Anon., British pacifist slogan, 1940.
102. Olivier (1989), op. cit., p. 2.
103. Ibid., p. 39.
104. Ibid., p. 103.
105. Ibid., p. 47.
106. Ibid., p. 46.
107. Ibid., pp. 48, 80.
108. Savona, J.L., *Jean Genet*, London: Macmillan, 1983, p. 108.
109. Olivier (1989), op. cit., p. 75.
110. Ibid., p. 75.
111. Ibid., p. 126.
112. Riviere (1929), op. cit., p. 303.
113. *The Guardian*, London: 17 March 2001.
114. Olivier (1989), op. cit., p. 125.
115. Pacteau, F., *The Symptom of Beauty*, London: Reaktion Books, 1994, p. 14.
116. Ibid., p. 16.
117. Ibid., p. 31.
118. Marlowe, C., *Dr Faustus* (1604), V.i; The Bible: I Kings, 11:3; The Song of Solomon, 6:13.
119. Pacteau (1994), op. cit., p. 156.
120. Ibid., p. 88.

121. Freud, S., 'Mourning and Melancholia' (1917), PFL 11, p. 250; SE 14, p. 249.
122. Pacteau (1994), op. cit., p. 91.
123. Milner, M., On Not Being Able to Paint, London: Heinemann, 1950.
124. Winnicott, D., 'Some Thoughts on the Word Democracy' (1950), in The Family and Individual Development, London: Tavistock, 1964.
125. Clendinnen, I., Reading the Holocaust, Cambridge: Cambridge University Press, 1999.
126. Borowski, T., This Way for the Gas, Ladies and Gentlemen, London: Penguin, 1976.
127. Lanzmann, C., 'The Obscenity of Understanding', in Caruth, C. (ed.), Trauma: Explorations in Memory, London: Johns Hopkins University Press, 1995, p. 204.
128. Geoghegan, V., Reason and Eros: The Social Theory of Herbert Marcuse, London: Pluto, 1981, pp. 56, 76–8.
129. Lanzmann, in Caruth (1995), op. cit., p. 204.
130. Benjamin, W., Illuminations, London: Fontana, 1973, p. 249.
131. Black, E., IBM and the Holocaust, London: Little, Brown, 2001.
132. Shorter, E., A History of Women's Bodies, London: Allen Lane, 1983.
133. 'Work liberates'; inscribed over the gates of Dachau concentration camp in 1933, and subsequently at Auschwitz and Sachsenhausen camps.
134. Theweleit, K., Male Fantasies, Oxford: Polity/Blackwell, 1987, p. 53.
135. Levi, P., If This Is A Man (1947), London: Abacus, 1987, p. 17.
136. Salinger, J.D., The Catcher in the Rye (1951), London: Penguin, 1984; Levi, P., The Drowned and the Saved, London: Abacus, 1988.

Further Reading

Adams, P., The Emptiness of the Image, London: Routledge, 1996.
Akerley, B.E., The X-Rated Bible, USA: Feral House, 1998.
Brantenberg, G., Egalia's Daughters, USA: Seal Press, 1985.
Bruce, V. and Young, A., In the Eye of the Beholder, Oxford: Oxford University Press, 1998.
Butler, J., Excitable Speech, London: Routledge, 1997.
Derrida, J., The Politics of Friendship, London: Verso, 1997.
Elias, N., The Civilizing Process, Oxford: Blackwell, 2000.
Greenfield, S., The Private Life of the Brain, London: Penguin, 2000.
Kovel, J., White Racism: A Psychohistory, London: Free Association Books, 1984.
Matte-Blanco, I., Thinking, Feeling and Being, London: Routledge, 1988.
MacDougall, J., The Many Faces of Eros, London: Free Association Books, 1995.
Mitchell, J., Psychoanalysis and Feminism, London: Penguin, 2000.
Paulos, J.A., Once Upon a Number, London: Penguin, 1998.
Phillips, A., The Beast in the Nursery, London: Faber and Faber, 1998.
Rodenburg, P., The Right to Speak, London: Methuen, 1992.
Walton, S., Out of It: A Cultural History of Intoxication, London: Hamish Hamilton, 2001.
Wurtzel, E., Bitch, London: Quartet, 1999.

Index